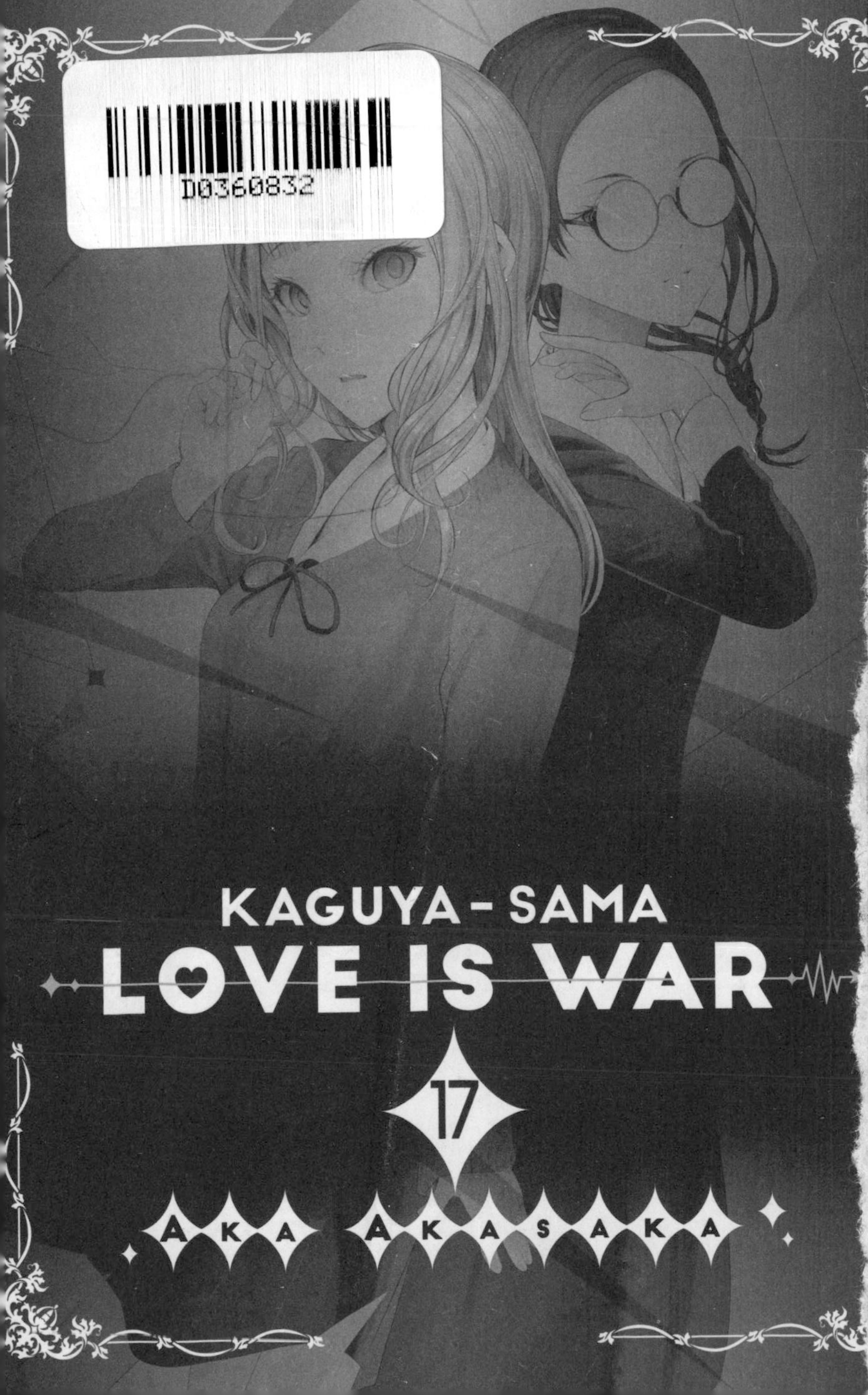
KAGUYA-SAMA
LOVE IS WAR
17
AKA AKASAKA

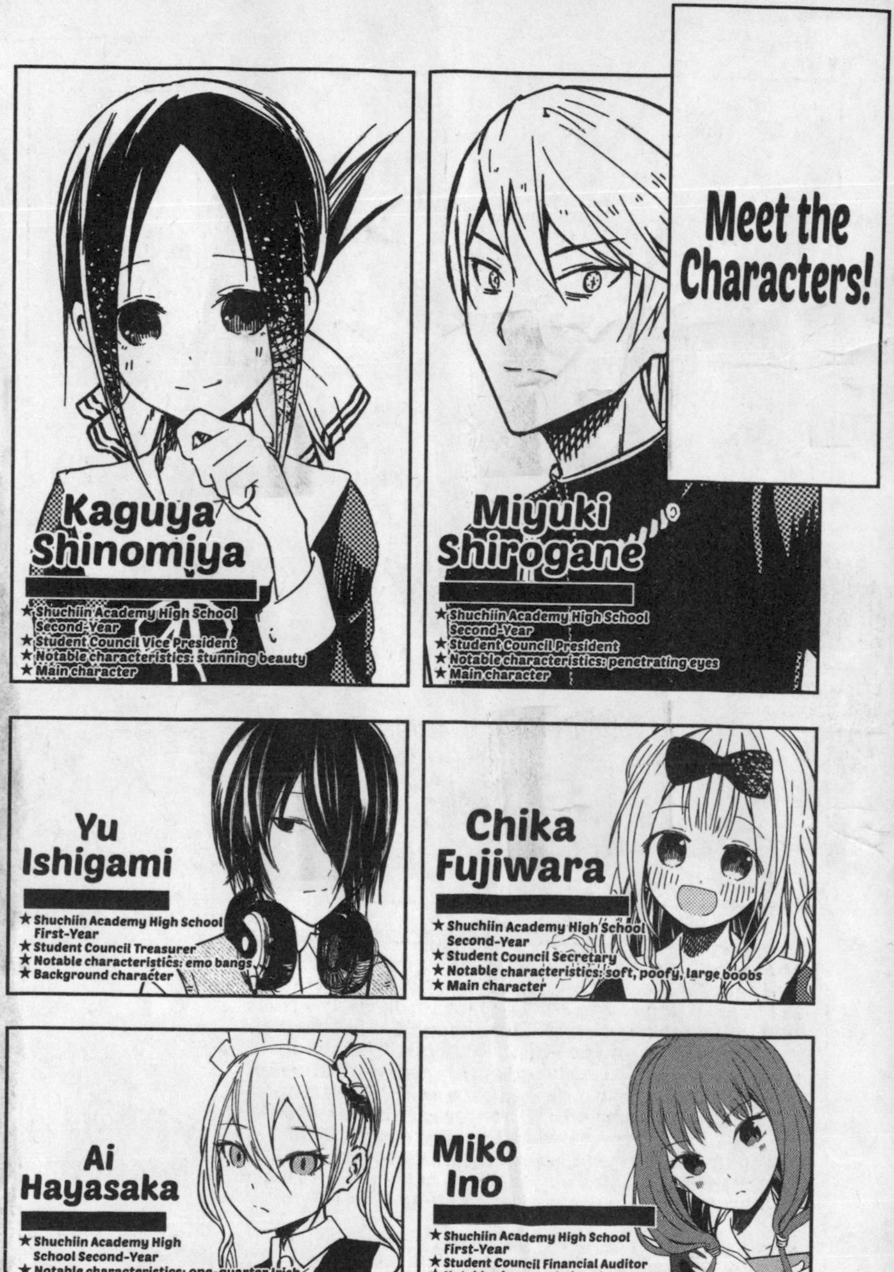
Meet the Characters!
Miyuki Shirogane
★ Shuchiin Academy High School Second-Year
★ Student Council President
★ Notable characteristics: penetrating eyes
★ Main character
Kaguya Shinomiya
★ Shuchiin Academy High School Second-Year
★ Student Council Vice President
★ Notable characteristics: stunning beauty
★ Main character
Chika Fujiwara
★ Shuchiin Academy High School Second-Year
★ Student Council Secretary
★ Notable characteristics: soft, poofy, large boobs
★ Main character
Yu Ishigami
★ Shuchiin Academy High School First-Year
★ Student Council Treasurer
★ Notable characteristics: emo bangs
★ Background character
Miko Ino
★ Shuchiin Academy High School First-Year
★ Student Council Financial Auditor
★ Notable characteristics: short
★ Background character
Ai Hayasaka
★ Shuchiin Academy High School Second-Year
★ Notable characteristics: one-quarter Irish
★ Profession: Kaguya Shinomiya's personal assistant

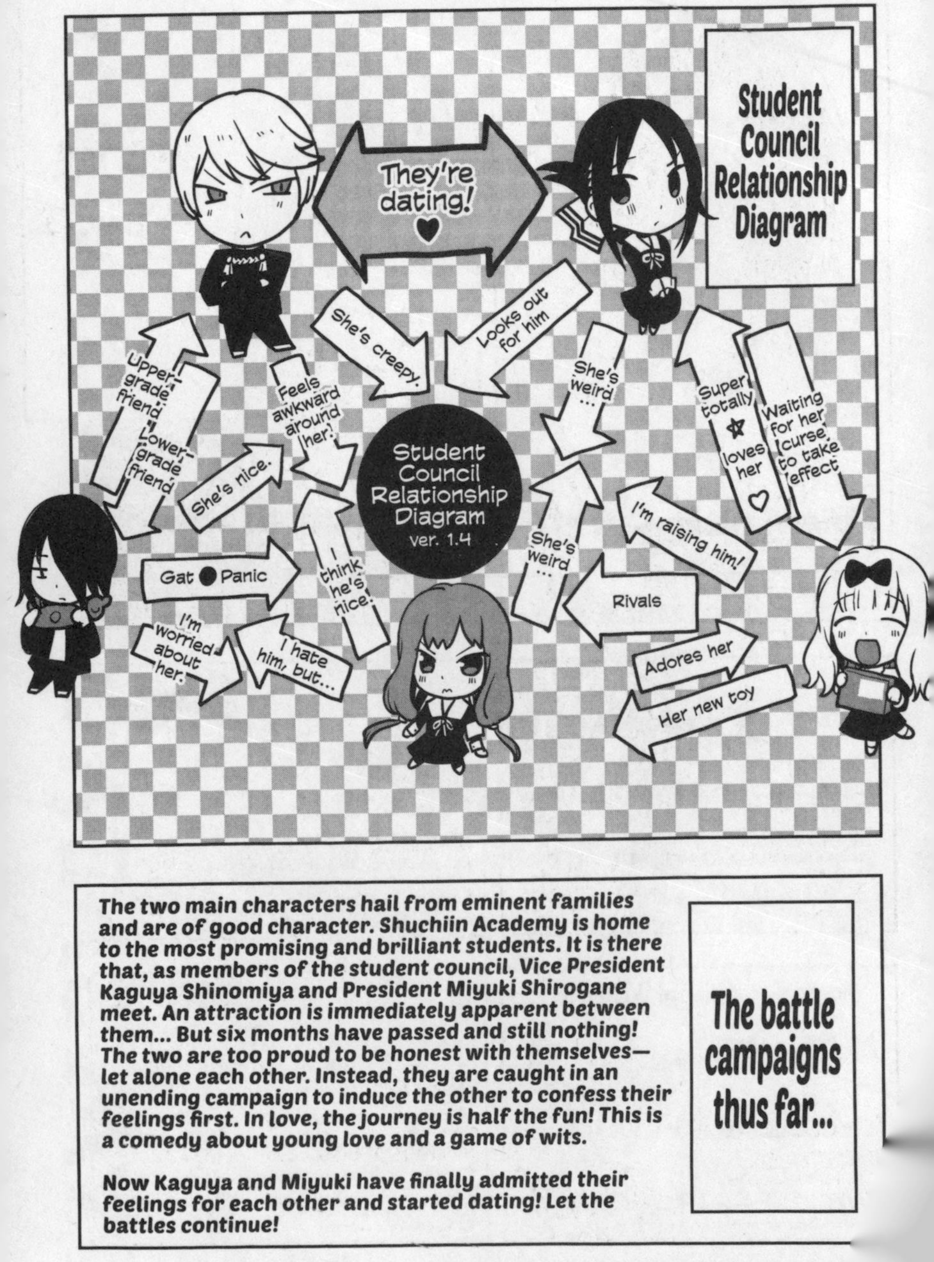
Student Council Relationship Diagram
They're dating!
She's creepy.
Looks out for him
Upper-grade friend
Lower-grade friend
Feels awkward around her.
She's nice.
She's weird...
Super totally ☆ loves her ♡
Waiting for her curse to take effect
Student Council Relationship Diagram ver. 1.4
I'm raising him!
She's weird...
Gat ● Panic
I think he's nice.
Rivals
I'm worried about her.
I hate him, but...
Adores her
Her new toy

The battle campaigns thus far...

The two main characters hail from eminent families and are of good character. Shuchiin Academy is home to the most promising and brilliant students. It is there that, as members of the student council, Vice President Kaguya Shinomiya and President Miyuki Shirogane meet. An attraction is immediately apparent between them... But six months have passed and still nothing! The two are too proud to be honest with themselves—let alone each other. Instead, they are caught in an unending campaign to induce the other to confess their feelings first. In love, the journey is half the fun! This is a comedy about young love and a game of wits.

Now Kaguya and Miyuki have finally admitted their feelings for each other and started dating! Let the battles continue!

KAGUYA-SAMA LOVE IS WA

BATTLE CAMPAIGNS 17

(1) Stray Bullet

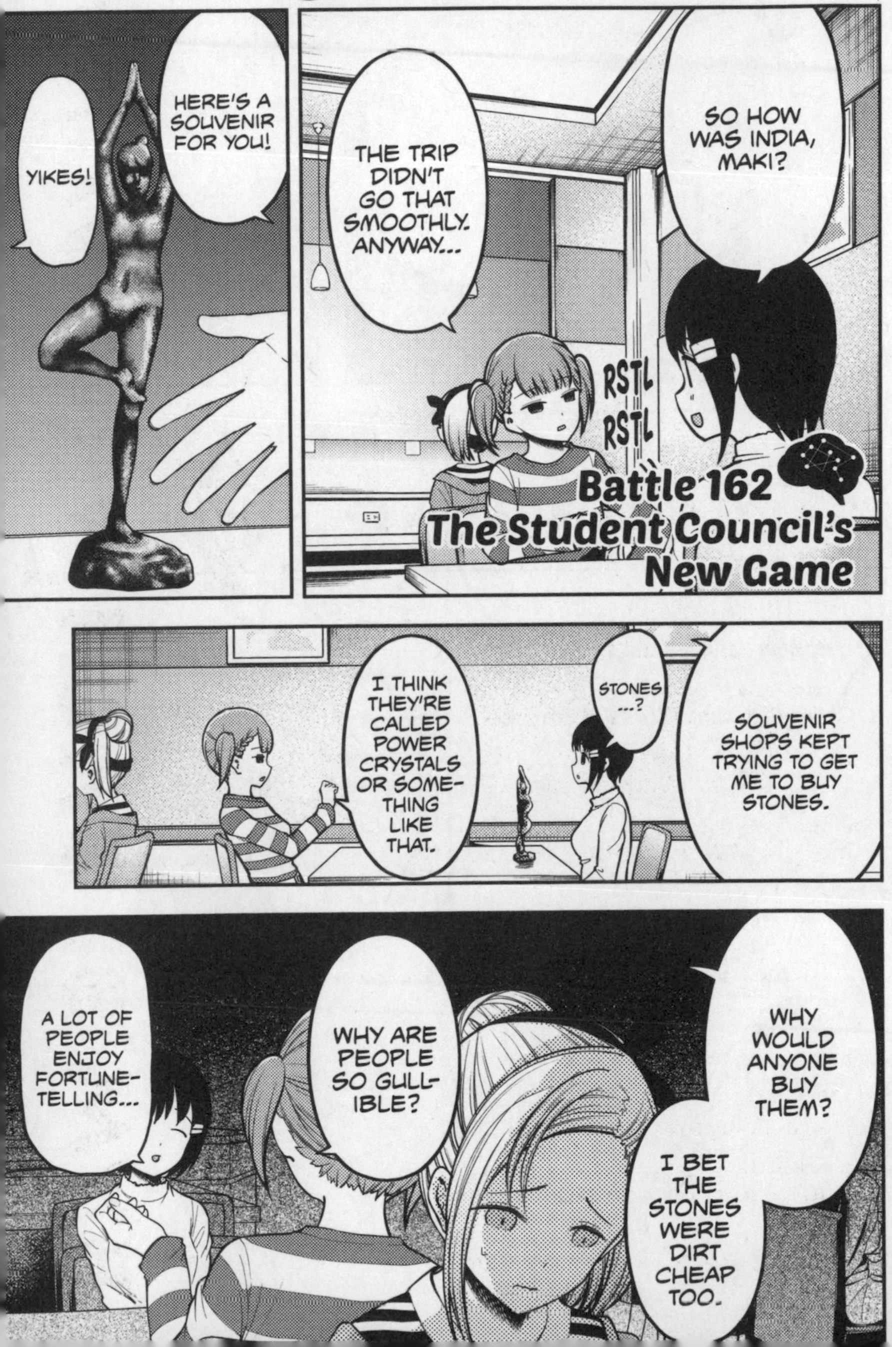
SO HOW WAS INDIA, MAKI?
THE TRIP DIDN'T GO THAT SMOOTHLY. ANYWAY...
RSTL
RSTL
Battle 162
The Student Council's New Game
HERE'S A SOUVENIR FOR YOU!
YIKES!
SOUVENIR SHOPS KEPT TRYING TO GET ME TO BUY STONES.
STONES ...?
I THINK THEY'RE CALLED POWER CRYSTALS OR SOME-THING LIKE THAT.
WHY WOULD ANYONE BUY THEM?
I BET THE STONES WERE DIRT CHEAP TOO.
WHY ARE PEOPLE SO GULL-IBLE?
A LOT OF PEOPLE ENJOY FORTUNE-TELLING...

② The Announcement

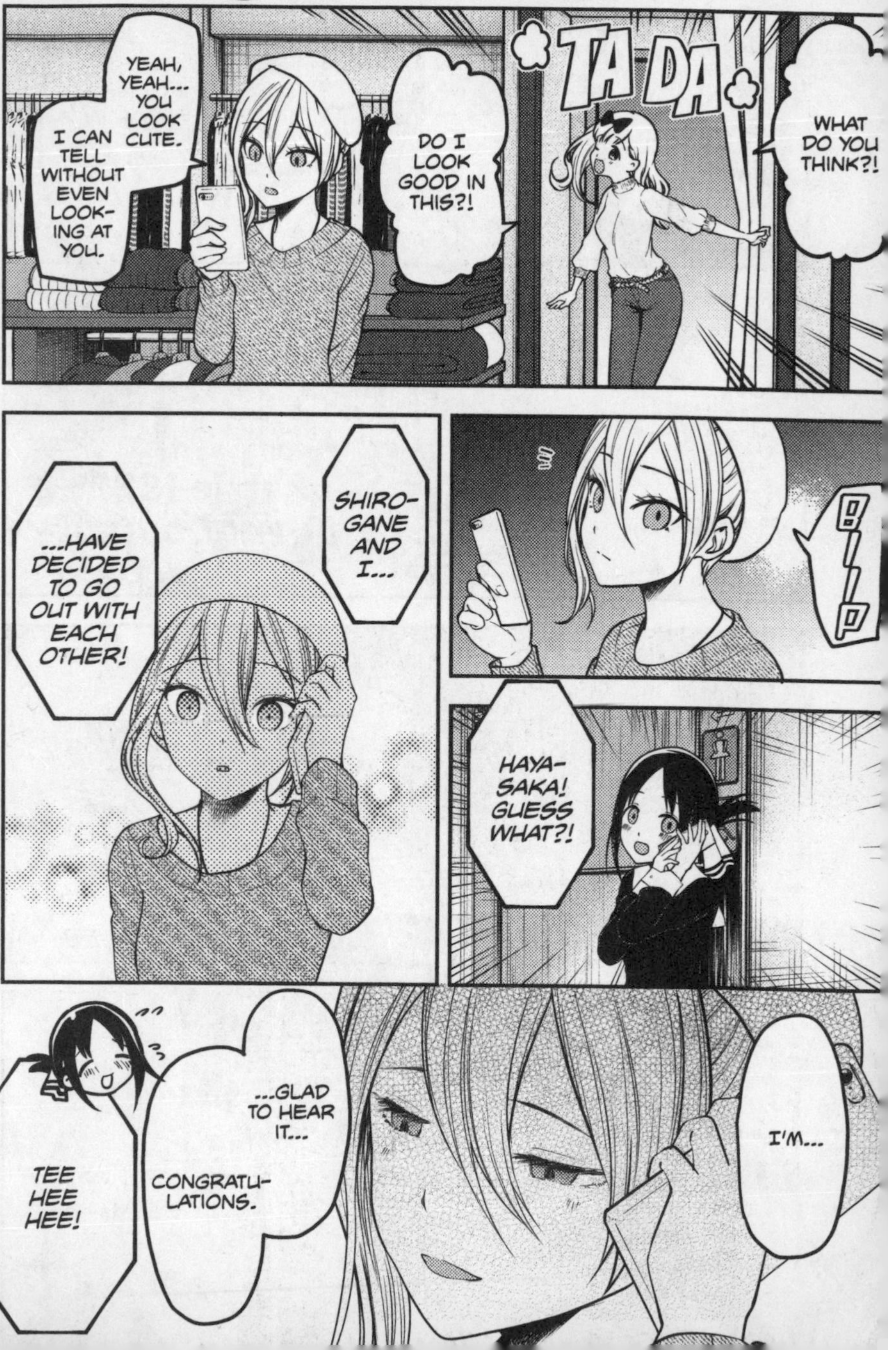
TA DA
WHAT DO YOU THINK?!
DO I LOOK GOOD IN THIS?!
YEAH, YEAH... YOU LOOK CUTE.
I CAN TELL WITHOUT EVEN LOOKING AT YOU.
BIP
HAYA-SAKA! GUESS WHAT?!
SHIRO-GANE AND I...
...HAVE DECIDED TO GO OUT WITH EACH OTHER!
I'M...
...GLAD TO HEAR IT...
CONGRATU-LATIONS.
TEE HEE HEE!

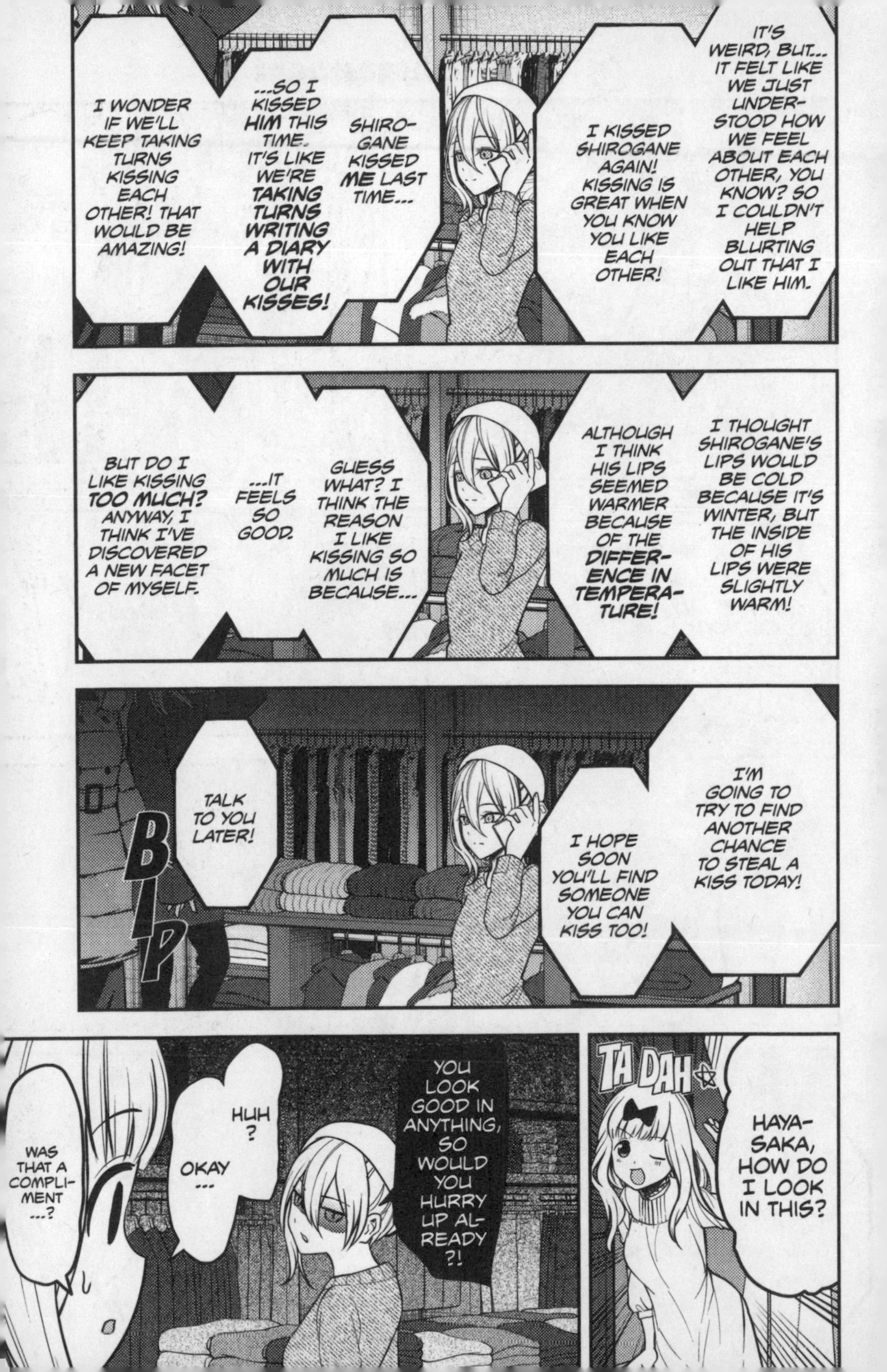
IT'S WEIRD, BUT... IT FELT LIKE WE JUST UNDERSTOOD HOW WE FEEL ABOUT EACH OTHER, YOU KNOW? SO I COULDN'T HELP BLURTING OUT THAT I LIKE HIM.
I KISSED SHIROGANE AGAIN! KISSING IS GREAT WHEN YOU KNOW YOU LIKE EACH OTHER!
SHIROGANE KISSED **ME** LAST TIME...
...SO I KISSED **HIM** THIS TIME. IT'S LIKE WE'RE **TAKING TURNS WRITING A DIARY WITH OUR KISSES!**
I WONDER IF WE'LL KEEP TAKING TURNS KISSING EACH OTHER! THAT WOULD BE AMAZING!
I THOUGHT SHIROGANE'S LIPS WOULD BE COLD BECAUSE IT'S WINTER, BUT THE INSIDE OF HIS LIPS WERE SLIGHTLY WARM!
ALTHOUGH I THINK HIS LIPS SEEMED WARMER BECAUSE OF THE **DIFFERENCE IN TEMPERATURE!**
GUESS WHAT? I THINK THE REASON I LIKE KISSING SO MUCH IS BECAUSE...
...IT FEELS SO GOOD.
BUT DO I LIKE KISSING **TOO MUCH?** ANYWAY, I THINK I'VE DISCOVERED A NEW FACET OF MYSELF.
I'M GOING TO TRY TO FIND ANOTHER CHANCE TO STEAL A KISS TODAY!
I HOPE SOON YOU'LL FIND SOMEONE YOU CAN KISS TOO!
TALK TO YOU LATER!
BIP
TA DAH
HAYASAKA, HOW DO I LOOK IN THIS?
YOU LOOK GOOD IN ANYTHING, SO WOULD YOU HURRY UP ALREADY?!
HUH?
OKAY...
WAS THAT A COMPLIMENT...?

③ Sho Is the Saltiest*

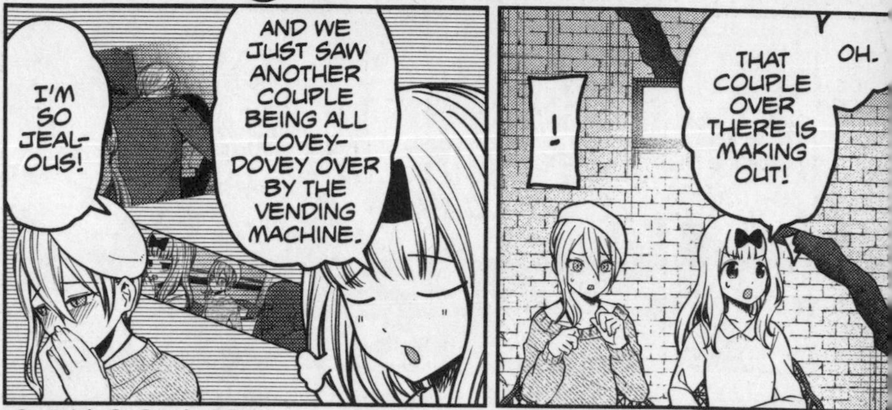
OH.
THAT COUPLE OVER THERE IS MAKING OUT!
!
AND WE JUST SAW ANOTHER COUPLE BEING ALL LOVEY-DOVEY OVER BY THE VENDING MACHINE.
I'M SO JEAL-OUS!

*See Vol. 3, Battle 22

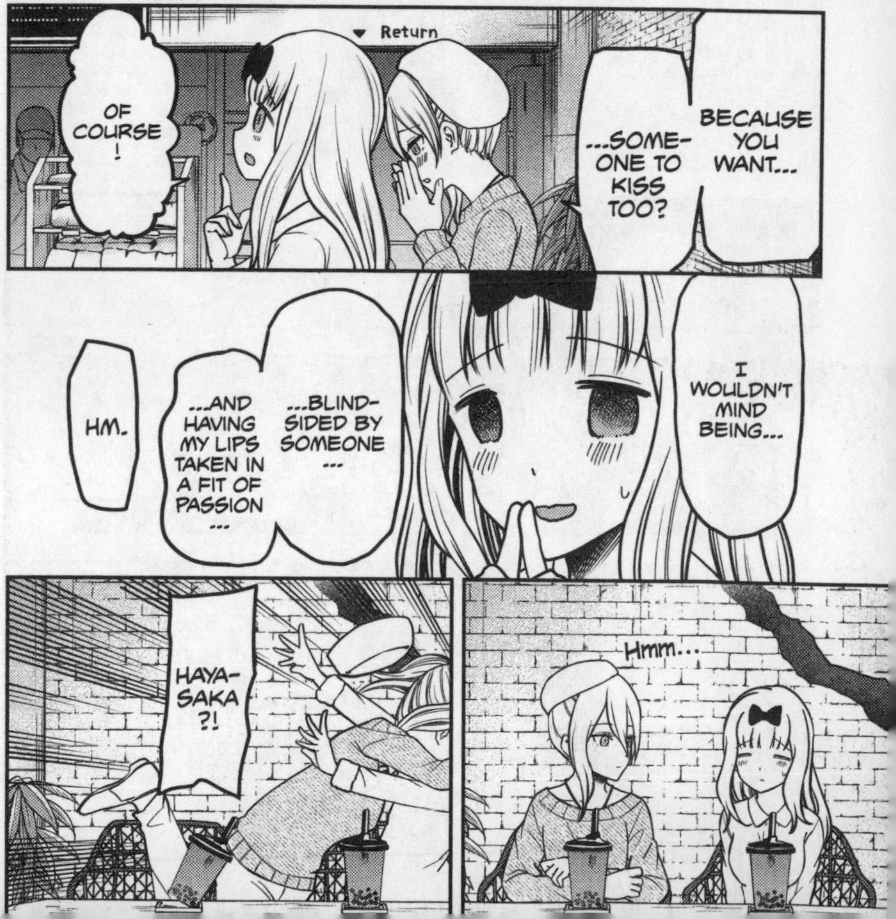
BECAUSE YOU WANT...
...SOME-ONE TO KISS TOO?
▼ Return
OF COURSE!
I WOULDN'T MIND BEING...
...BLIND-SIDED BY SOMEONE...
...AND HAVING MY LIPS TAKEN IN A FIT OF PASSION...
HM.
Hmm...
HAYA-SAKA?!

4 For Some Reason, Middle-Aged Men Have a Talent for Predicting How Other People's Relationships Will Develop Based on Just a Few Basic Facts

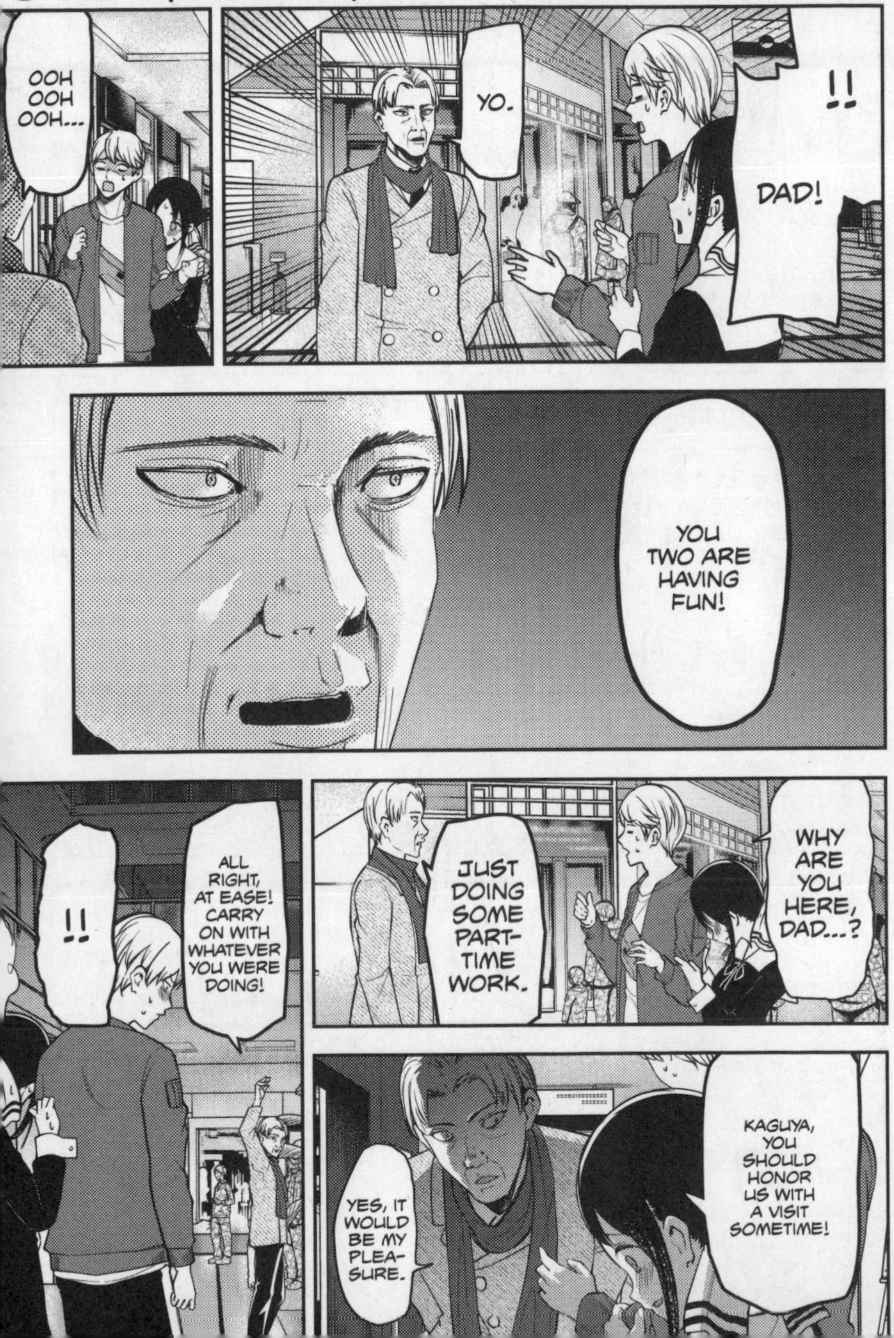

YO.
!!
DAD!
OOH OOH OOH...
YOU TWO ARE HAVING FUN!
WHY ARE YOU HERE, DAD...?
JUST DOING SOME PART-TIME WORK.
KAGUYA, YOU SHOULD HONOR US WITH A VISIT SOMETIME!
YES, IT WOULD BE MY PLEASURE.
ALL RIGHT, AT EASE! CARRY ON WITH WHATEVER YOU WERE DOING!
!!

5 Preparing to Study Overseas

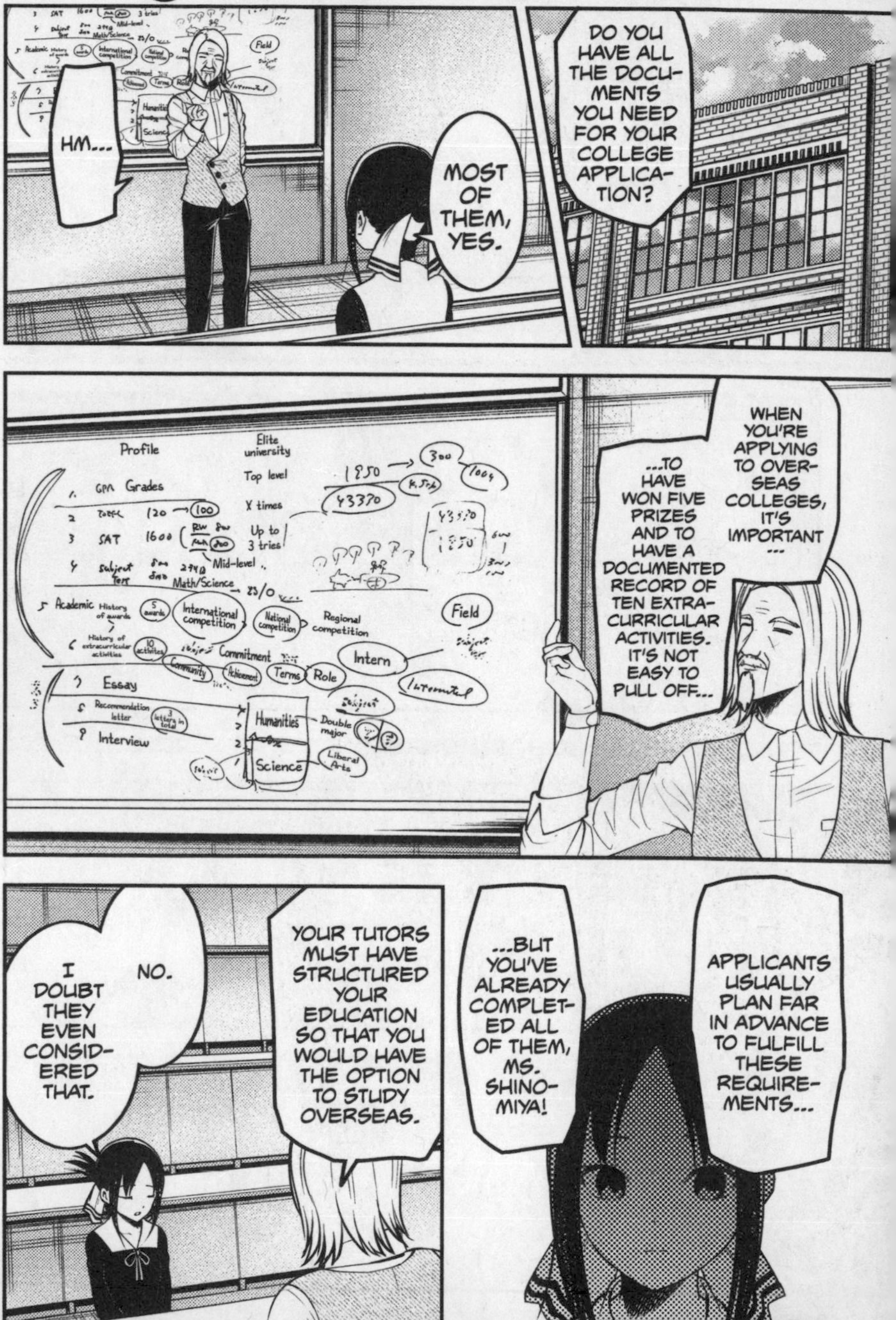
DO YOU HAVE ALL THE DOCUMENTS YOU NEED FOR YOUR COLLEGE APPLICATION?
MOST OF THEM, YES.
HM...
WHEN YOU'RE APPLYING TO OVERSEAS COLLEGES, IT'S IMPORTANT...
...TO HAVE WON FIVE PRIZES AND TO HAVE A DOCUMENTED RECORD OF TEN EXTRACURRICULAR ACTIVITIES. IT'S NOT EASY TO PULL OFF...
APPLICANTS USUALLY PLAN FAR IN ADVANCE TO FULFILL THESE REQUIREMENTS...
...BUT YOU'VE ALREADY COMPLETED ALL OF THEM, MS. SHINOMIYA!
YOUR TUTORS MUST HAVE STRUCTURED YOUR EDUCATION SO THAT YOU WOULD HAVE THE OPTION TO STUDY OVERSEAS.
NO.
I DOUBT THEY EVEN CONSIDERED THAT.

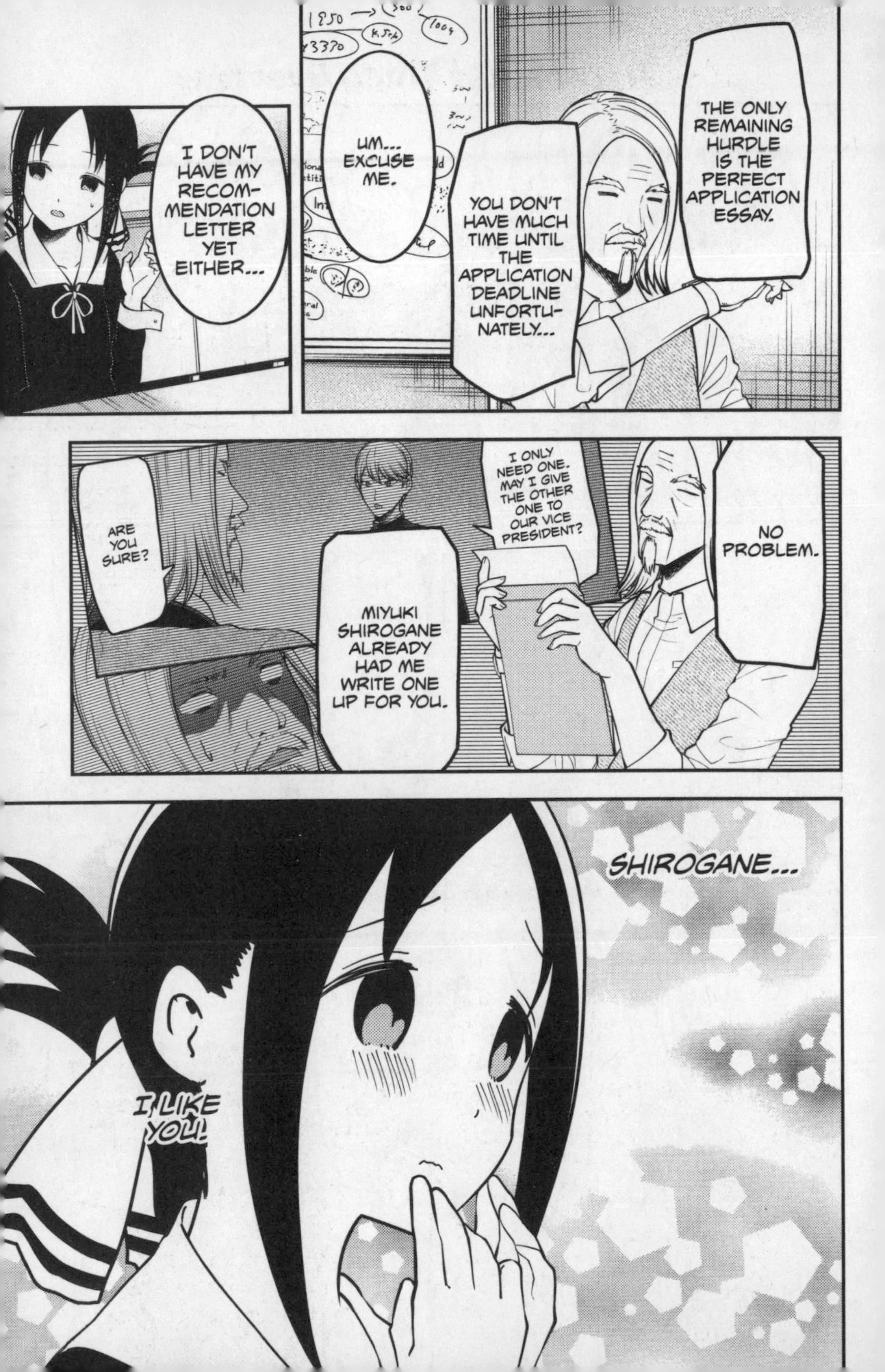
THE ONLY REMAINING HURDLE IS THE PERFECT APPLICATION ESSAY.
YOU DON'T HAVE MUCH TIME UNTIL THE APPLICATION DEADLINE UNFORTUNATELY...
UM... EXCUSE ME.
I DON'T HAVE MY RECOMMENDATION LETTER YET EITHER...
I ONLY NEED ONE. MAY I GIVE THE OTHER ONE TO OUR VICE PRESIDENT?
NO PROBLEM.
ARE YOU SURE?
MIYUKI SHIROGANE ALREADY HAD ME WRITE ONE UP FOR YOU.
SHIROGANE...
I LIKE YOU.

6 Enemy of World Peace

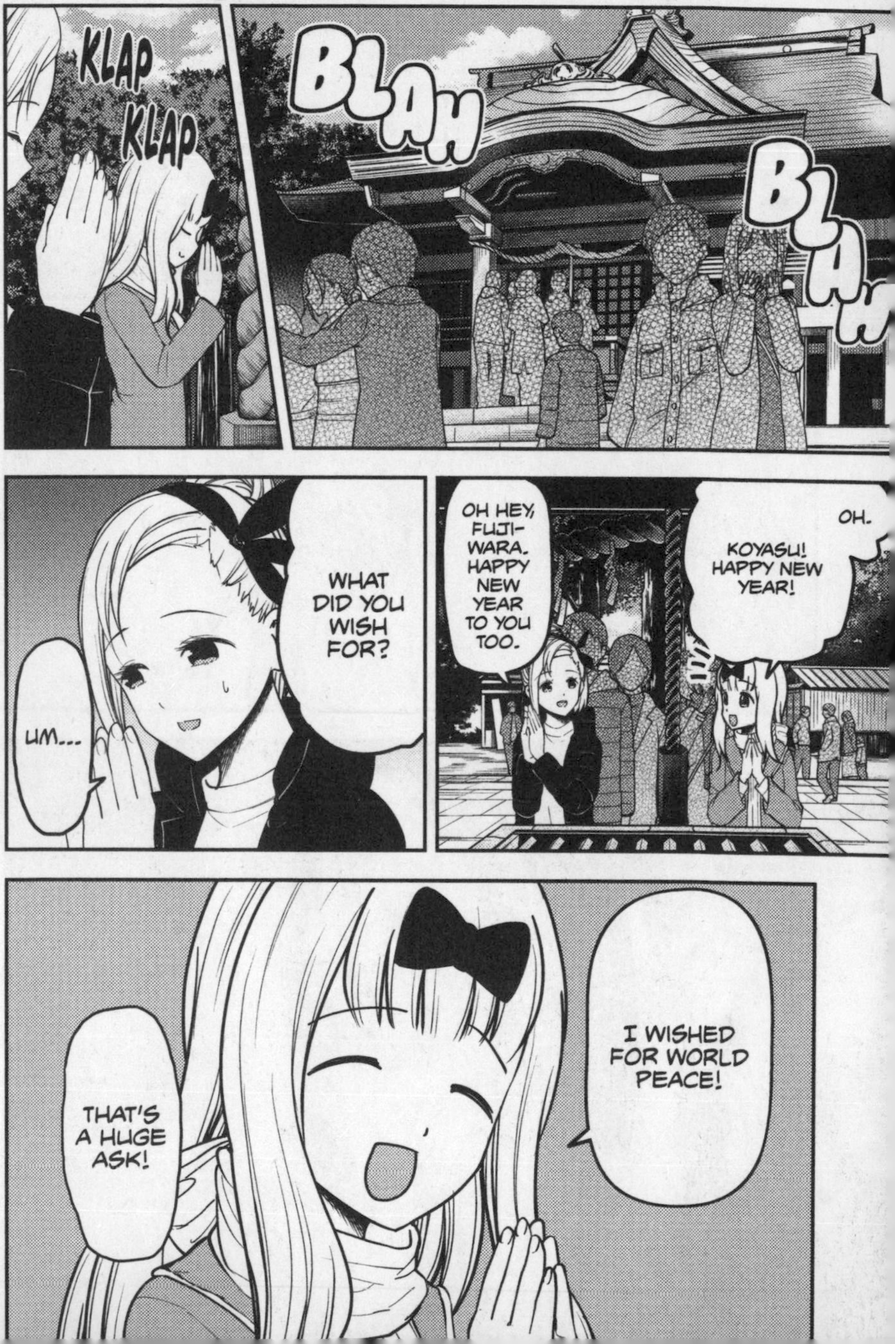
BLAH
BLAH
KLAP
KLAP
OH.
KOYASU! HAPPY NEW YEAR!
OH HEY, FUJI-WARA. HAPPY NEW YEAR TO YOU TOO.
WHAT DID YOU WISH FOR?
UM...
I WISHED FOR WORLD PEACE!
THAT'S A HUGE ASK!

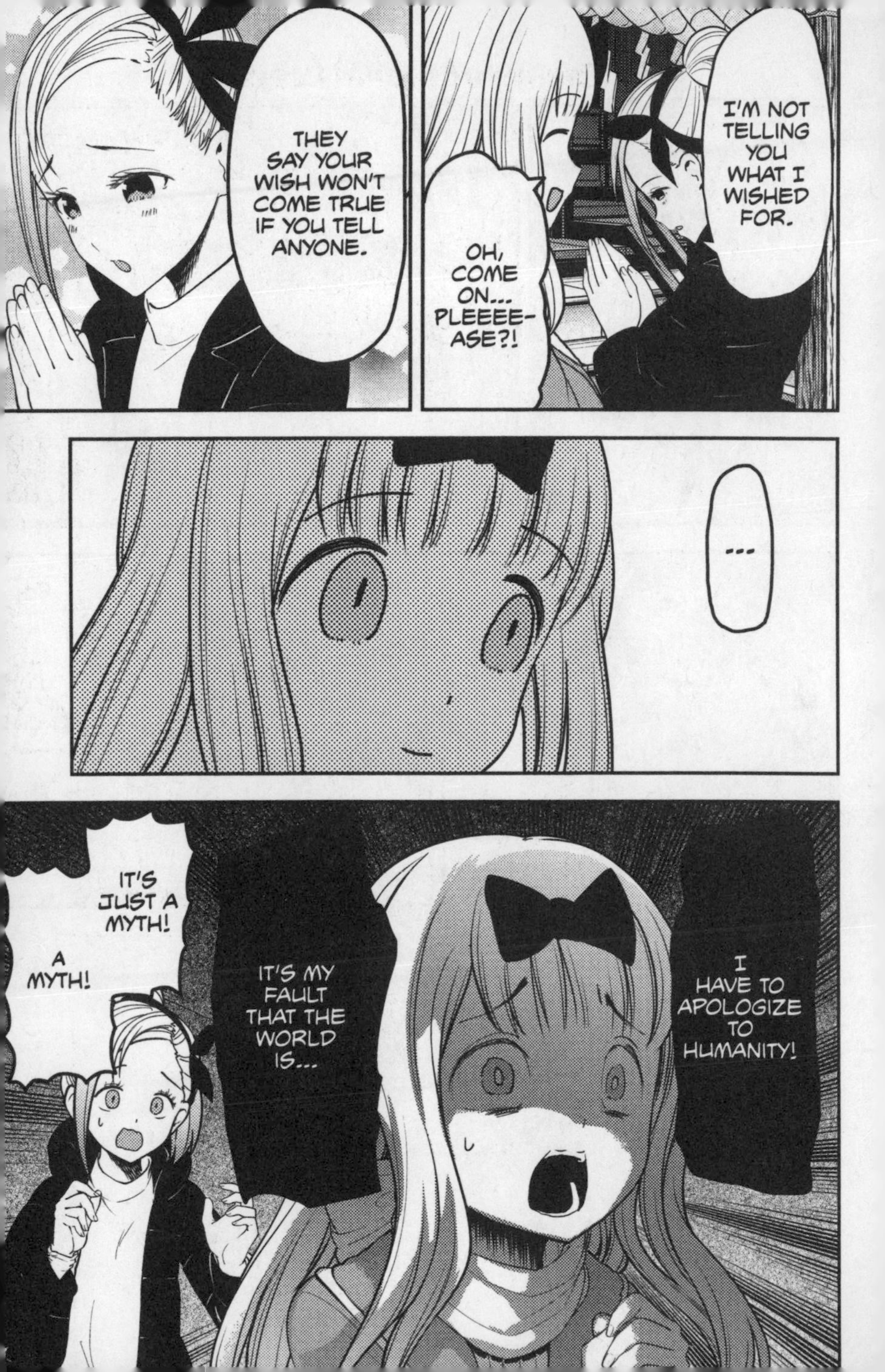
I'M NOT TELLING YOU WHAT I WISHED FOR.
OH, COME ON... PLEEEEASE?!
THEY SAY YOUR WISH WON'T COME TRUE IF YOU TELL ANYONE.
...
I HAVE TO APOLOGIZE TO HUMANITY!
IT'S MY FAULT THAT THE WORLD IS...
IT'S JUST A MYTH!
A MYTH!

⑦ At the Shinomiya's Kyoto Estate

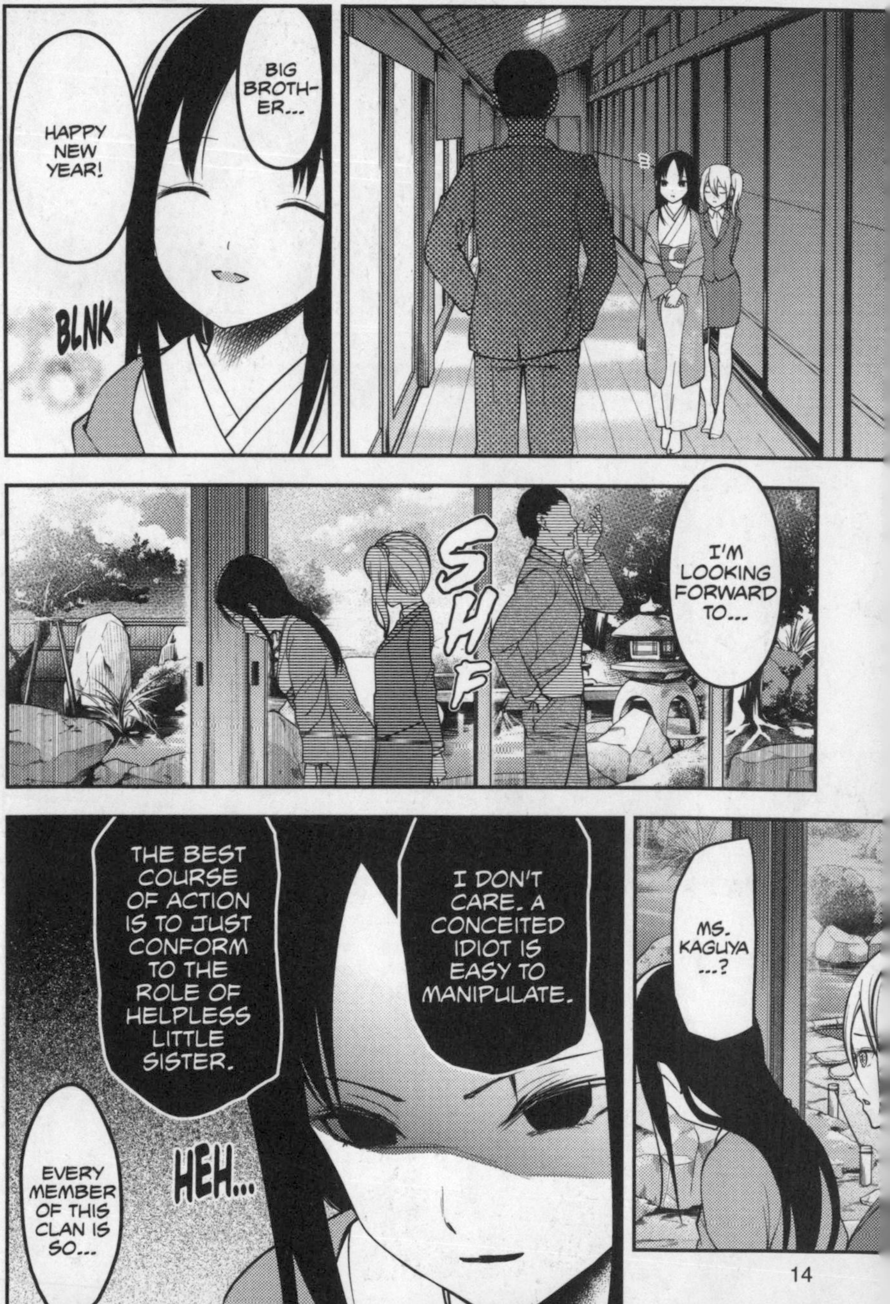
BIG BROTHER-ER...
HAPPY NEW YEAR!
BLNK
I'M LOOKING FORWARD TO...
SHF
MS. KAGUYA ...?
I DON'T CARE. A CONCEITED IDIOT IS EASY TO MANIPULATE.
THE BEST COURSE OF ACTION IS TO JUST CONFORM TO THE ROLE OF HELPLESS LITTLE SISTER.
HEH...
EVERY MEMBER OF THIS CLAN IS SO...

⑧ Yu Ishigami Wants to Make Her Confess

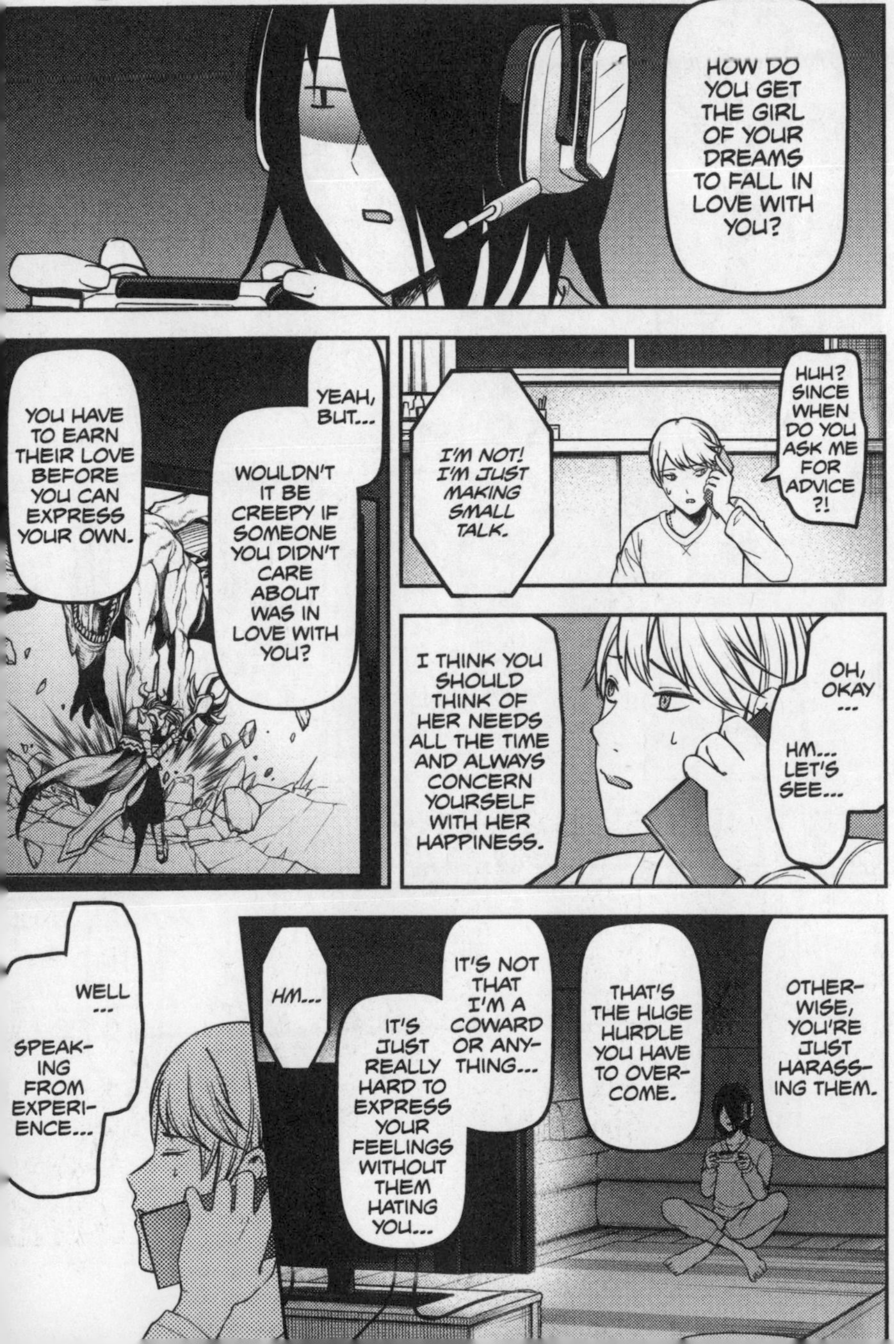
HOW DO YOU GET THE GIRL OF YOUR DREAMS TO FALL IN LOVE WITH YOU?
HUH? SINCE WHEN DO YOU ASK ME FOR ADVICE?!
I'M NOT! I'M JUST MAKING SMALL TALK.
OH, OKAY...
HM... LET'S SEE...
I THINK YOU SHOULD THINK OF HER NEEDS ALL THE TIME AND ALWAYS CONCERN YOURSELF WITH HER HAPPINESS.
YEAH, BUT...
WOULDN'T IT BE CREEPY IF SOMEONE YOU DIDN'T CARE ABOUT WAS IN LOVE WITH YOU?
YOU HAVE TO EARN THEIR LOVE BEFORE YOU CAN EXPRESS YOUR OWN.
OTHER-WISE, YOU'RE JUST HARASS-ING THEM.
THAT'S THE HUGE HURDLE YOU HAVE TO OVER-COME.
IT'S NOT THAT I'M A COWARD OR ANY-THING...
IT'S JUST REALLY HARD TO EXPRESS YOUR FEELINGS WITHOUT THEM HATING YOU...
HM...
WELL...
SPEAK-ING FROM EXPERI-ENCE...

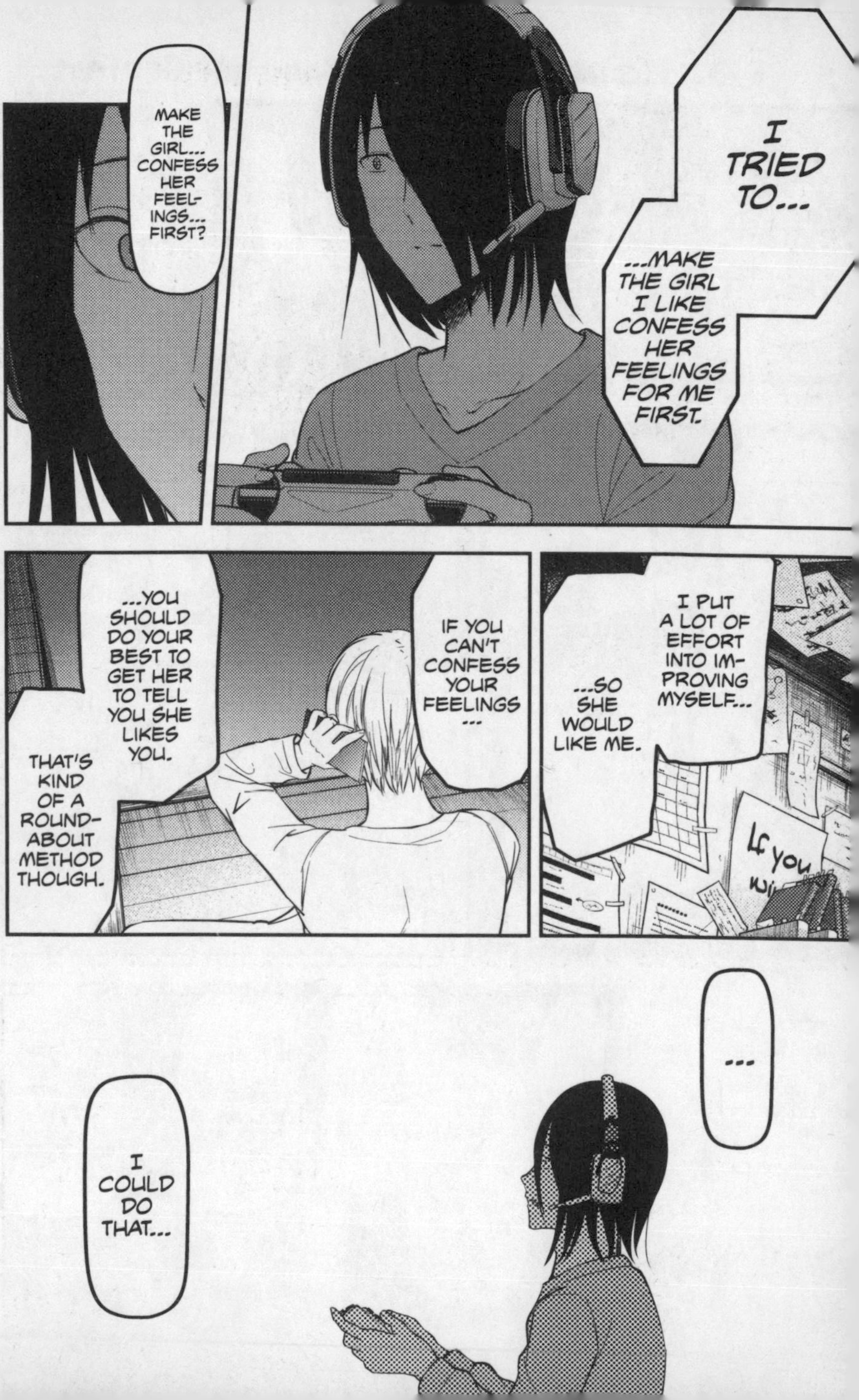
I TRIED TO...
...MAKE THE GIRL I LIKE CONFESS HER FEELINGS FOR ME FIRST.
MAKE THE GIRL... CONFESS HER FEELINGS... FIRST?
I PUT A LOT OF EFFORT INTO IMPROVING MYSELF...
...SO SHE WOULD LIKE ME.
IF YOU CAN'T CONFESS YOUR FEELINGS...
...YOU SHOULD DO YOUR BEST TO GET HER TO TELL YOU SHE LIKES YOU.
THAT'S KIND OF A ROUNDABOUT METHOD THOUGH.
...
I COULD DO THAT...

⑨ Kaguya's Christmas Gift

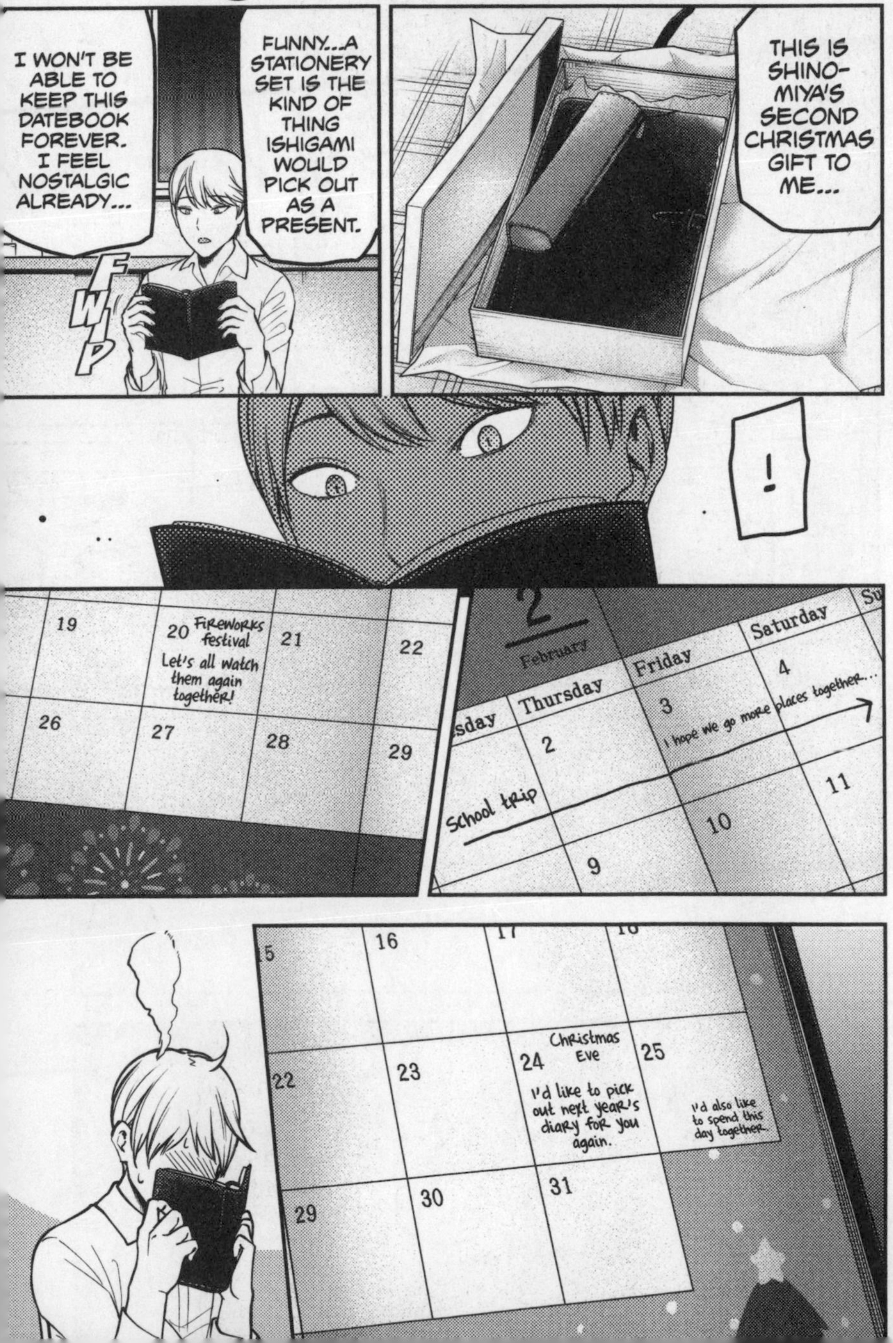
THIS IS SHINOMIYA'S SECOND CHRISTMAS GIFT TO ME...
FUNNY...A STATIONERY SET IS THE KIND OF THING ISHIGAMI WOULD PICK OUT AS A PRESENT.
I WON'T BE ABLE TO KEEP THIS DATEBOOK FOREVER. I FEEL NOSTALGIC ALREADY...
FWIP
!
February
Thursday
Friday
Saturday
I hope we go more places together...
School trip
Fireworks festival
Let's all watch them again together!
Christmas Eve
I'd like to pick out next year's diary for you again.
I'd also like to spend this day together.

⑩ Shirogane's Birthday Gift

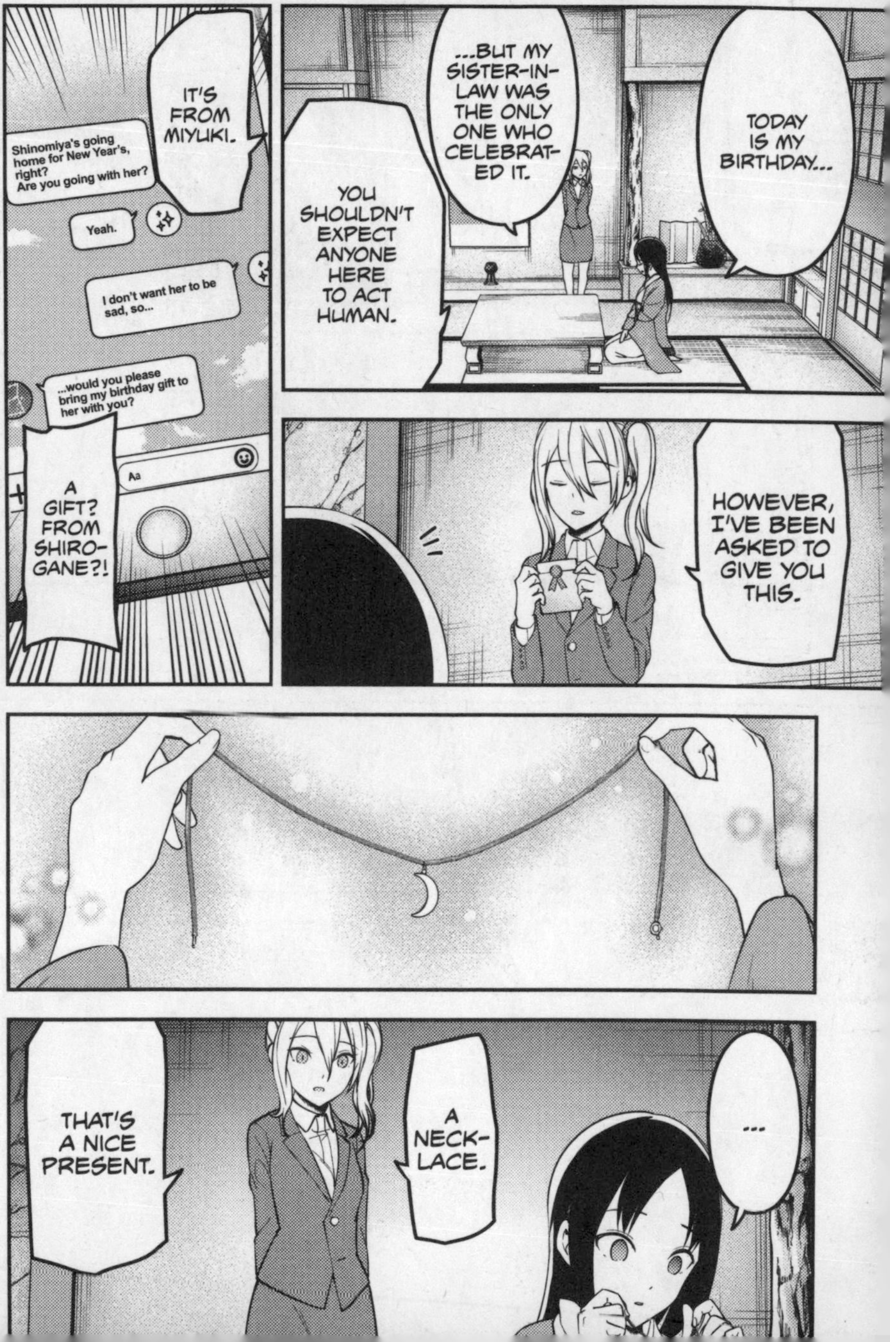
TODAY IS MY BIRTHDAY...
...BUT MY SISTER-IN-LAW WAS THE ONLY ONE WHO CELEBRATED IT.
YOU SHOULDN'T EXPECT ANYONE HERE TO ACT HUMAN.
HOWEVER, I'VE BEEN ASKED TO GIVE YOU THIS.
IT'S FROM MIYUKI.
Shinomiya's going home for New Year's, right? Are you going with her?
Yeah.
I don't want her to be sad, so...
...would you please bring my birthday gift to her with you?
Aa
A GIFT? FROM SHIROGANE?!
...
A NECKLACE.
THAT'S A NICE PRESENT.

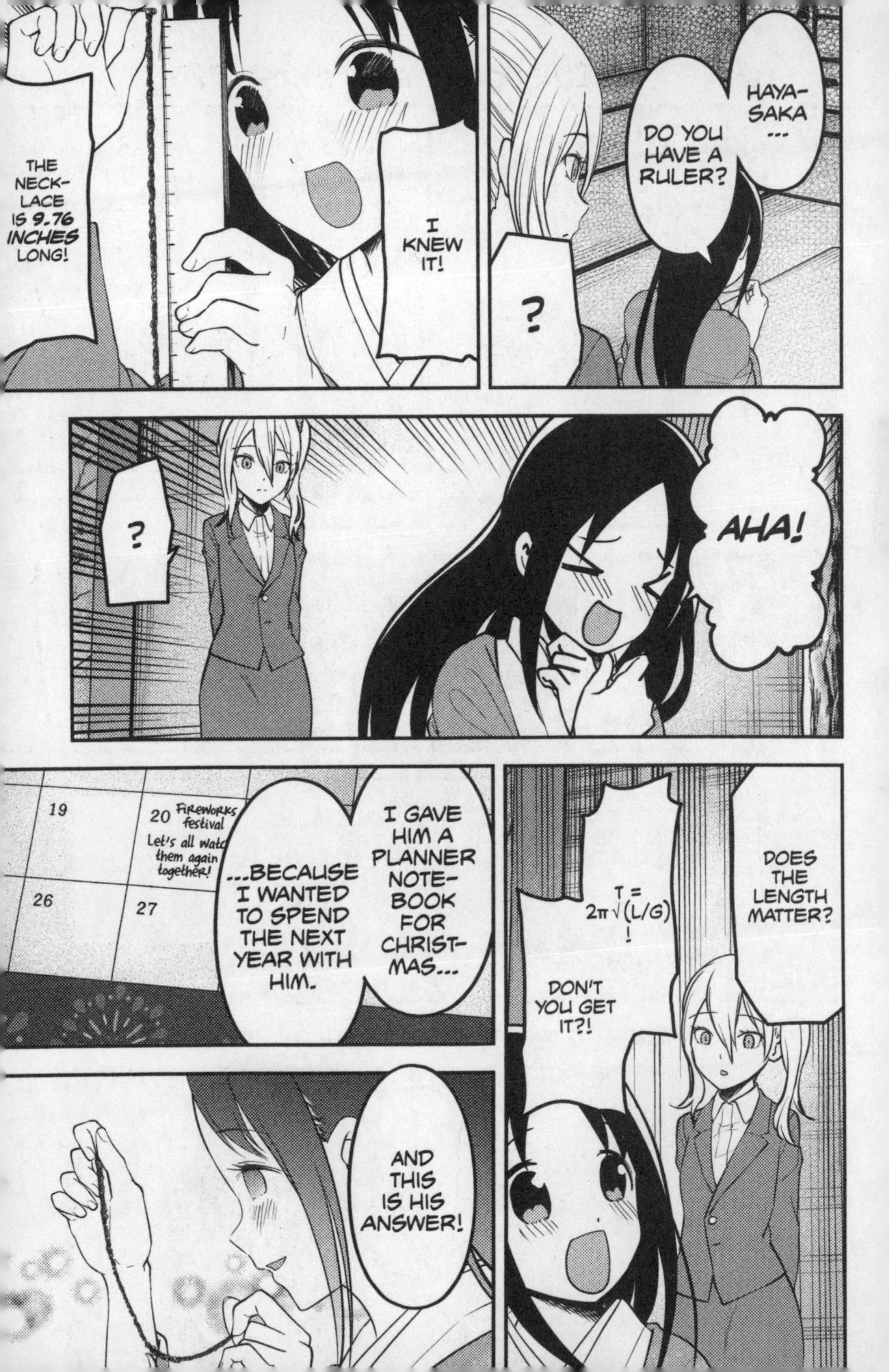
HAYA-SAKA...
DO YOU HAVE A RULER?
?
I KNEW IT!
THE NECK-LACE IS 9.76 INCHES LONG!
AHA!
?
DOES THE LENGTH MATTER?
T = 2π√(L/G)!
DON'T YOU GET IT?!
I GAVE HIM A PLANNER NOTE-BOOK FOR CHRIST-MAS...
...BECAUSE I WANTED TO SPEND THE NEXT YEAR WITH HIM.
19
20 Fireworks festival
Let's all watc them again together!
26
27
AND THIS IS HIS ANSWER!

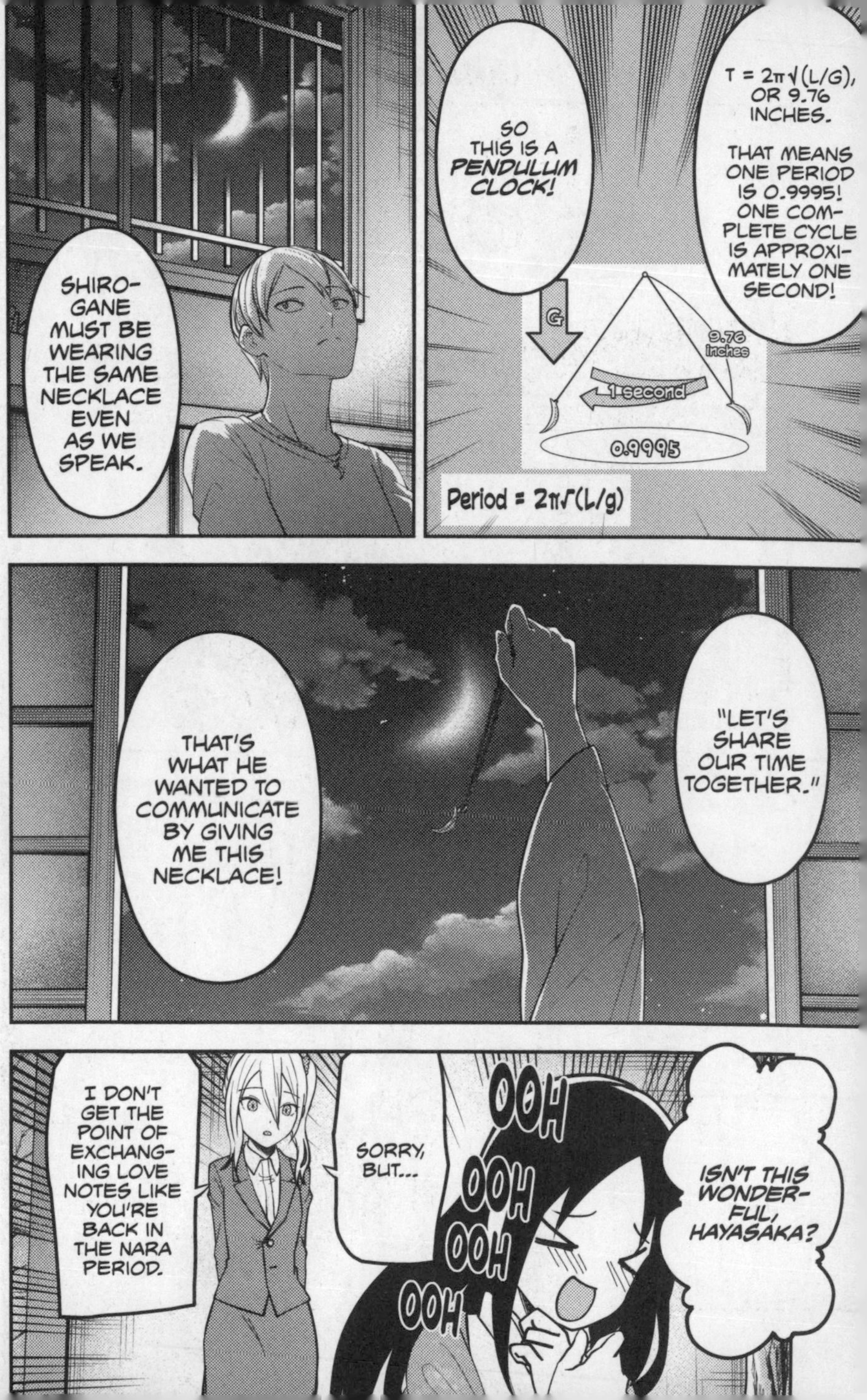
T = 2π√(L/G), OR 9.76 INCHES.
THAT MEANS ONE PERIOD IS 0.9995! ONE COM-PLETE CYCLE IS APPROXI-MATELY ONE SECOND!
SO THIS IS A *PENDULUM CLOCK!*
G
9.76 inches
1 second
0.9995
Period = 2π√(L/g)
SHIRO-GANE MUST BE WEARING THE SAME NECKLACE EVEN AS WE SPEAK.
"LET'S SHARE OUR TIME TOGETHER."
THAT'S WHAT HE WANTED TO COMMUNICATE BY GIVING ME THIS NECKLACE!
ISN'T THIS WONDER-FUL, HAYASAKA?
OOH HOO
OOH HOO
OOH HOO
OOH HOO
SORRY, BUT...
I DON'T GET THE POINT OF EXCHANG-ING LOVE NOTES LIKE YOU'RE BACK IN THE NARA PERIOD.

⑪ End of the New Game Chapter

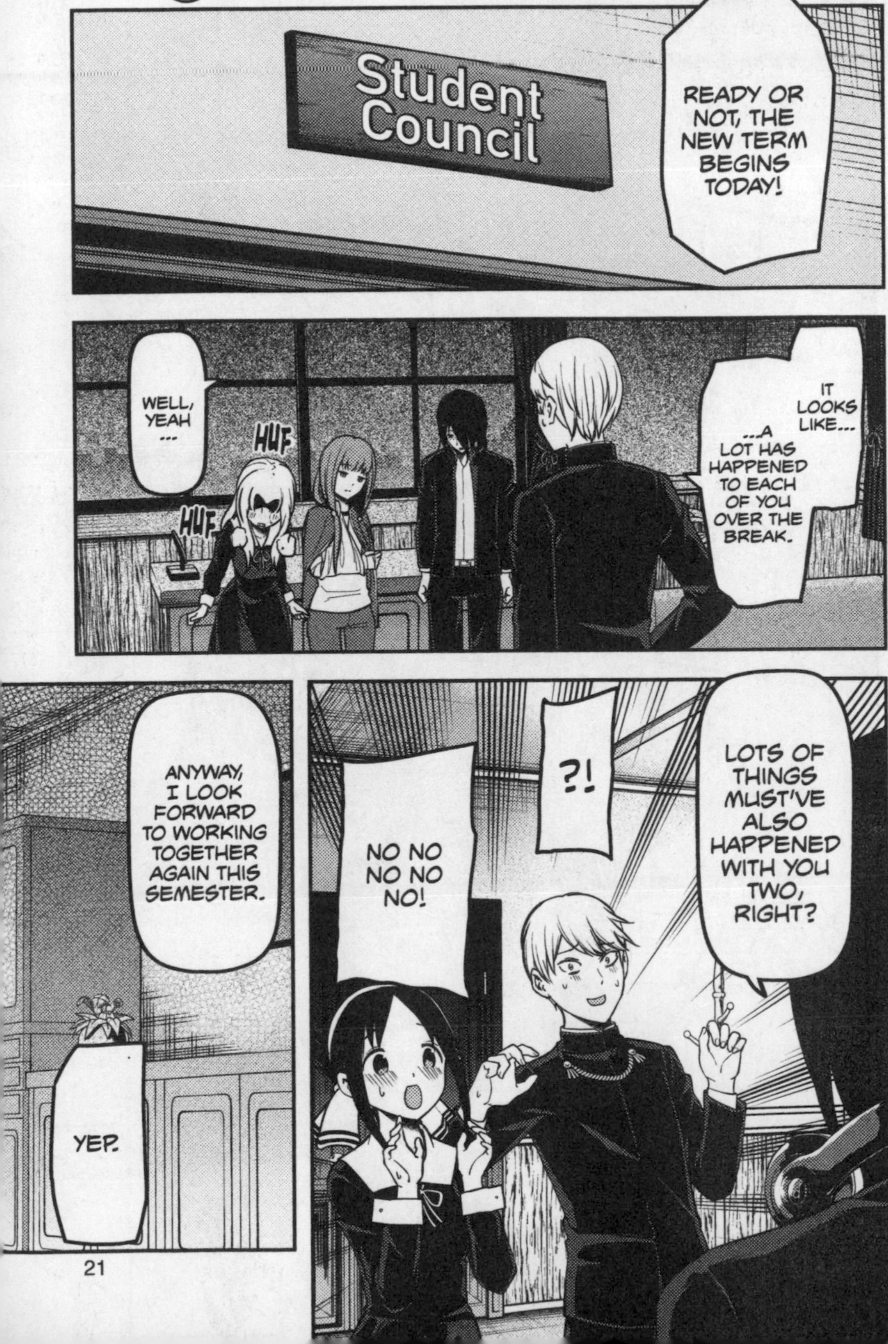
Student Council
READY OR NOT, THE NEW TERM BEGINS TODAY!
IT LOOKS LIKE...
...A LOT HAS HAPPENED TO EACH OF YOU OVER THE BREAK.
HUF
HUF
WELL, YEAH ...
LOTS OF THINGS MUST'VE ALSO HAPPENED WITH YOU TWO, RIGHT?
?!
NO NO NO NO NO!
ANYWAY, I LOOK FORWARD TO WORKING TOGETHER AGAIN THIS SEMESTER.
YEP.

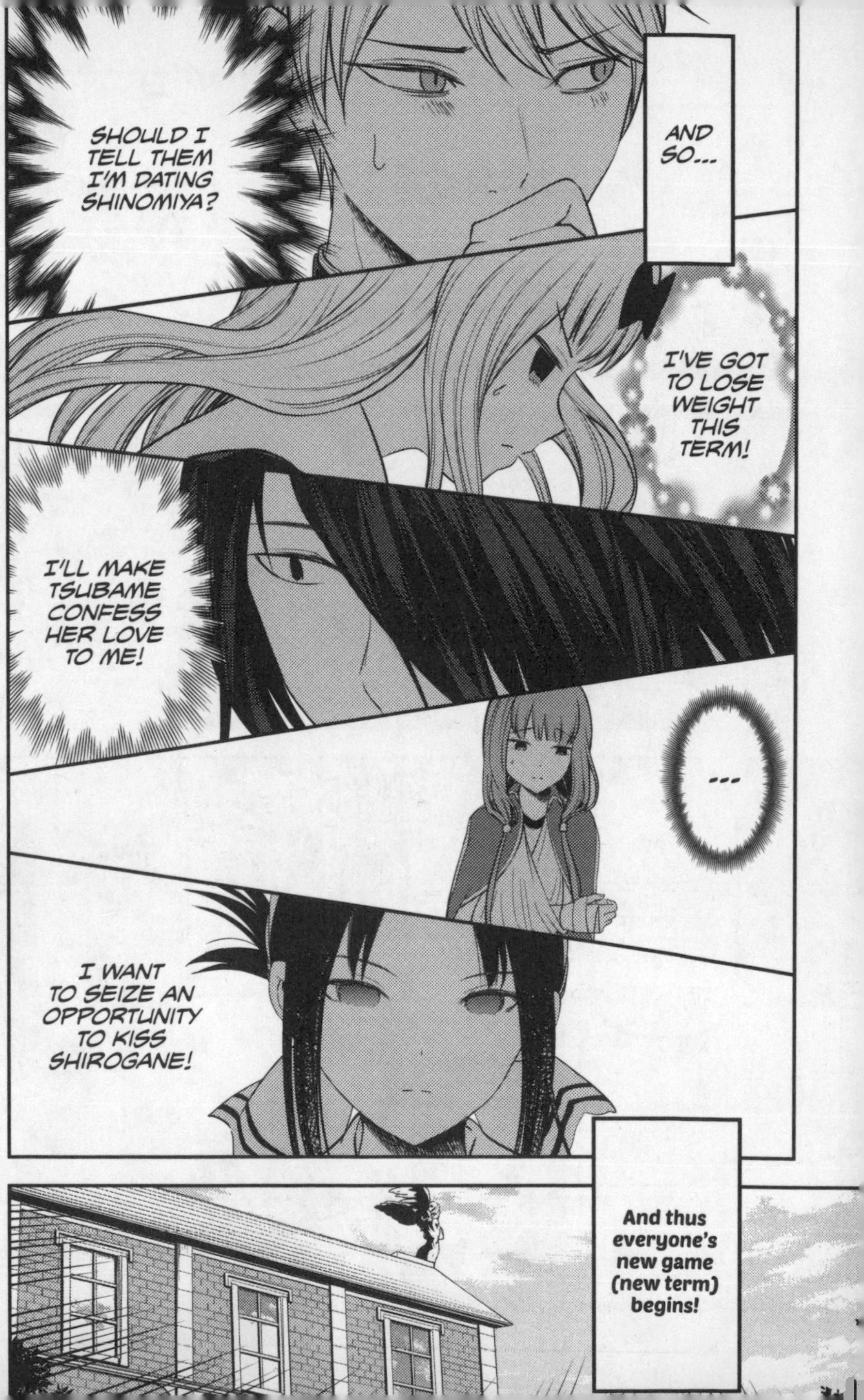
AND SO...
SHOULD I TELL THEM I'M DATING SHINOMIYA?
I'VE GOT TO LOSE WEIGHT THIS TERM!
I'LL MAKE TSUBAME CONFESS HER LOVE TO ME!
...
I WANT TO SEIZE AN OPPORTUNITY TO KISS SHIROGANE!
And thus everyone's new game (new term) begins!

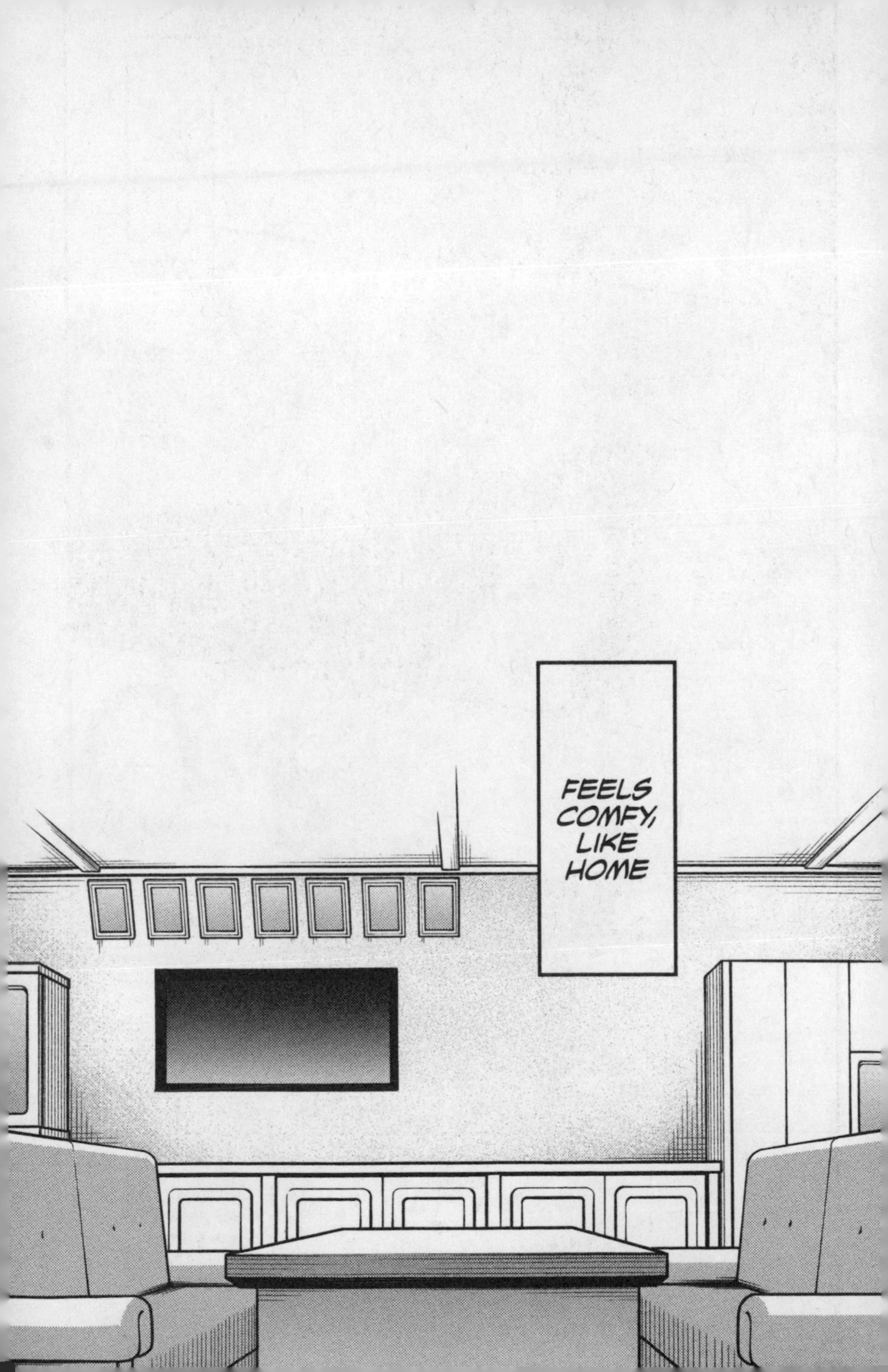
FEELS COMFY, LIKE HOME

KAGUYA-SAMA
LOVE IS WAR

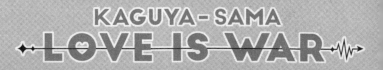

Battle 163 Chika Fujiwara Wants to Surprise

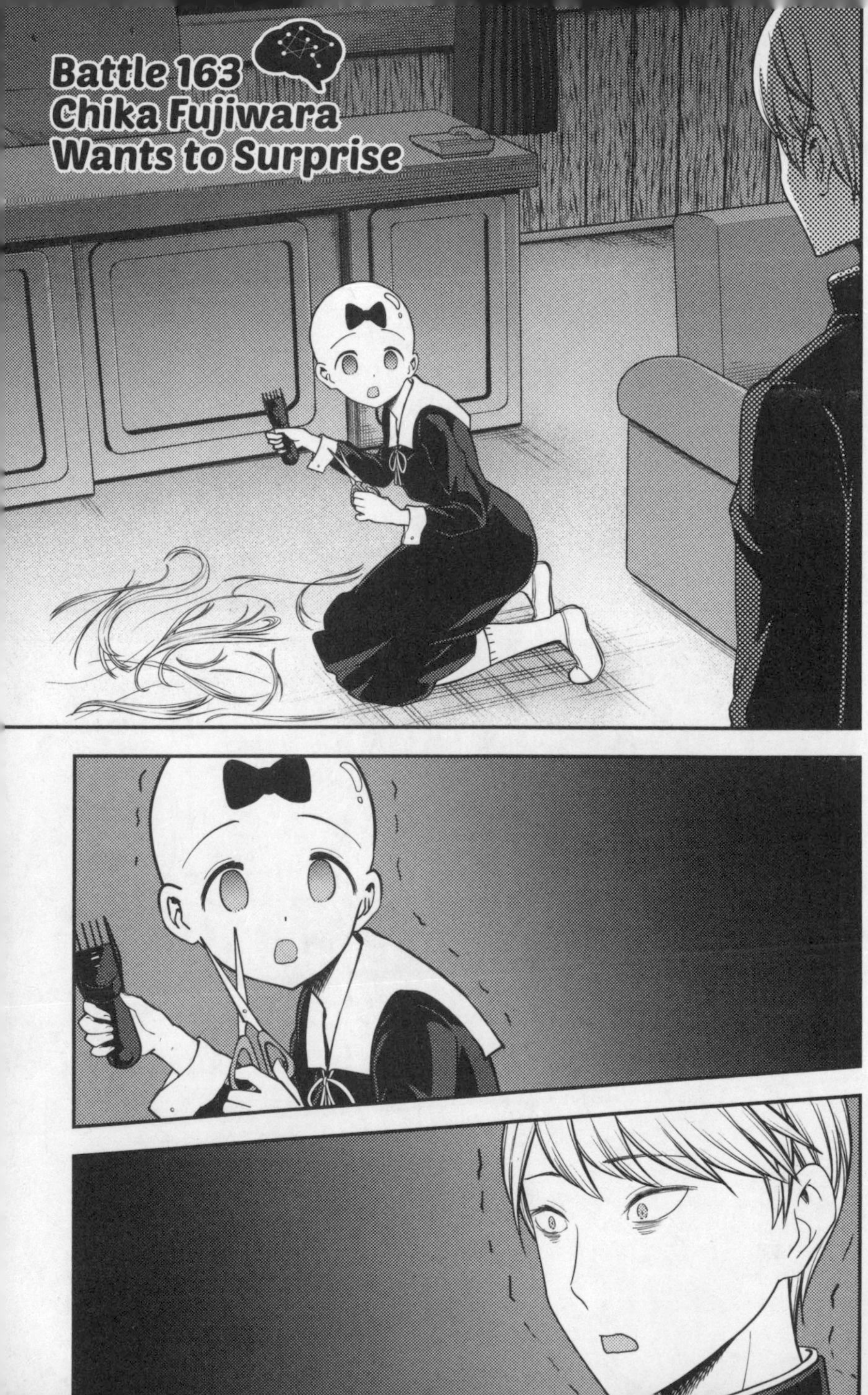

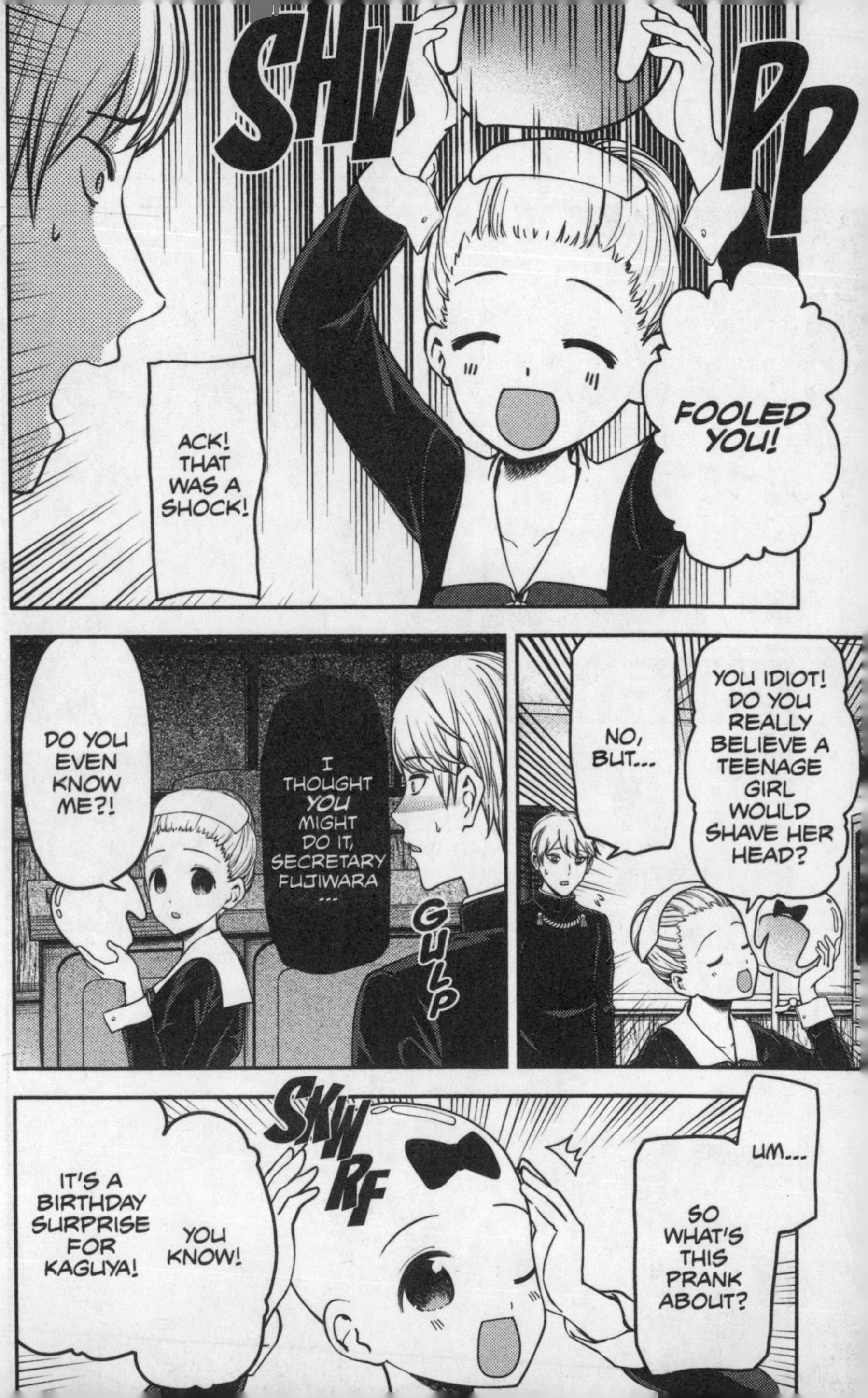
SHI
PP
FOOLED YOU!
ACK! THAT WAS A SHOCK!
YOU IDIOT! DO YOU REALLY BELIEVE A TEENAGE GIRL WOULD SHAVE HER HEAD?
NO, BUT...
I THOUGHT YOU MIGHT DO IT, SECRETARY FUJIWARA...
GULP
DO YOU EVEN KNOW ME?!
UM...
SO WHAT'S THIS PRANK ABOUT?
SKWRF
YOU KNOW!
IT'S A BIRTHDAY SURPRISE FOR KAGUYA!

BIRTHDAY SURPRISES!

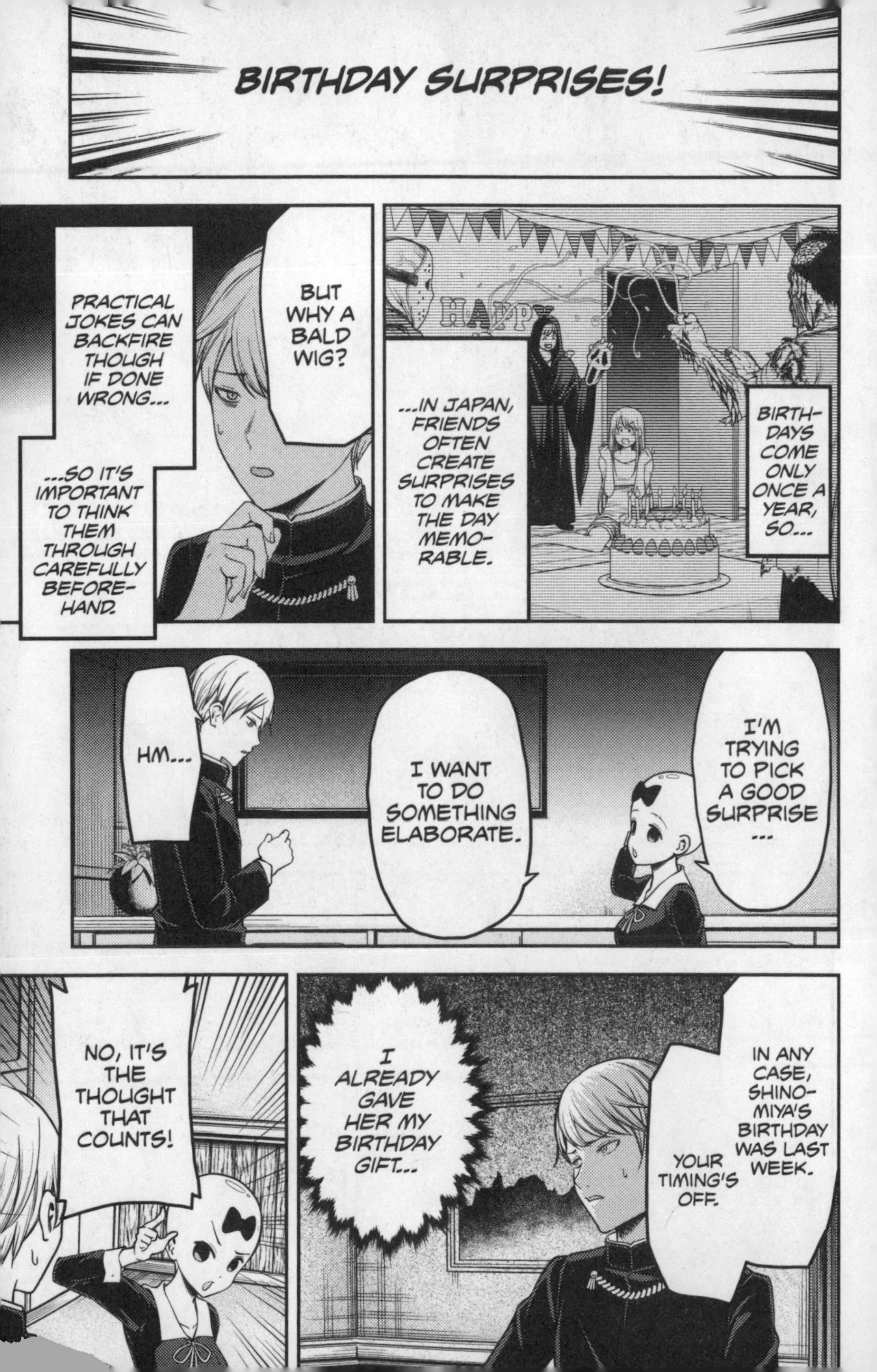
BIRTHDAY SURPRISES!
BIRTHDAYS COME ONLY ONCE A YEAR, SO...
HAPPY
...IN JAPAN, FRIENDS OFTEN CREATE SURPRISES TO MAKE THE DAY MEMORABLE.
BUT WHY A BALD WIG?
PRACTICAL JOKES CAN BACKFIRE THOUGH IF DONE WRONG...
...SO IT'S IMPORTANT TO THINK THEM THROUGH CAREFULLY BEFOREHAND.
I'M TRYING TO PICK A GOOD SURPRISE...
I WANT TO DO SOMETHING ELABORATE.
HM...
IN ANY CASE, SHINOMIYA'S BIRTHDAY WAS LAST WEEK.
YOUR TIMING'S OFF.
I ALREADY GAVE HER MY BIRTHDAY GIFT...
NO, IT'S THE THOUGHT THAT COUNTS!

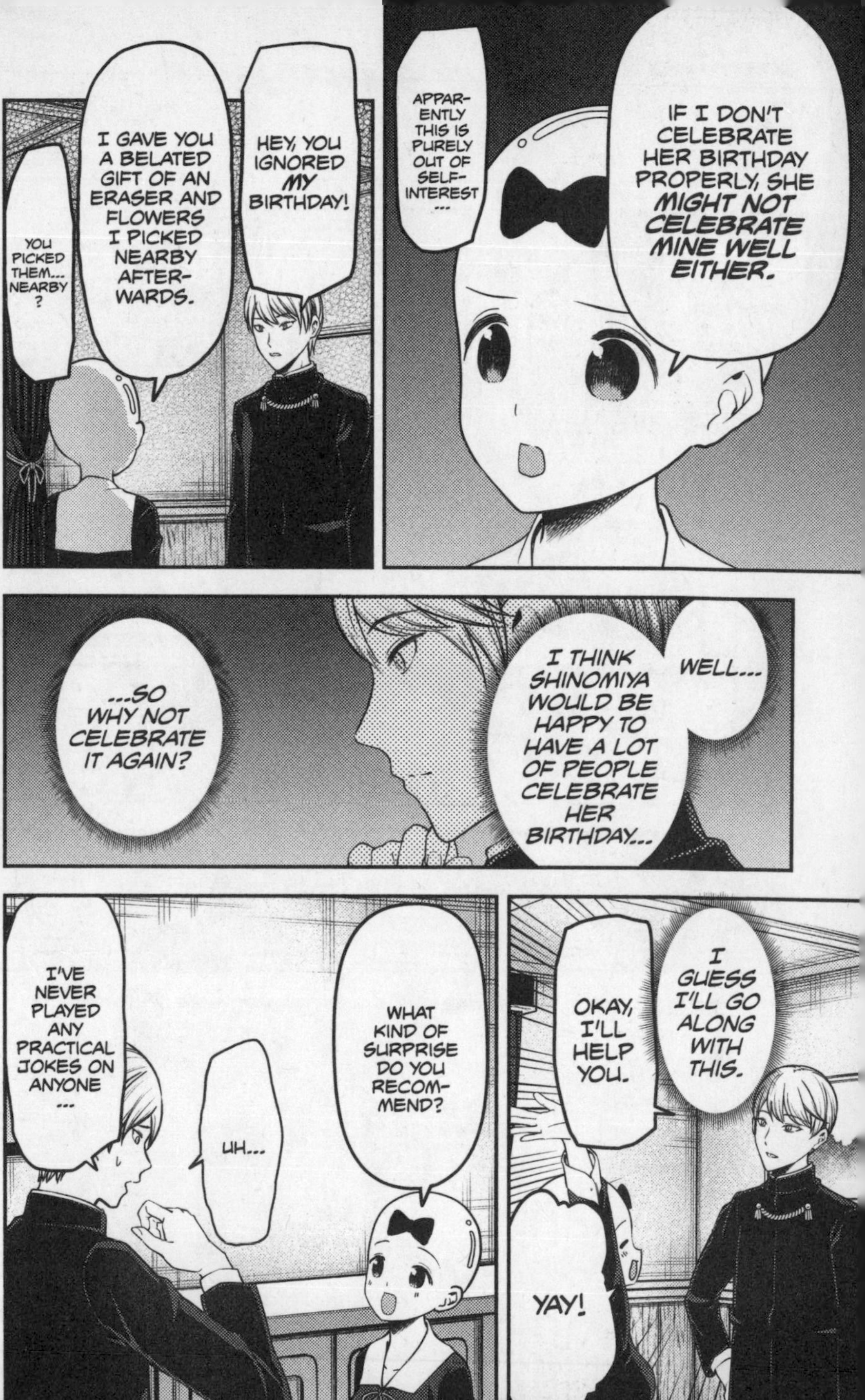
IF I DON'T CELEBRATE HER BIRTHDAY PROPERLY, SHE MIGHT NOT CELEBRATE MINE WELL EITHER.
APPARENTLY THIS IS PURELY OUT OF SELF-INTEREST...
HEY, YOU IGNORED MY BIRTHDAY!
I GAVE YOU A BELATED GIFT OF AN ERASER AND FLOWERS I PICKED NEARBY AFTERWARDS.
YOU PICKED THEM... NEARBY?
WELL...
I THINK SHINOMIYA WOULD BE HAPPY TO HAVE A LOT OF PEOPLE CELEBRATE HER BIRTHDAY...
...SO WHY NOT CELEBRATE IT AGAIN?
I GUESS I'LL GO ALONG WITH THIS.
OKAY, I'LL HELP YOU.
YAY!
WHAT KIND OF SURPRISE DO YOU RECOMMEND?
UH...
I'VE NEVER PLAYED ANY PRACTICAL JOKES ON ANYONE...

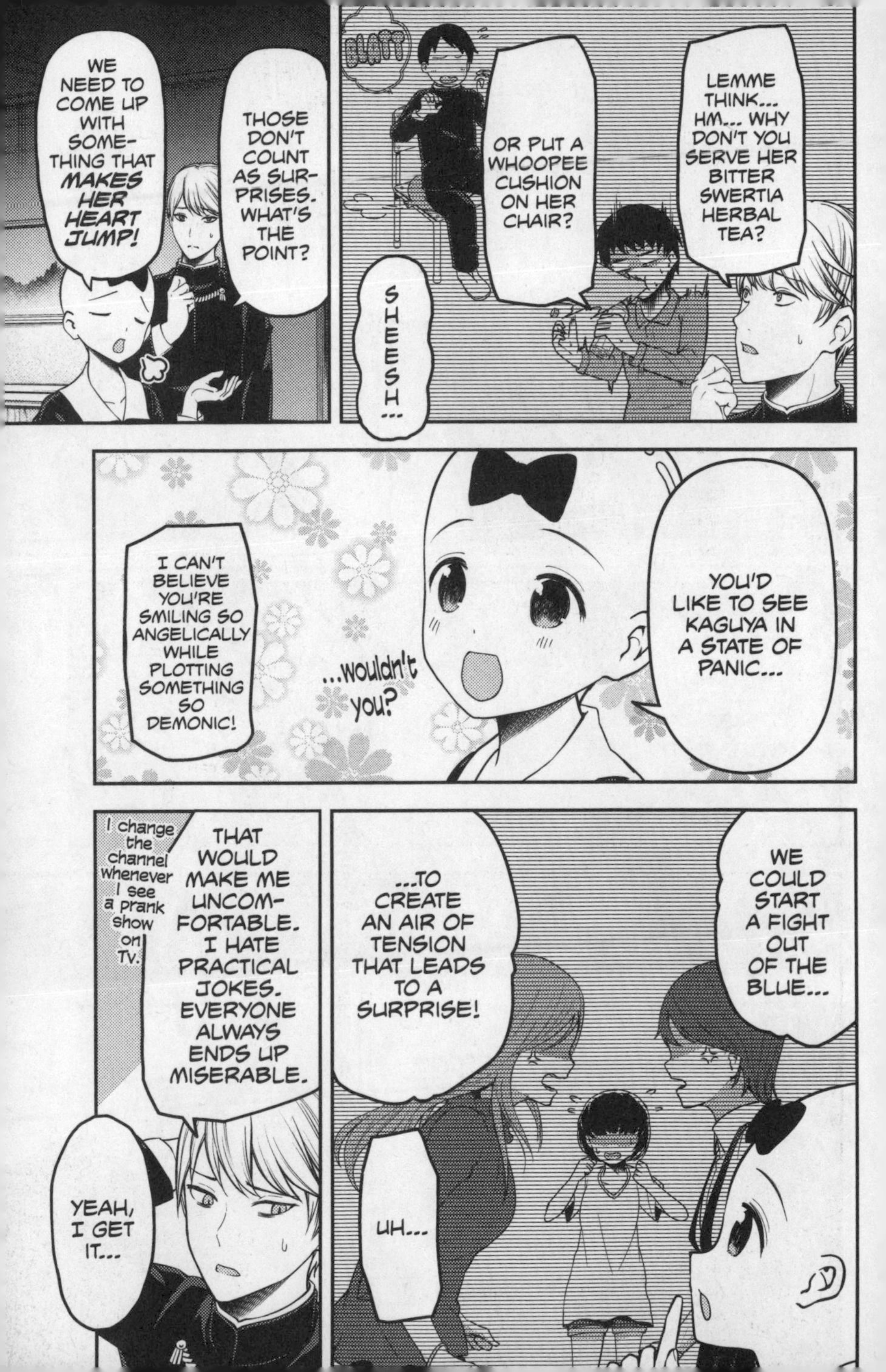
LEMME THINK... HM... WHY DON'T YOU SERVE HER BITTER SWERTIA HERBAL TEA?
OR PUT A WHOOPEE CUSHION ON HER CHAIR?
SHEESH...
THOSE DON'T COUNT AS SURPRISES. WHAT'S THE POINT?
WE NEED TO COME UP WITH SOMETHING THAT MAKES HER HEART JUMP!
YOU'D LIKE TO SEE KAGUYA IN A STATE OF PANIC...
...wouldn't you?
I CAN'T BELIEVE YOU'RE SMILING SO ANGELICALLY WHILE PLOTTING SOMETHING SO DEMONIC!
WE COULD START A FIGHT OUT OF THE BLUE...
...TO CREATE AN AIR OF TENSION THAT LEADS TO A SURPRISE!
UH...
THAT WOULD MAKE ME UNCOMFORTABLE. I HATE PRACTICAL JOKES. EVERYONE ALWAYS ENDS UP MISERABLE.
I change the channel whenever I see a prank show on TV.
YEAH, I GET IT...

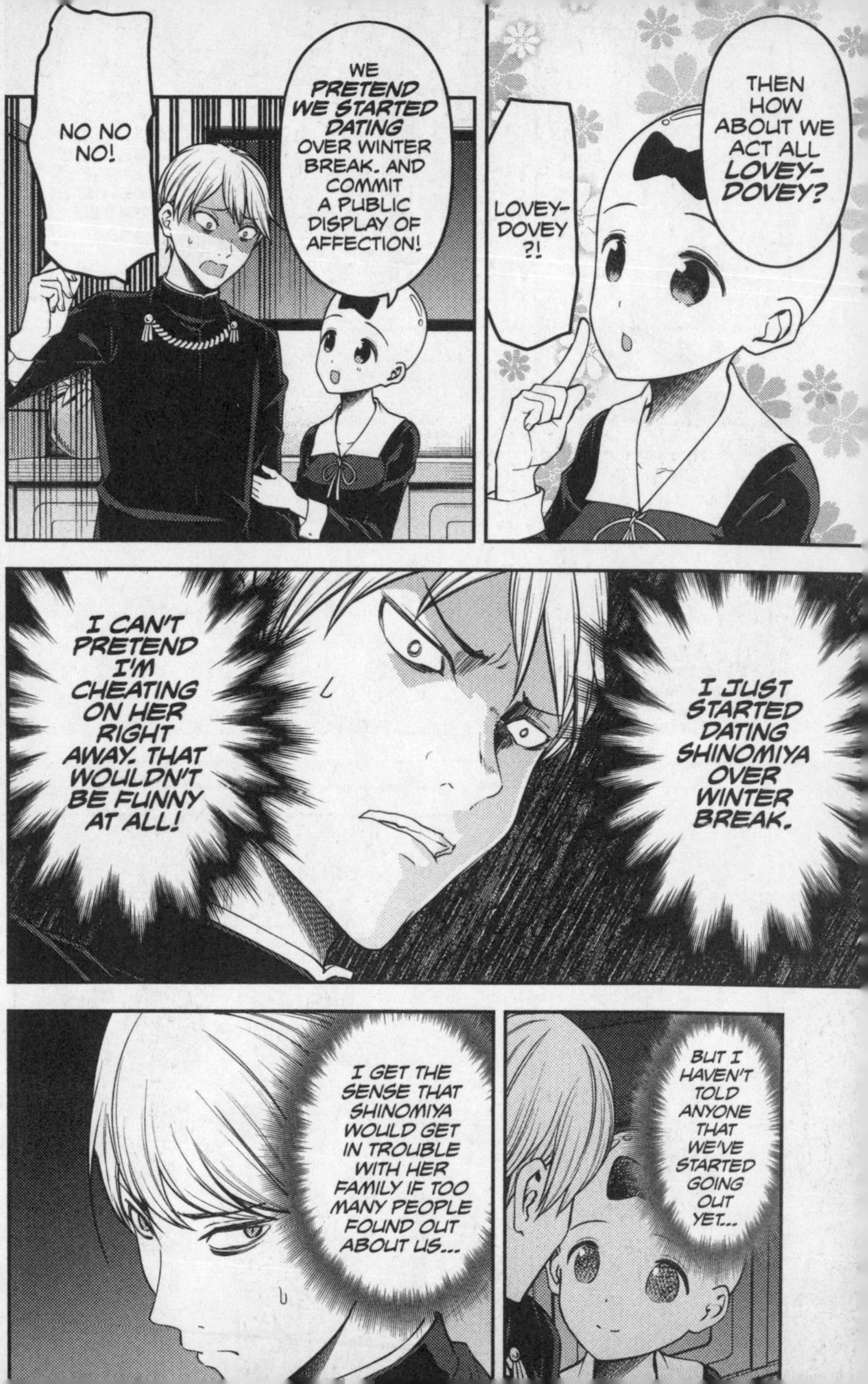
THEN HOW ABOUT WE ACT ALL LOVEY-DOVEY?
LOVEY-DOVEY ?!
WE PRETEND WE STARTED DATING OVER WINTER BREAK. AND COMMIT A PUBLIC DISPLAY OF AFFECTION!
NO NO NO!
I JUST STARTED DATING SHINOMIYA OVER WINTER BREAK.
I CAN'T PRETEND I'M CHEATING ON HER RIGHT AWAY. THAT WOULDN'T BE FUNNY AT ALL!
BUT I HAVEN'T TOLD ANYONE THAT WE'VE STARTED GOING OUT YET...
I GET THE SENSE THAT SHINOMIYA WOULD GET IN TROUBLE WITH HER FAMILY IF TOO MANY PEOPLE FOUND OUT ABOUT US...

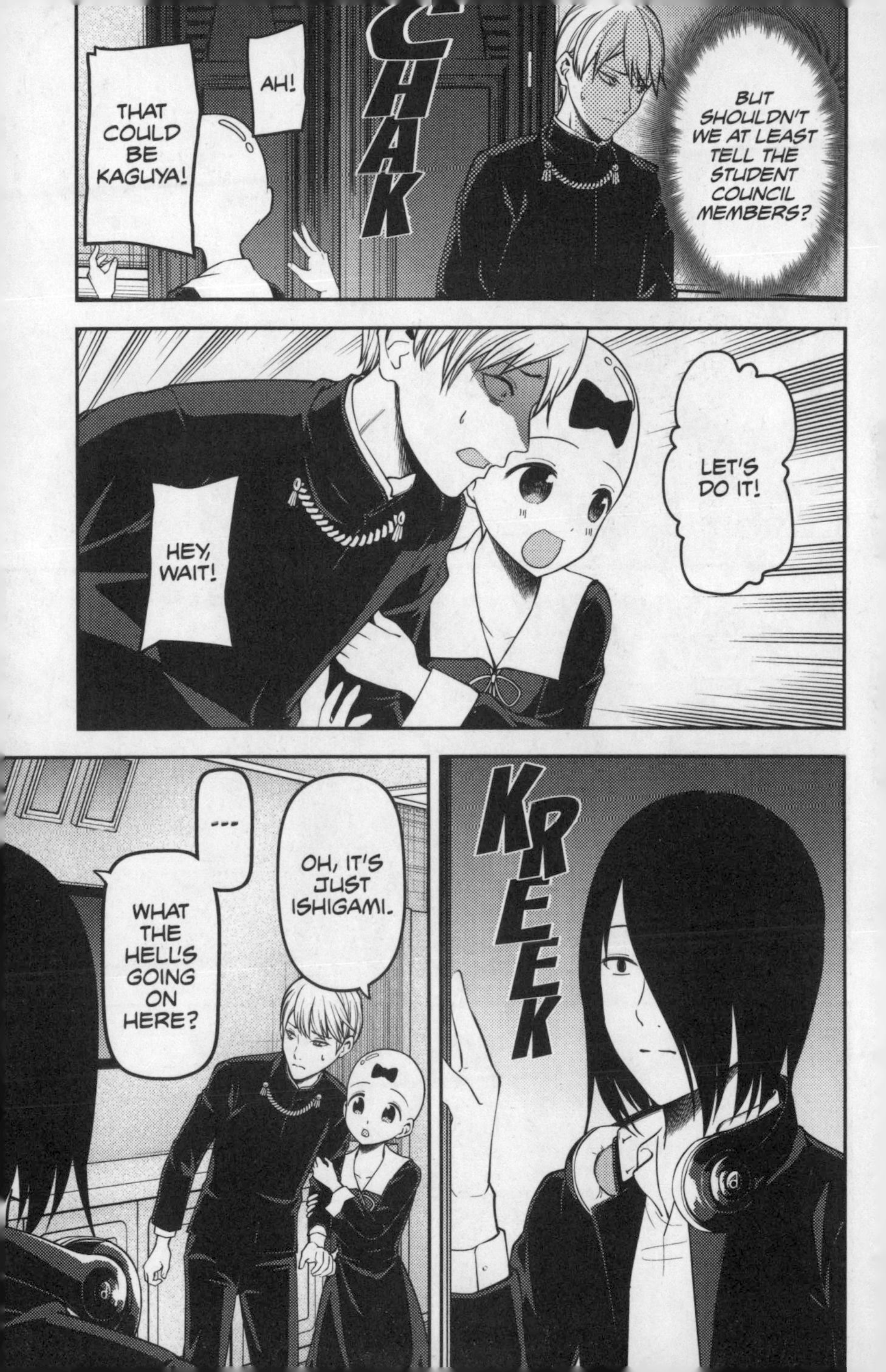
BUT SHOULDN'T WE AT LEAST TELL THE STUDENT COUNCIL MEMBERS?
CHAK
AH!
THAT COULD BE KAGUYA!
LET'S DO IT!
HEY, WAIT!
KREEK
OH, IT'S JUST ISHIGAMI.
...
WHAT THE HELL'S GOING ON HERE?

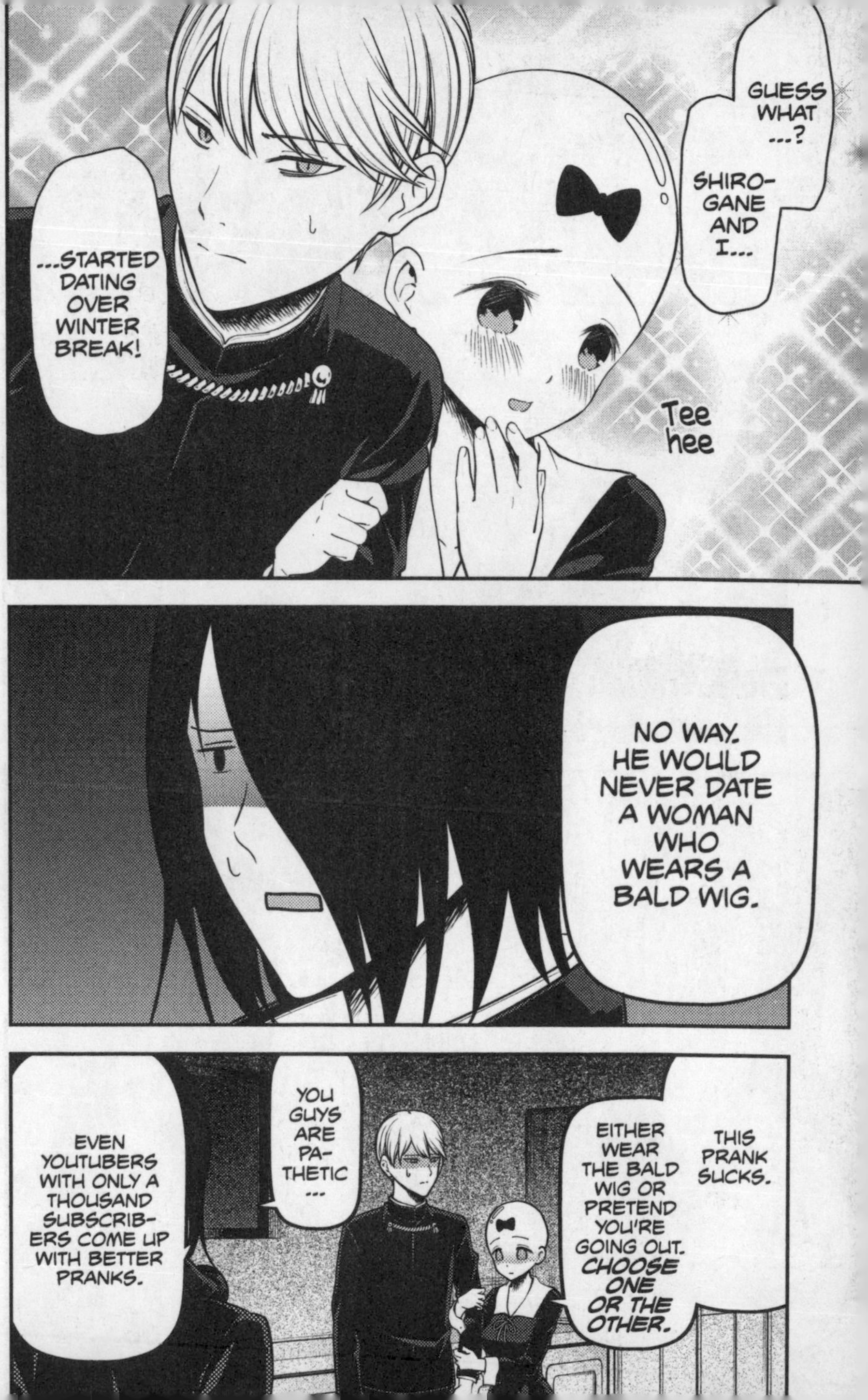
GUESS WHAT ...?
SHIRO-GANE AND I...
Tee hee
...STARTED DATING OVER WINTER BREAK!
NO WAY. HE WOULD NEVER DATE A WOMAN WHO WEARS A BALD WIG.
THIS PRANK SUCKS.
EITHER WEAR THE BALD WIG OR PRETEND YOU'RE GOING OUT. CHOOSE ONE OR THE OTHER.
YOU GUYS ARE PATHETIC ...
EVEN YOUTUBERS WITH ONLY A THOUSAND SUBSCRIB-ERS COME UP WITH BETTER PRANKS.

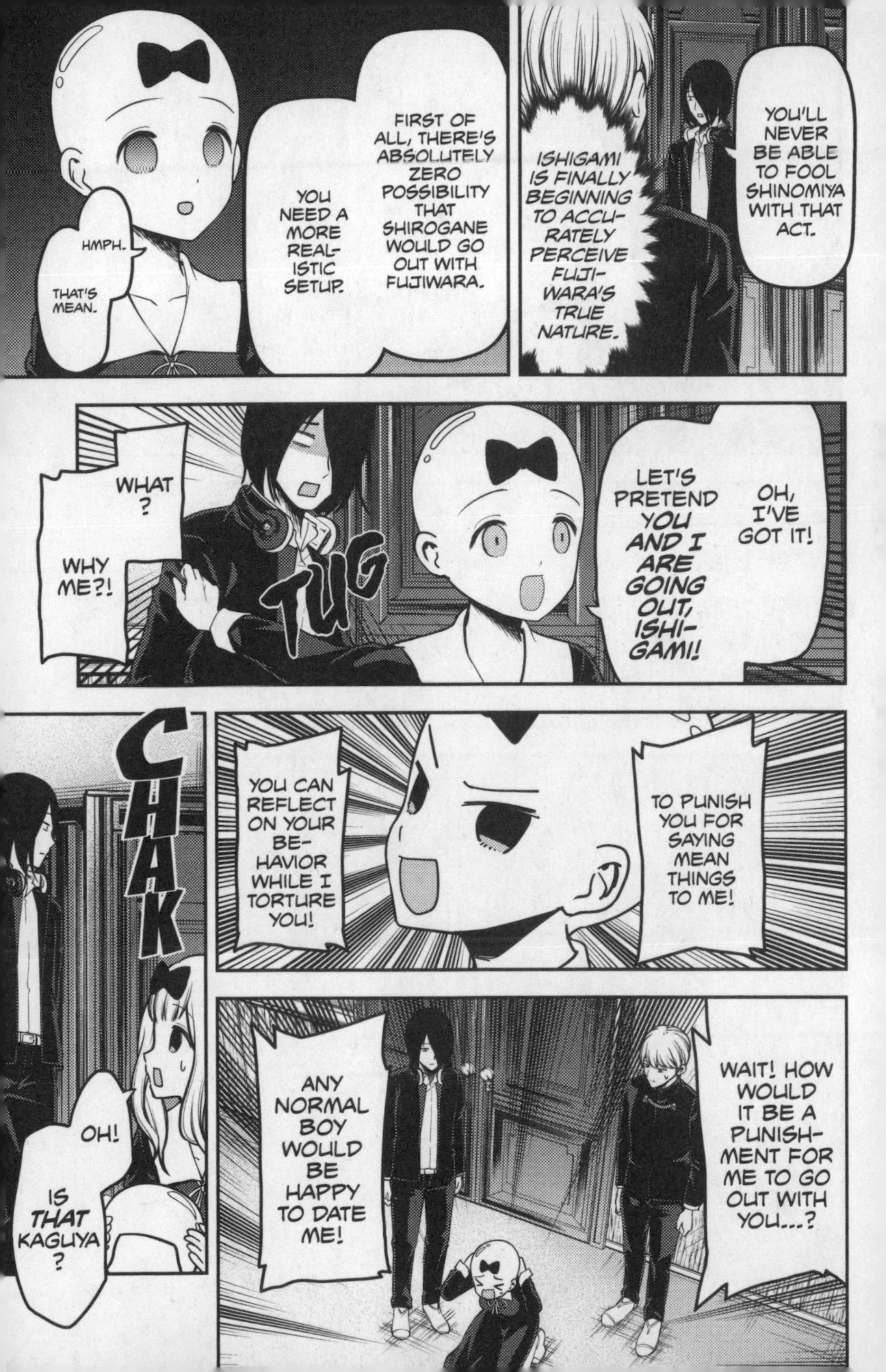
YOU'LL NEVER BE ABLE TO FOOL SHINOMIYA WITH THAT ACT.
ISHIGAMI IS FINALLY BEGINNING TO ACCURATELY PERCEIVE FUJIWARA'S TRUE NATURE.
FIRST OF ALL, THERE'S ABSOLUTELY ZERO POSSIBILITY THAT SHIROGANE WOULD GO OUT WITH FUJIWARA.
YOU NEED A MORE REALISTIC SETUP.
HMPH.
THAT'S MEAN.
OH, I'VE GOT IT!
LET'S PRETEND *YOU AND I* ARE GOING OUT, ISHIGAMI!
TUG
WHAT? WHY ME?!
TO PUNISH YOU FOR SAYING MEAN THINGS TO ME!
YOU CAN REFLECT ON YOUR BEHAVIOR WHILE I TORTURE YOU!
WAIT! HOW WOULD IT BE A PUNISHMENT FOR ME TO GO OUT WITH YOU...?
ANY NORMAL BOY WOULD BE HAPPY TO DATE ME!
CHAK
OH!
IS *THAT* KAGUYA?

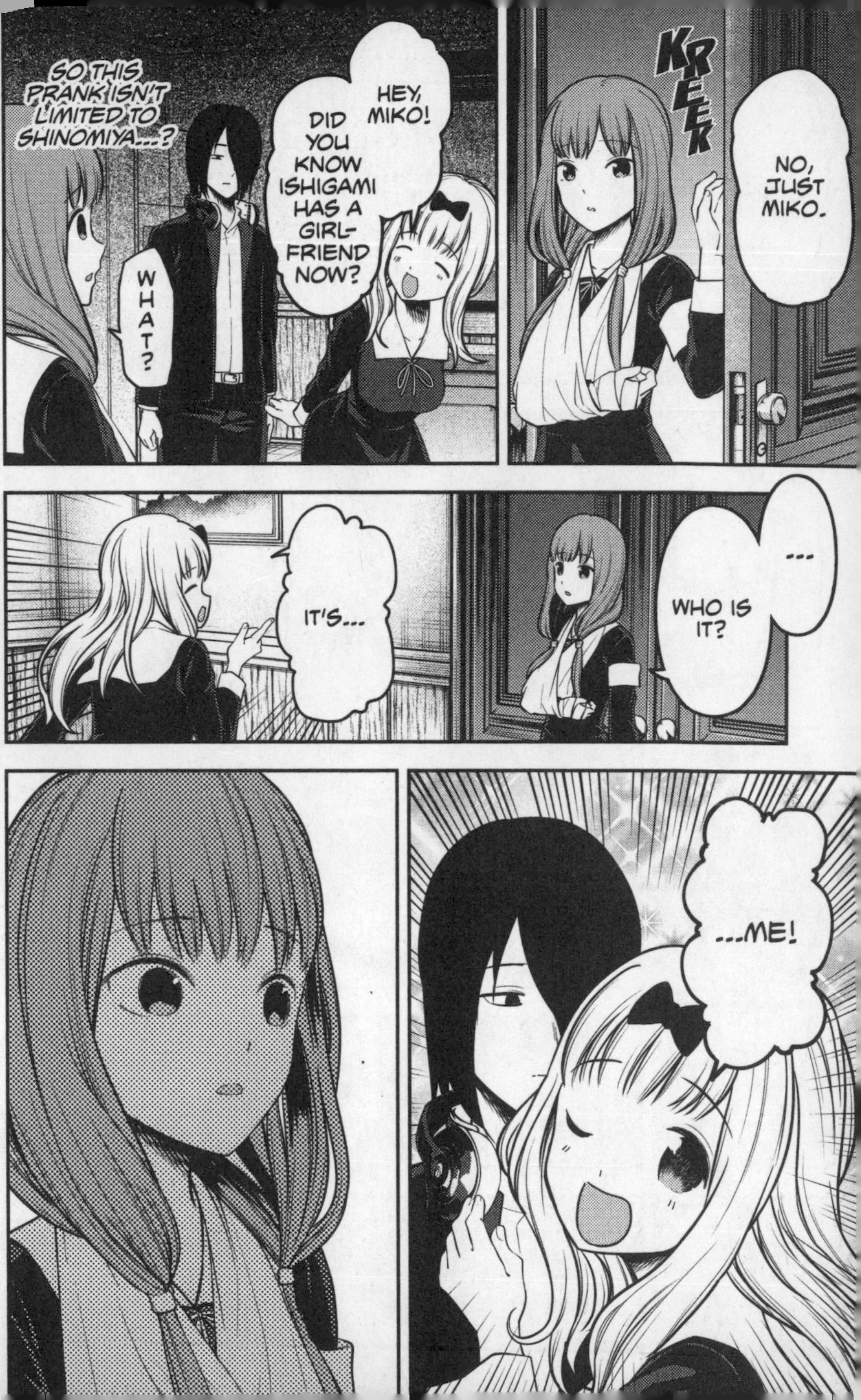
KREEK
NO, JUST MIKO.
HEY, MIKO! DID YOU KNOW ISHIGAMI HAS A GIRL-FRIEND NOW?
WHAT?
SO THIS PRANK ISN'T LIMITED TO SHINOMIYA...?
... WHO IS IT?
IT'S...
...ME!

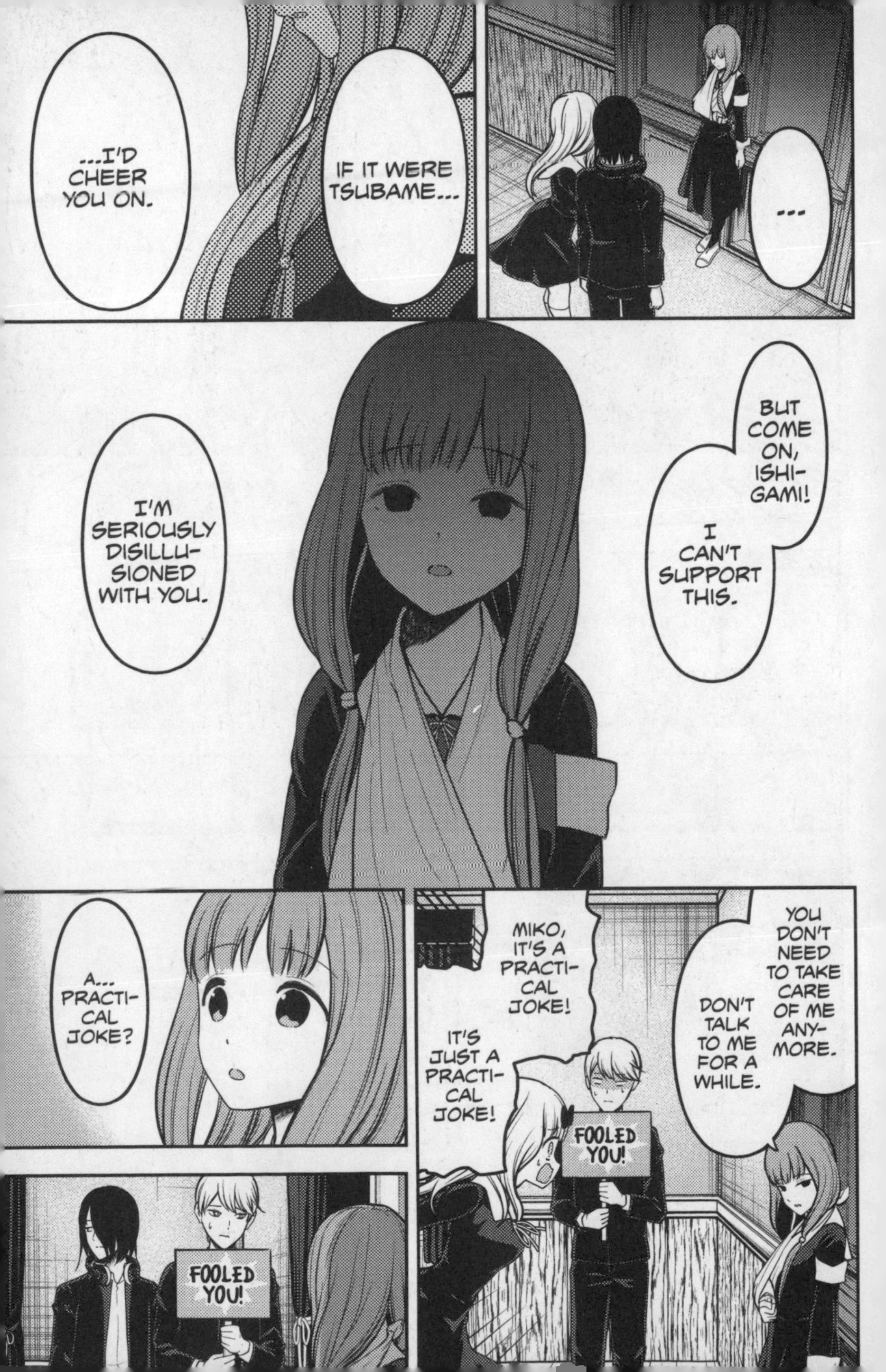
...
IF IT WERE TSUBAME...
...I'D CHEER YOU ON.
BUT COME ON, ISHIGAMI!
I CAN'T SUPPORT THIS.
I'M SERIOUSLY DISILLUSIONED WITH YOU.
YOU DON'T NEED TO TAKE CARE OF ME ANYMORE.
DON'T TALK TO ME FOR A WHILE.
MIKO, IT'S A PRACTICAL JOKE!
IT'S JUST A PRACTICAL JOKE!
FOOLED YOU!
A... PRACTICAL JOKE?
FOOLED YOU!

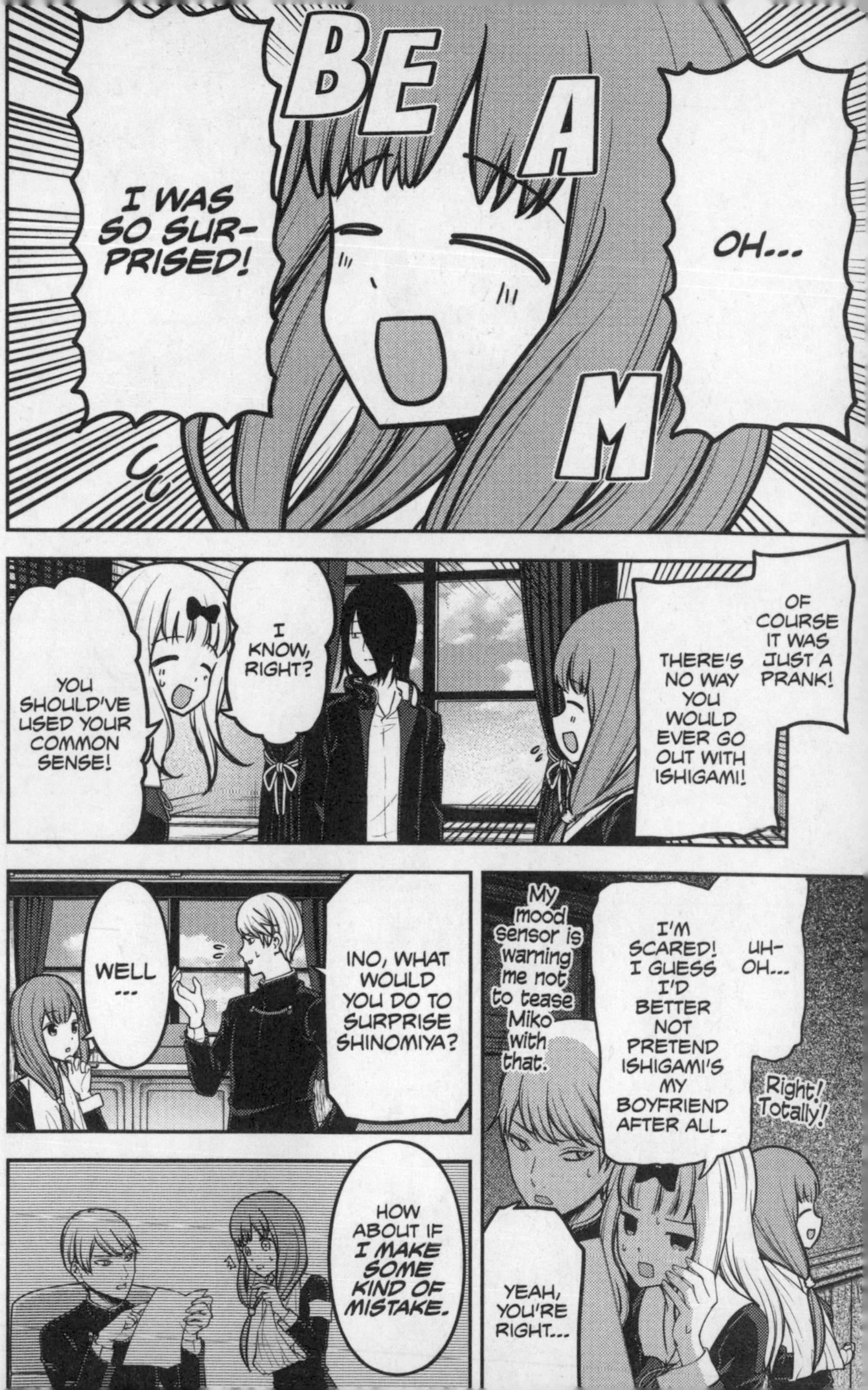
OH...
BEAM
I WAS SO SURPRISED!
OF COURSE IT WAS JUST A PRANK!
THERE'S NO WAY YOU WOULD EVER GO OUT WITH ISHIGAMI!
I KNOW, RIGHT?
YOU SHOULD'VE USED YOUR COMMON SENSE!
UH-OH...
I'M SCARED! I GUESS I'D BETTER NOT PRETEND ISHIGAMI'S MY BOYFRIEND AFTER ALL.
My mood sensor is warning me not to tease Miko with that.
Right! Totally!
YEAH, YOU'RE RIGHT...
INO, WHAT WOULD YOU DO TO SURPRISE SHINOMIYA?
WELL...
HOW ABOUT IF *I MAKE SOME KIND OF MISTAKE.*

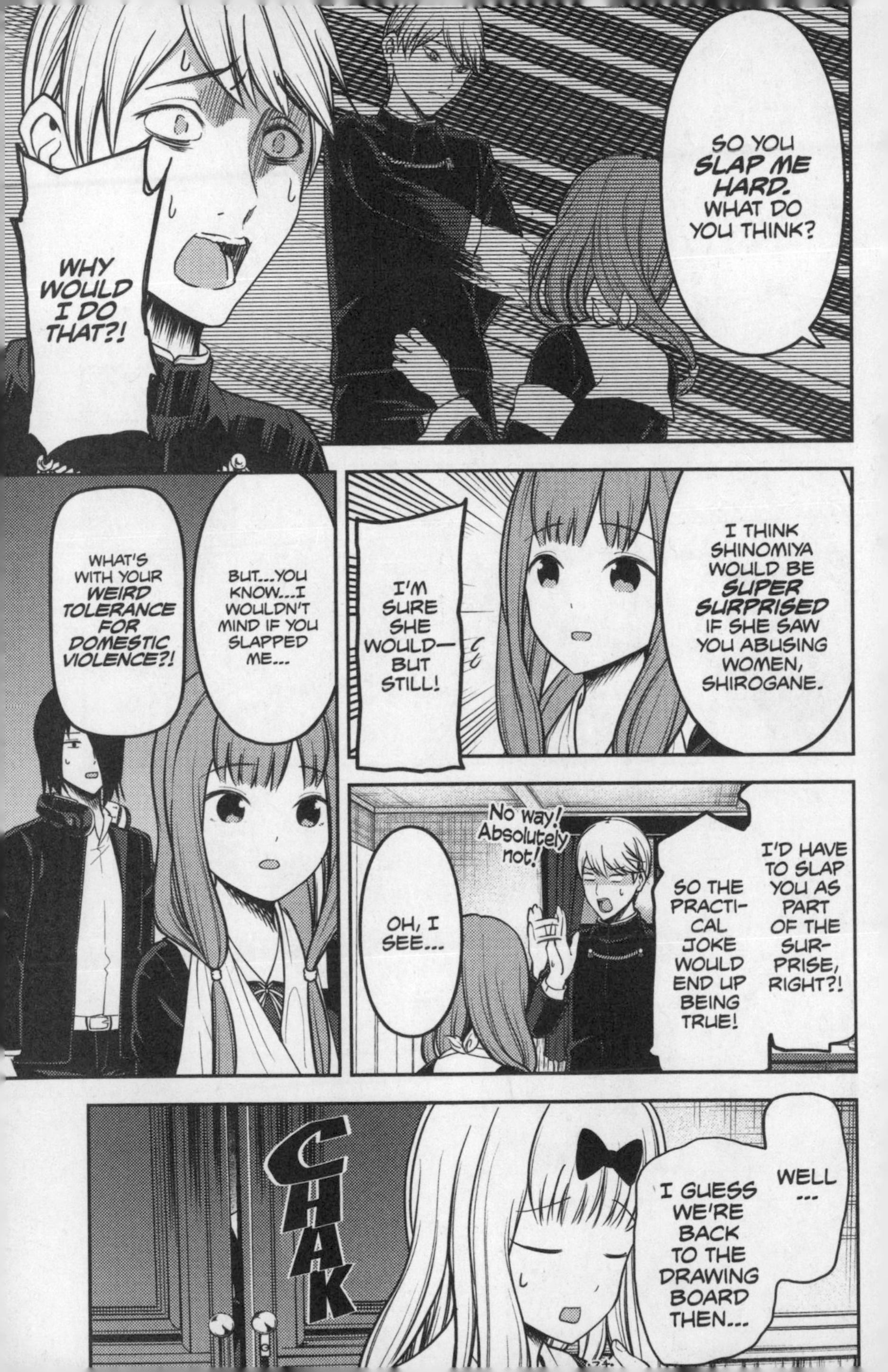
SO YOU SLAP ME HARD. WHAT DO YOU THINK?
WHY WOULD I DO THAT?!
I THINK SHINOMIYA WOULD BE SUPER SURPRISED IF SHE SAW YOU ABUSING WOMEN, SHIROGANE.
I'M SURE SHE WOULD— BUT STILL!
I'D HAVE TO SLAP YOU AS PART OF THE SURPRISE, RIGHT?!
SO THE PRACTICAL JOKE WOULD END UP BEING TRUE!
No way! Absolutely not!
OH, I SEE...
BUT...YOU KNOW...I WOULDN'T MIND IF YOU SLAPPED ME...
WHAT'S WITH YOUR WEIRD TOLERANCE FOR DOMESTIC VIOLENCE?!
WELL...
I GUESS WE'RE BACK TO THE DRAWING BOARD THEN...
CHAK

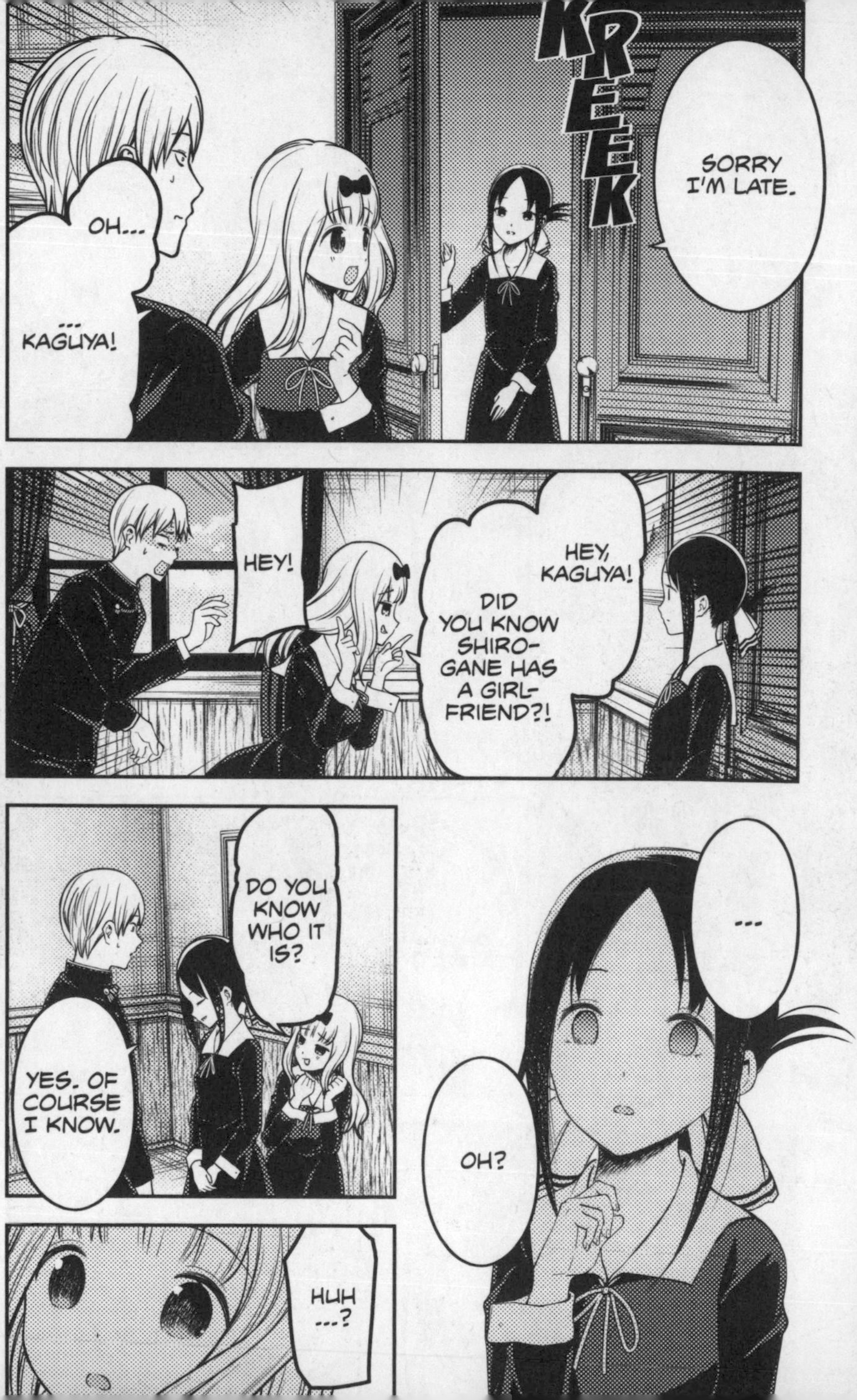
KREEK
SORRY I'M LATE.
OH...
... KAGUYA!
HEY, KAGUYA!
DID YOU KNOW SHIRO-GANE HAS A GIRL-FRIEND?!
HEY!
...
OH?
DO YOU KNOW WHO IT IS?
YES. OF COURSE I KNOW.
HUH ...?

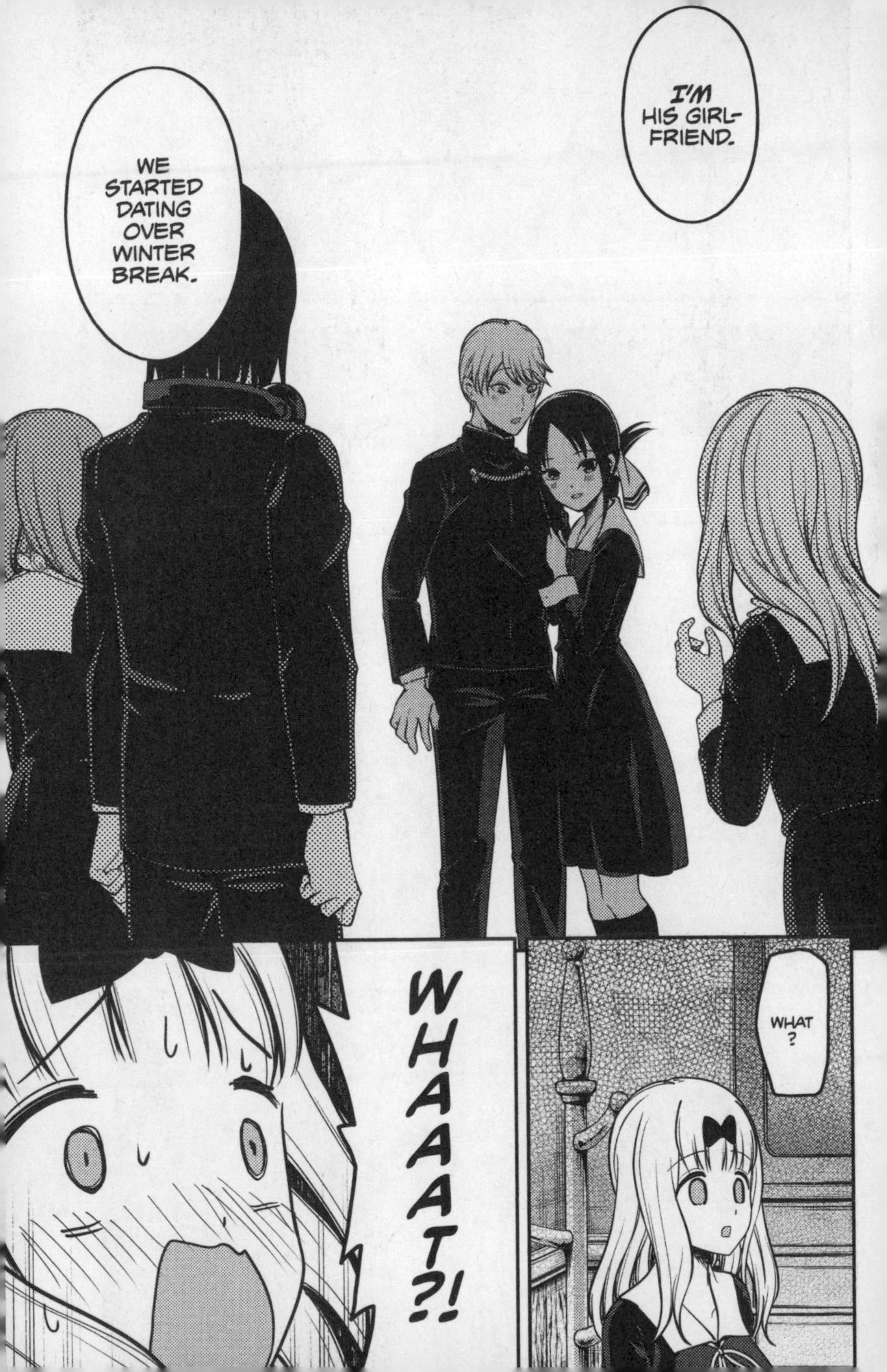
I'M HIS GIRL-FRIEND.
WE STARTED DATING OVER WINTER BREAK.
WHAT?
WHAAAAT?!

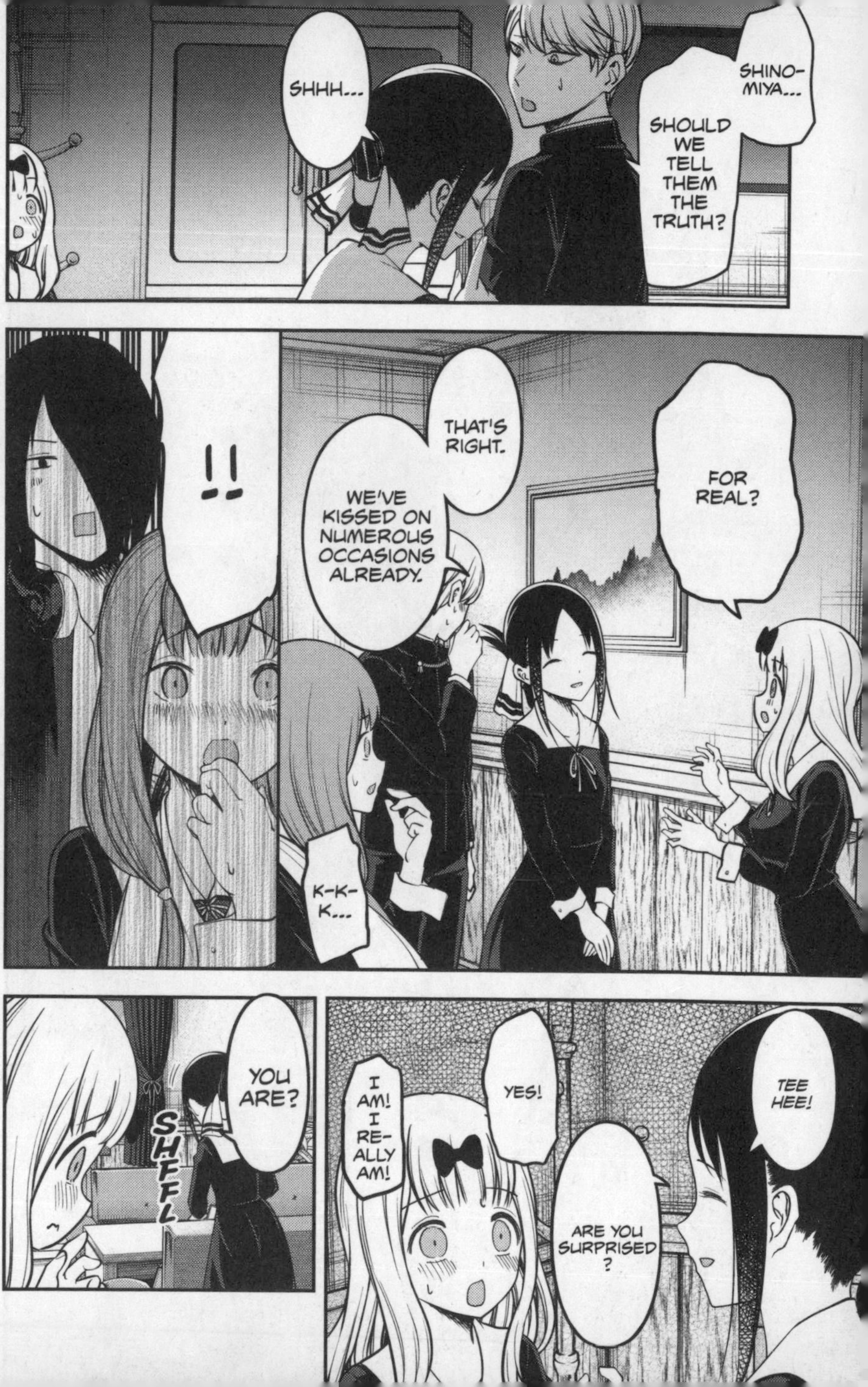
SHINO-MIYA...
SHOULD WE TELL THEM THE TRUTH?
SHHH...
FOR REAL?
THAT'S RIGHT.
WE'VE KISSED ON NUMEROUS OCCASIONS ALREADY.
K-K-K...
!!
TEE HEE!
ARE YOU SURPRISED?
YES!
I AM! I RE-ALLY AM!
YOU ARE?
SHFFL

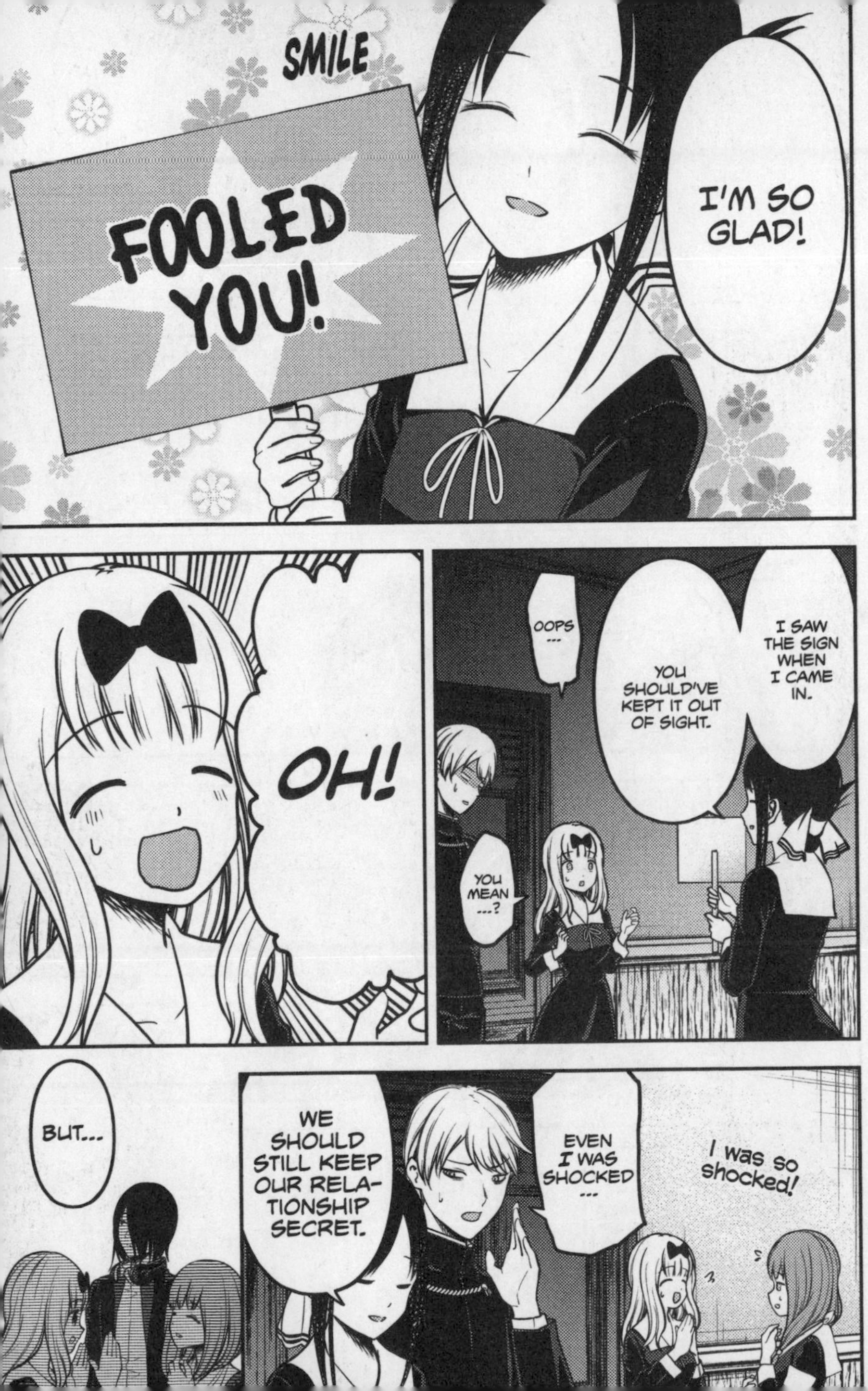
I'M SO GLAD!
SMILE
FOOLED YOU!
I SAW THE SIGN WHEN I CAME IN.
YOU SHOULD'VE KEPT IT OUT OF SIGHT.
OOPS...
YOU MEAN...?
OH!
I was so shocked!
EVEN I WAS SHOCKED...
WE SHOULD STILL KEEP OUR RELA-TIONSHIP SECRET.
BUT...

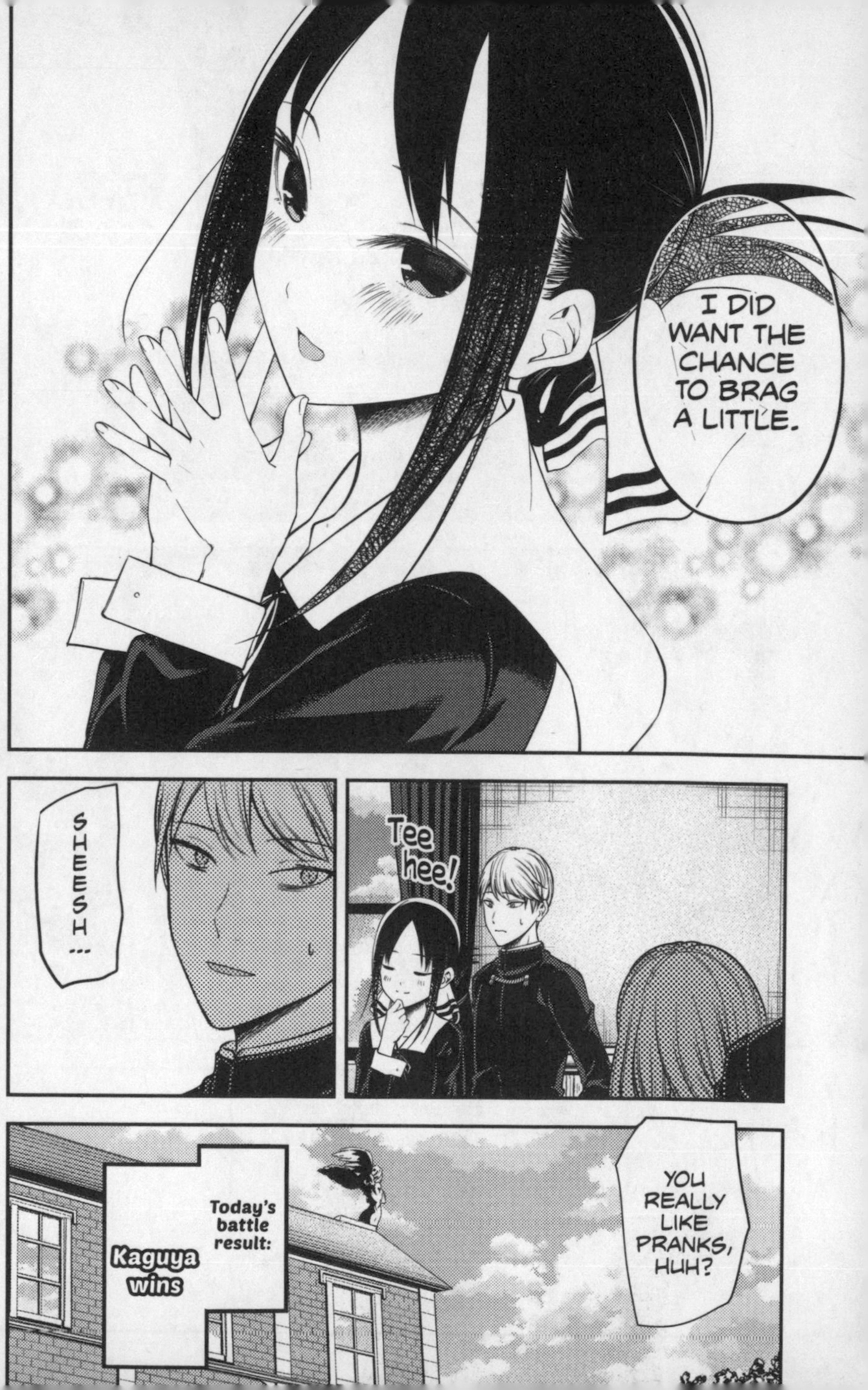
I DID WANT THE CHANCE TO BRAG A LITTLE.
Tee hee!
SHEESH...
YOU REALLY LIKE PRANKS, HUH?
Today's battle result:
Kaguya wins

You enjoy pain?
Yeah.
Doesn't pain make you feel safe somehow?
Huh? Um...

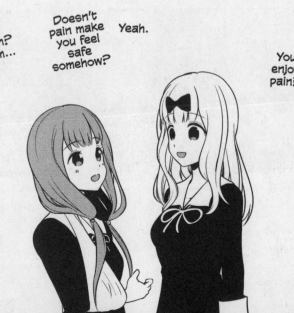

KAGUYA-SAMA

LOVE IS WAR

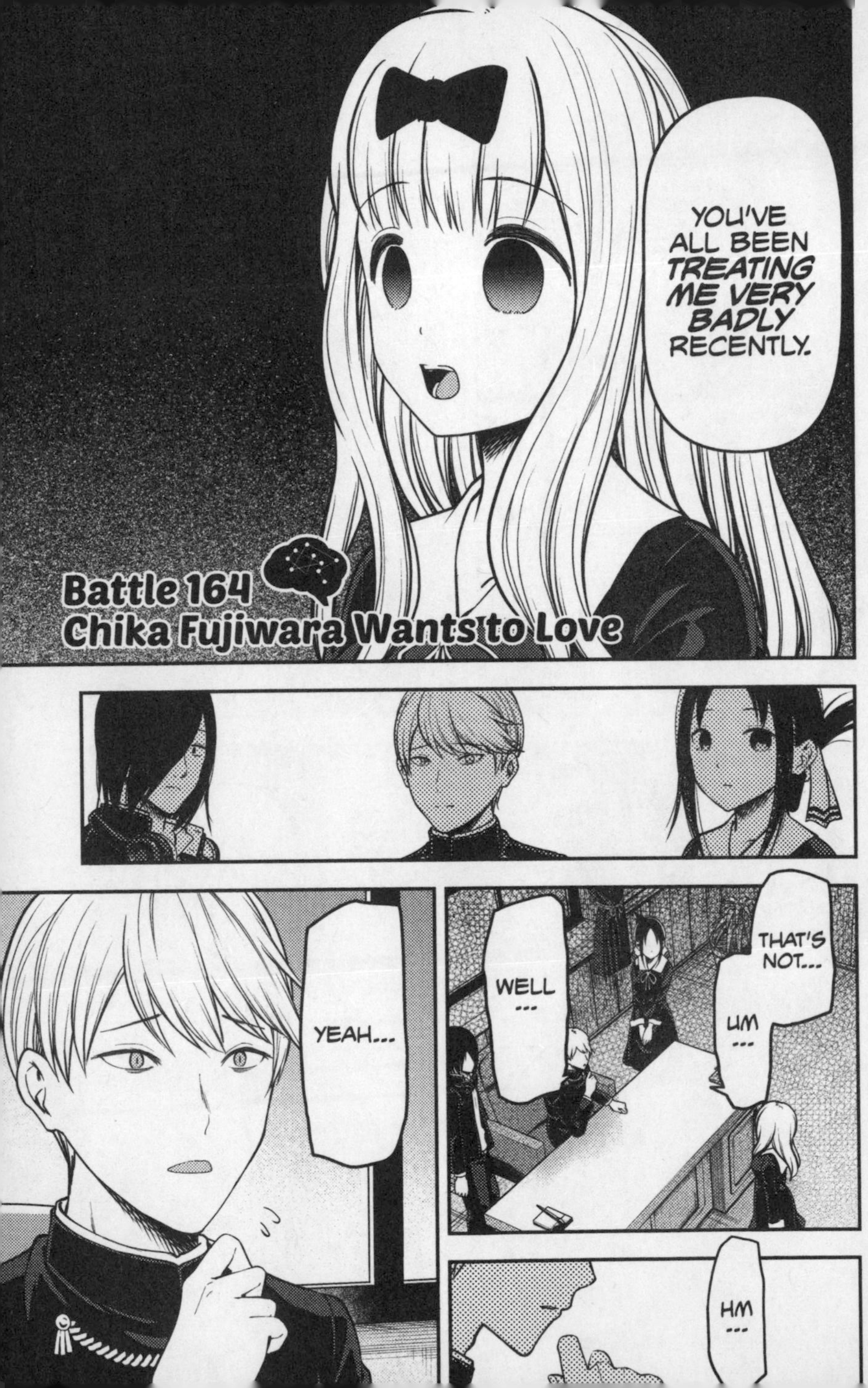
YOU'VE ALL BEEN TREATING ME VERY BADLY RECENTLY.
Battle 164
Chika Fujiwara Wants to Love
THAT'S NOT...
UM ...
WELL ...
HM ...
YEAH...

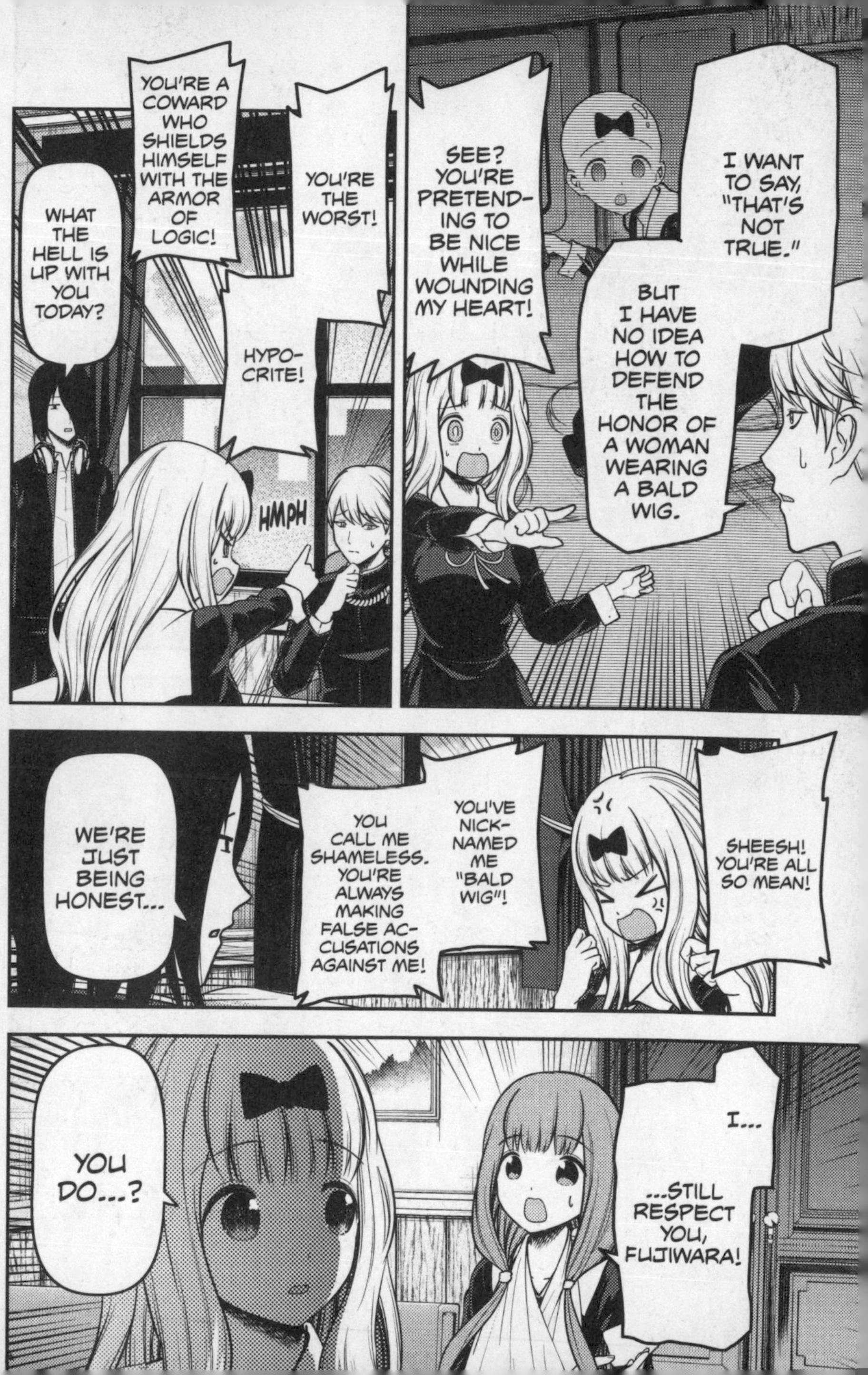
I WANT TO SAY, "THAT'S NOT TRUE."
BUT I HAVE NO IDEA HOW TO DEFEND THE HONOR OF A WOMAN WEARING A BALD WIG.
SEE? YOU'RE PRETENDING TO BE NICE WHILE WOUNDING MY HEART!
YOU'RE THE WORST!
YOU'RE A COWARD WHO SHIELDS HIMSELF WITH THE ARMOR OF LOGIC!
HYPOCRITE!
HMPH
WHAT THE HELL IS UP WITH YOU TODAY?
SHEESH! YOU'RE ALL SO MEAN!
YOU'VE NICKNAMED ME "BALD WIG"!
YOU CALL ME SHAMELESS. YOU'RE ALWAYS MAKING FALSE ACCUSATIONS AGAINST ME!
WE'RE JUST BEING HONEST...
I...
...STILL RESPECT YOU, FUJIWARA!
YOU DO...?

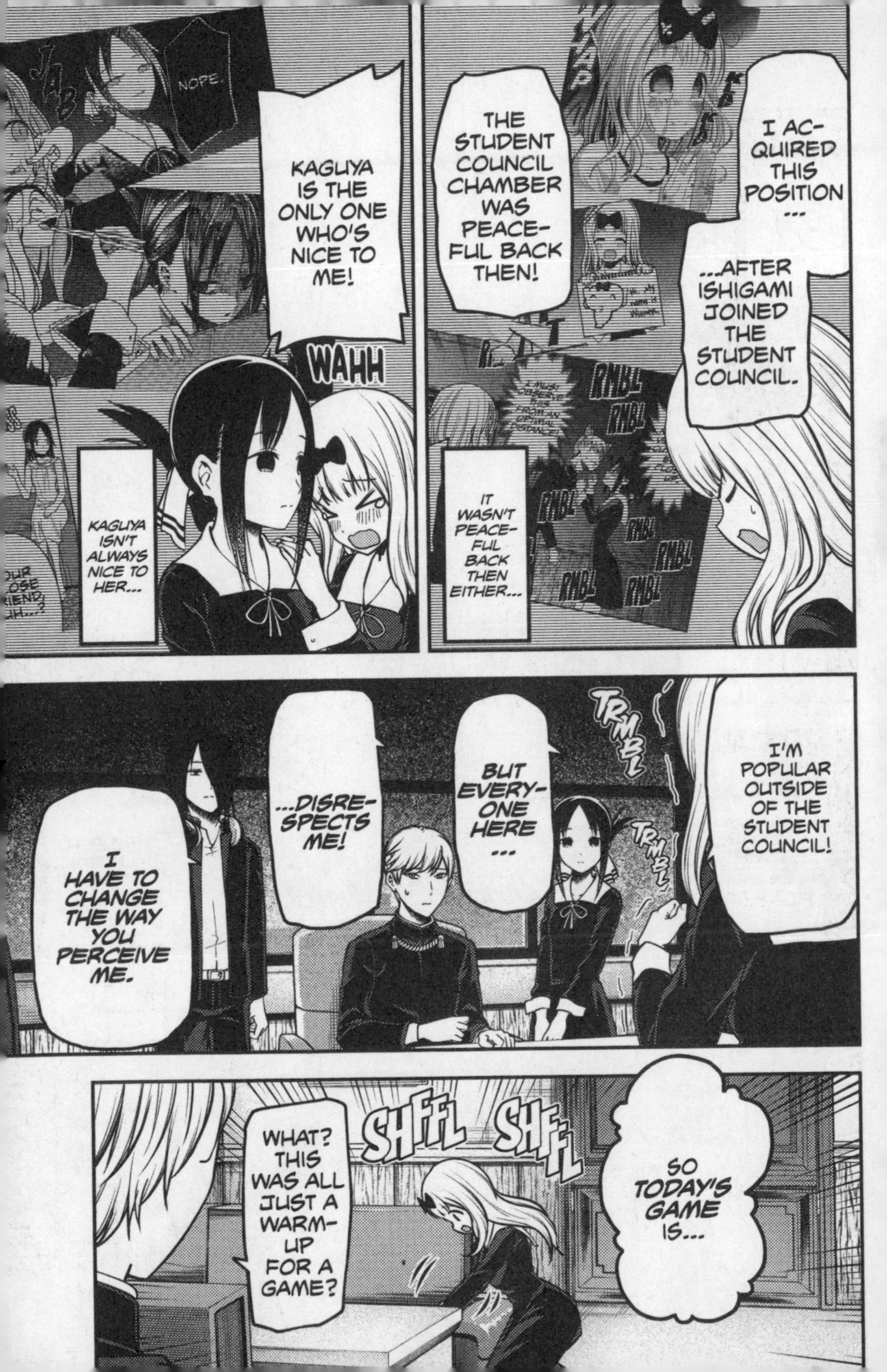
I ACQUIRED THIS POSITION...
THE STUDENT COUNCIL CHAMBER WAS PEACEFUL BACK THEN!
...AFTER ISHIGAMI JOINED THE STUDENT COUNCIL.
RMBL RMBL RMBL RMBL RMBL RMBL RMBL
I MUST OBSERVE THIS FROM AN OPTIMAL DISTANCE!
IT WASN'T PEACEFUL BACK THEN EITHER...
NOPE.
JAB
KAGUYA IS THE ONLY ONE WHO'S NICE TO ME!
WAHH
KAGUYA ISN'T ALWAYS NICE TO HER...
I'M POPULAR OUTSIDE OF THE STUDENT COUNCIL!
TRMBL TRMBL
BUT EVERYONE HERE...
...DISRESPECTS ME!
I HAVE TO CHANGE THE WAY YOU PERCEIVE ME.
SO TODAY'S GAME IS...
SHFFL SHFFL
WHAT? THIS WAS ALL JUST A WARM-UP FOR A GAME?

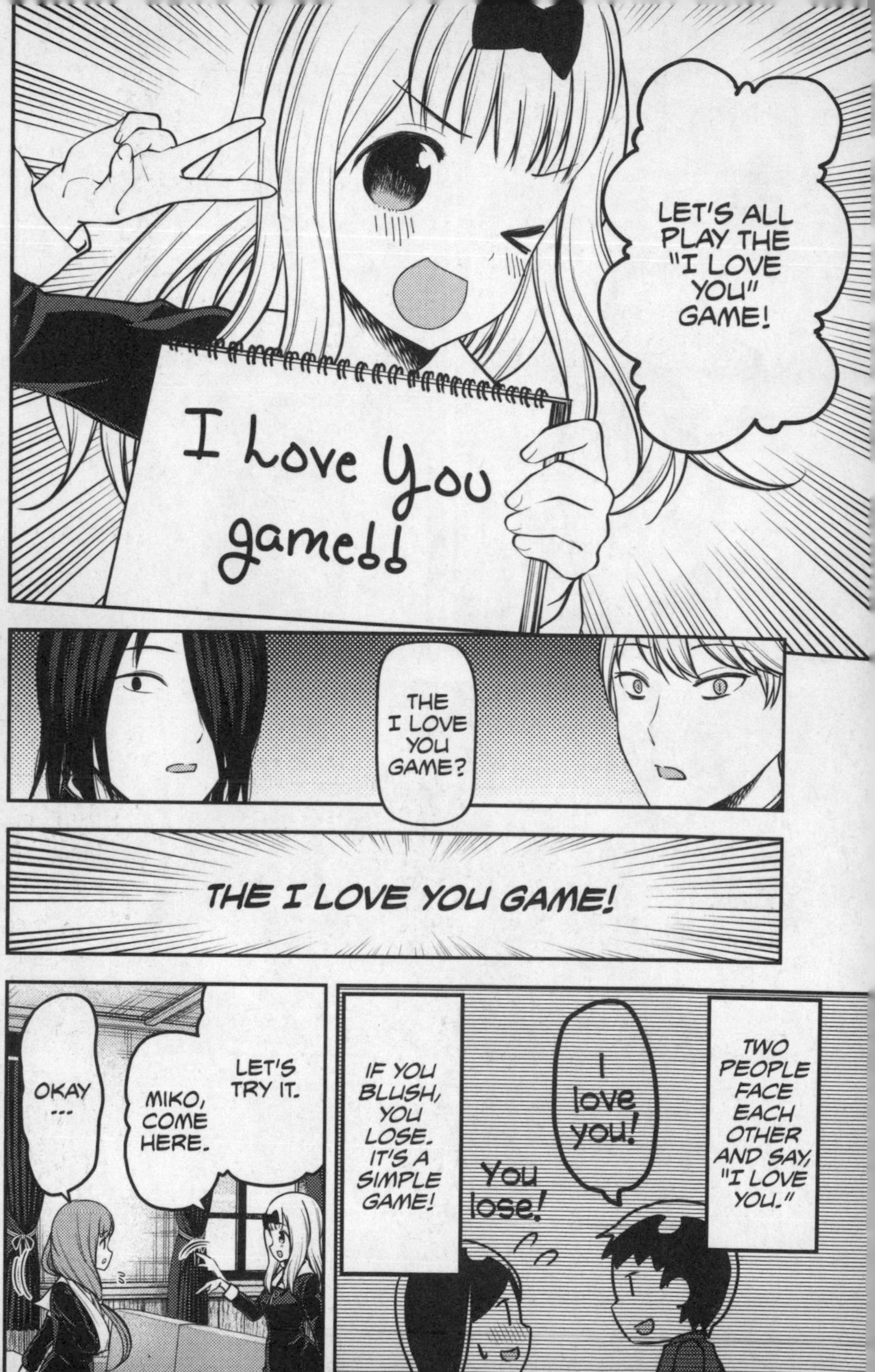
LET'S ALL PLAY THE "I LOVE YOU" GAME!
I Love You game!!
THE I LOVE YOU GAME?
THE I LOVE YOU GAME!
TWO PEOPLE FACE EACH OTHER AND SAY, "I LOVE YOU."
I love you!
You lose!
IF YOU BLUSH, YOU LOSE. IT'S A SIMPLE GAME!
LET'S TRY IT.
MIKO, COME HERE.
OKAY ...

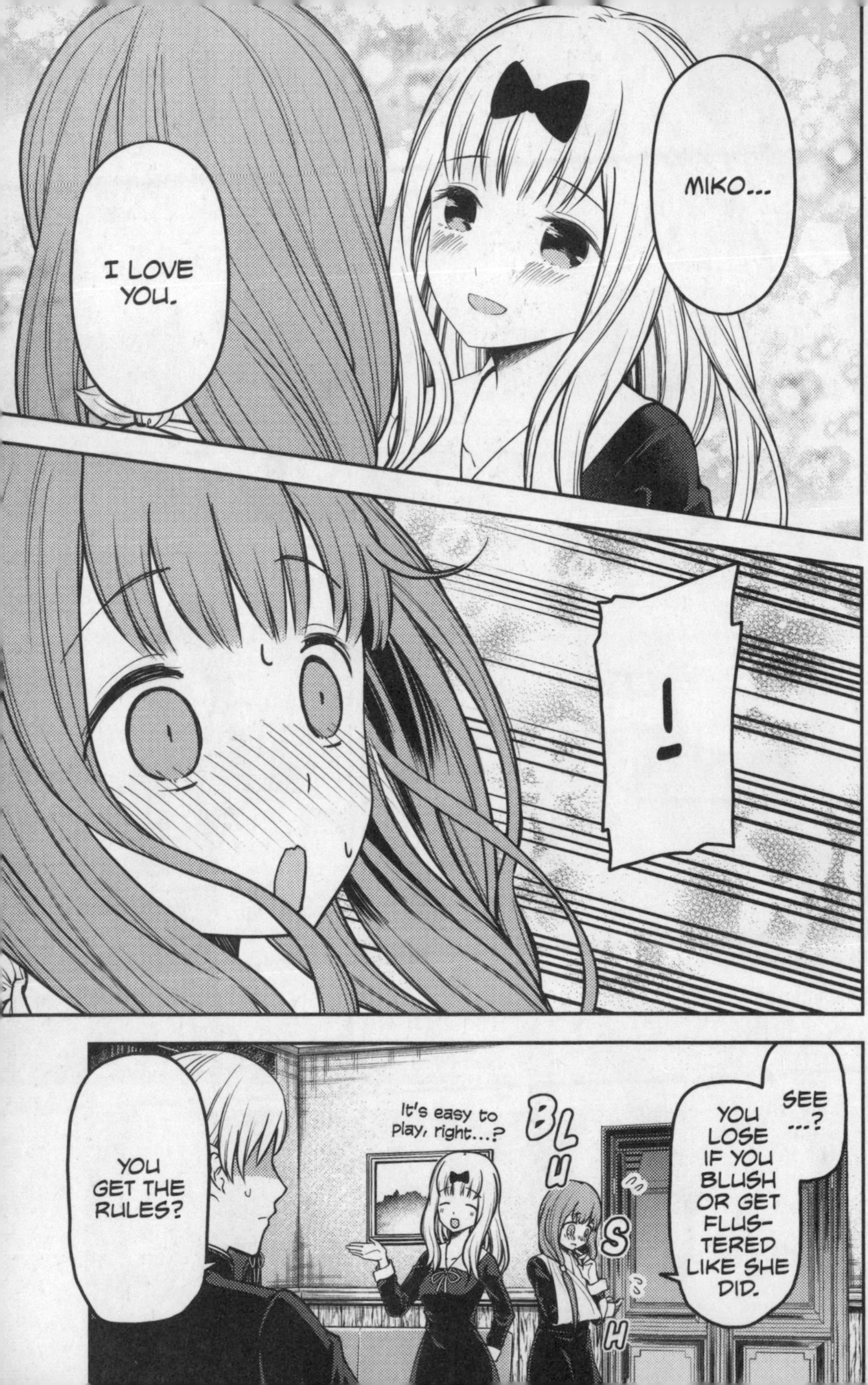
MIKO...
I LOVE YOU.
!
SEE...?
YOU LOSE IF YOU BLUSH OR GET FLUS-TERED LIKE SHE DID.
BLUSH
It's easy to play, right...?
YOU GET THE RULES?

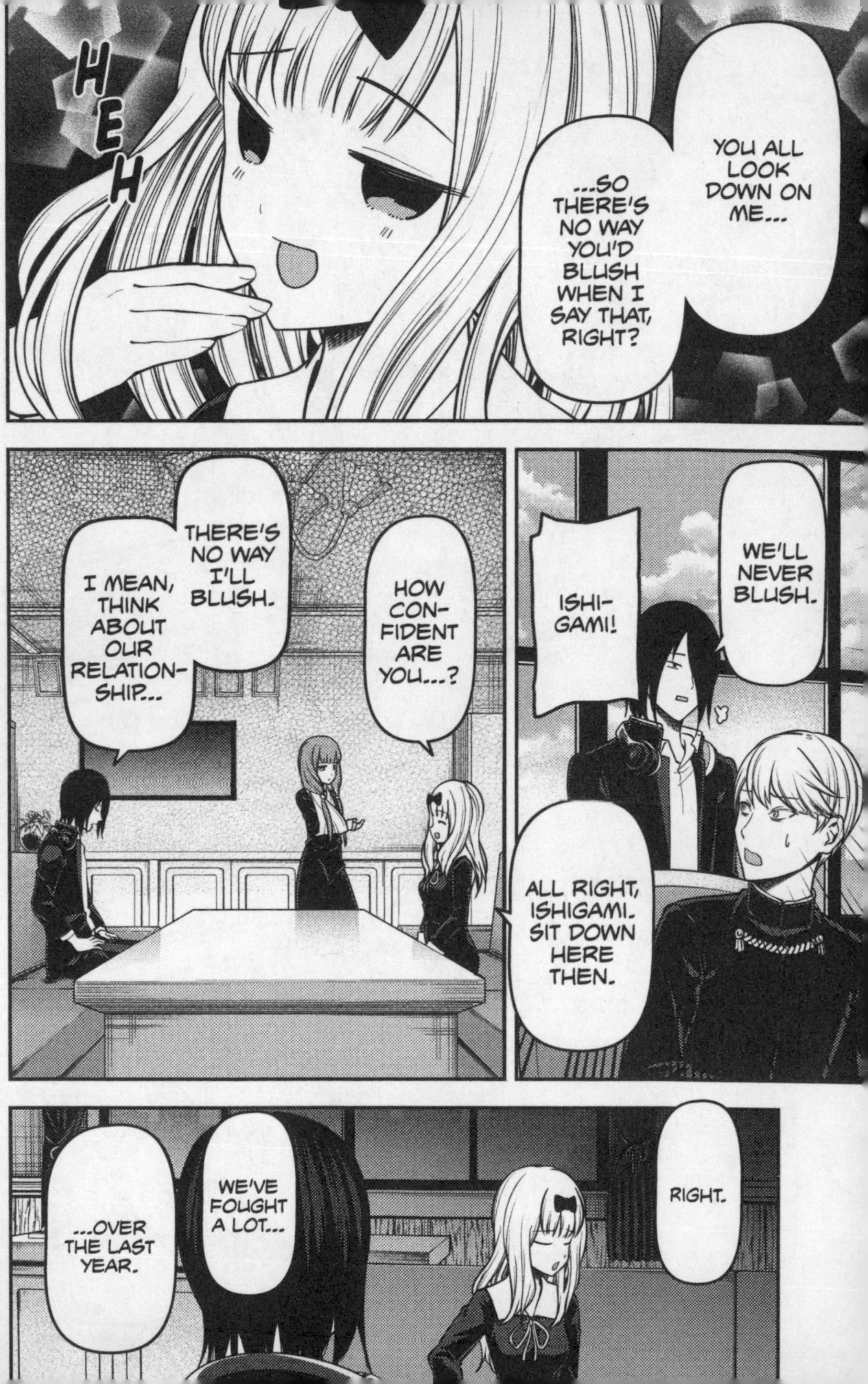
HEH
YOU ALL LOOK DOWN ON ME...
...SO THERE'S NO WAY YOU'D BLUSH WHEN I SAY THAT, RIGHT?
WE'LL NEVER BLUSH.
ISHIGAMI!
ALL RIGHT, ISHIGAMI. SIT DOWN HERE THEN.
HOW CONFIDENT ARE YOU...?
THERE'S NO WAY I'LL BLUSH.
I MEAN, THINK ABOUT OUR RELATIONSHIP...
RIGHT.
WE'VE FOUGHT A LOT...
...OVER THE LAST YEAR.

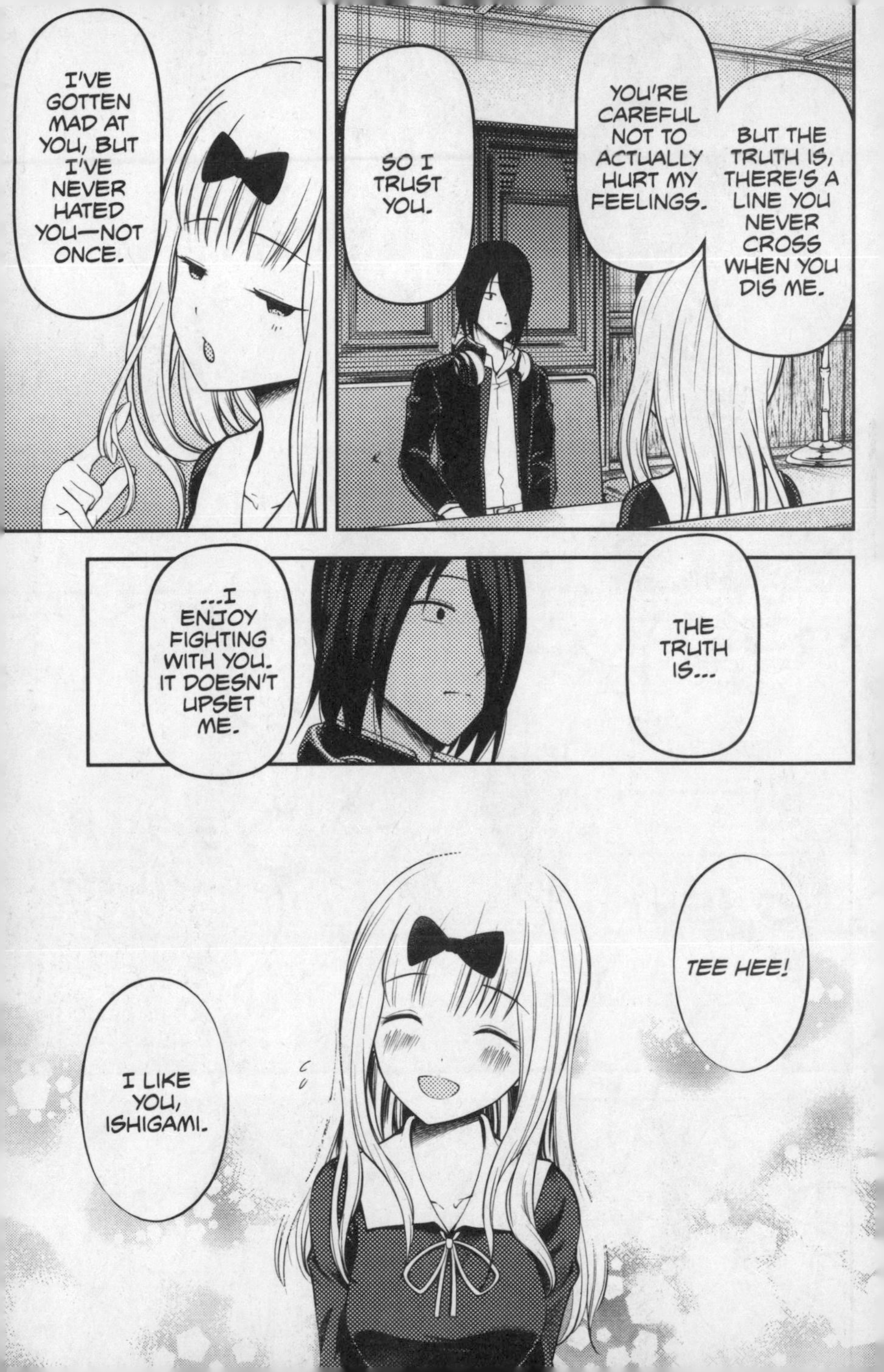
BUT THE TRUTH IS, THERE'S A LINE YOU NEVER CROSS WHEN YOU DIS ME.
YOU'RE CAREFUL NOT TO ACTUALLY HURT MY FEELINGS.
SO I TRUST YOU.
I'VE GOTTEN MAD AT YOU, BUT I'VE NEVER HATED YOU—NOT ONCE.
THE TRUTH IS...
...I ENJOY FIGHTING WITH YOU. IT DOESN'T UPSET ME.
TEE HEE!
I LIKE YOU, ISHIGAMI.

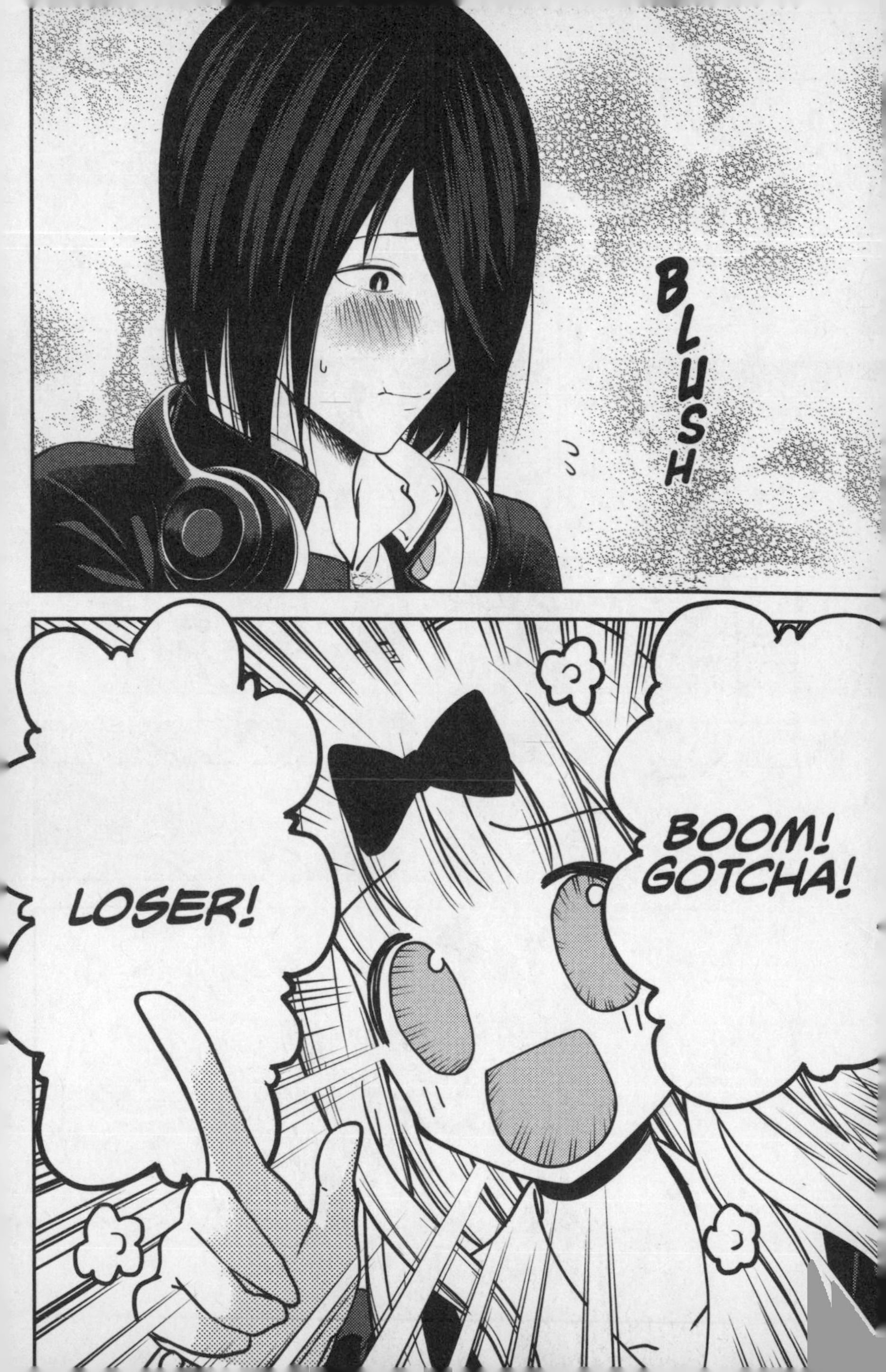
BLUSH
BOOM! GOTCHA!
LOSER!

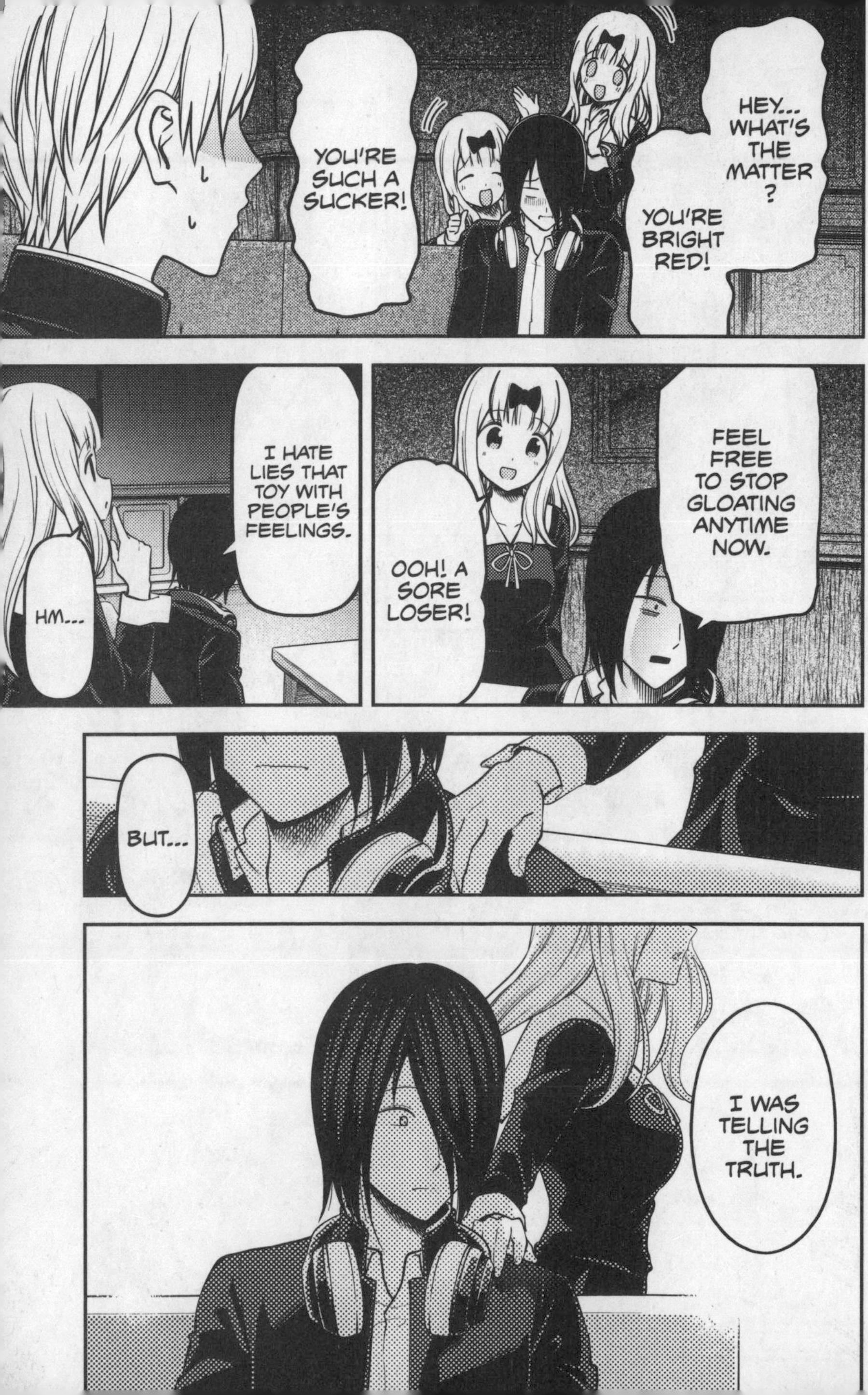
HEY... WHAT'S THE MATTER?
YOU'RE BRIGHT RED!
YOU'RE SUCH A SUCKER!
FEEL FREE TO STOP GLOATING ANYTIME NOW.
OOH! A SORE LOSER!
I HATE LIES THAT TOY WITH PEOPLE'S FEELINGS.
HM...
BUT...
I WAS TELLING THE TRUTH.

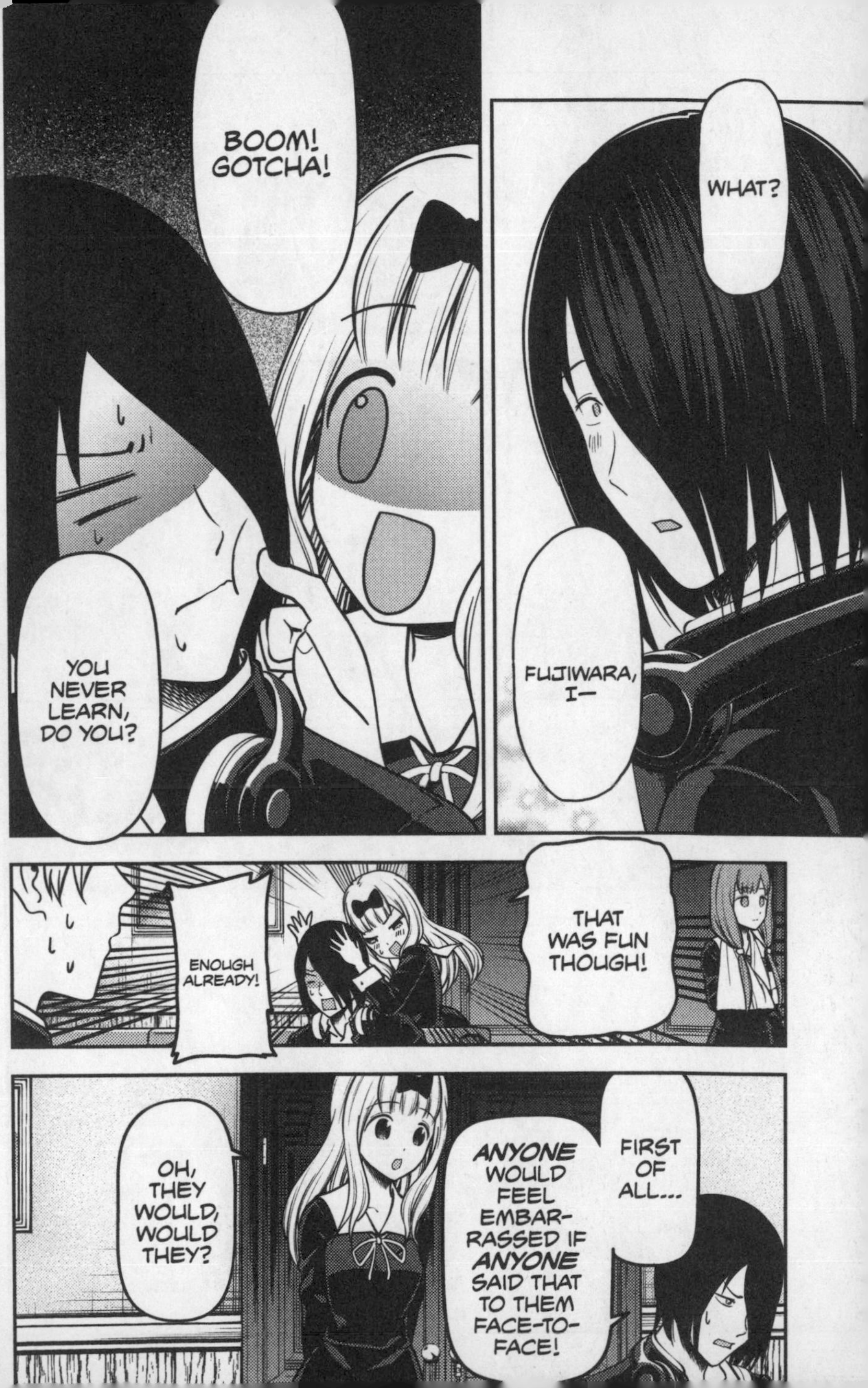
WHAT?
FUJIWARA, I—
BOOM! GOTCHA!
YOU NEVER LEARN, DO YOU?
THAT WAS FUN THOUGH!
ENOUGH ALREADY!
FIRST OF ALL...
ANYONE WOULD FEEL EMBARRASSED IF *ANYONE* SAID THAT TO THEM FACE-TO-FACE!
OH, THEY WOULD, WOULD THEY?

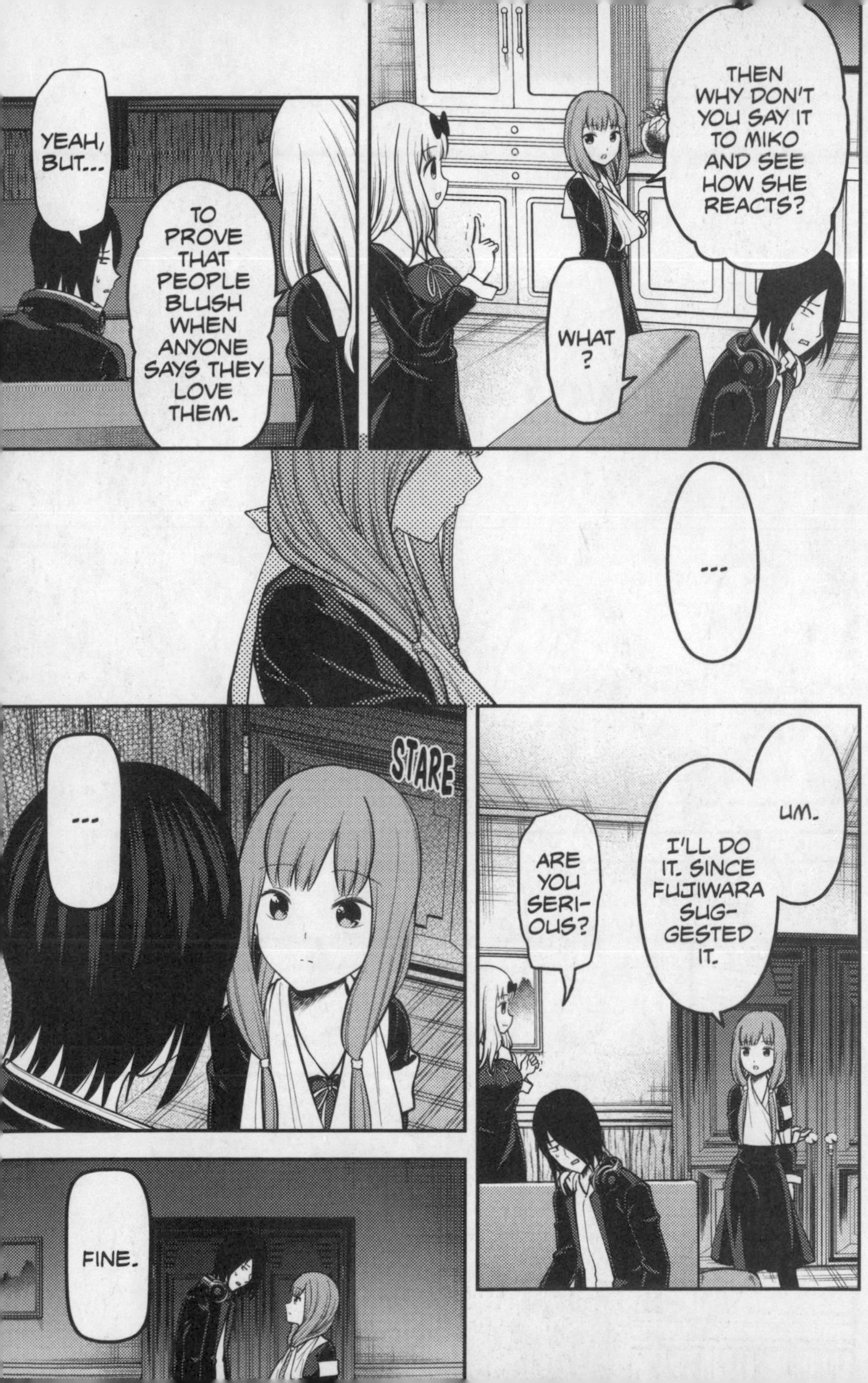
THEN WHY DON'T YOU SAY IT TO MIKO AND SEE HOW SHE REACTS?
WHAT?
YEAH, BUT...
TO PROVE THAT PEOPLE BLUSH WHEN ANYONE SAYS THEY LOVE THEM.
...
UM.
I'LL DO IT. SINCE FUJIWARA SUG-GESTED IT.
ARE YOU SERI-OUS?
STARE
...
FINE.

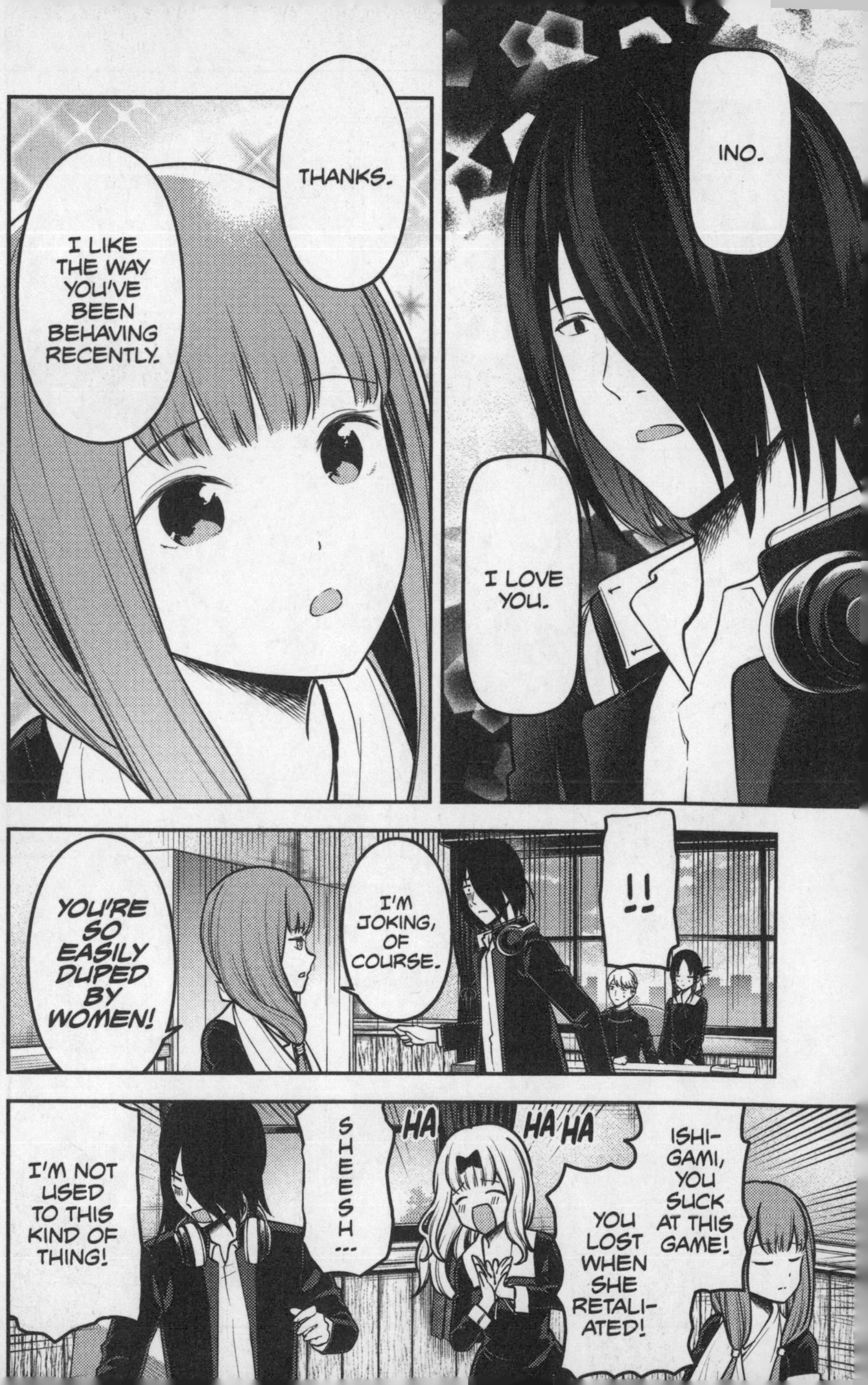
INO.
I LOVE YOU.
THANKS.
I LIKE THE WAY YOU'VE BEEN BEHAVING RECENTLY.
!!
I'M JOKING, OF COURSE.
YOU'RE SO EASILY DUPED BY WOMEN!
ISHI-GAMI, YOU SUCK AT THIS GAME!
YOU LOST WHEN SHE RETALI-ATED!
HA HA HA
SHEESH...
I'M NOT USED TO THIS KIND OF THING!

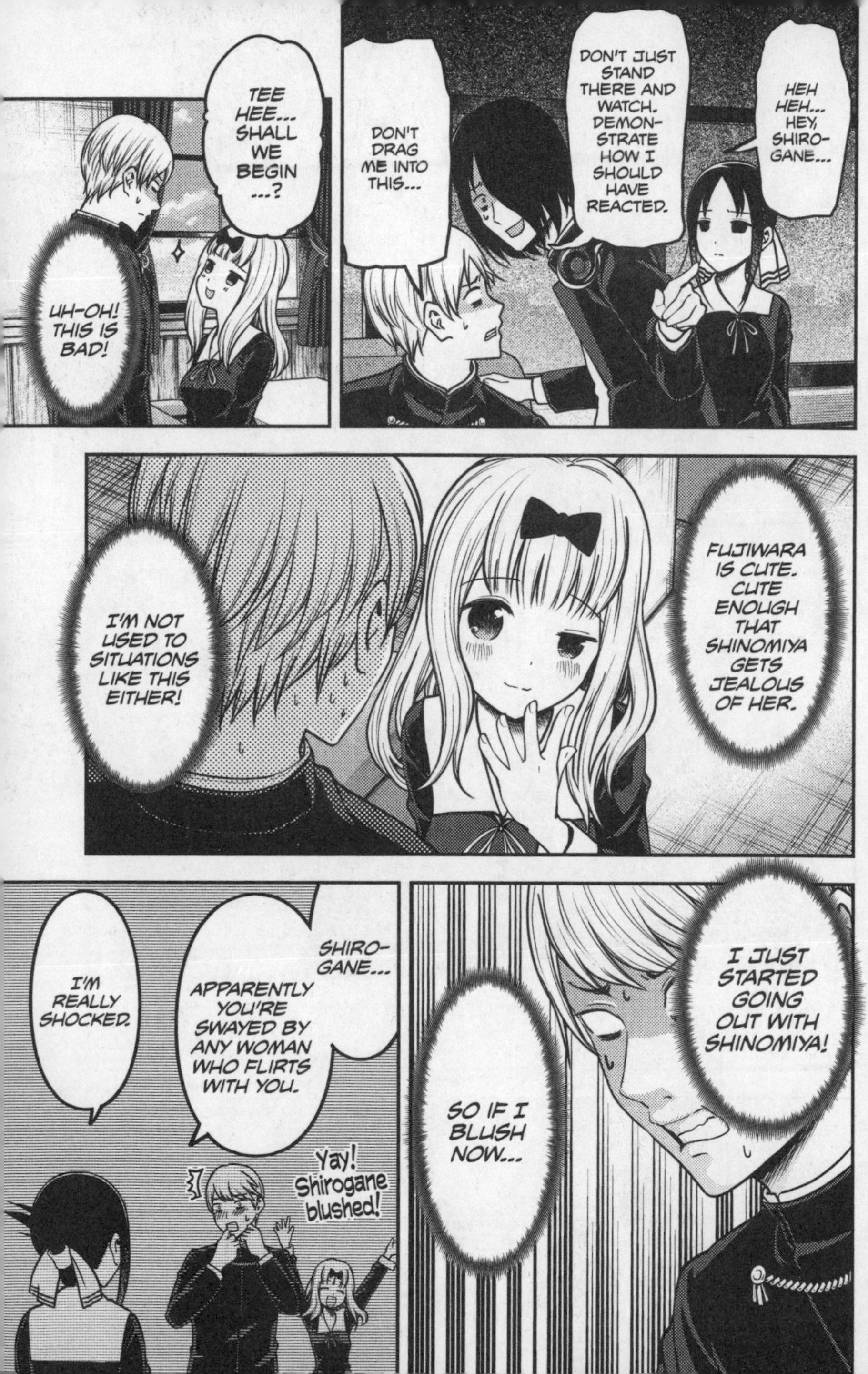
HEH HEH... HEY, SHIRO-GANE...
DON'T JUST STAND THERE AND WATCH. DEMON-STRATE HOW I SHOULD HAVE REACTED.
DON'T DRAG ME INTO THIS...
TEE HEE... SHALL WE BEGIN...?
UH-OH! THIS IS BAD!
FUJIWARA IS CUTE. CUTE ENOUGH THAT SHINOMIYA GETS JEALOUS OF HER.
I'M NOT USED TO SITUATIONS LIKE THIS EITHER!
I JUST STARTED GOING OUT WITH SHINOMIYA!
SO IF I BLUSH NOW...
SHIRO-GANE...
APPARENTLY YOU'RE SWAYED BY ANY WOMAN WHO FLIRTS WITH YOU.
I'M REALLY SHOCKED.
Yay! Shirogane blushed!

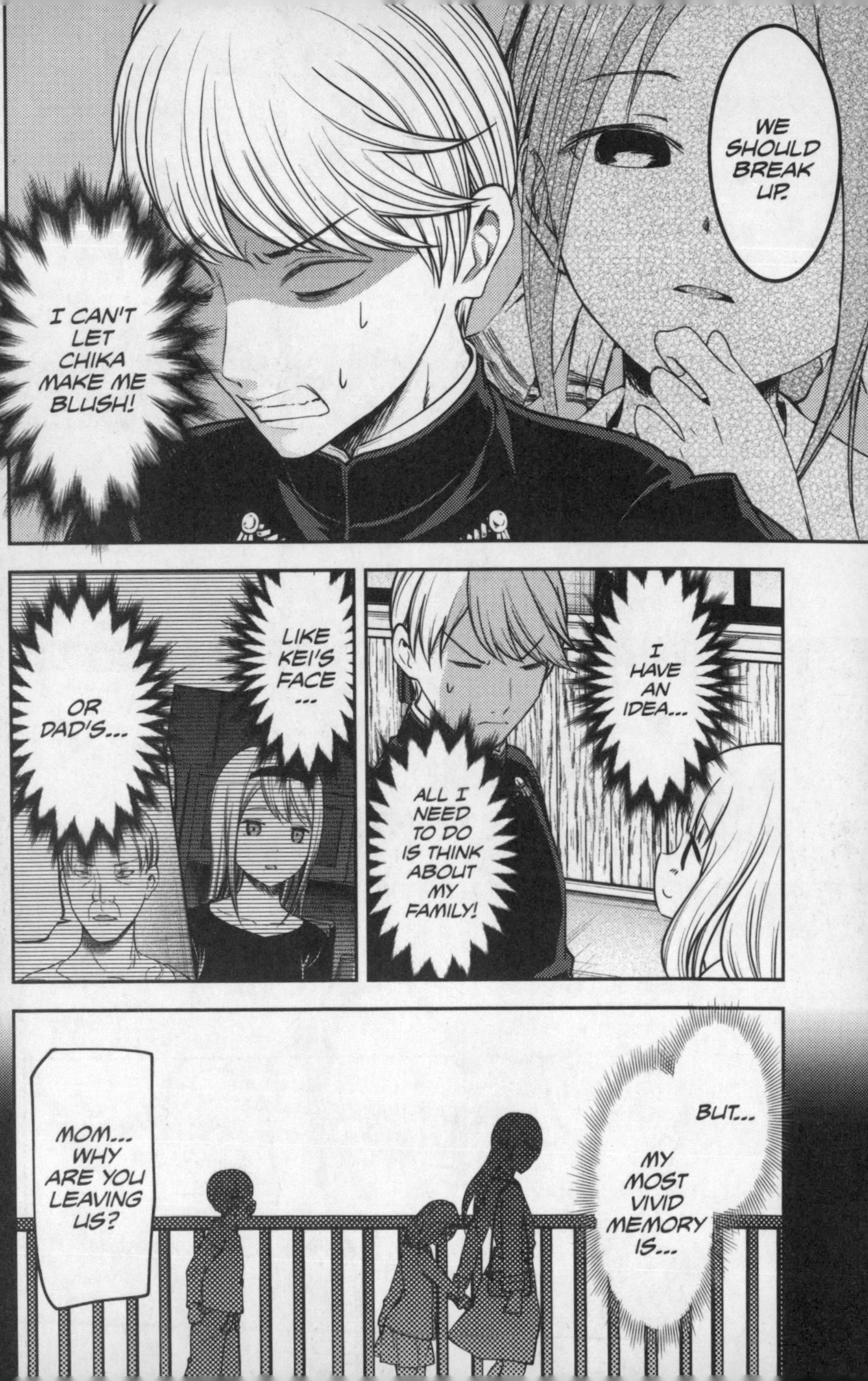
WE SHOULD BREAK UP.
I CAN'T LET CHIKA MAKE ME BLUSH!
I HAVE AN IDEA...
ALL I NEED TO DO IS THINK ABOUT MY FAMILY!
LIKE KEI'S FACE...
OR DAD'S...
BUT...
MY MOST VIVID MEMORY IS...
MOM... WHY ARE YOU LEAVING US?

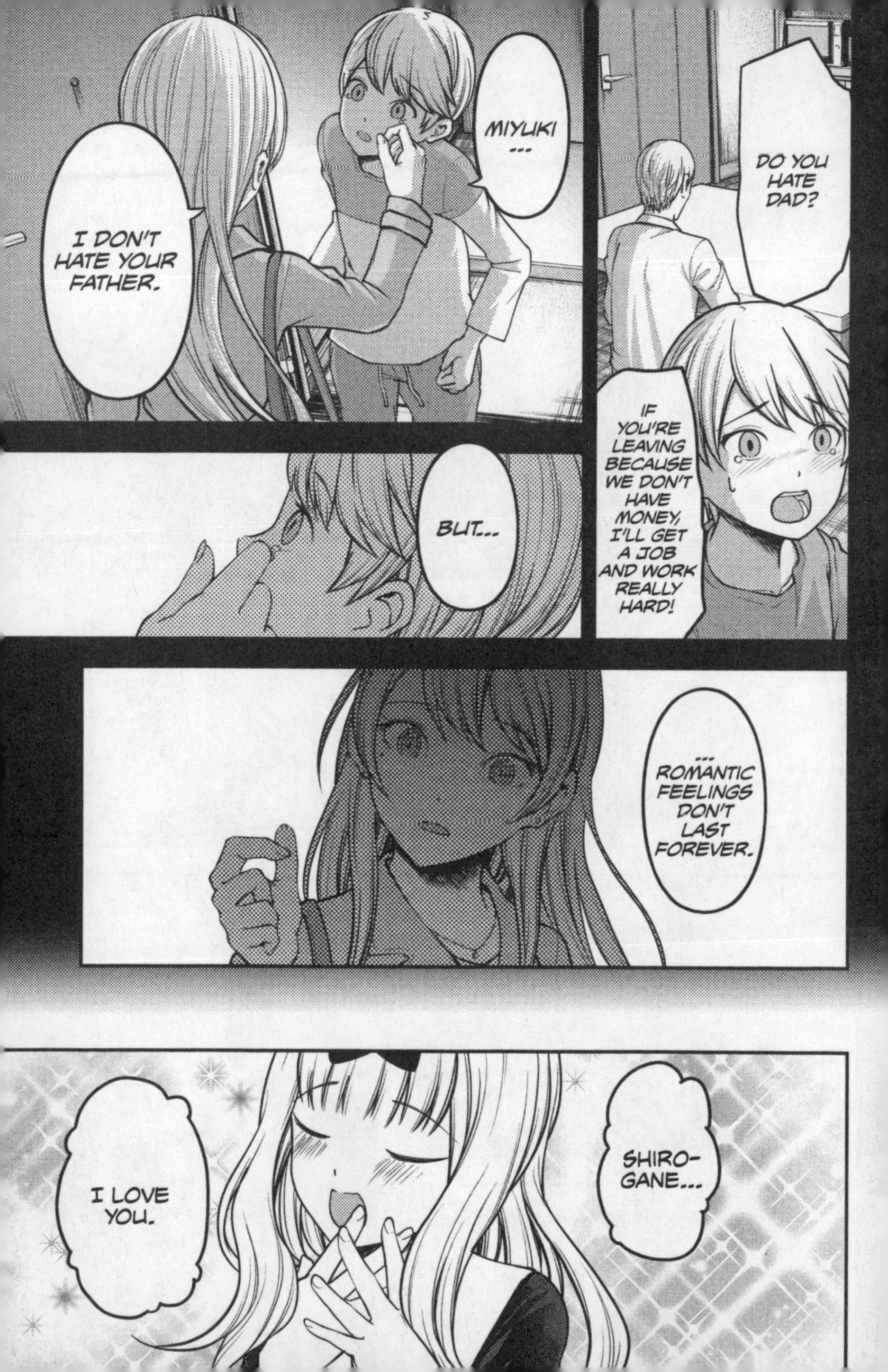
DO YOU HATE DAD?
IF YOU'RE LEAVING BECAUSE WE DON'T HAVE MONEY, I'LL GET A JOB AND WORK REALLY HARD!
MIYUKI...
I DON'T HATE YOUR FATHER.
BUT...
...ROMANTIC FEELINGS DON'T LAST FOREVER.
SHIRO-GANE...
I LOVE YOU.

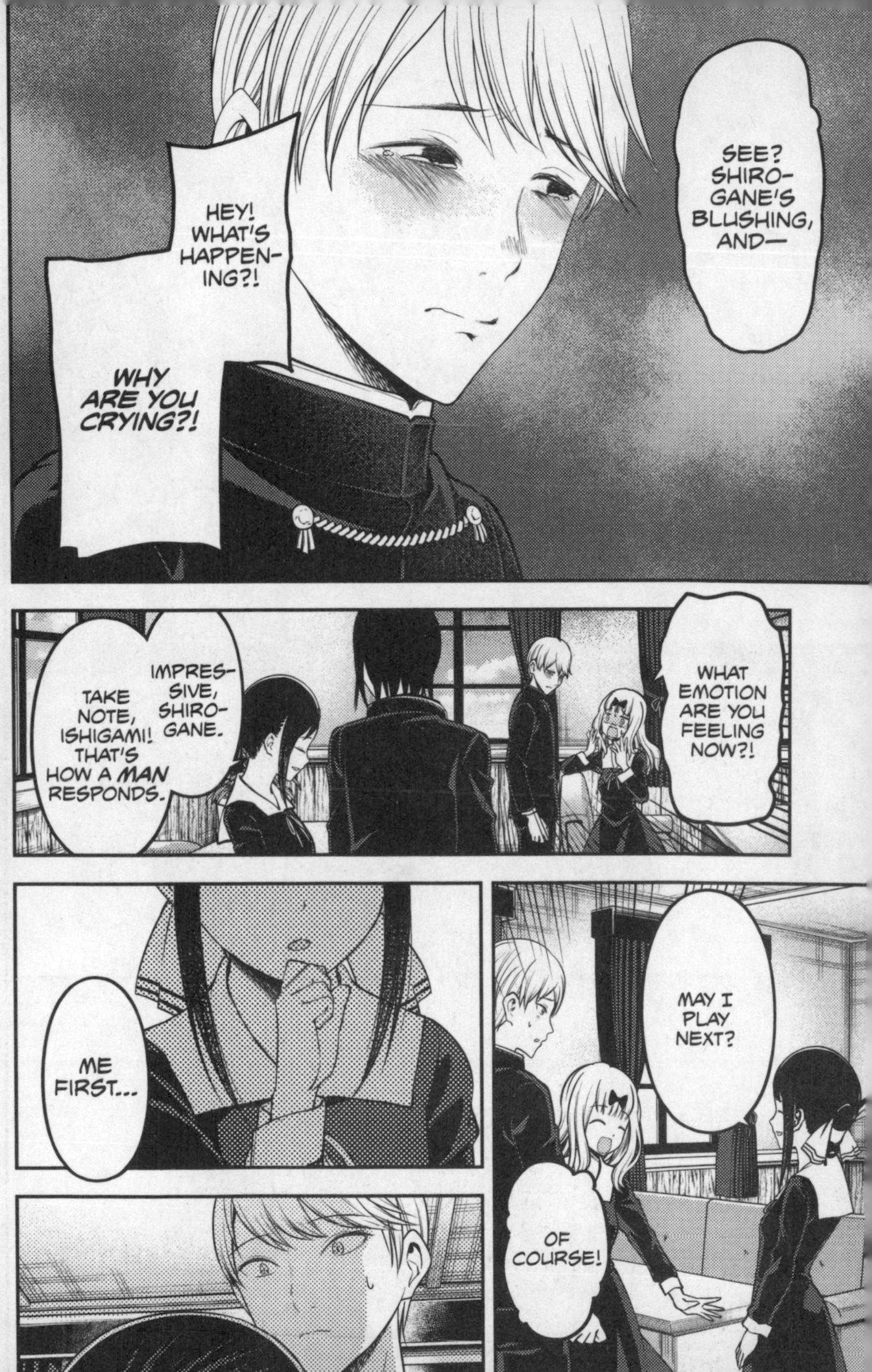

SEE? SHIRO-GANE'S BLUSHING, AND—
HEY! WHAT'S HAPPEN-ING?!
WHY ARE YOU CRYING?!
WHAT EMOTION ARE YOU FEELING NOW?!
IMPRES-SIVE, SHIRO-GANE.
TAKE NOTE, ISHIGAMI! THAT'S HOW A *MAN* RESPONDS.
MAY I PLAY NEXT?
OF COURSE!
ME FIRST...

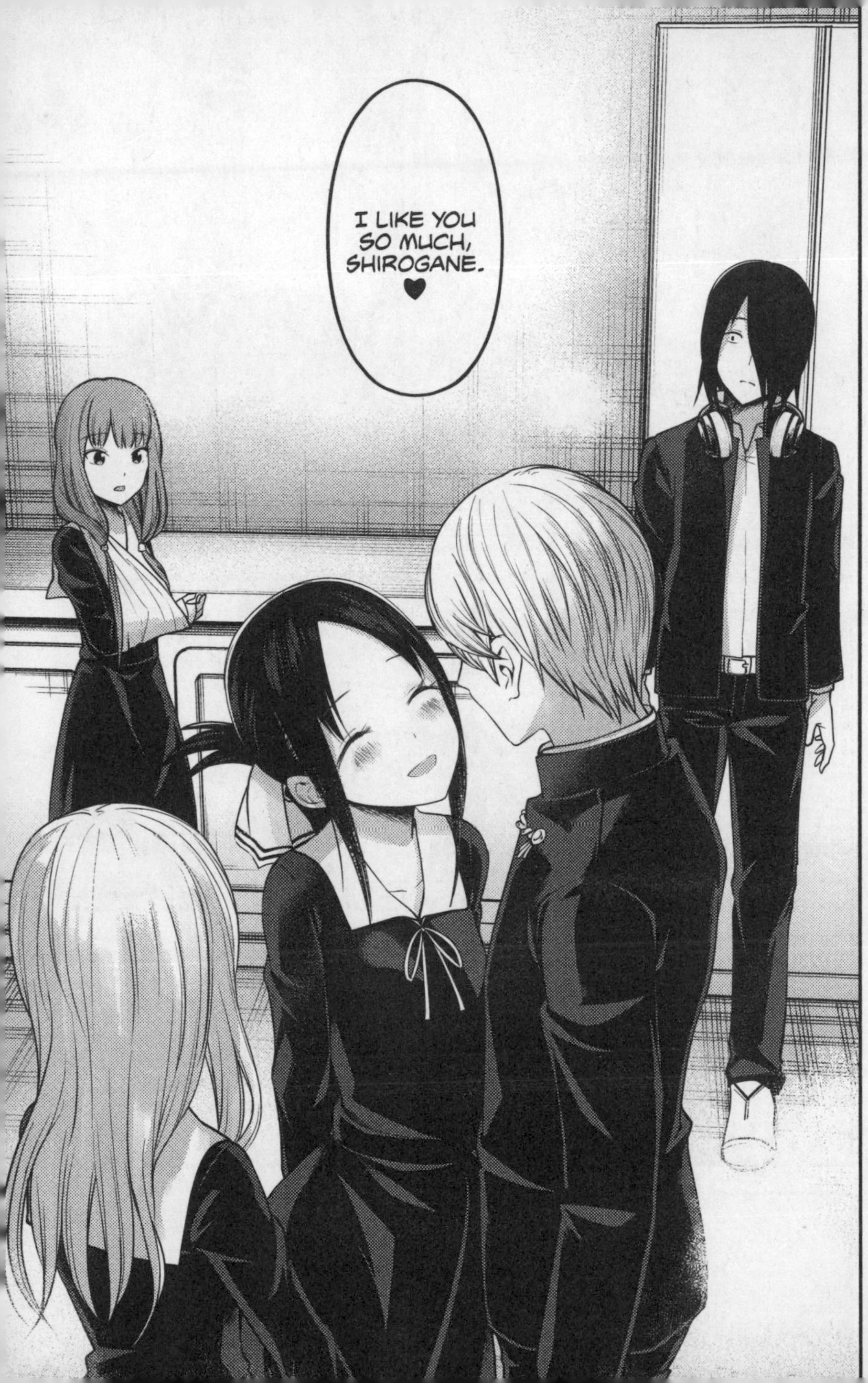
I LIKE YOU SO MUCH, SHIROGANE. ♥

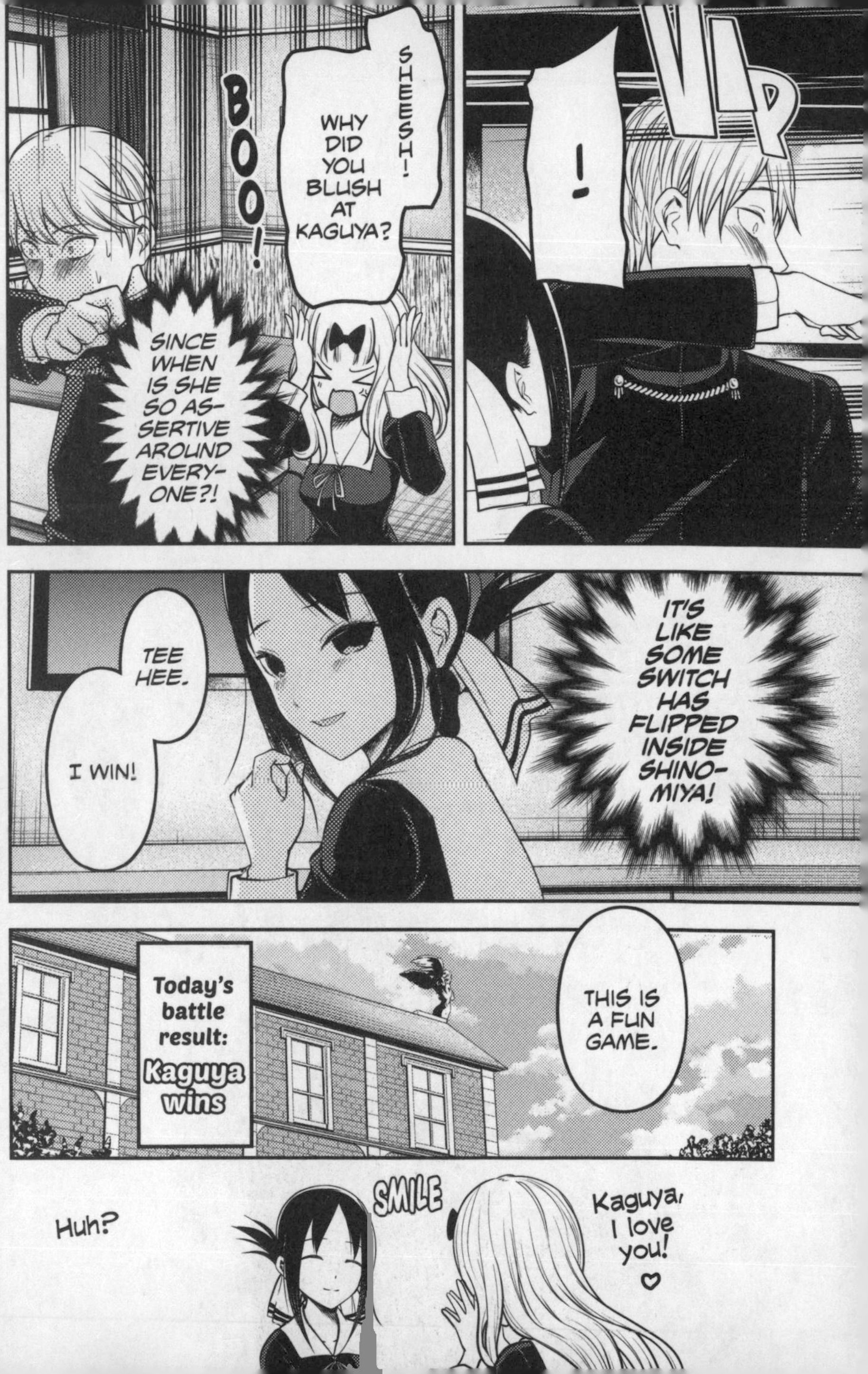

VIP
!
SHEESH!
WHY DID YOU BLUSH AT KAGUYA?
BOO!
SINCE WHEN IS SHE SO ASSERTIVE AROUND EVERYONE?!
IT'S LIKE SOME SWITCH HAS FLIPPED INSIDE SHINOMIYA!
TEE HEE.
I WIN!
THIS IS A FUN GAME.
Today's battle result: Kaguya wins
Kaguya, I love you! ♡
SMILE
Huh?

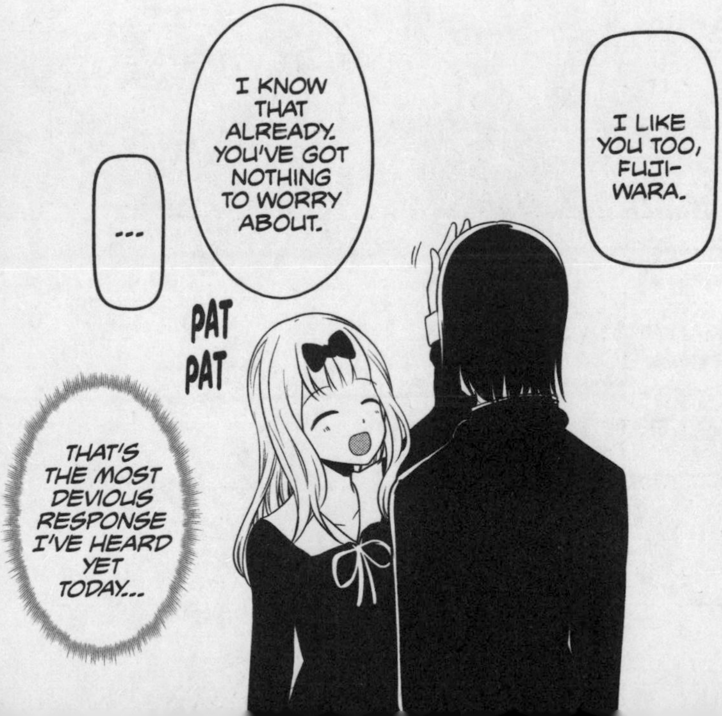
I LIKE YOU TOO, FUJI-WARA.
I KNOW THAT ALREADY. YOU'VE GOT NOTHING TO WORRY ABOUT.
...
PAT PAT
THAT'S THE MOST DEVIOUS RESPONSE I'VE HEARD YET TODAY...

KAGUYA-SAMA
LOVE IS WAR

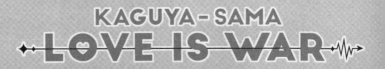

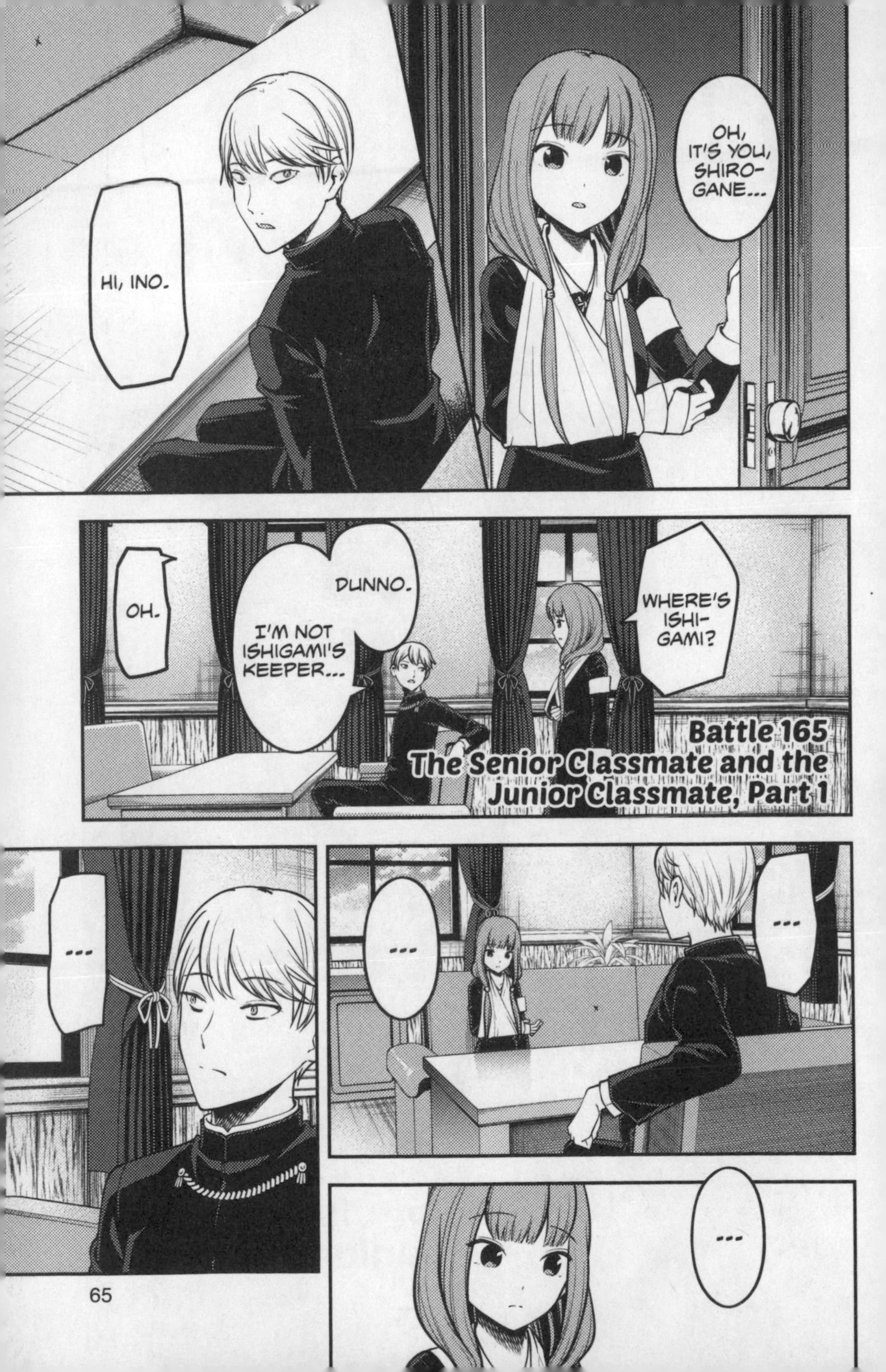
OH, IT'S YOU, SHIRO-GANE...
HI, INO.
WHERE'S ISHI-GAMI?
DUNNO.
I'M NOT ISHIGAMI'S KEEPER...
OH.
Battle 165 The Senior Classmate and the Junior Classmate, Part 1
...
...
...
...

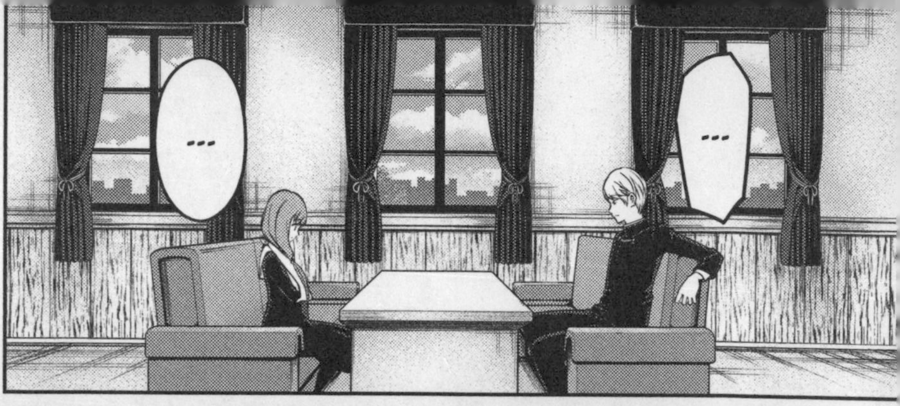
...
...

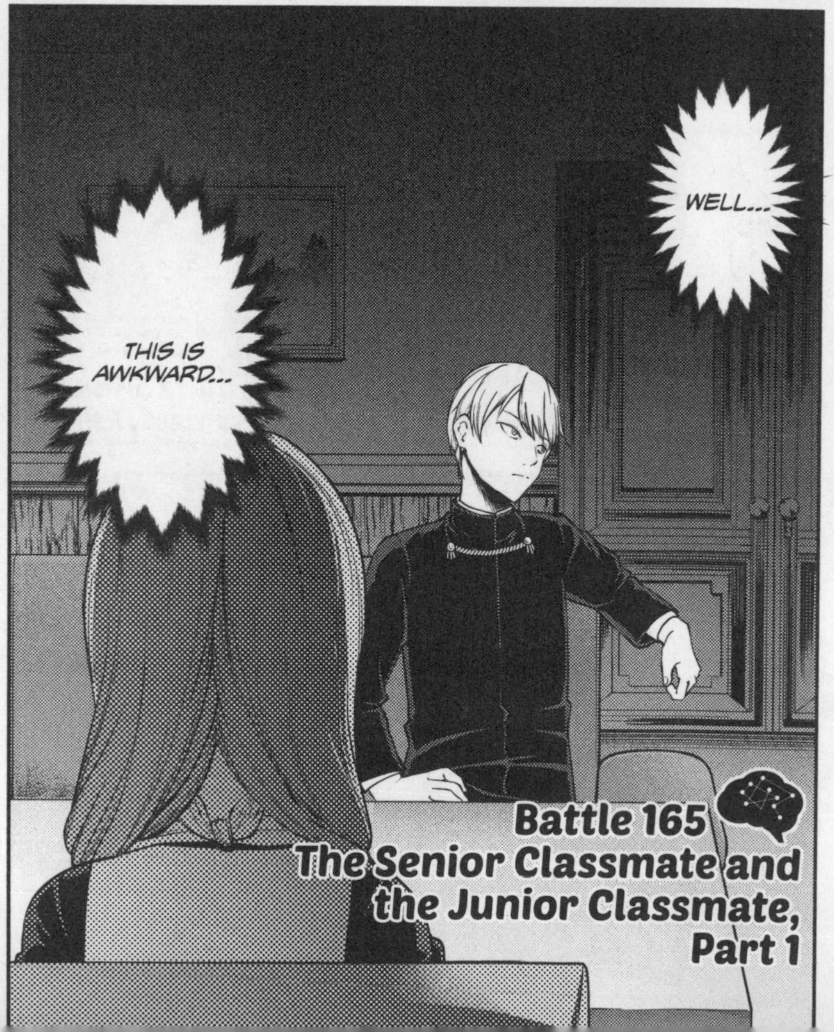
WELL...
THIS IS AWKWARD...

Battle 165
The Senior Classmate and the Junior Classmate, Part 1

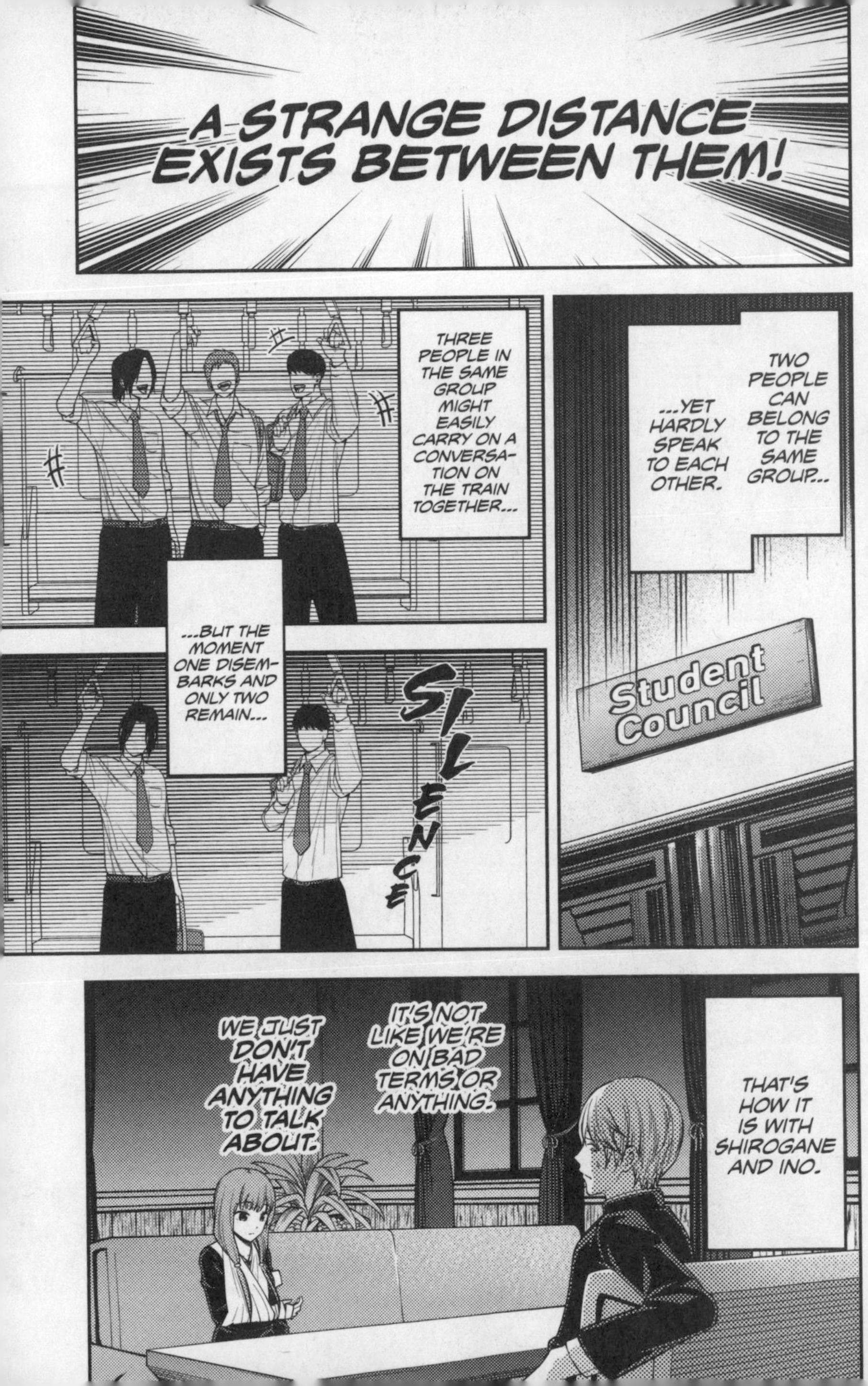
A STRANGE DISTANCE EXISTS BETWEEN THEM!
TWO PEOPLE CAN BELONG TO THE SAME GROUP...
...YET HARDLY SPEAK TO EACH OTHER.
Student Council
THREE PEOPLE IN THE SAME GROUP MIGHT EASILY CARRY ON A CONVERSATION ON THE TRAIN TOGETHER...
...BUT THE MOMENT ONE DISEMBARKS AND ONLY TWO REMAIN...
SILENCE
THAT'S HOW IT IS WITH SHIROGANE AND INO.
IT'S NOT LIKE WE'RE ON BAD TERMS OR ANYTHING.
WE JUST DON'T HAVE ANYTHING TO TALK ABOUT.

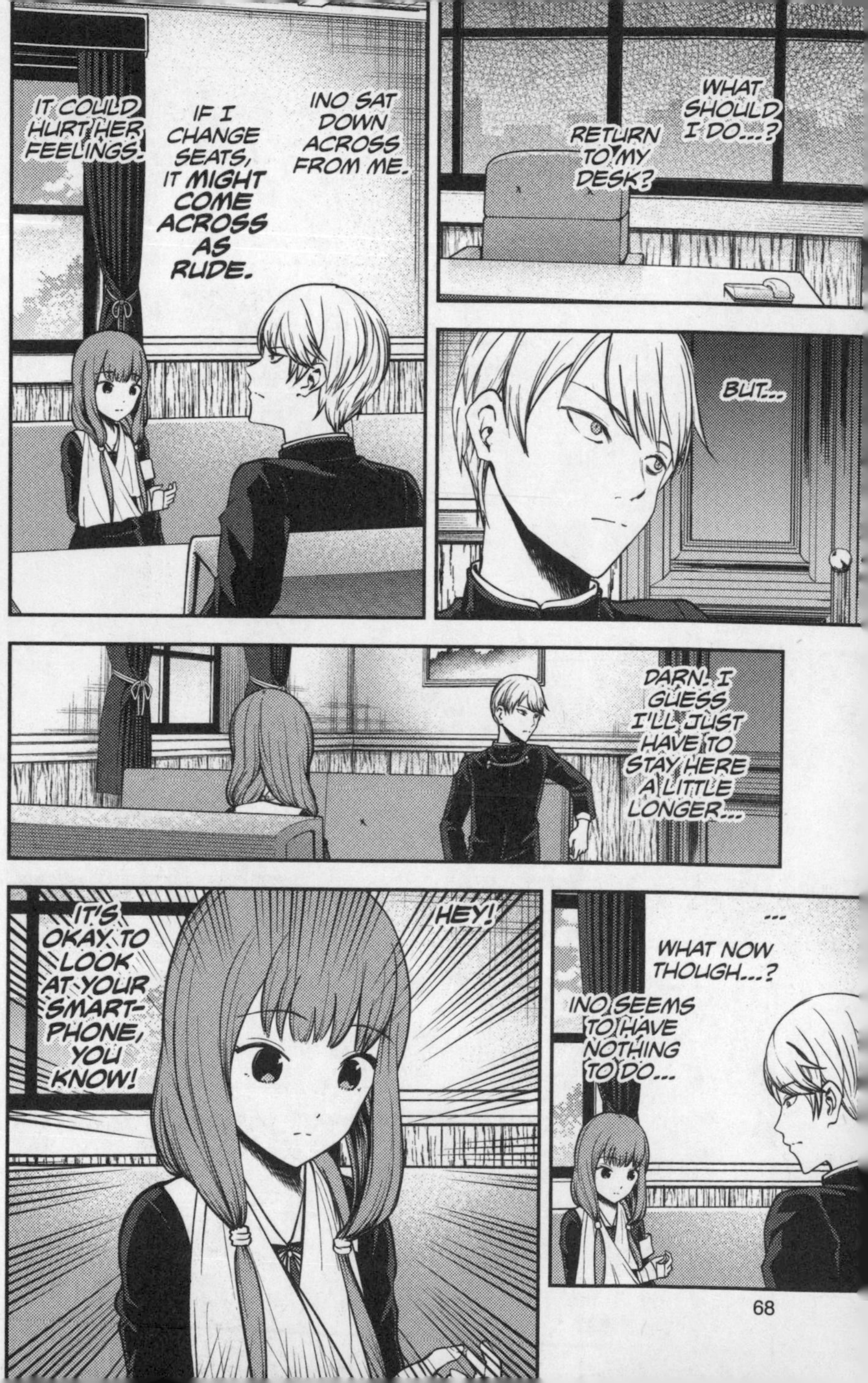
WHAT SHOULD I DO...?
RETURN TO MY DESK?
BUT...
INO SAT DOWN ACROSS FROM ME.
IF I CHANGE SEATS, IT MIGHT COME ACROSS AS RUDE.
IT COULD HURT HER FEELINGS.
DARN. I GUESS I'LL JUST HAVE TO STAY HERE A LITTLE LONGER...
...
WHAT NOW THOUGH...?
INO SEEMS TO HAVE NOTHING TO DO...
HEY!
IT'S OKAY TO LOOK AT YOUR SMARTPHONE, YOU KNOW!

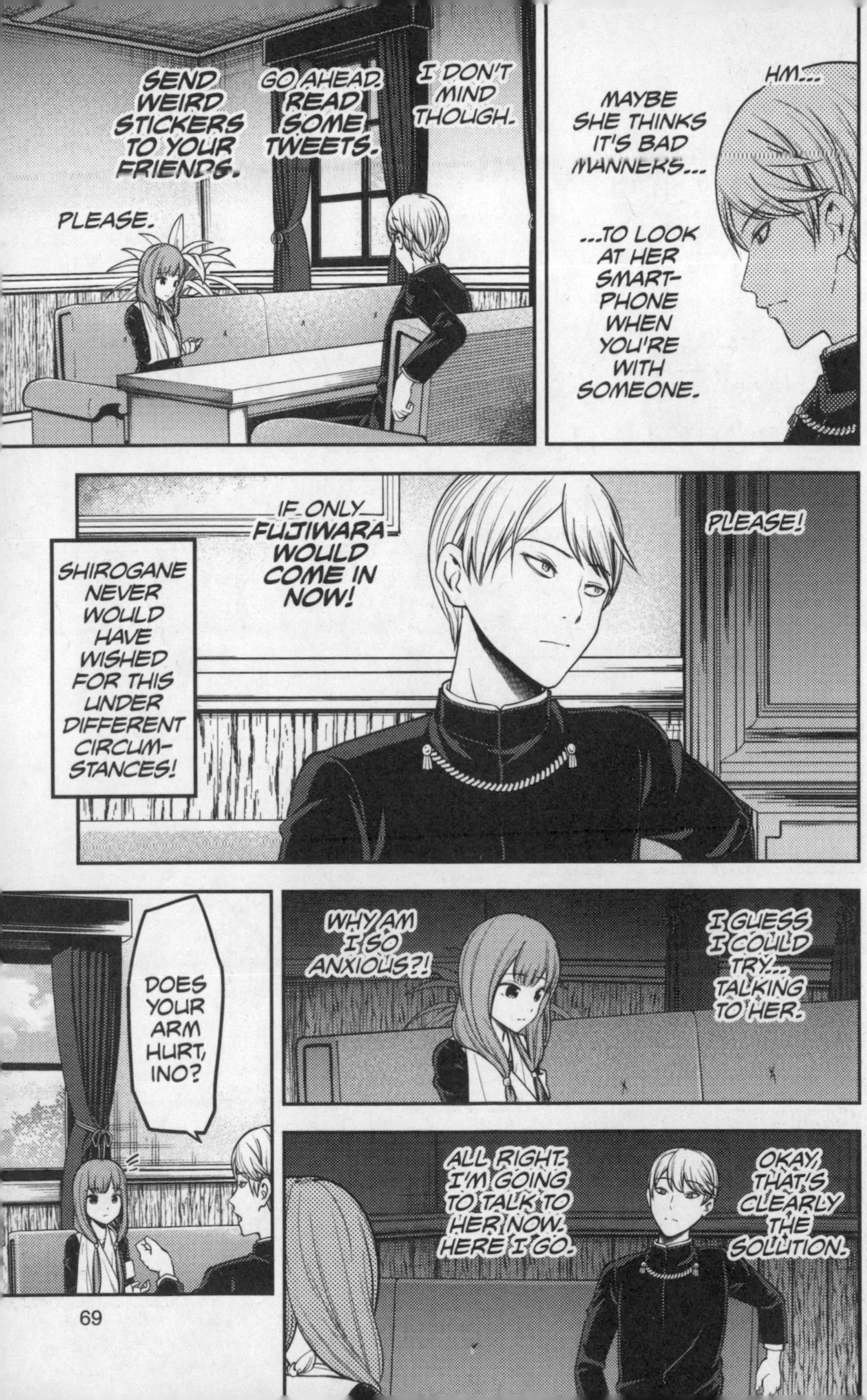
HM...
MAYBE SHE THINKS IT'S BAD MANNERS...
...TO LOOK AT HER SMARTPHONE WHEN YOU'RE WITH SOMEONE.
I DON'T MIND THOUGH.
GO AHEAD. READ SOME TWEETS.
SEND WEIRD STICKERS TO YOUR FRIENDS.
PLEASE.
PLEASE!
IF ONLY FUJIWARA WOULD COME IN NOW!
SHIROGANE NEVER WOULD HAVE WISHED FOR THIS UNDER DIFFERENT CIRCUMSTANCES!
I GUESS I COULD TRY... TALKING TO HER.
WHY AM I SO ANXIOUS?!
OKAY, THAT'S CLEARLY THE SOLUTION.
ALL RIGHT. I'M GOING TO TALK TO HER NOW. HERE I GO.
DOES YOUR ARM HURT, INO?

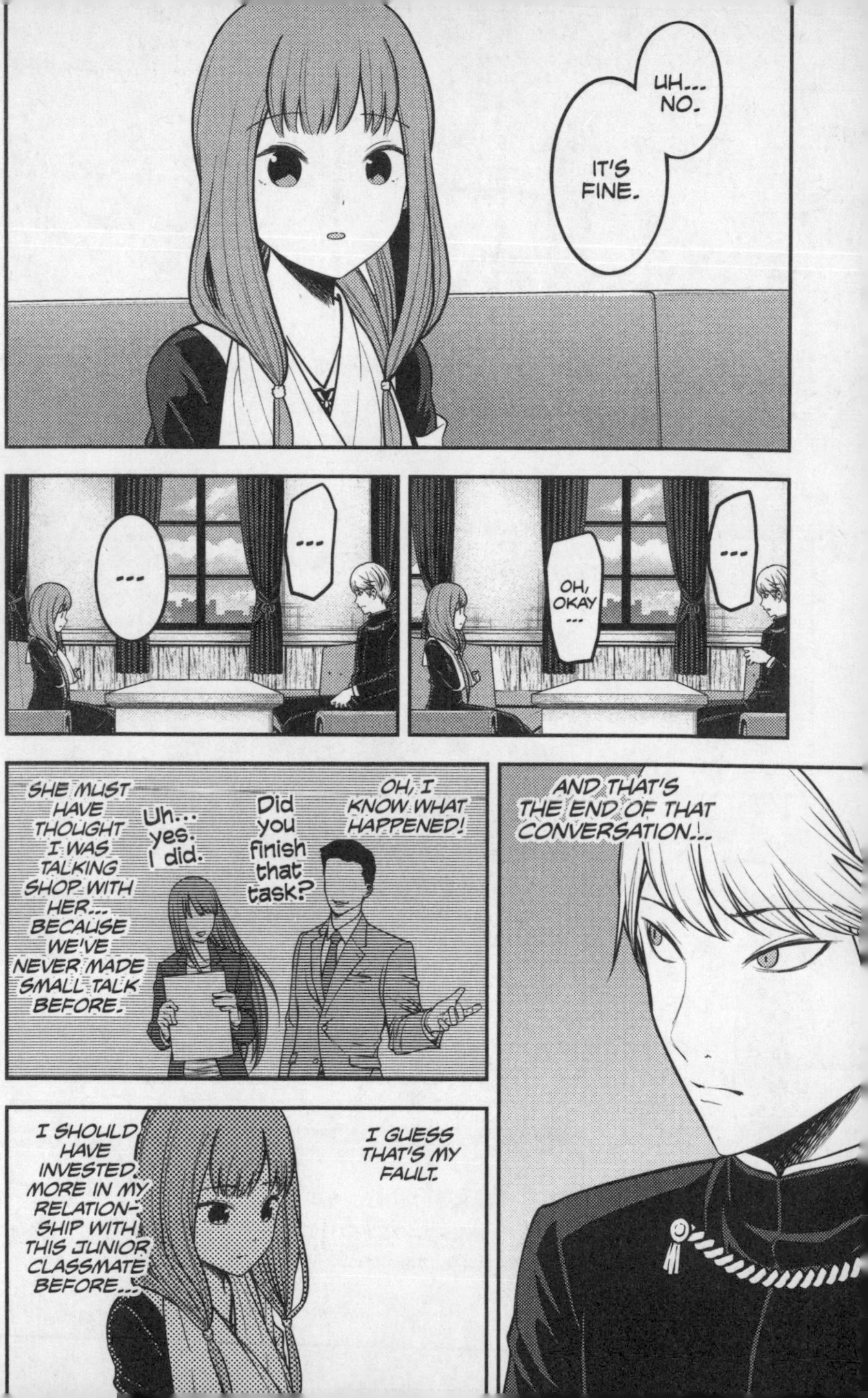
UH... NO.
IT'S FINE.
...
OH, OKAY ...
...
...
AND THAT'S THE END OF THAT CONVERSATION...
OH, I KNOW WHAT HAPPENED!
Did you finish that task?
Uh... yes. I did.
SHE MUST HAVE THOUGHT I WAS TALKING SHOP WITH HER... BECAUSE WE'VE NEVER MADE SMALL TALK BEFORE.
I GUESS THAT'S MY FAULT.
I SHOULD HAVE INVESTED MORE IN MY RELATION-SHIP WITH THIS JUNIOR CLASSMATE BEFORE...

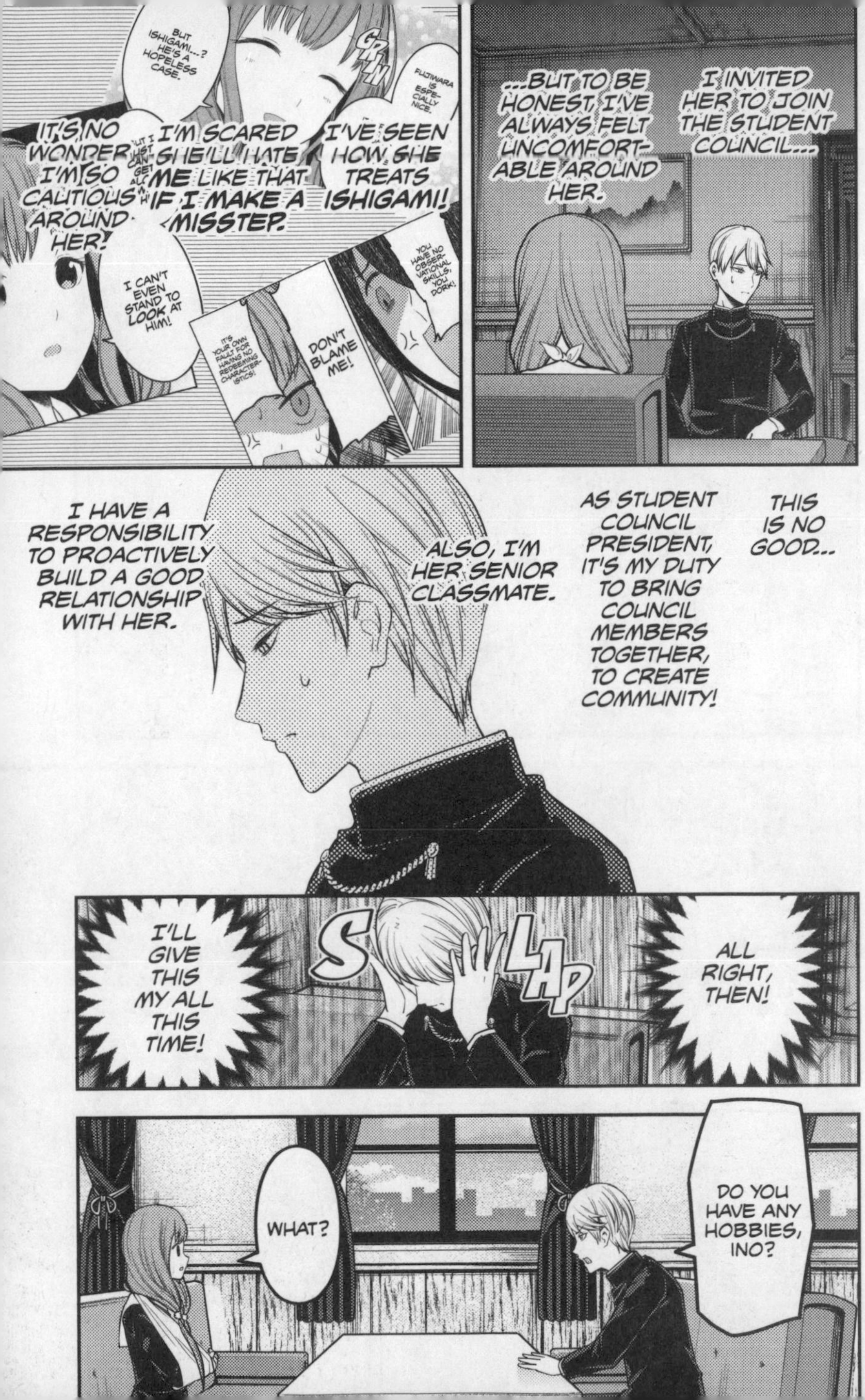
I INVITED HER TO JOIN THE STUDENT COUNCIL...
...BUT TO BE HONEST, I'VE ALWAYS FELT UNCOMFORT-ABLE AROUND HER.
I'VE SEEN HOW SHE TREATS ISHIGAMI!
FUJIWARA IS ESPE-CIALLY NICE.
GRIN
BUT ISHIGAMI...? HE'S A HOPELESS CASE.
I'M SCARED SHE'LL HATE ME LIKE THAT IF I MAKE A MISSTEP.
IT'S NO WONDER I'M SO CAUTIOUS AROUND HER!
YOU HAVE NO OBSER-VATIONAL SKILLS, YOU DORK!
DON'T BLAME ME!
IT'S YOUR OWN FAULT FOR HAVING NO REDEEMING CHARACTER-ISTICS!
I CAN'T EVEN STAND TO LOOK AT HIM!
THIS IS NO GOOD...
AS STUDENT COUNCIL PRESIDENT, IT'S MY DUTY TO BRING COUNCIL MEMBERS TOGETHER, TO CREATE COMMUNITY!
ALSO, I'M HER SENIOR CLASSMATE.
I HAVE A RESPONSIBILITY TO PROACTIVELY BUILD A GOOD RELATIONSHIP WITH HER.
ALL RIGHT, THEN!
SLAP
I'LL GIVE THIS MY ALL THIS TIME!
DO YOU HAVE ANY HOBBIES, INO?
WHAT?

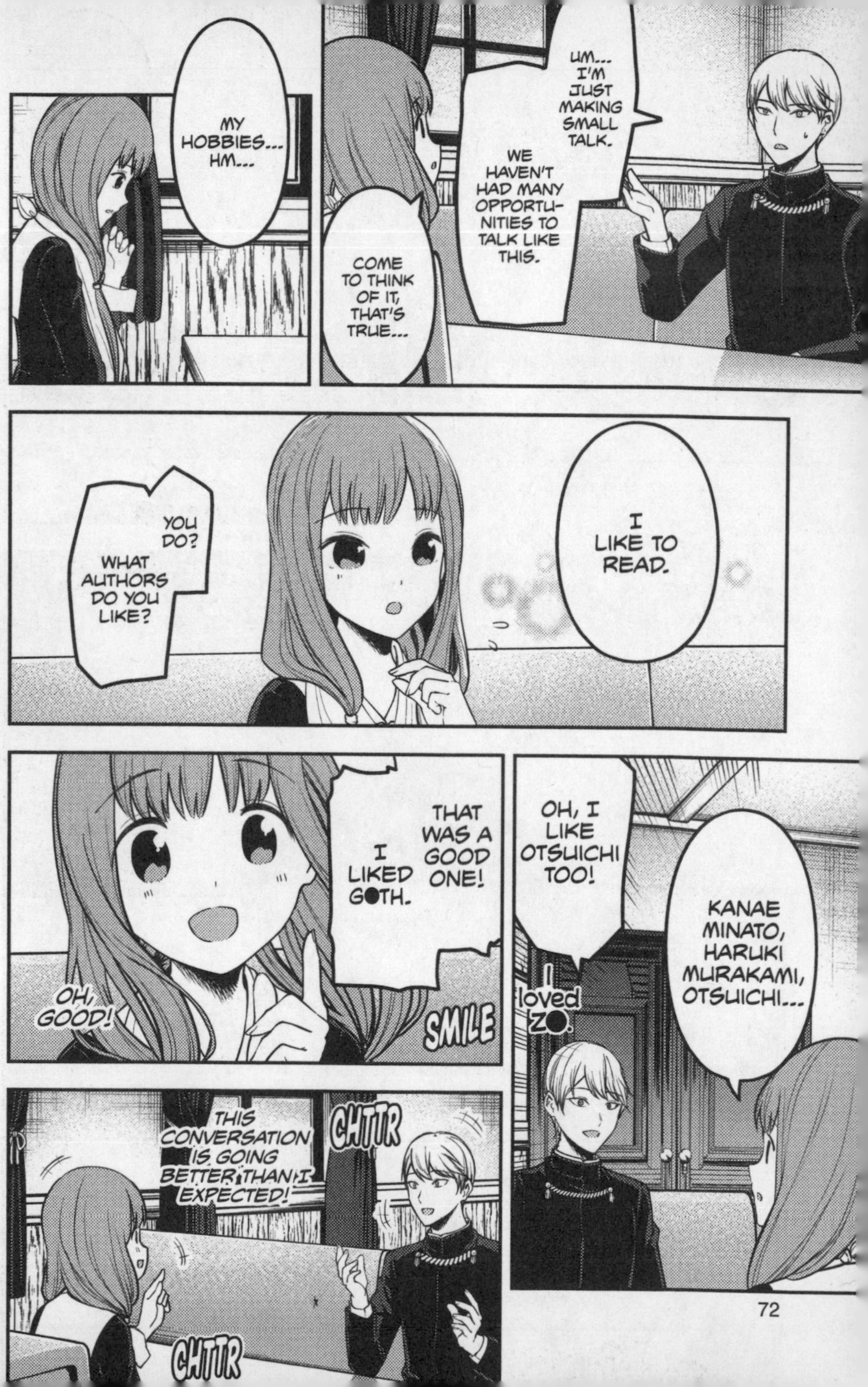
UM... I'M JUST MAKING SMALL TALK.
WE HAVEN'T HAD MANY OPPORTUNITIES TO TALK LIKE THIS.
COME TO THINK OF IT, THAT'S TRUE...
MY HOBBIES... HM...
I LIKE TO READ.
YOU DO? WHAT AUTHORS DO YOU LIKE?
KANAE MINATO, HARUKI MURAKAMI, OTSUICHI...
OH, I LIKE OTSUICHI TOO!
I loved ZO.
THAT WAS A GOOD ONE!
I LIKED G●TH.
SMILE
OH, GOOD!
CHTTR
THIS CONVERSATION IS GOING BETTER THAN I EXPECTED!
CHTTR

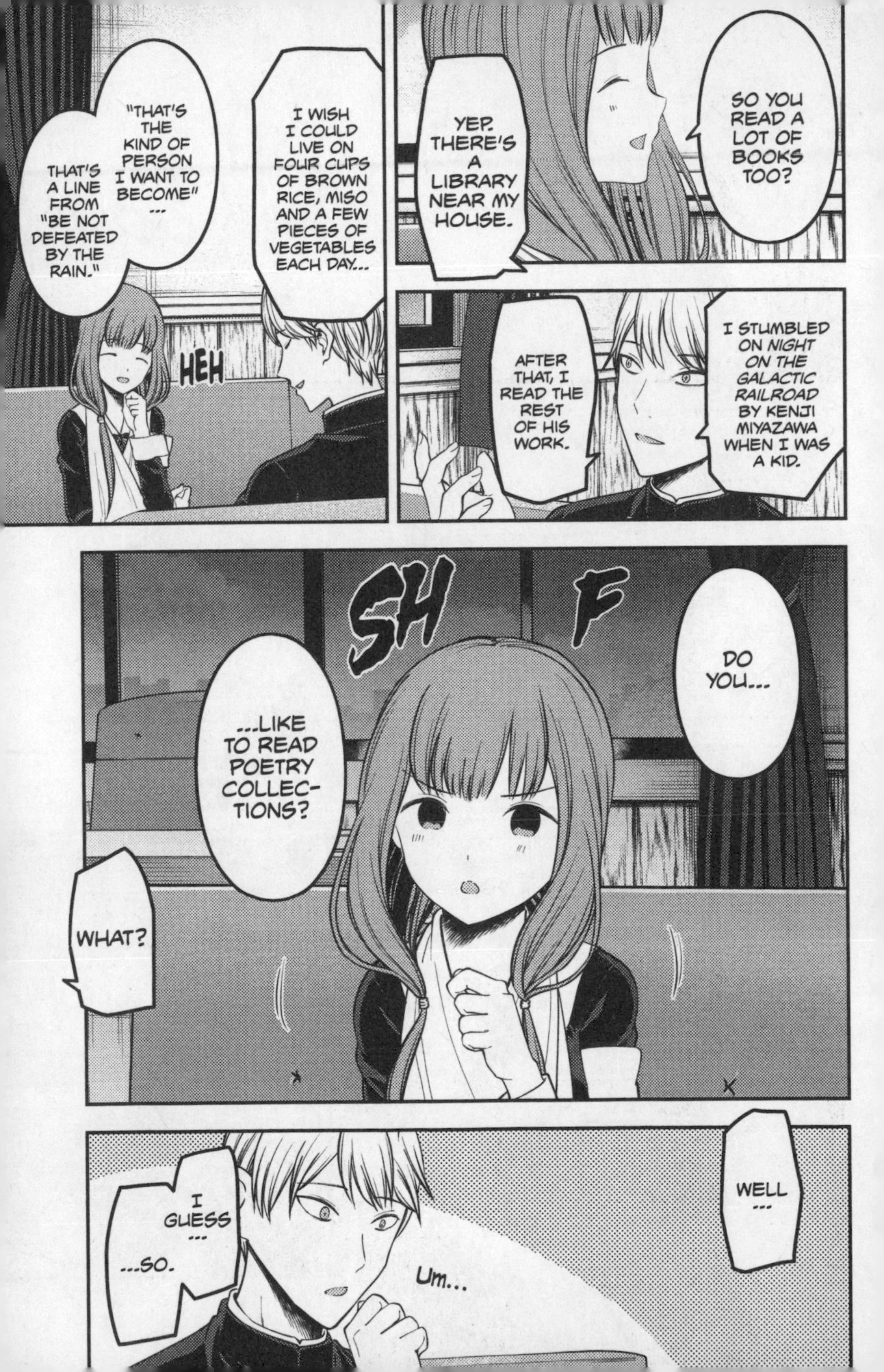
SO YOU READ A LOT OF BOOKS TOO?
YEP. THERE'S A LIBRARY NEAR MY HOUSE.
I STUMBLED ON *NIGHT ON THE GALACTIC RAILROAD* BY KENJI MIYAZAWA WHEN I WAS A KID.
AFTER THAT, I READ THE REST OF HIS WORK.
I WISH I COULD LIVE ON FOUR CUPS OF BROWN RICE, MISO AND A FEW PIECES OF VEGETABLES EACH DAY...
"THAT'S THE KIND OF PERSON I WANT TO BECOME"...
THAT'S A LINE FROM "BE NOT DEFEATED BY THE RAIN."
HEH
DO YOU...
SH
F
...LIKE TO READ POETRY COLLEC-TIONS?
WHAT?
WELL...
I GUESS...
...SO.
Um...

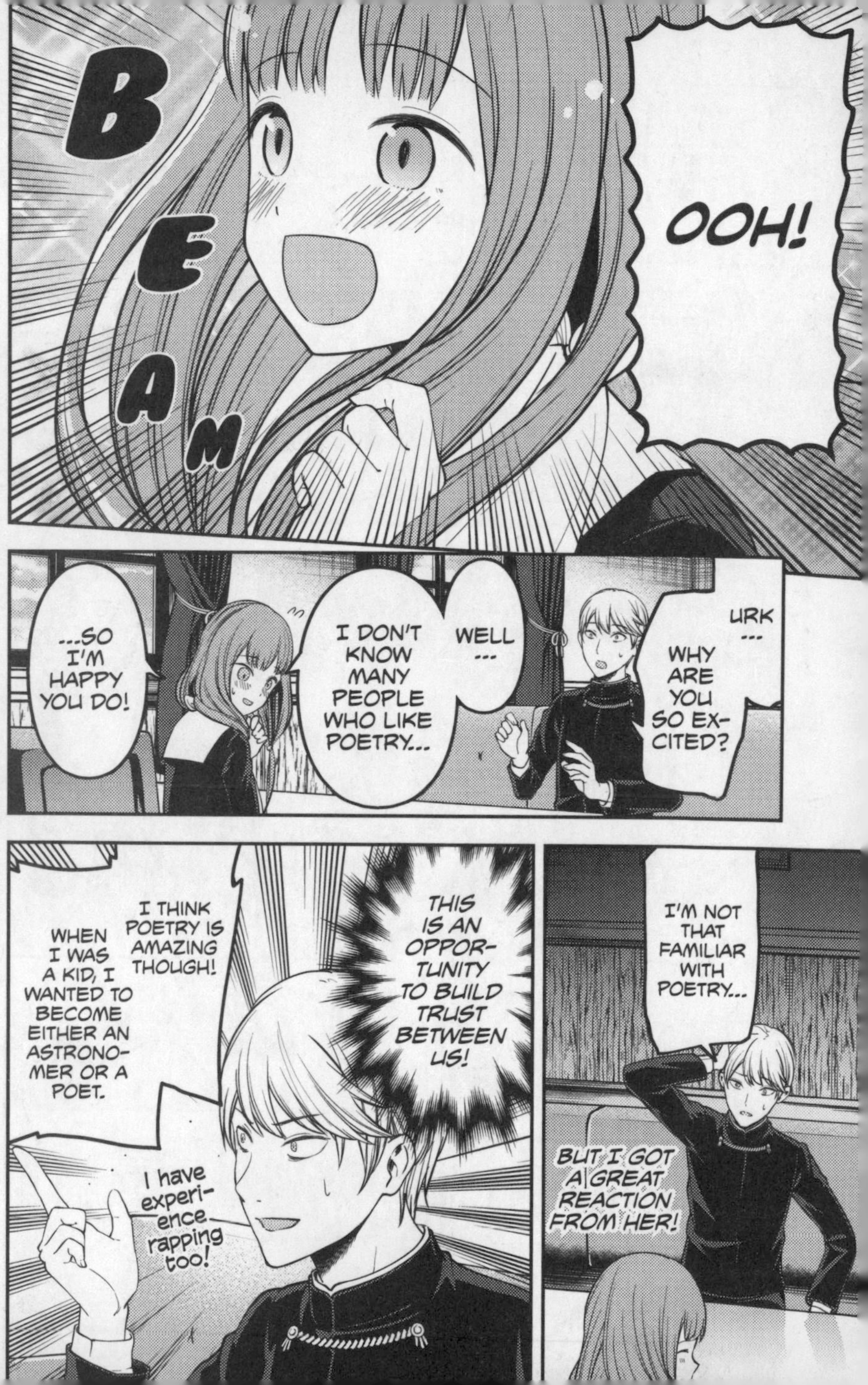
OOH!
BEAM
URK --- WHY ARE YOU SO EXCITED?
WELL ---
I DON'T KNOW MANY PEOPLE WHO LIKE POETRY...
...SO I'M HAPPY YOU DO!
I'M NOT THAT FAMILIAR WITH POETRY...
BUT I GOT A GREAT REACTION FROM HER!
THIS IS AN OPPORTUNITY TO BUILD TRUST BETWEEN US!
I THINK POETRY IS AMAZING THOUGH!
WHEN I WAS A KID, I WANTED TO BECOME EITHER AN ASTRONOMER OR A POET.
I have experience rapping too!

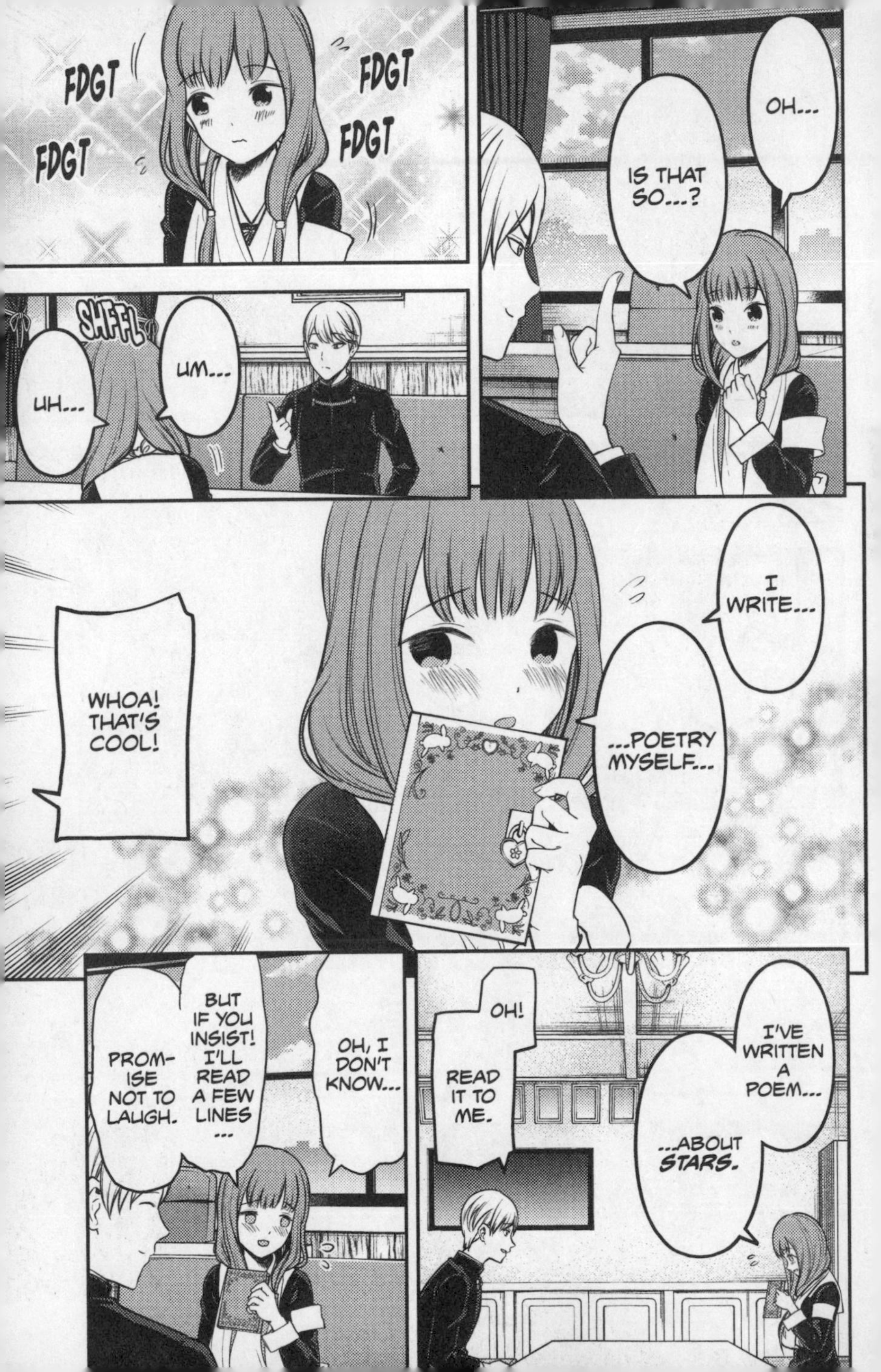
OH...
IS THAT SO...?
FDGT
FDGT
FDGT
FDGT
SHFFL
UM...
UH...
I WRITE...
...POETRY MYSELF...
WHOA! THAT'S COOL!
I'VE WRITTEN A POEM...
...ABOUT STARS.
OH!
READ IT TO ME.
OH, I DON'T KNOW...
BUT IF YOU INSIST! I'LL READ A FEW LINES...
PROMISE NOT TO LAUGH.

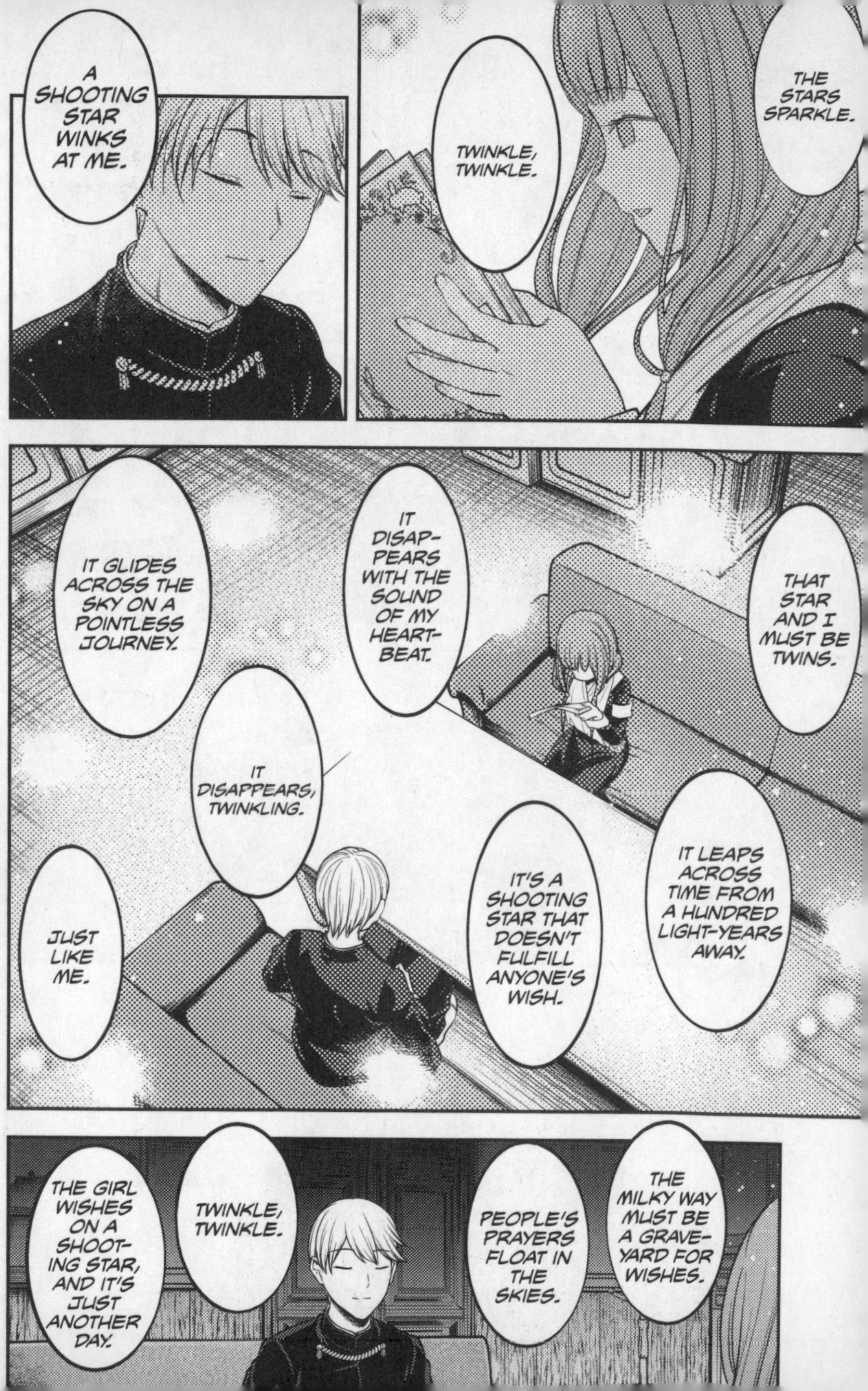
THE STARS SPARKLE.
TWINKLE, TWINKLE.
A SHOOTING STAR WINKS AT ME.
THAT STAR AND I MUST BE TWINS.
IT DISAPPEARS WITH THE SOUND OF MY HEARTBEAT.
IT GLIDES ACROSS THE SKY ON A POINTLESS JOURNEY.
IT LEAPS ACROSS TIME FROM A HUNDRED LIGHT-YEARS AWAY.
IT'S A SHOOTING STAR THAT DOESN'T FULFILL ANYONE'S WISH.
IT DISAPPEARS, TWINKLING.
JUST LIKE ME.
THE MILKY WAY MUST BE A GRAVEYARD FOR WISHES.
PEOPLE'S PRAYERS FLOAT IN THE SKIES.
TWINKLE, TWINKLE.
THE GIRL WISHES ON A SHOOTING STAR, AND IT'S JUST ANOTHER DAY.

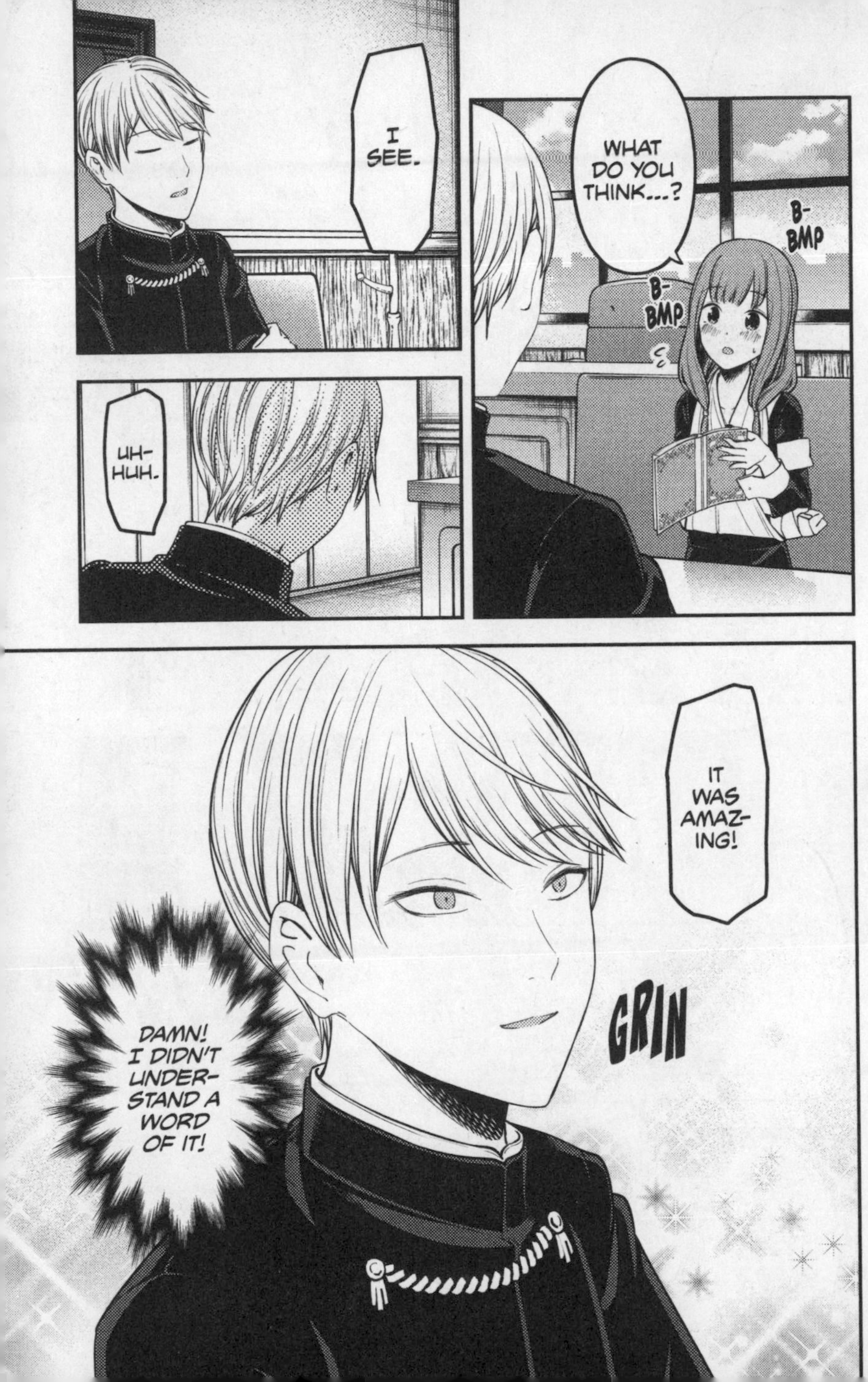
WHAT DO YOU THINK...?
B-BMP
B-BMP
I SEE.
UH-HUH.
IT WAS AMAZ-ING!
GRIN
DAMN! I DIDN'T UNDER-STAND A WORD OF IT!

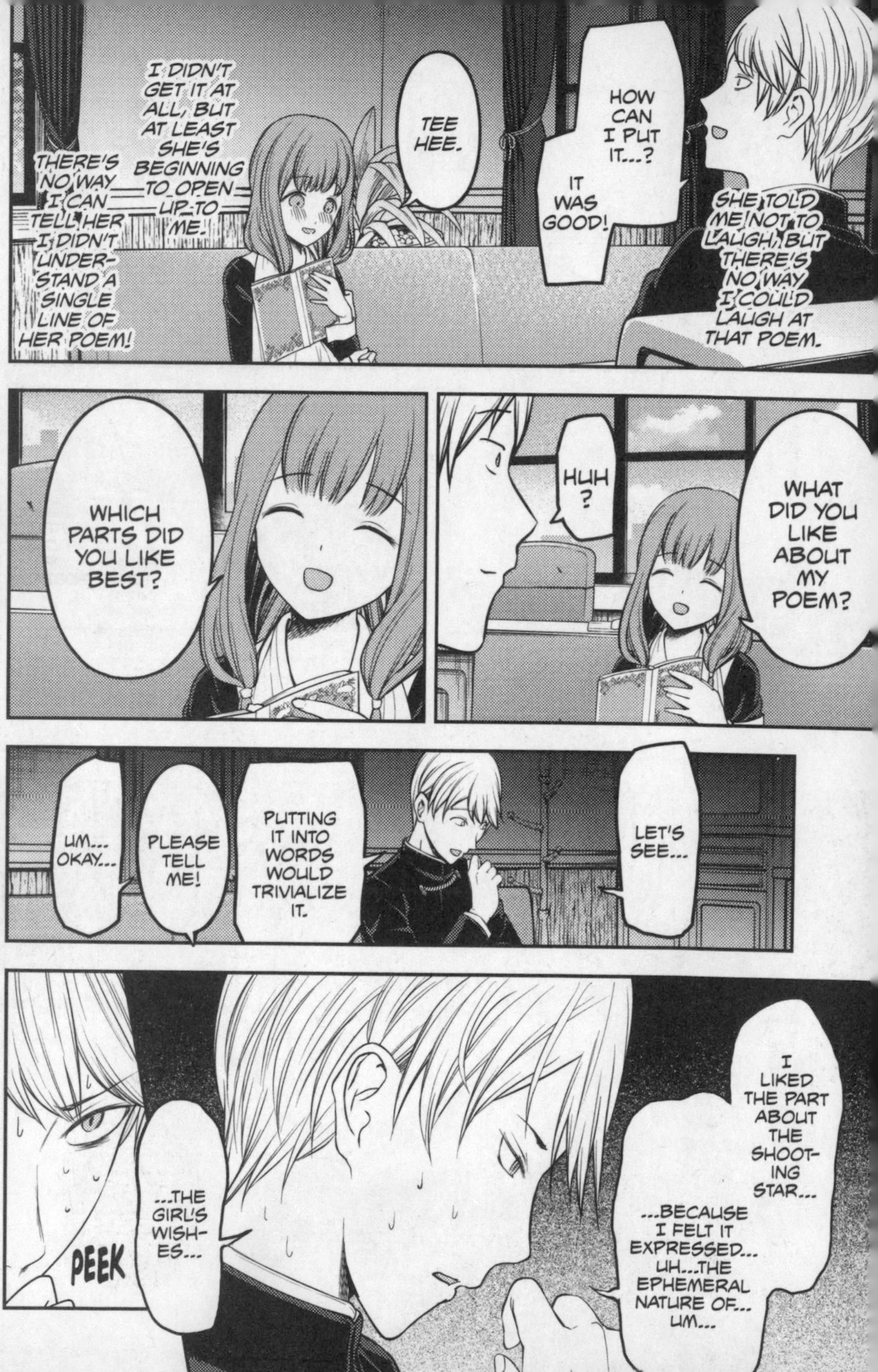
HOW CAN I PUT IT...? IT WAS GOOD!
SHE TOLD ME NOT TO LAUGH, BUT THERE'S NO WAY I COULD LAUGH AT THAT POEM.
TEE HEE.
I DIDN'T GET IT AT ALL, BUT AT LEAST SHE'S BEGINNING TO OPEN UP TO ME.
THERE'S NO WAY I CAN TELL HER I DIDN'T UNDER-STAND A SINGLE LINE OF HER POEM!
WHAT DID YOU LIKE ABOUT MY POEM?
HUH?
WHICH PARTS DID YOU LIKE BEST?
LET'S SEE...
PUTTING IT INTO WORDS WOULD TRIVIALIZE IT.
PLEASE TELL ME!
UM... OKAY...
I LIKED THE PART ABOUT THE SHOOT-ING STAR...
...BECAUSE I FELT IT EXPRESSED... UH...THE EPHEMERAL NATURE OF... UM...
...THE GIRL'S WISH-ES...
PEEK

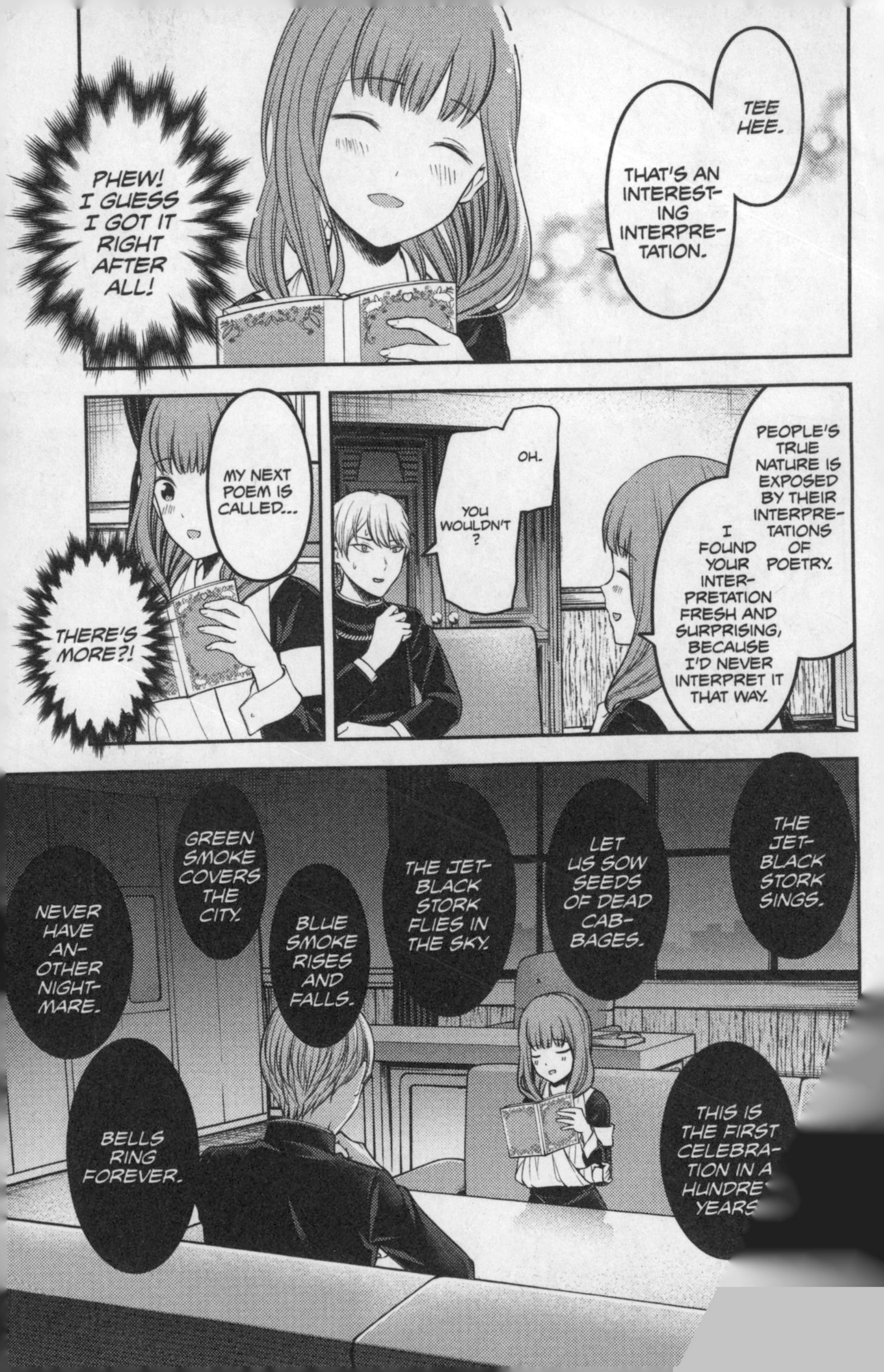
TEE HEE.
THAT'S AN INTERESTING INTERPRETATION.
PHEW! I GUESS I GOT IT RIGHT AFTER ALL!
PEOPLE'S TRUE NATURE IS EXPOSED BY THEIR INTERPRETATIONS OF POETRY.
I FOUND YOUR INTERPRETATION FRESH AND SURPRISING, BECAUSE I'D NEVER INTERPRET IT THAT WAY.
OH.
YOU WOULDN'T?
MY NEXT POEM IS CALLED...
THERE'S MORE?!
THE JET-BLACK STORK SINGS.
LET US SOW SEEDS OF DEAD CABBAGES.
THE JET-BLACK STORK FLIES IN THE SKY.
GREEN SMOKE COVERS THE CITY.
BLUE SMOKE RISES AND FALLS.
NEVER HAVE ANOTHER NIGHTMARE.
THIS IS THE FIRST CELEBRATION IN A HUNDRE YEARS
BELLS RING FOREVER.

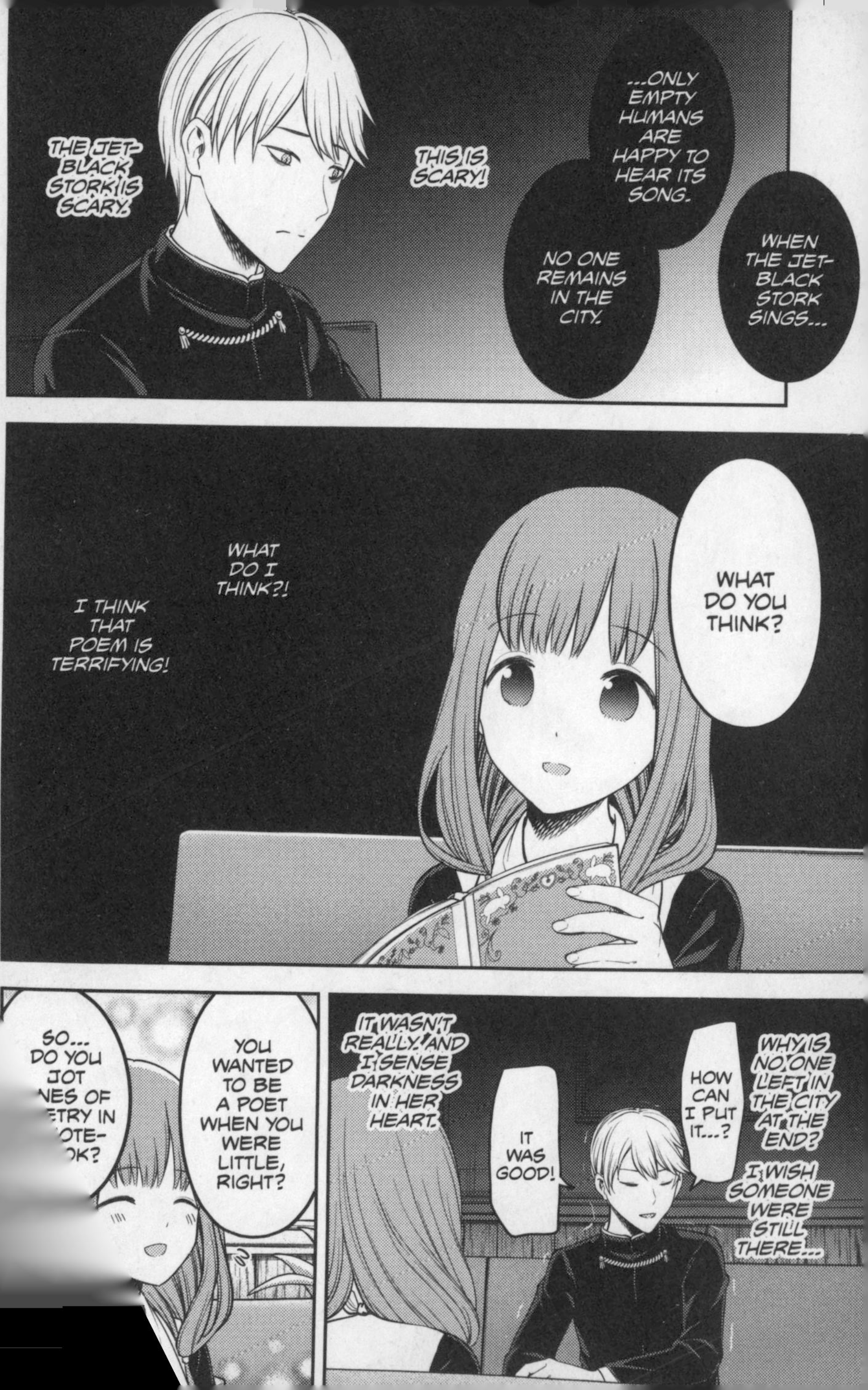
WHEN THE JET-BLACK STORK SINGS...
NO ONE REMAINS IN THE CITY.
...ONLY EMPTY HUMANS ARE HAPPY TO HEAR ITS SONG.
THIS IS SCARY!
THE JET-BLACK STORK IS SCARY.
WHAT DO YOU THINK?
WHAT DO I THINK?!
I THINK THAT POEM IS TERRIFYING!
WHY IS NO ONE LEFT IN THE CITY AT THE END?
I WISH SOMEONE WERE STILL THERE...
HOW CAN I PUT IT...?
IT WAS GOOD!
IT WASN'T REALLY. AND I SENSE DARKNESS IN HER HEART.
YOU WANTED TO BE A POET WHEN YOU WERE LITTLE, RIGHT?
SO... DO YOU JOT NES OF ETRY IN OTE- OK?

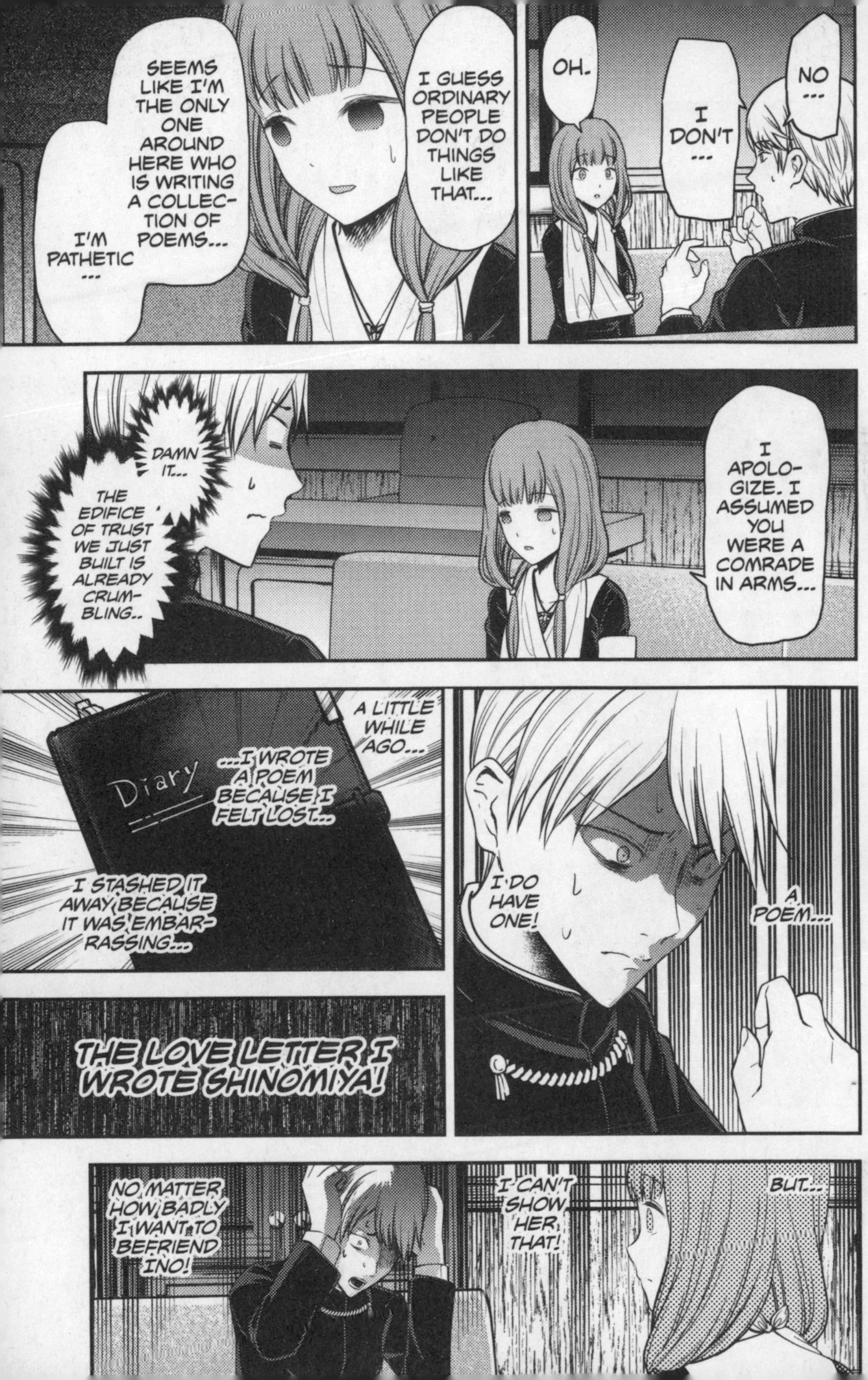
NO ---
I DON'T ---
OH.
I GUESS ORDINARY PEOPLE DON'T DO THINGS LIKE THAT...
SEEMS LIKE I'M THE ONLY ONE AROUND HERE WHO IS WRITING A COLLECTION OF POEMS...
I'M PATHETIC ---
I APOLOGIZE. I ASSUMED YOU WERE A COMRADE IN ARMS...
DAMN IT...
THE EDIFICE OF TRUST WE JUST BUILT IS ALREADY CRUMBLING.
A POEM...
I DO HAVE ONE!
A LITTLE WHILE AGO...
...I WROTE A POEM BECAUSE I FELT LOST...
Diary
I STASHED IT AWAY BECAUSE IT WAS EMBARRASSING...
THE LOVE LETTER I WROTE SHINOMIYA!
BUT...
I CAN'T SHOW HER THAT!
NO MATTER HOW BADLY I WANT TO BEFRIEND INO!

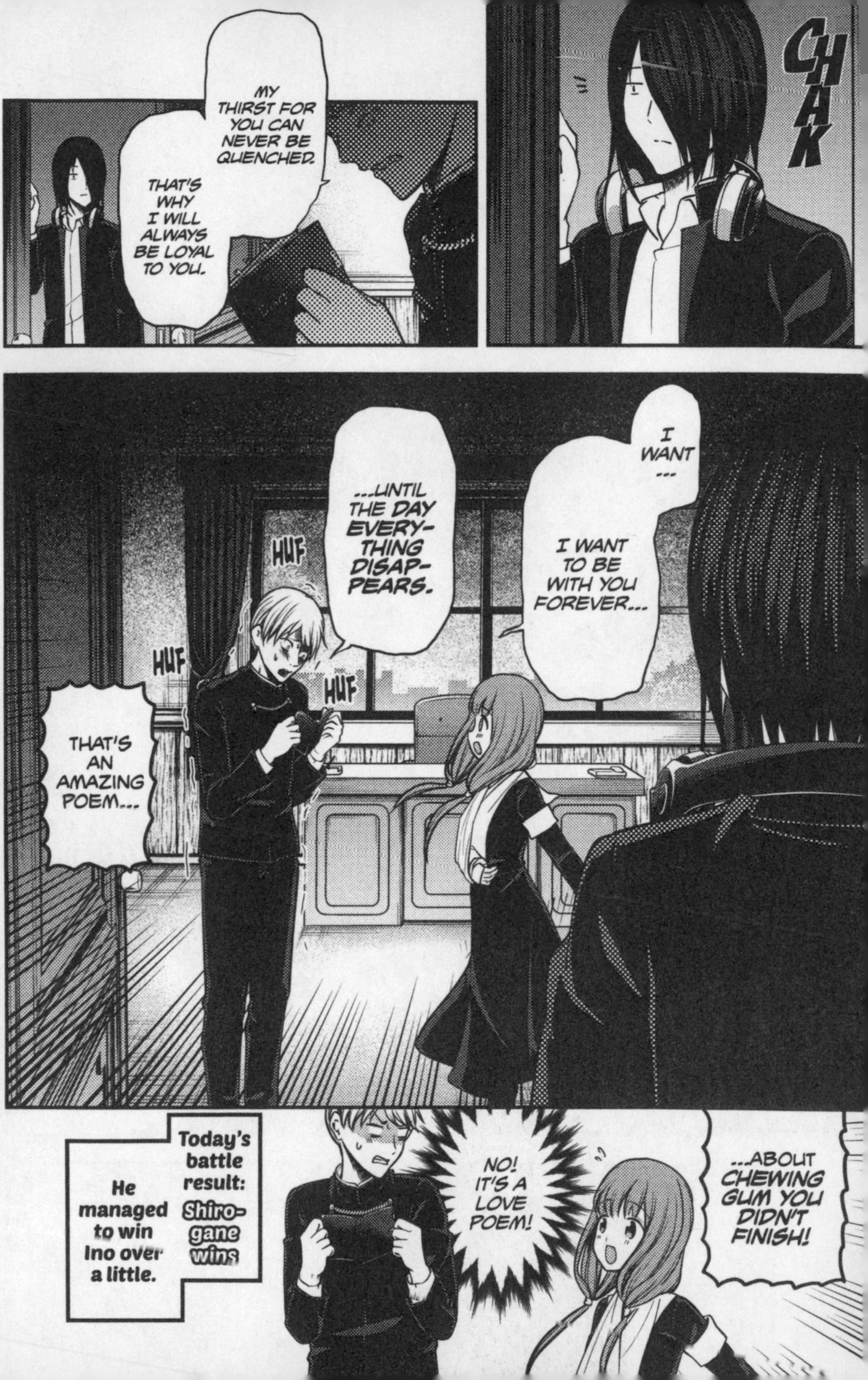
CHAK
MY THIRST FOR YOU CAN NEVER BE QUENCHED.
THAT'S WHY I WILL ALWAYS BE LOYAL TO YOU.
I WANT...
I WANT TO BE WITH YOU FOREVER...
...UNTIL THE DAY EVERYTHING DISAPPEARS.
HUF
HUF
HUF
THAT'S AN AMAZING POEM...
...ABOUT CHEWING GUM YOU DIDN'T FINISH!
NO! IT'S A LOVE POEM!
Today's battle result: Shirogane wins
He managed to win Ino over a little.

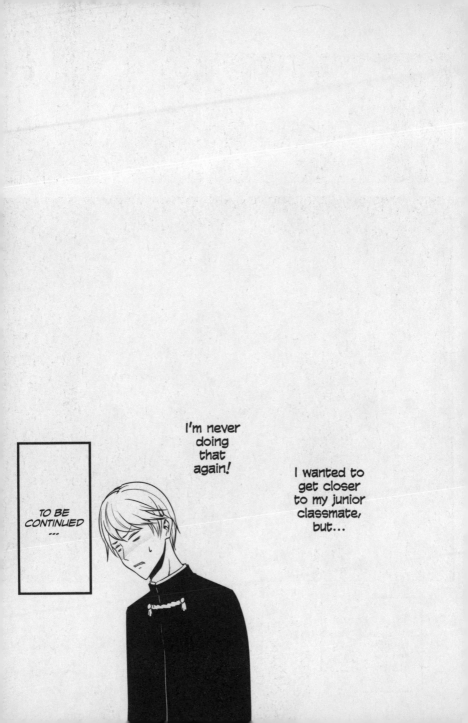

I wanted to get closer to my junior classmate, but...
I'm never doing that again!
TO BE CONTINUED ...

KAGUYA-SAMA

LOVE IS WAR

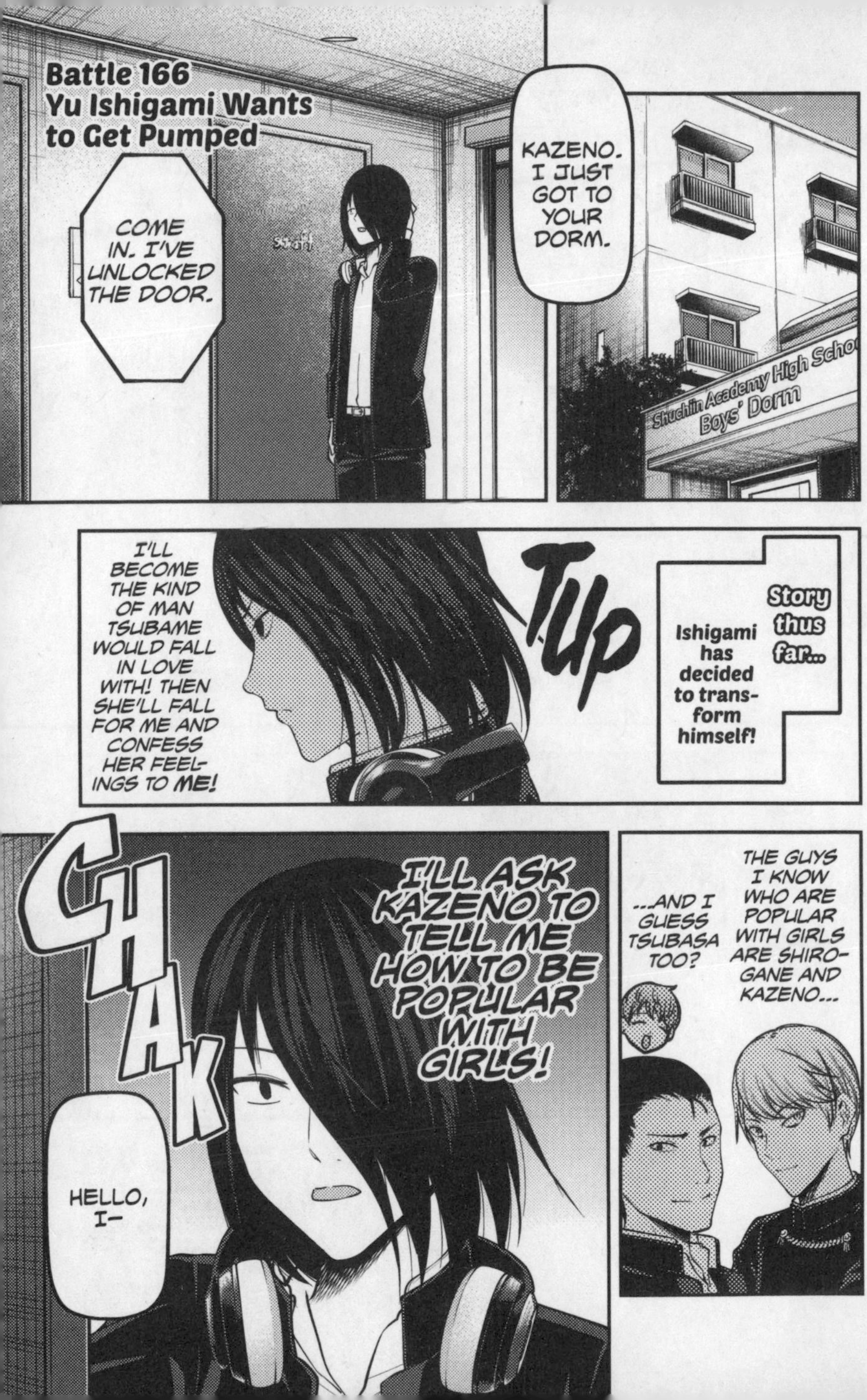
KAZENO. I JUST GOT TO YOUR DORM.
Shuchiin Academy High Scho
Boys' Dorm
Battle 166
Yu Ishigami Wants to Get Pumped
COME IN. I'VE UNLOCKED THE DOOR.
Story thus far...
Ishigami has decided to transform himself!
TUP
I'LL BECOME THE KIND OF MAN TSUBAME WOULD FALL IN LOVE WITH! THEN SHE'LL FALL FOR ME AND CONFESS HER FEELINGS TO ME!
THE GUYS I KNOW WHO ARE POPULAR WITH GIRLS ARE SHIROGANE AND KAZENO...
...AND I GUESS TSUBASA TOO?
I'LL ASK KAZENO TO TELL ME HOW TO BE POPULAR WITH GIRLS!
CHAK
HELLO, I–

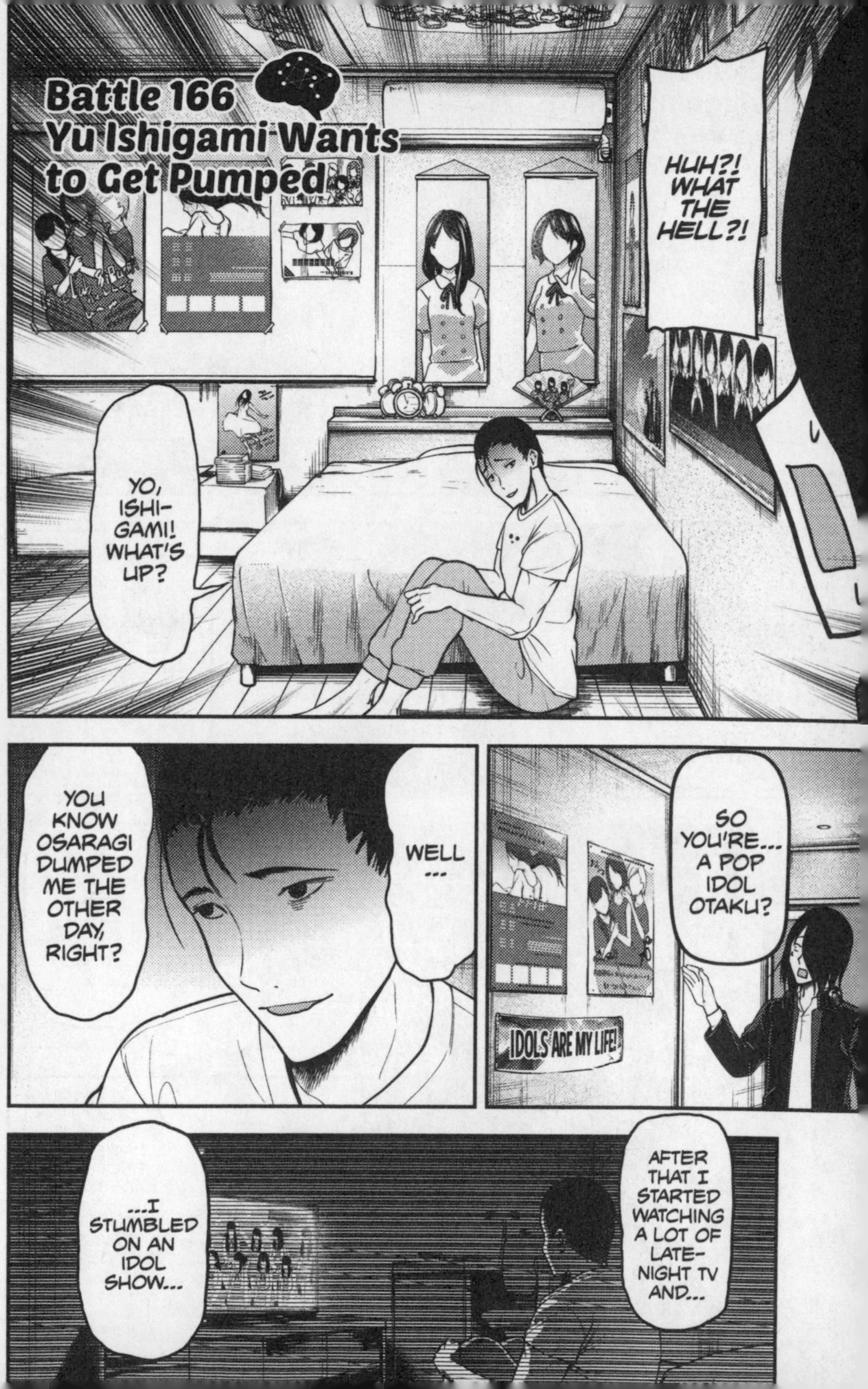
Battle 166
Yu Ishigami Wants to Get Pumped
HUH?! WHAT THE HELL?!
YO, ISHIGAMI! WHAT'S UP?
SO YOU'RE... A POP IDOL OTAKU?
IDOLS ARE MY LIFE!
WELL ---
YOU KNOW OSARAGI DUMPED ME THE OTHER DAY, RIGHT?
AFTER THAT I STARTED WATCHING A LOT OF LATE-NIGHT TV AND...
...I STUMBLED ON AN IDOL SHOW...

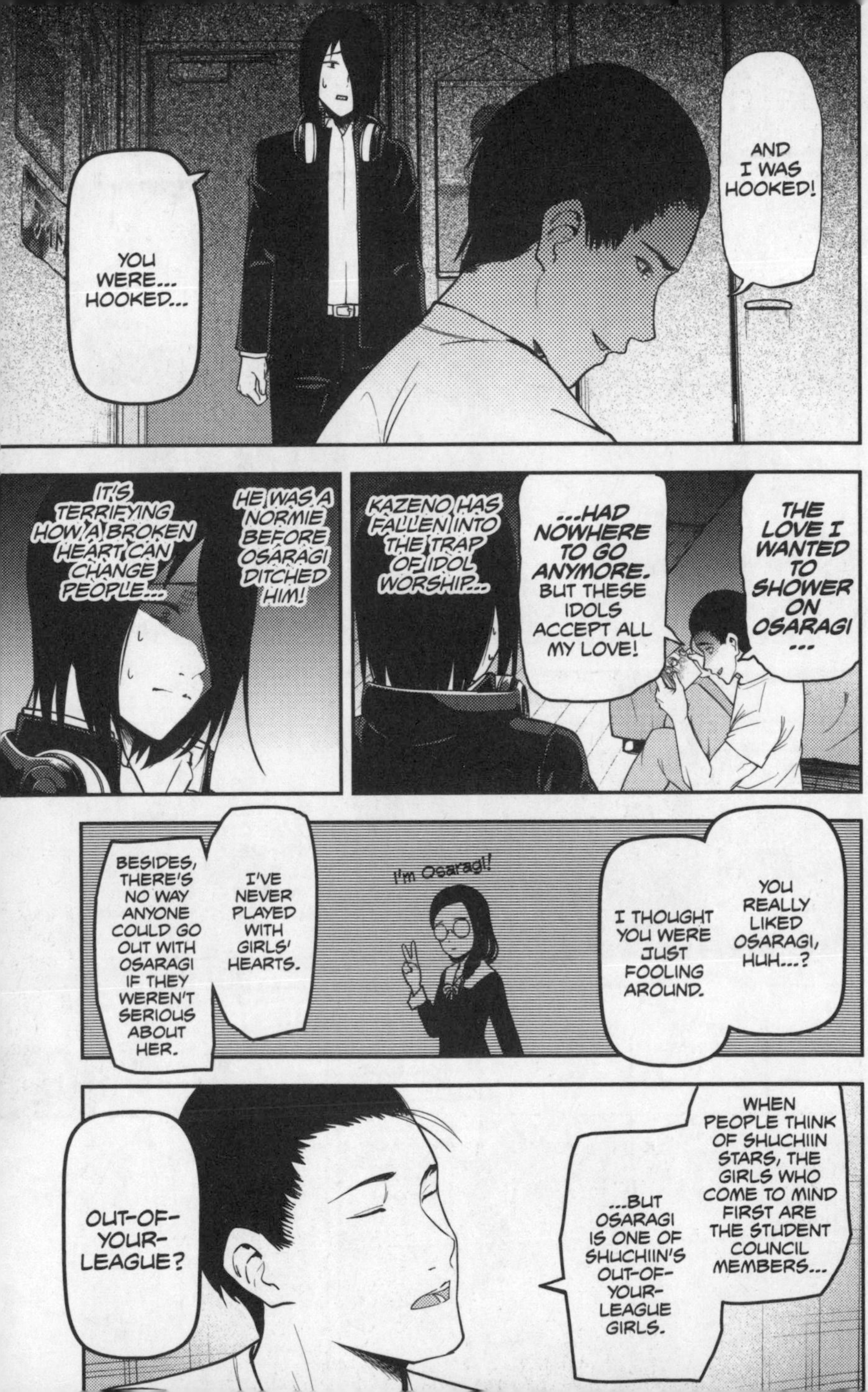
AND I WAS HOOKED!
YOU WERE... HOOKED...
THE LOVE I WANTED TO SHOWER ON OSARAGI...
...HAD NOWHERE TO GO ANYMORE. BUT THESE IDOLS ACCEPT ALL MY LOVE!
KAZENO HAS FALLEN INTO THE TRAP OF IDOL WORSHIP...
HE WAS A NORMIE BEFORE OSARAGI DITCHED HIM!
IT'S TERRIFYING HOW A BROKEN HEART CAN CHANGE PEOPLE...
YOU REALLY LIKED OSARAGI, HUH...?
I THOUGHT YOU WERE JUST FOOLING AROUND.
I'm Osaragi!
I'VE NEVER PLAYED WITH GIRLS' HEARTS.
BESIDES, THERE'S NO WAY ANYONE COULD GO OUT WITH OSARAGI IF THEY WEREN'T SERIOUS ABOUT HER.
WHEN PEOPLE THINK OF SHUCHIIN STARS, THE GIRLS WHO COME TO MIND FIRST ARE THE STUDENT COUNCIL MEMBERS...
...BUT OSARAGI IS ONE OF SHUCHIIN'S OUT-OF-YOUR-LEAGUE GIRLS.
OUT-OF-YOUR-LEAGUE?

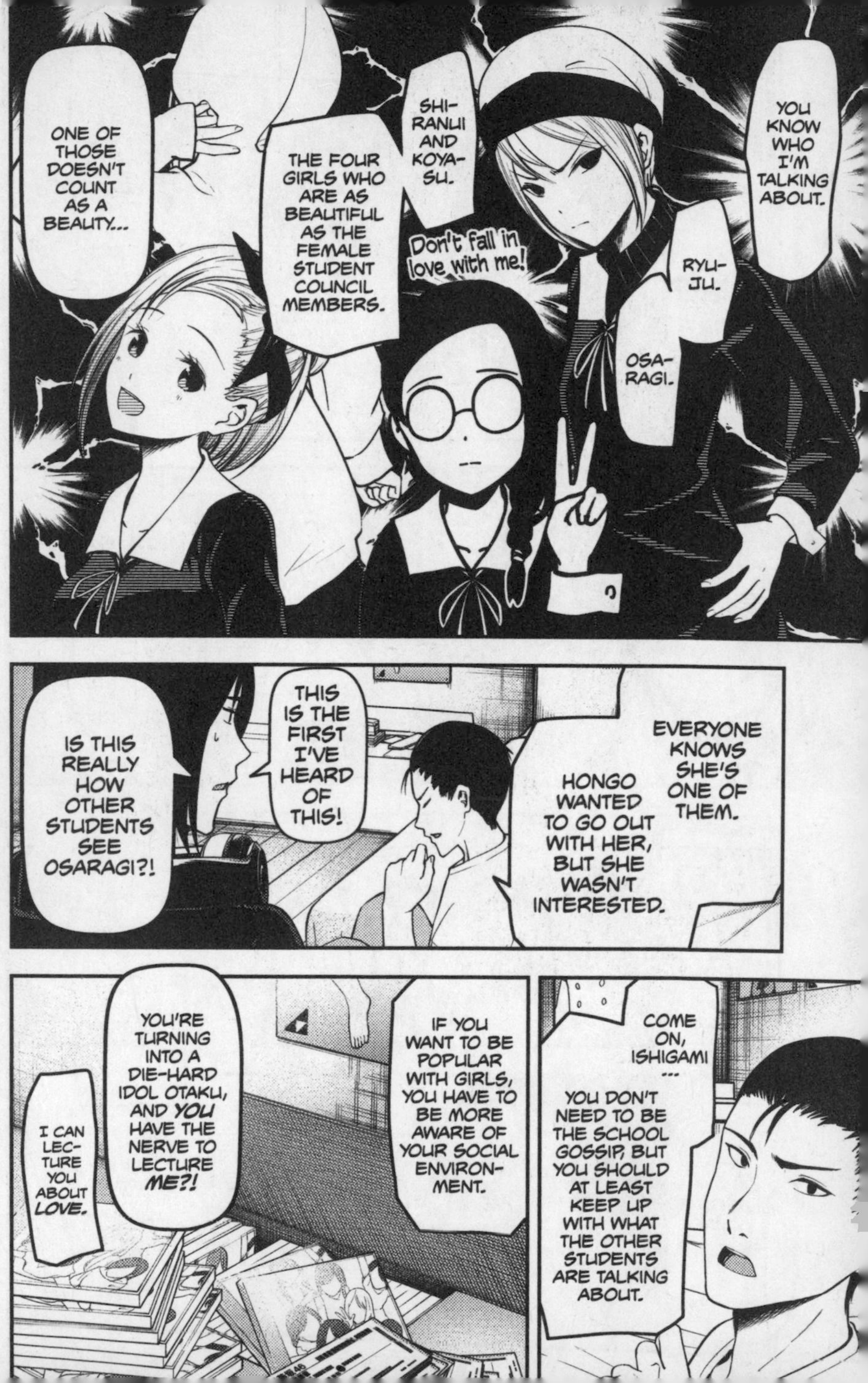
YOU KNOW WHO I'M TALKING ABOUT.
RYUJU.
OSARAGI.
SHIRANUI AND KOYASU.
THE FOUR GIRLS WHO ARE AS BEAUTIFUL AS THE FEMALE STUDENT COUNCIL MEMBERS.
Don't fall in love with me!
ONE OF THOSE DOESN'T COUNT AS A BEAUTY...
EVERYONE KNOWS SHE'S ONE OF THEM.
HONGO WANTED TO GO OUT WITH HER, BUT SHE WASN'T INTERESTED.
THIS IS THE FIRST I'VE HEARD OF THIS!
IS THIS REALLY HOW OTHER STUDENTS SEE OSARAGI?!
COME ON, ISHIGAMI...
YOU DON'T NEED TO BE THE SCHOOL GOSSIP, BUT YOU SHOULD AT LEAST KEEP UP WITH WHAT THE OTHER STUDENTS ARE TALKING ABOUT.
IF YOU WANT TO BE POPULAR WITH GIRLS, YOU HAVE TO BE MORE AWARE OF YOUR SOCIAL ENVIRONMENT.
YOU'RE TURNING INTO A DIE-HARD IDOL OTAKU, AND *YOU* HAVE THE NERVE TO LECTURE *ME?!*
I CAN LECTURE YOU ABOUT *LOVE.*

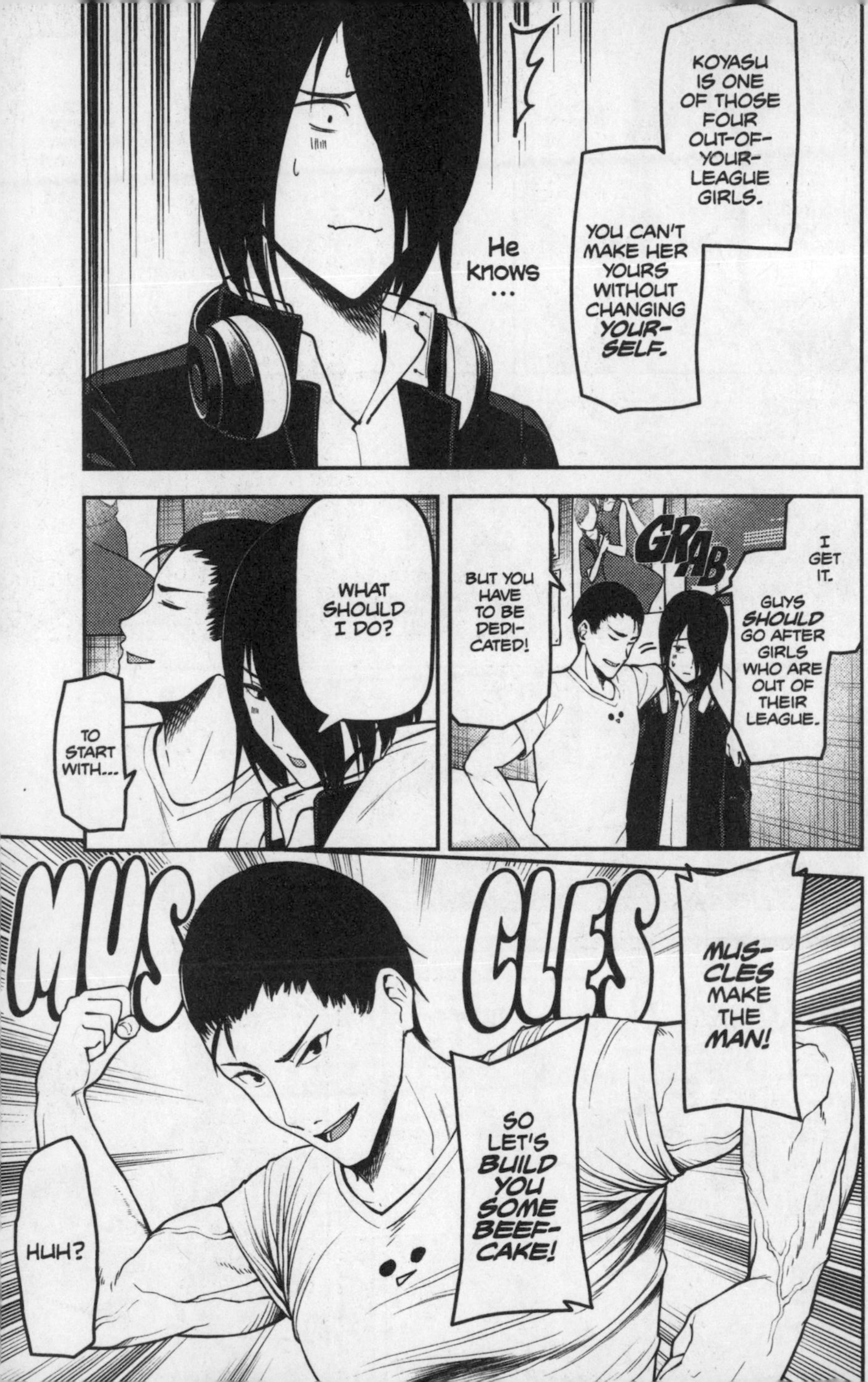
KOYASU IS ONE OF THOSE FOUR OUT-OF-YOUR-LEAGUE GIRLS.
YOU CAN'T MAKE HER YOURS WITHOUT CHANGING *YOURSELF.*
He knows...
GRAB
I GET IT.
GUYS *SHOULD* GO AFTER GIRLS WHO ARE OUT OF THEIR LEAGUE.
BUT YOU HAVE TO BE DEDICATED!
WHAT SHOULD I DO?
TO START WITH...
MUSCLES
MUSCLES MAKE THE *MAN!*
SO LET'S *BUILD YOU SOME BEEFCAKE!*
HUH?

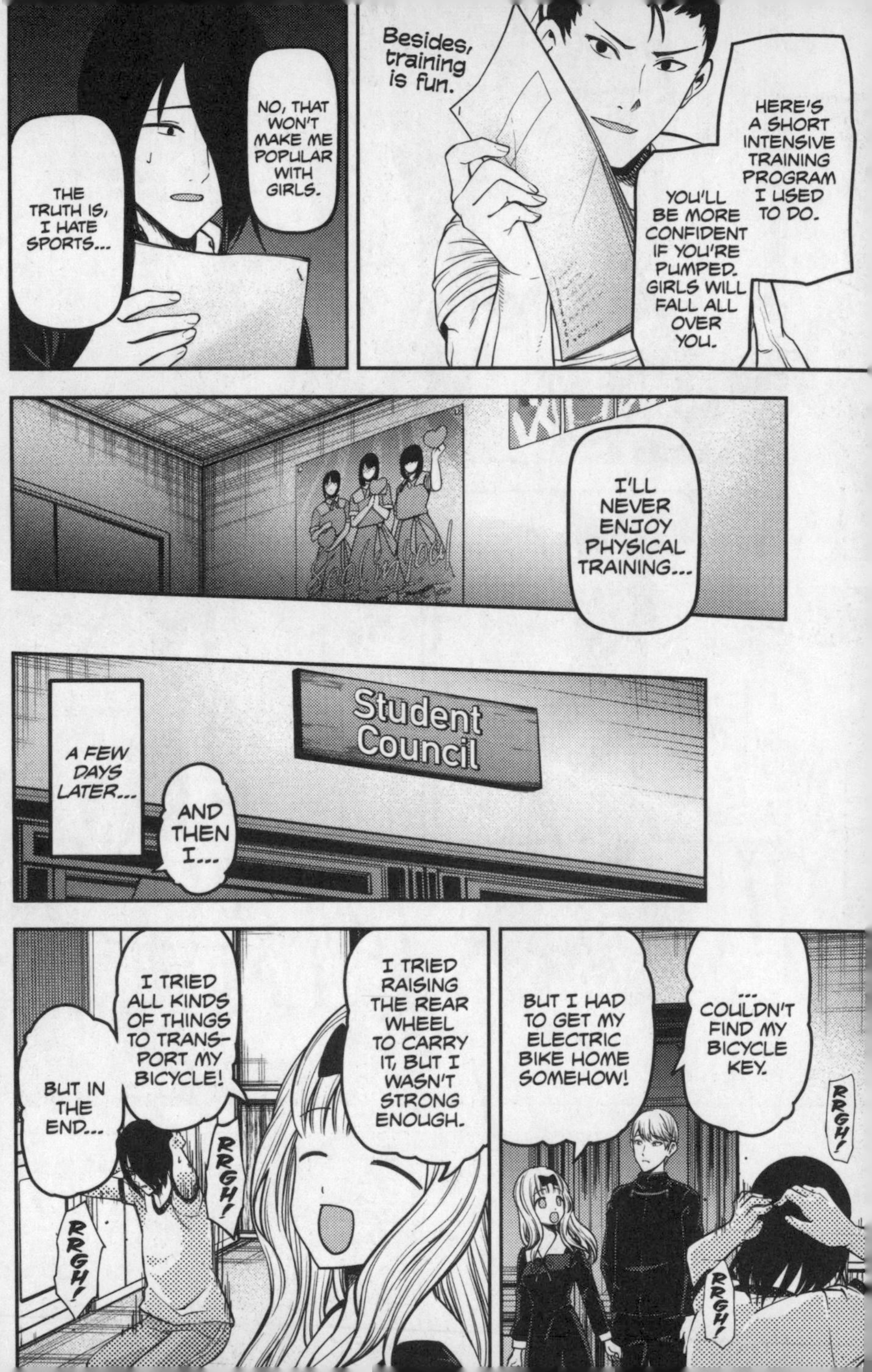
HERE'S A SHORT INTENSIVE TRAINING PROGRAM I USED TO DO.
YOU'LL BE MORE CONFIDENT IF YOU'RE PUMPED. GIRLS WILL FALL ALL OVER YOU.
Besides, training is fun.
NO, THAT WON'T MAKE ME POPULAR WITH GIRLS.
THE TRUTH IS, I HATE SPORTS...
I'LL NEVER ENJOY PHYSICAL TRAINING...
Student Council
A FEW DAYS LATER...
AND THEN I...
... COULDN'T FIND MY BICYCLE KEY.
RRGH!
BUT I HAD TO GET MY ELECTRIC BIKE HOME SOMEHOW!
RRGH!
I TRIED RAISING THE REAR WHEEL TO CARRY IT, BUT I WASN'T STRONG ENOUGH.
I TRIED ALL KINDS OF THINGS TO TRANS-PORT MY BICYCLE!
RRGH!
BUT IN THE END...
RRGH!

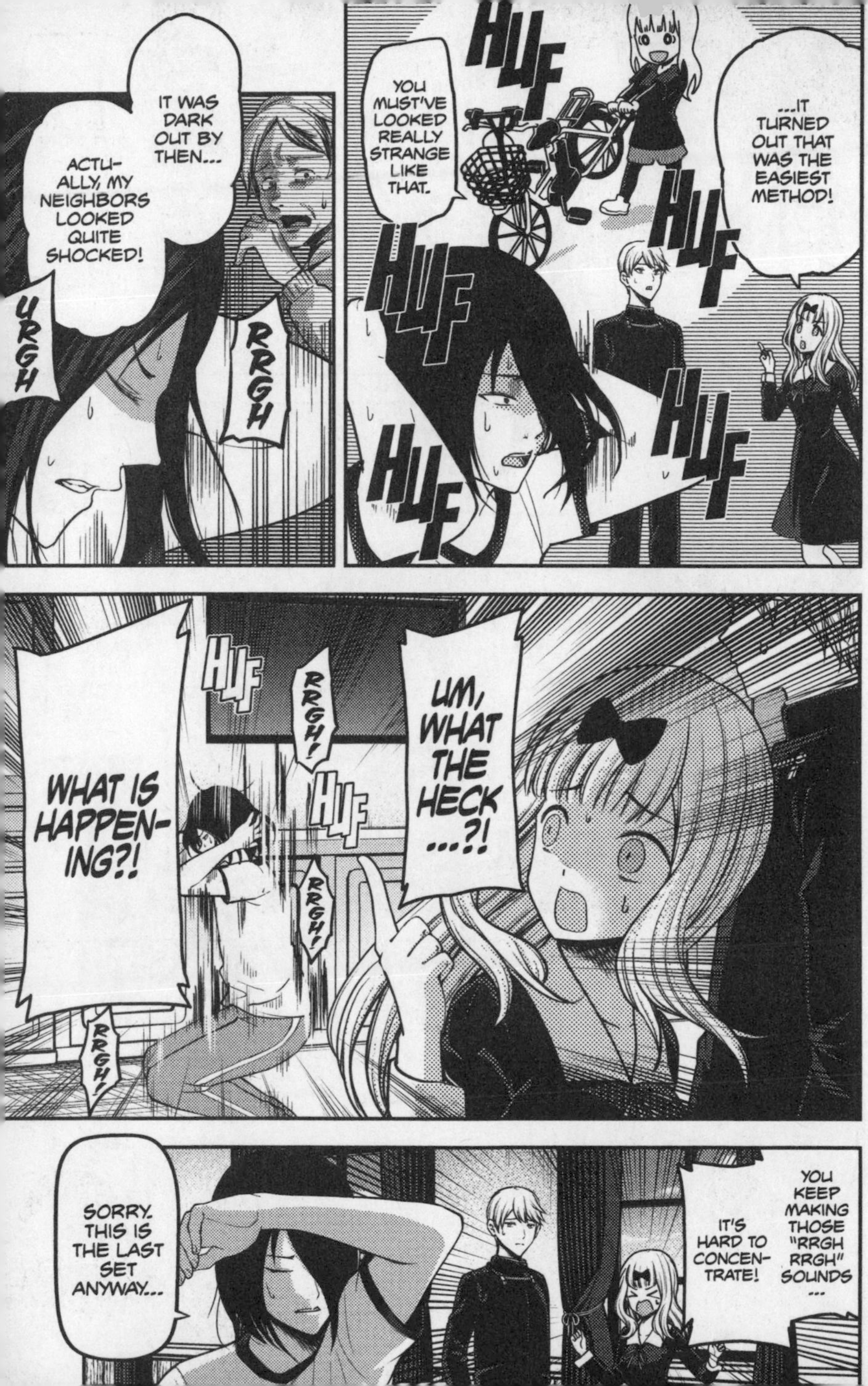

...IT TURNED OUT THAT WAS THE EASIEST METHOD!
HUF
HUF
YOU MUST'VE LOOKED REALLY STRANGE LIKE THAT.
HUF
HUF
HUF
IT WAS DARK OUT BY THEN...
ACTUALLY, MY NEIGHBORS LOOKED QUITE SHOCKED!
RRGH
URGH
UM, WHAT THE HECK...?!
RRGH!
HUF
HUF
RRGH!
WHAT IS HAPPENING?!
RRGH!
YOU KEEP MAKING THOSE "RRGH RRGH" SOUNDS...
IT'S HARD TO CONCENTRATE!
SORRY. THIS IS THE LAST SET ANYWAY...

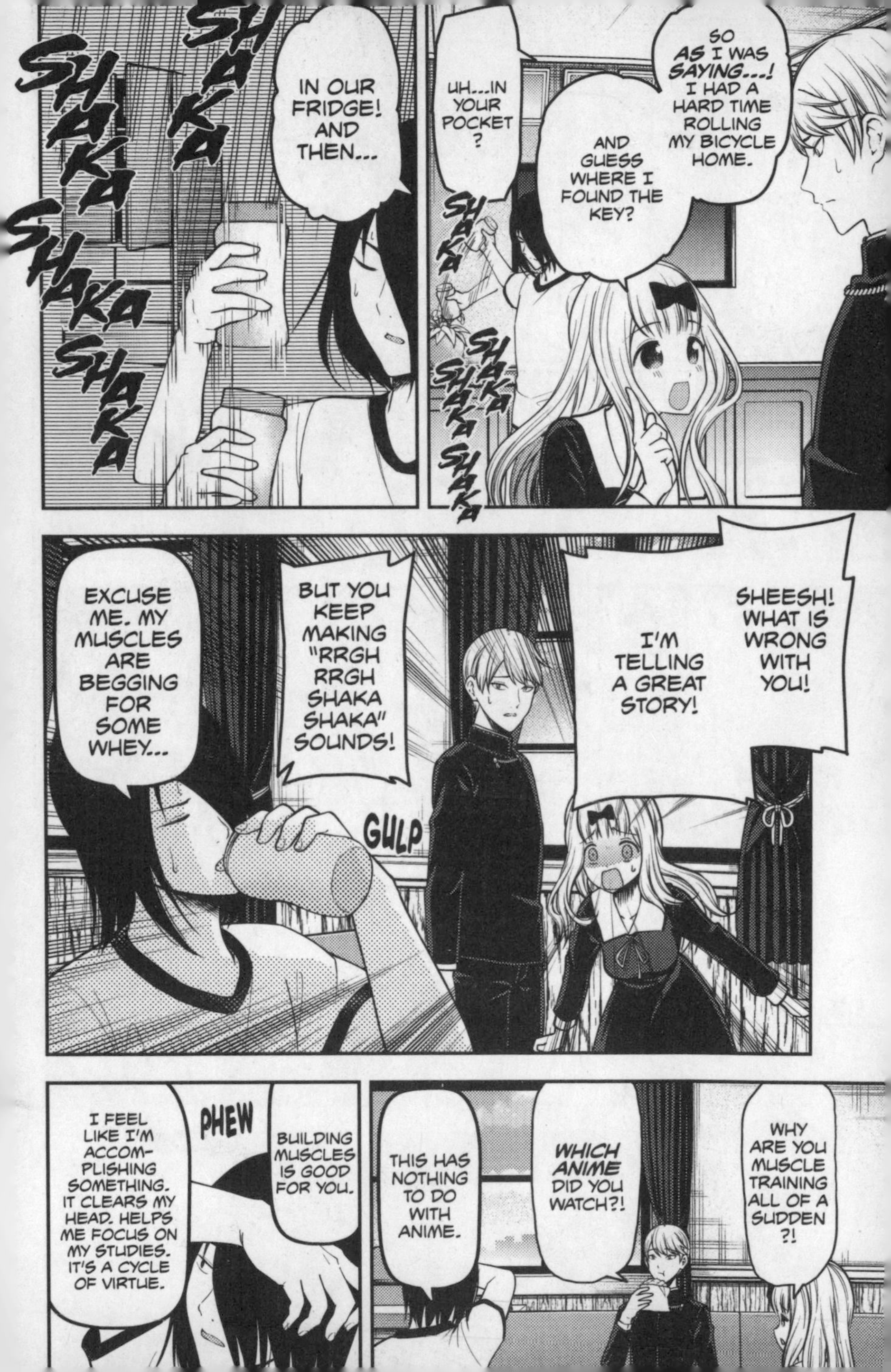
SO AS I WAS SAYING...! I HAD A HARD TIME ROLLING MY BICYCLE HOME.
AND GUESS WHERE I FOUND THE KEY?
UH...IN YOUR POCKET?
SHAKA SHAKA SHAKA SHAKA
IN OUR FRIDGE! AND THEN...
SHAKA SHAKA SHAKA SHAKA SHAKA
SHEESH! WHAT IS WRONG WITH YOU!
I'M TELLING A GREAT STORY!
BUT YOU KEEP MAKING "RRGH RRGH SHAKA SHAKA" SOUNDS!
EXCUSE ME. MY MUSCLES ARE BEGGING FOR SOME WHEY...
GULP
WHY ARE YOU MUSCLE TRAINING ALL OF A SUDDEN?!
WHICH ANIME DID YOU WATCH?!
THIS HAS NOTHING TO DO WITH ANIME.
BUILDING MUSCLES IS GOOD FOR YOU.
PHEW
I FEEL LIKE I'M ACCOMPLISHING SOMETHING. IT CLEARS MY HEAD. HELPS ME FOCUS ON MY STUDIES. IT'S A CYCLE OF VIRTUE.

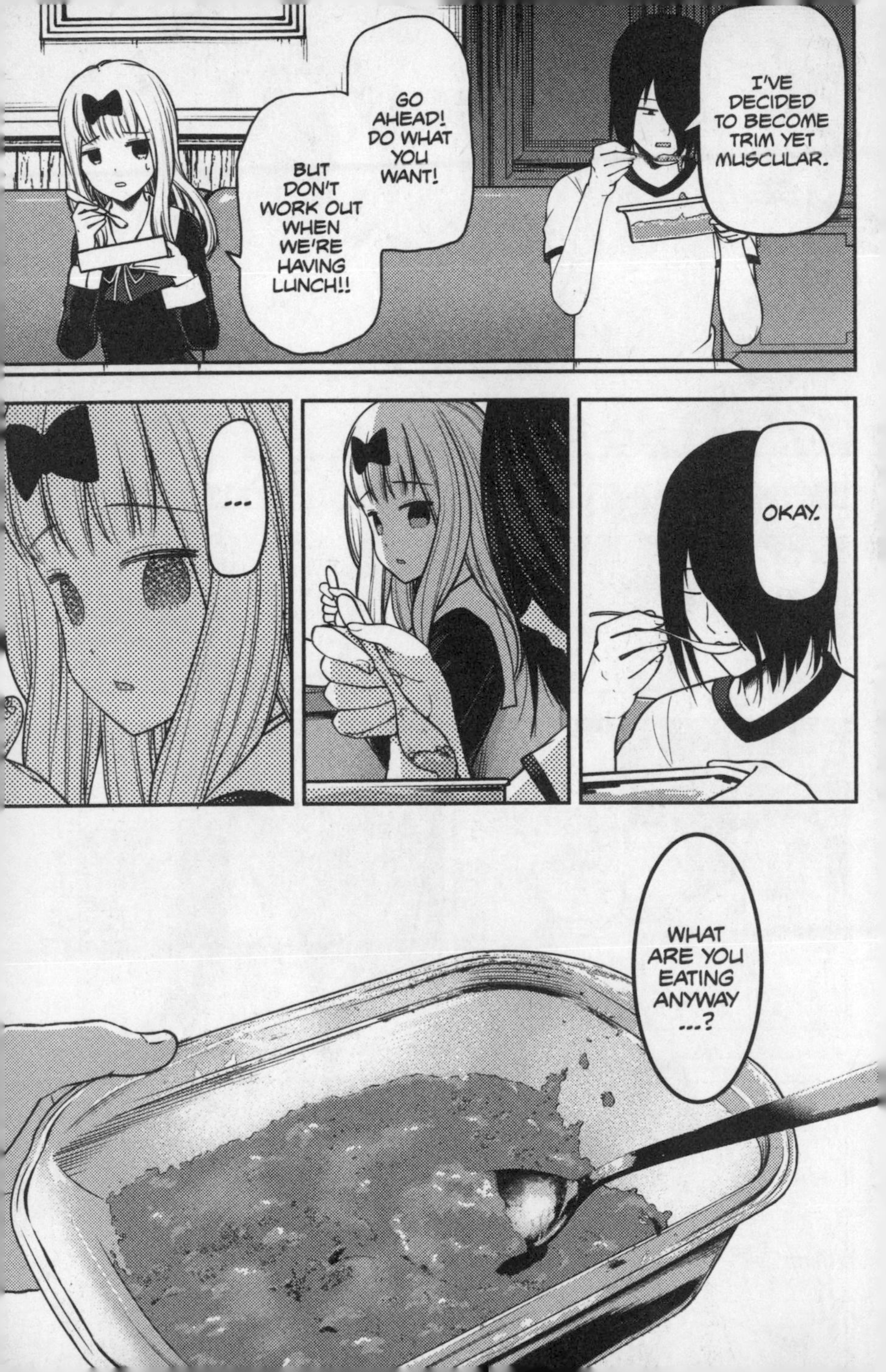
I'VE DECIDED TO BECOME TRIM YET MUSCULAR.
GO AHEAD! DO WHAT YOU WANT!
BUT DON'T WORK OUT WHEN WE'RE HAVING LUNCH!!
OKAY.
...
WHAT ARE YOU EATING ANYWAY ...?

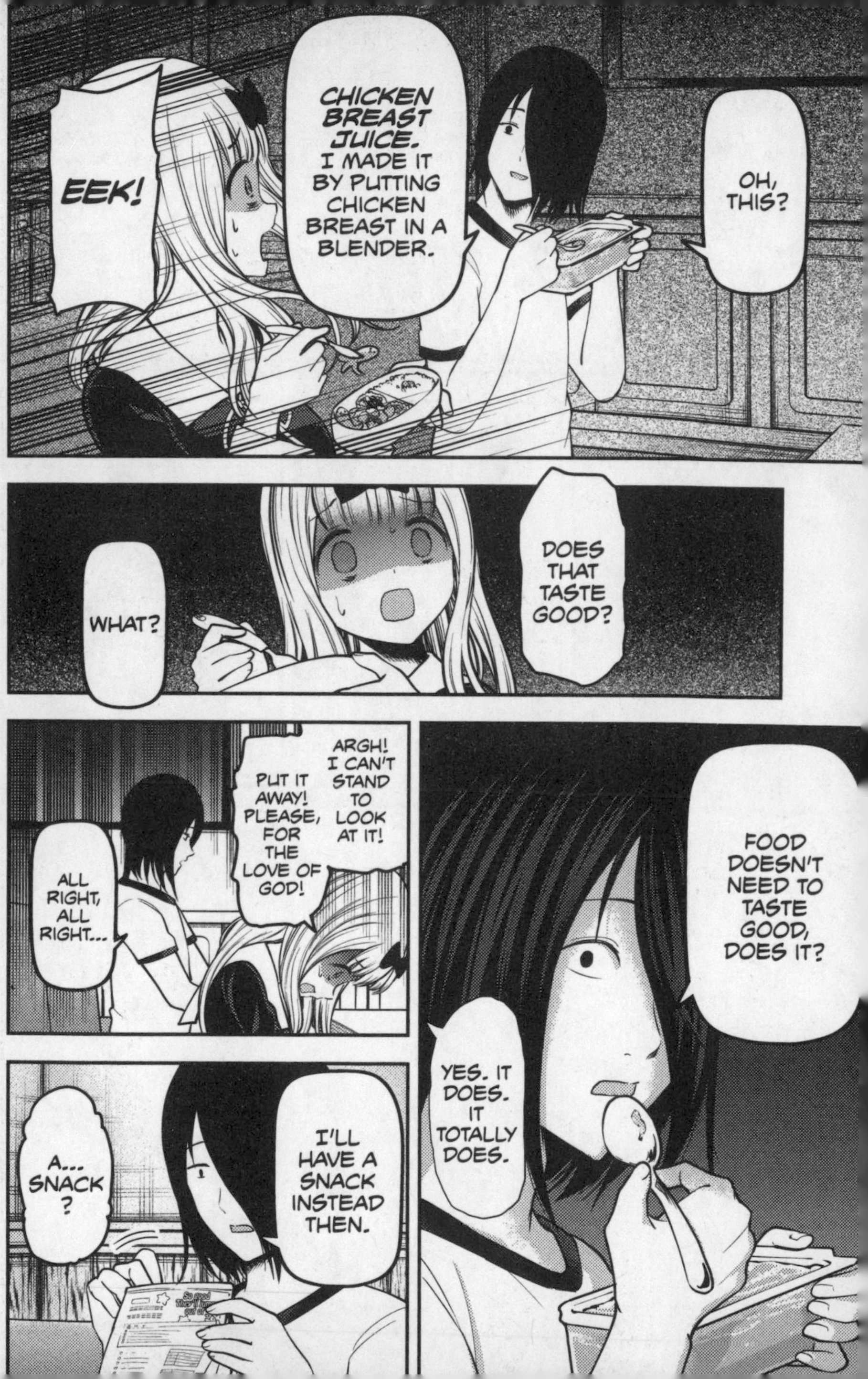
OH, THIS?
CHICKEN BREAST JUICE. I MADE IT BY PUTTING CHICKEN BREAST IN A BLENDER.
EEK!
DOES THAT TASTE GOOD?
WHAT?
FOOD DOESN'T NEED TO TASTE GOOD, DOES IT?
YES. IT DOES. IT TOTALLY DOES.
ARGH! I CAN'T STAND TO LOOK AT IT!
PUT IT AWAY! PLEASE, FOR THE LOVE OF GOD!
ALL RIGHT, ALL RIGHT...
I'LL HAVE A SNACK INSTEAD THEN.
A... SNACK?

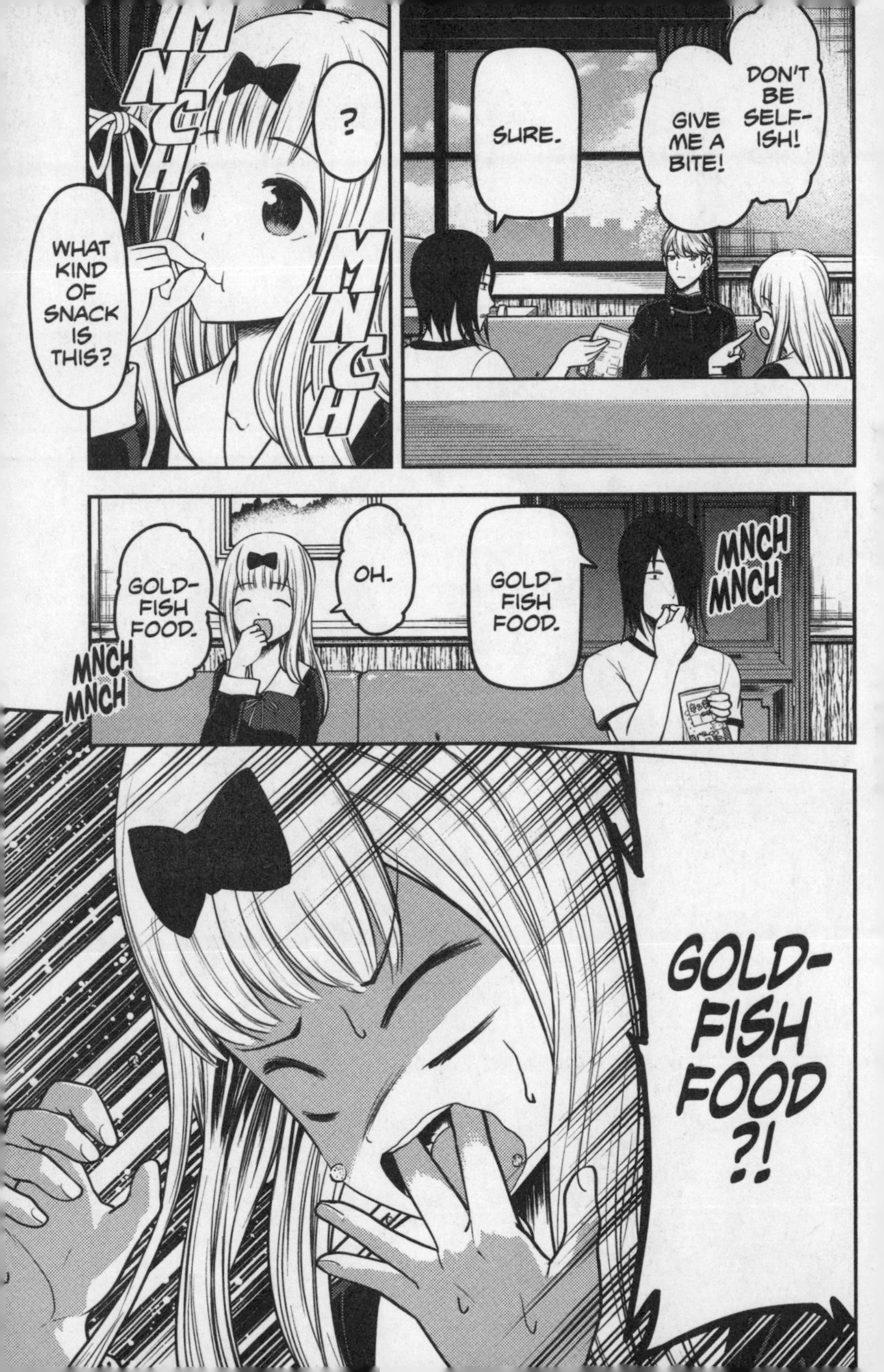
DON'T BE SELF-ISH!
GIVE ME A BITE!
SURE.
?
MNCH
WHAT KIND OF SNACK IS THIS?
MNCH
MNCH MNCH
GOLD-FISH FOOD.
OH.
GOLD-FISH FOOD.
MNCH MNCH
GOLD-FISH FOOD?!

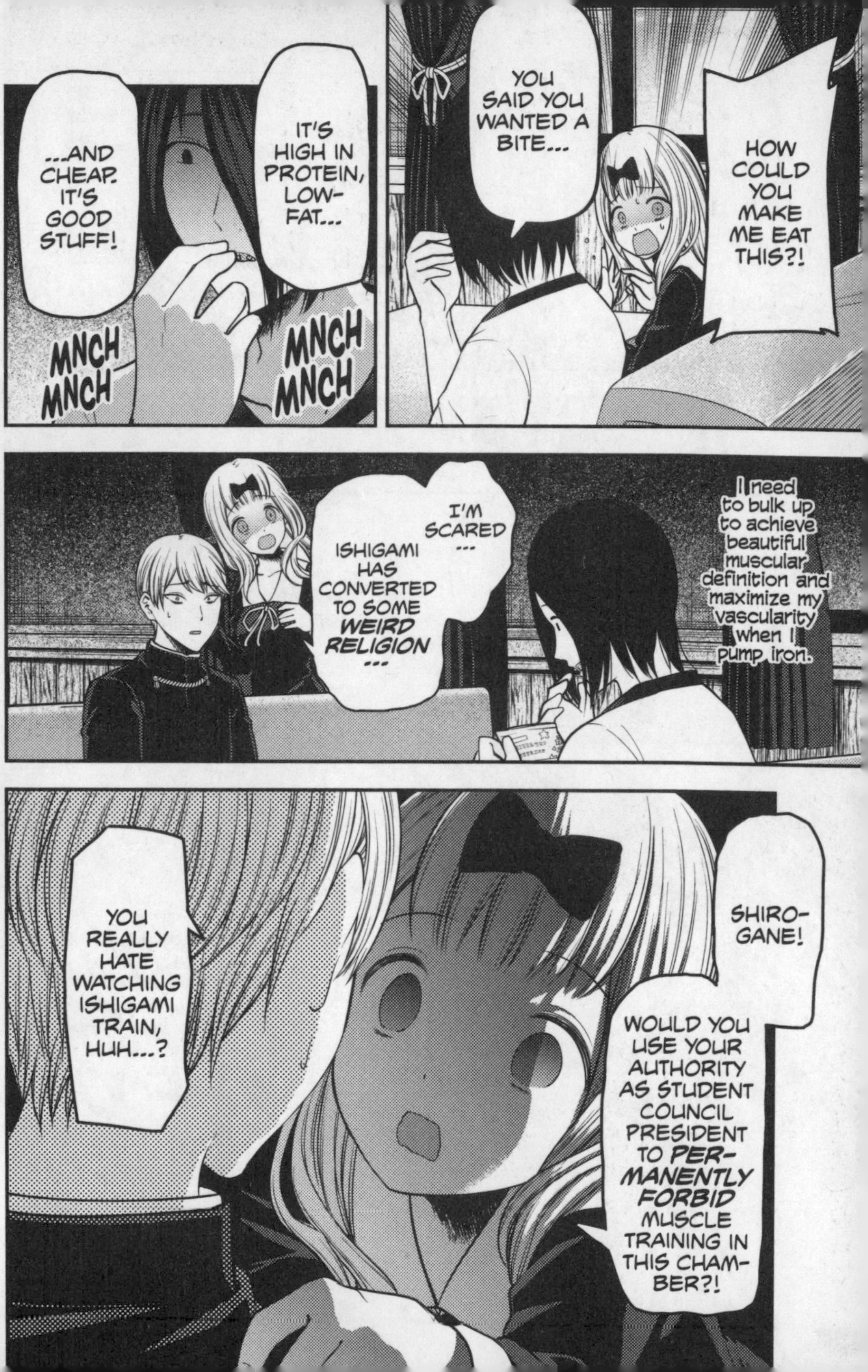
HOW COULD YOU MAKE ME EAT THIS?!
YOU SAID YOU WANTED A BITE...
IT'S HIGH IN PROTEIN, LOW-FAT...
MNCH MNCH
...AND CHEAP. IT'S GOOD STUFF!
MNCH MNCH
I need to bulk up to achieve beautiful muscular definition and maximize my vascularity when I pump iron.
I'M SCARED...
ISHIGAMI HAS CONVERTED TO SOME WEIRD RELIGION...
SHIRO-GANE!
WOULD YOU USE YOUR AUTHORITY AS STUDENT COUNCIL PRESIDENT TO PER-MANENTLY FORBID MUSCLE TRAINING IN THIS CHAM-BER?!
YOU REALLY HATE WATCHING ISHIGAMI TRAIN, HUH...?

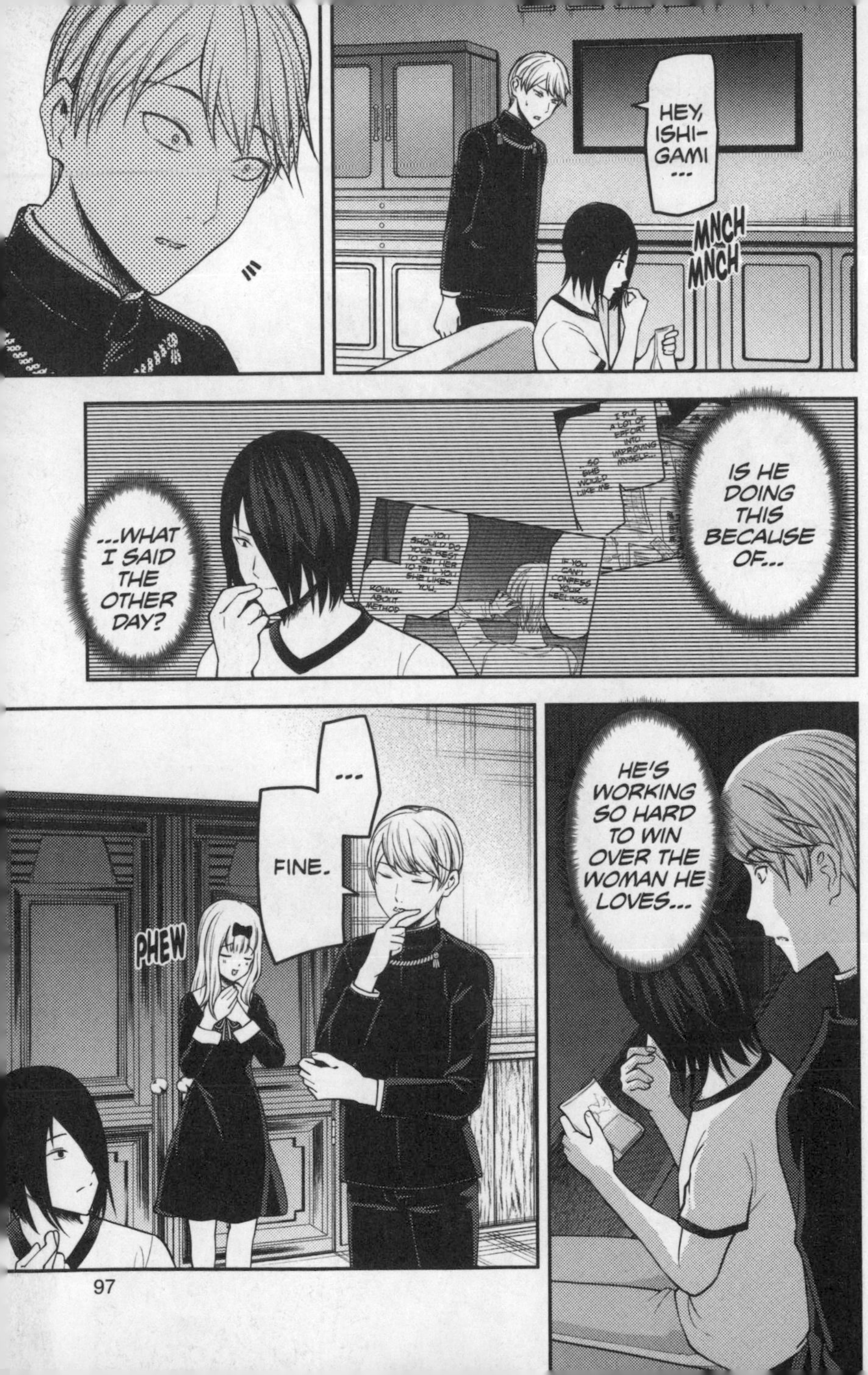

HEY, ISHIGAMI...
MNCH MNCH
IS HE DOING THIS BECAUSE OF...
I PUT A LOT OF EFFORT INTO IMPROVING MYSELF...
...SO SHE WOULD LIKE ME
IF YOU CAN'T CONFESS YOUR FEELINGS
...YOU SHOULD DO YOUR BEST TO GET HER TO TELL YOU SHE LIKES YOU.
ROUNDABOUT METHOD
...WHAT I SAID THE OTHER DAY?
HE'S WORKING SO HARD TO WIN OVER THE WOMAN HE LOVES...
...
FINE.
PHEW

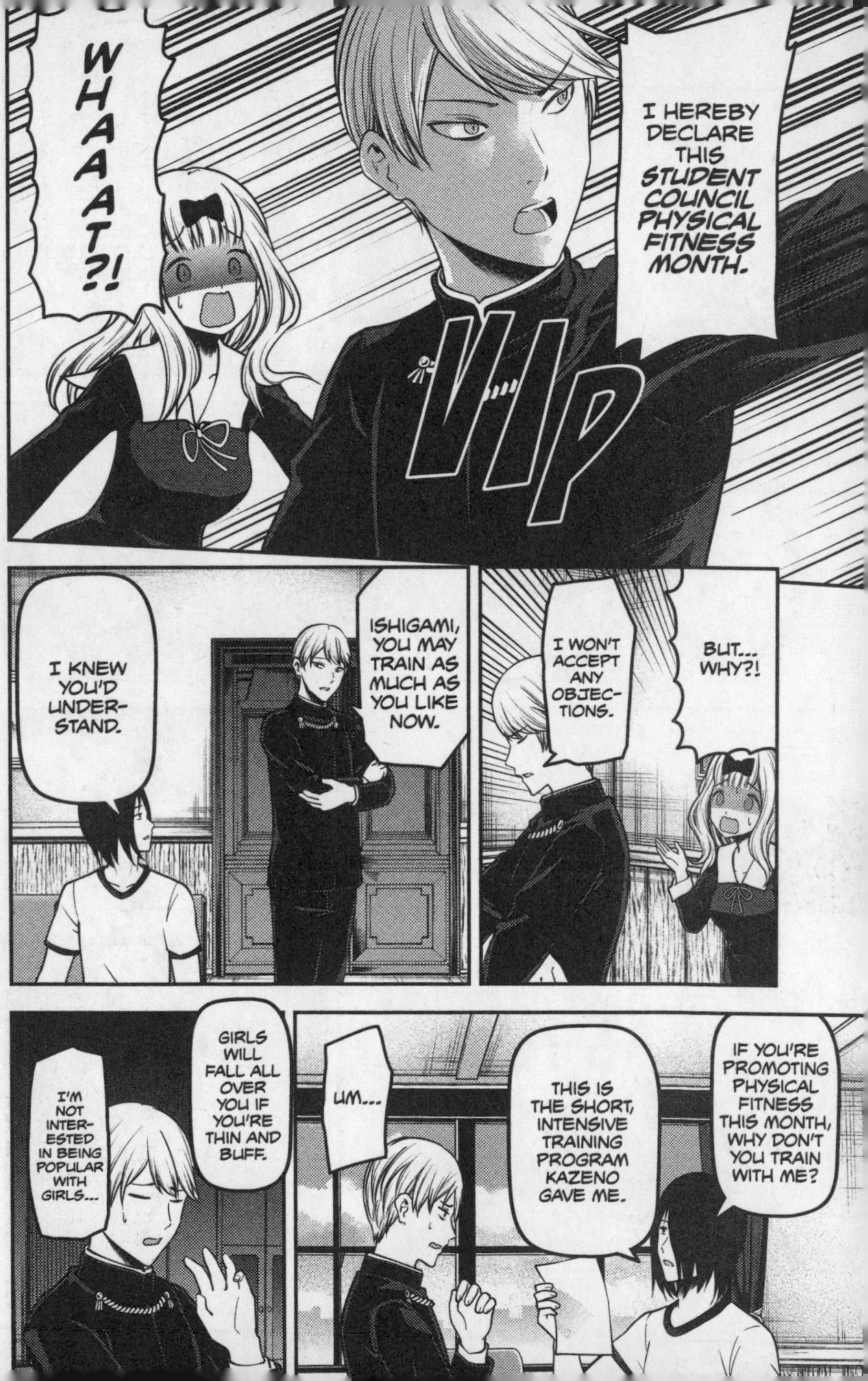
I HEREBY DECLARE THIS STUDENT COUNCIL PHYSICAL FITNESS MONTH.
VIP
WHAAAT?!
BUT... WHY?!
I WON'T ACCEPT ANY OBJECTIONS.
ISHIGAMI, YOU MAY TRAIN AS MUCH AS YOU LIKE NOW.
I KNEW YOU'D UNDERSTAND.
IF YOU'RE PROMOTING PHYSICAL FITNESS THIS MONTH, WHY DON'T YOU TRAIN WITH ME?
THIS IS THE SHORT, INTENSIVE TRAINING PROGRAM KAZENO GAVE ME.
UM...
GIRLS WILL FALL ALL OVER YOU IF YOU'RE THIN AND BUFF.
I'M NOT INTERESTED IN BEING POPULAR WITH GIRLS...

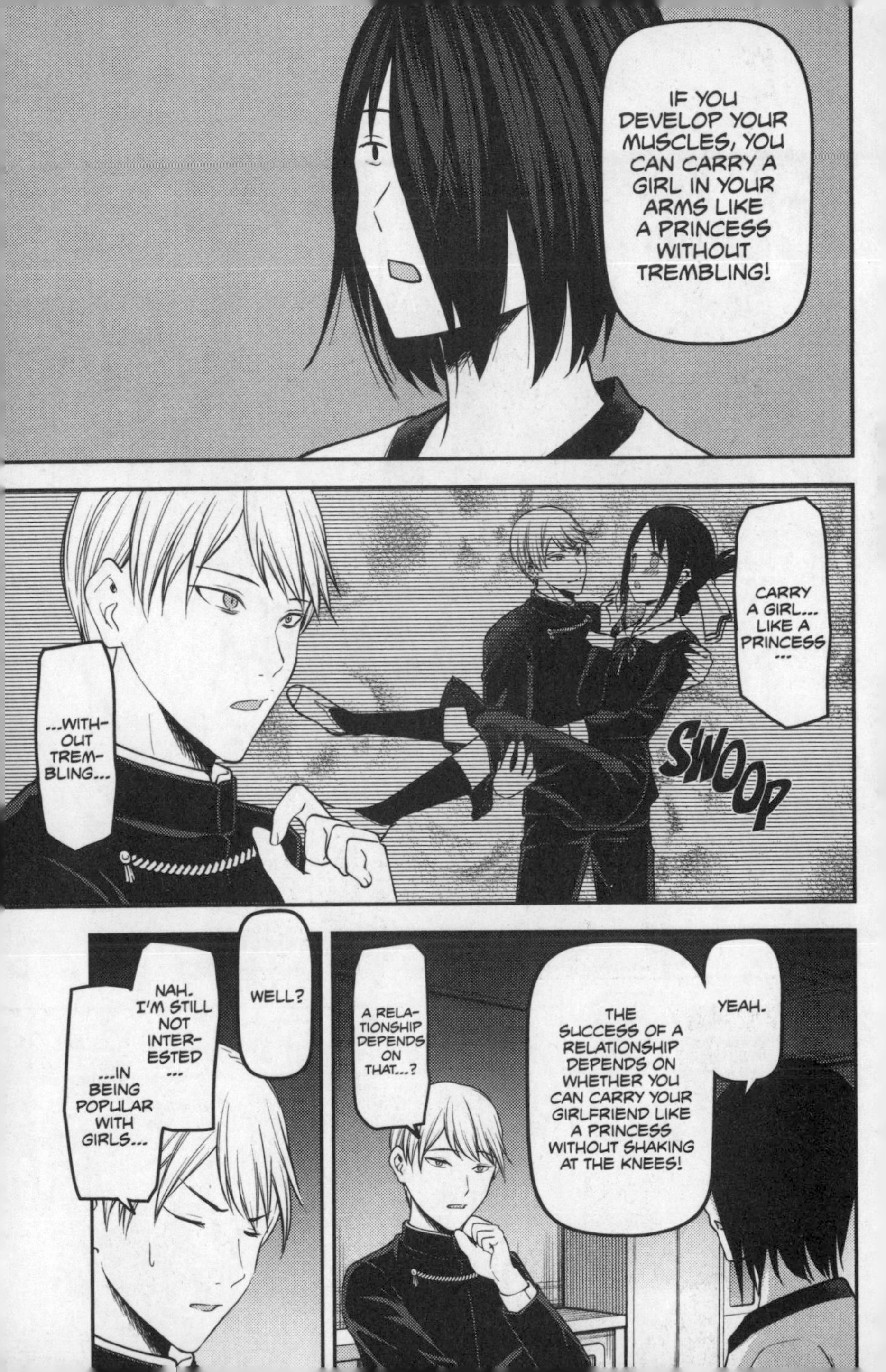
IF YOU DEVELOP YOUR MUSCLES, YOU CAN CARRY A GIRL IN YOUR ARMS LIKE A PRINCESS WITHOUT TREMBLING!
CARRY A GIRL... LIKE A PRINCESS ...
SWOOP
...WITHOUT TREMBLING...
YEAH.
THE SUCCESS OF A RELATIONSHIP DEPENDS ON WHETHER YOU CAN CARRY YOUR GIRLFRIEND LIKE A PRINCESS WITHOUT SHAKING AT THE KNEES!
A RELATIONSHIP DEPENDS ON THAT...?
WELL?
NAH. I'M STILL NOT INTERESTED ...
...IN BEING POPULAR WITH GIRLS...

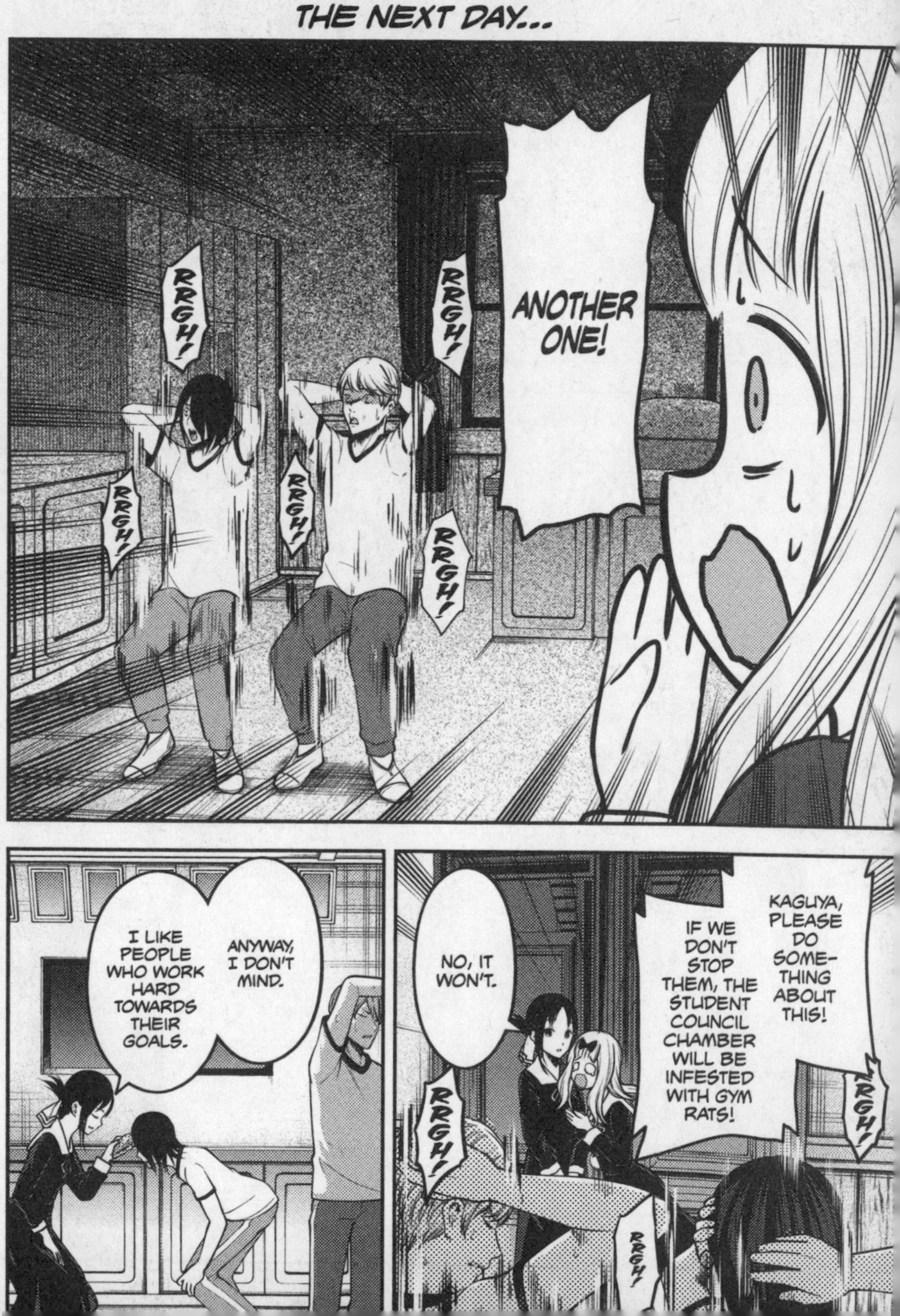
THE NEXT DAY...
ANOTHER ONE!
RRGH!
RRGH!
RRGH!
RRGH!
RRGH!
KAGUYA, PLEASE DO SOMETHING ABOUT THIS!
IF WE DON'T STOP THEM, THE STUDENT COUNCIL CHAMBER WILL BE INFESTED WITH GYM RATS!
RRGH!
NO, IT WON'T.
RRGH!
RRGH!
ANYWAY, I DON'T MIND.
I LIKE PEOPLE WHO WORK HARD TOWARDS THEIR GOALS.

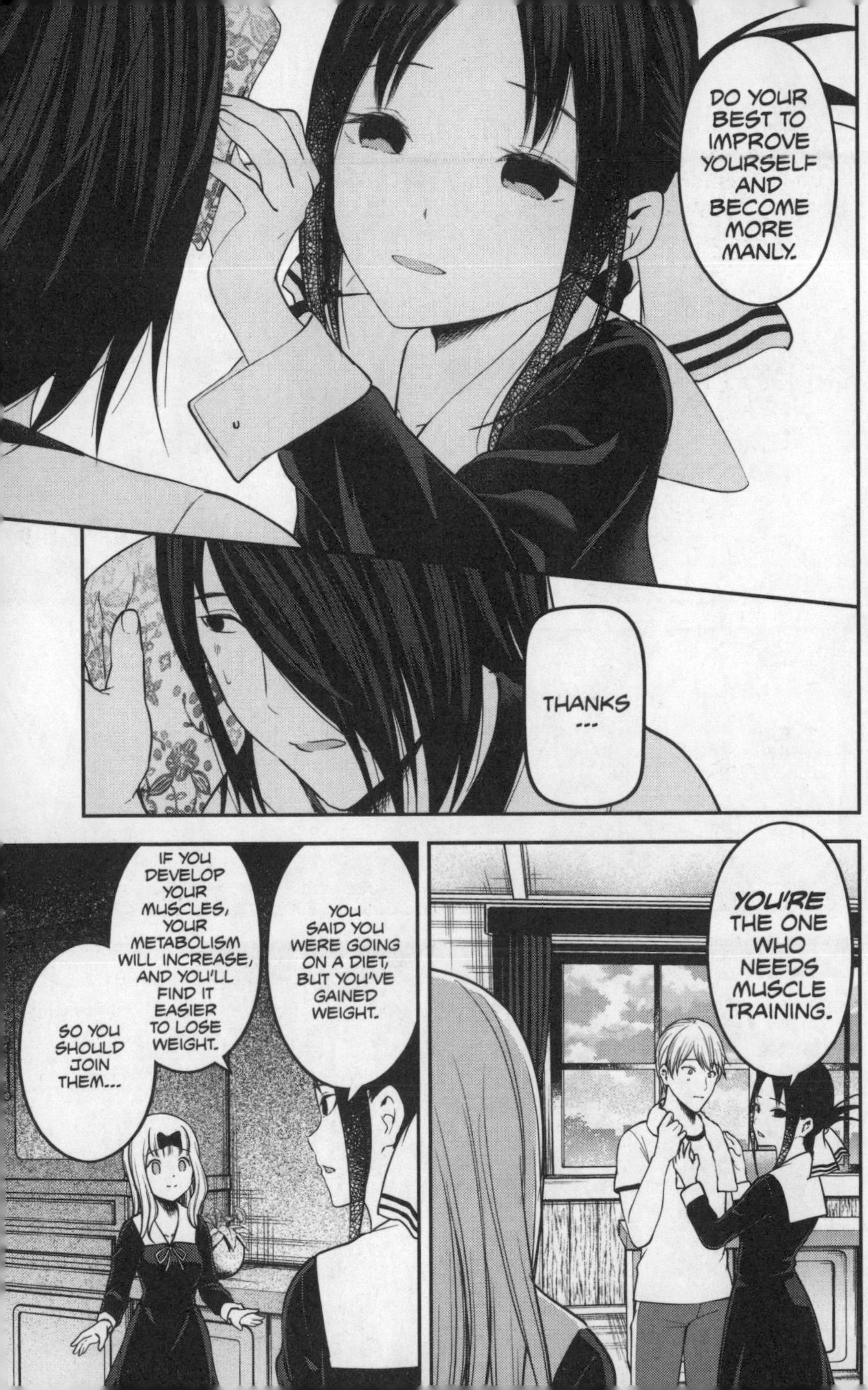
DO YOUR BEST TO IMPROVE YOURSELF AND BECOME MORE MANLY.
THANKS...
YOU'RE THE ONE WHO NEEDS MUSCLE TRAINING.
YOU SAID YOU WERE GOING ON A DIET, BUT YOU'VE GAINED WEIGHT.
IF YOU DEVELOP YOUR MUSCLES, YOUR METABOLISM WILL INCREASE, AND YOU'LL FIND IT EASIER TO LOSE WEIGHT.
SO YOU SHOULD JOIN THEM...

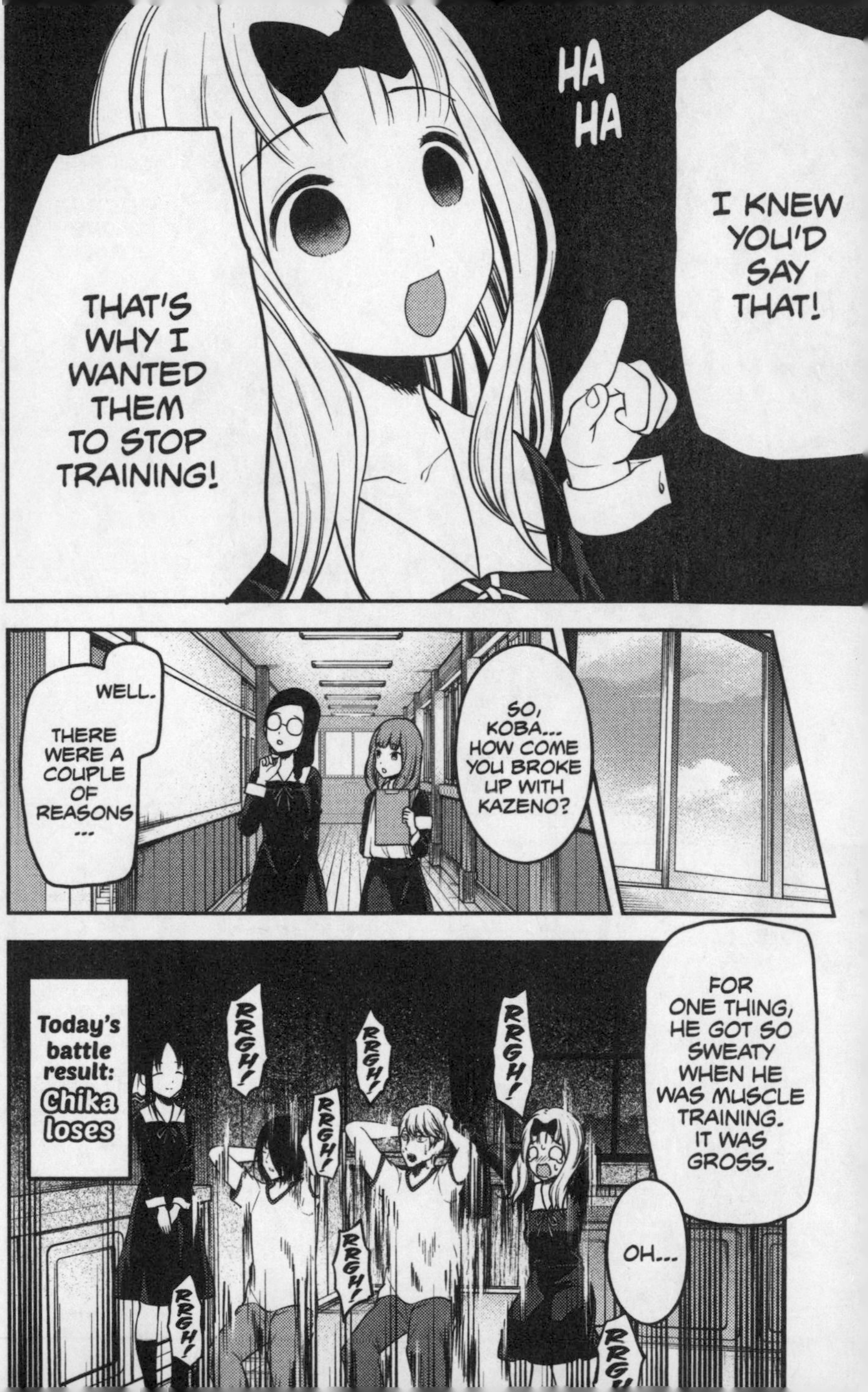
I KNEW YOU'D SAY THAT!
HA HA
THAT'S WHY I WANTED THEM TO STOP TRAINING!
SO, KOBA... HOW COME YOU BROKE UP WITH KAZENO?
WELL.
THERE WERE A COUPLE OF REASONS...
FOR ONE THING, HE GOT SO SWEATY WHEN HE WAS MUSCLE TRAINING. IT WAS GROSS.
OH...
RRGH!
RRGH!
RRGH!
RRGH!
RRGH!
RRGH!
Today's battle result: Chika loses

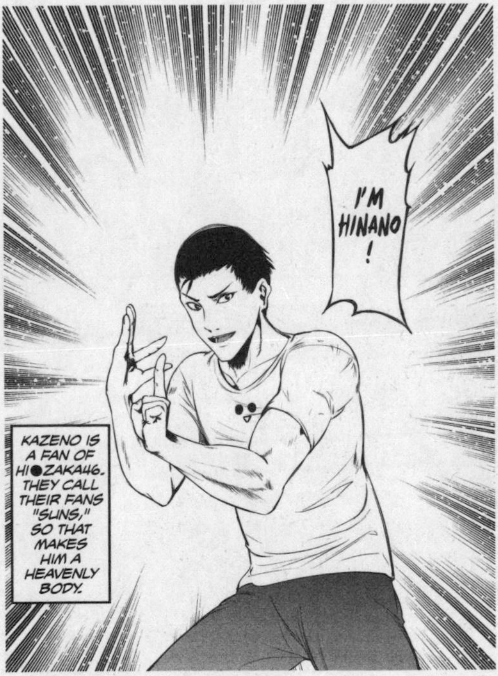
I'M HINANO!
KAZENO IS A FAN OF HI●ZAKA46. THEY CALL THEIR FANS "SUNS," SO THAT MAKES HIM A HEAVENLY BODY.

KAGUYA-SAMA
LOVE IS WAR

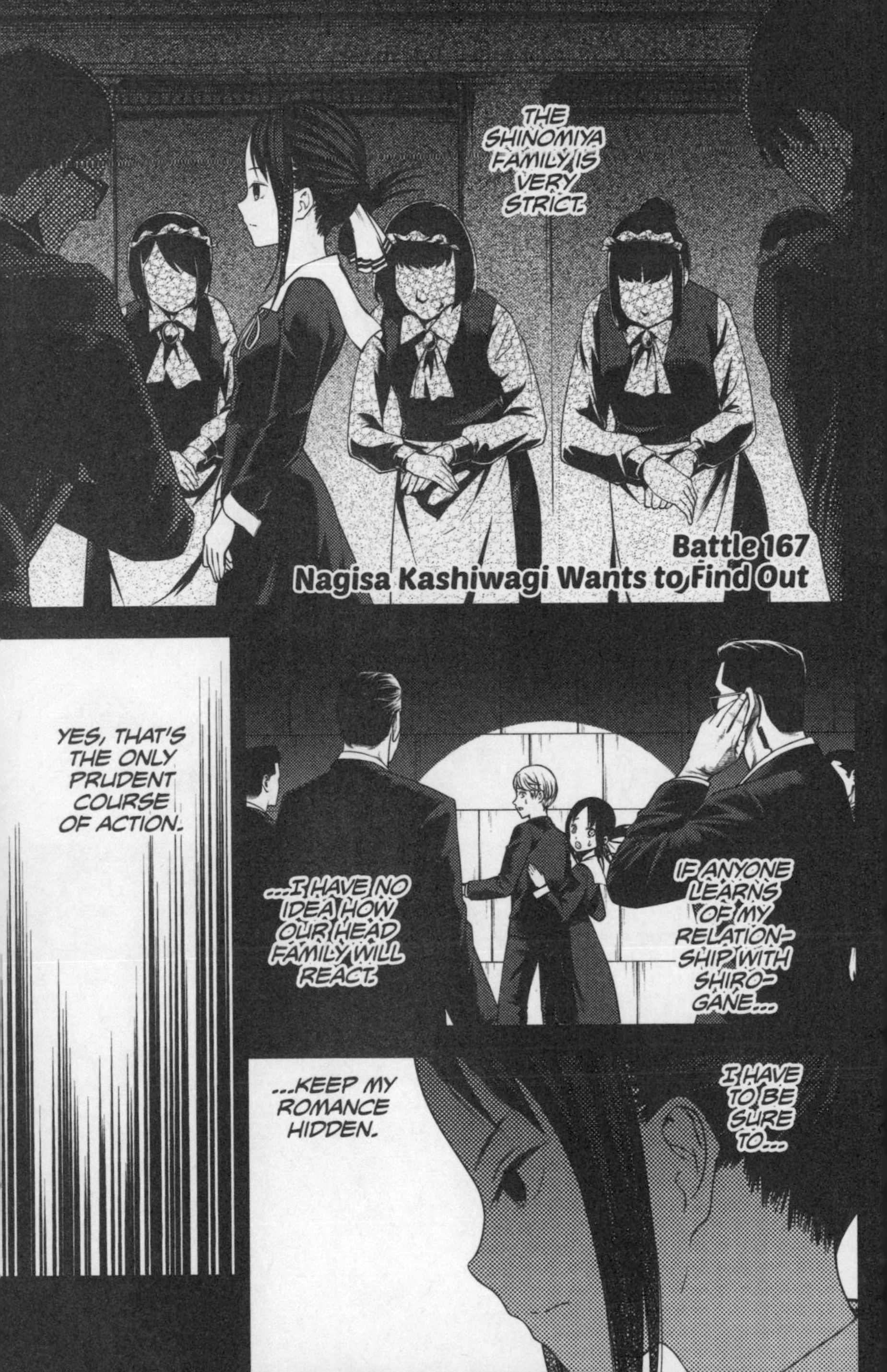
THE SHINOMIYA FAMILY IS VERY STRICT.
Battle 167
Nagisa Kashiwagi Wants to Find Out
IF ANYONE LEARNS OF MY RELATION-SHIP WITH SHIRO-GANE...
...I HAVE NO IDEA HOW OUR HEAD FAMILY WILL REACT.
I HAVE TO BE SURE TO...
...KEEP MY ROMANCE HIDDEN.
YES, THAT'S THE ONLY PRUDENT COURSE OF ACTION.

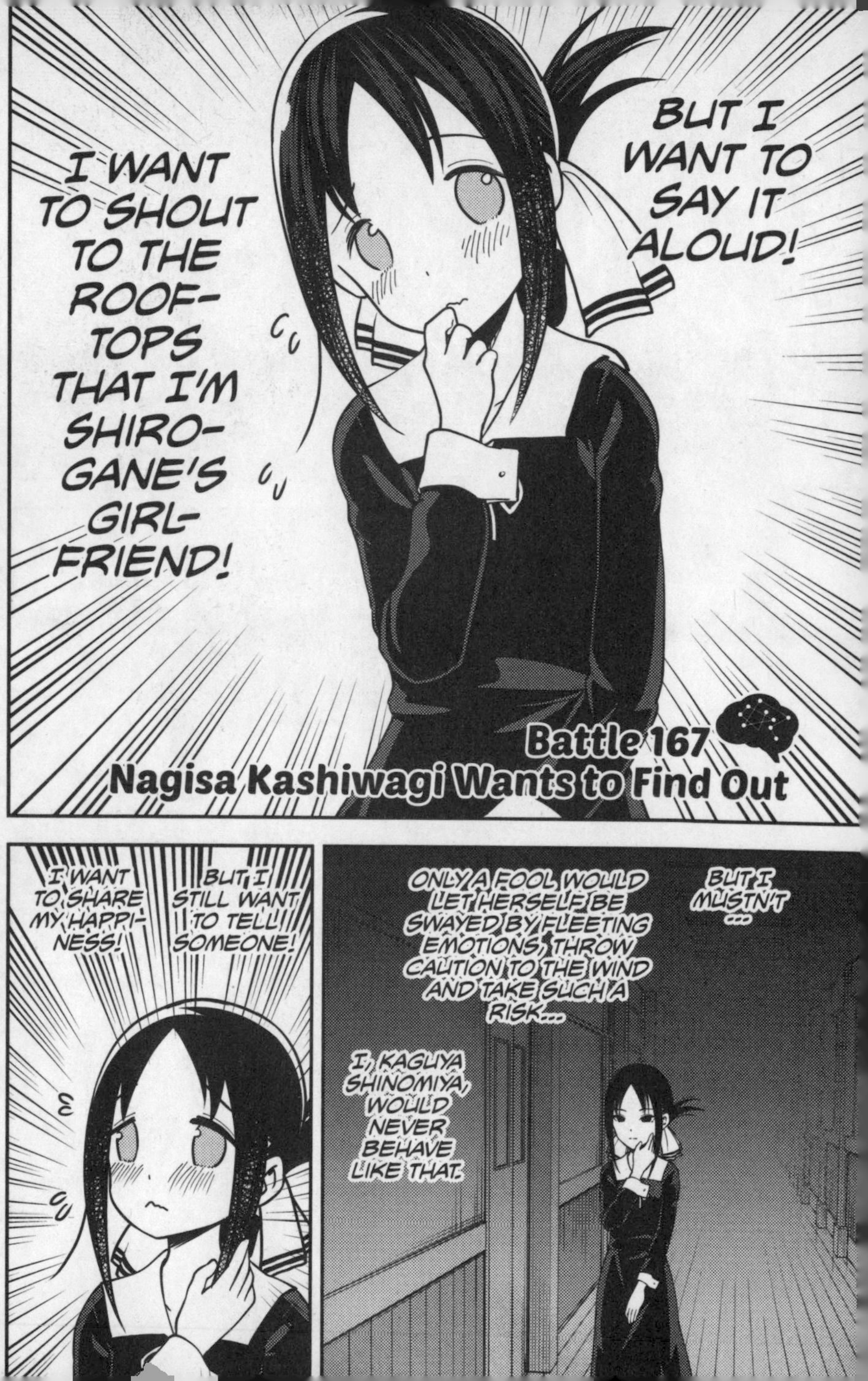
BUT I WANT TO SAY IT ALOUD!
I WANT TO SHOUT TO THE ROOF-TOPS THAT I'M SHIRO-GANE'S GIRL-FRIEND!
Battle 167
Nagisa Kashiwagi Wants to Find Out
BUT I MUSTN'T...
ONLY A FOOL WOULD LET HERSELF BE SWAYED BY FLEETING EMOTIONS, THROW CAUTION TO THE WIND AND TAKE SUCH A RISK...
I, KAGUYA SHINOMIYA, WOULD NEVER BEHAVE LIKE THAT.
BUT I STILL WANT TO TELL SOMEONE!
I WANT TO SHARE MY HAPPI-NESS!

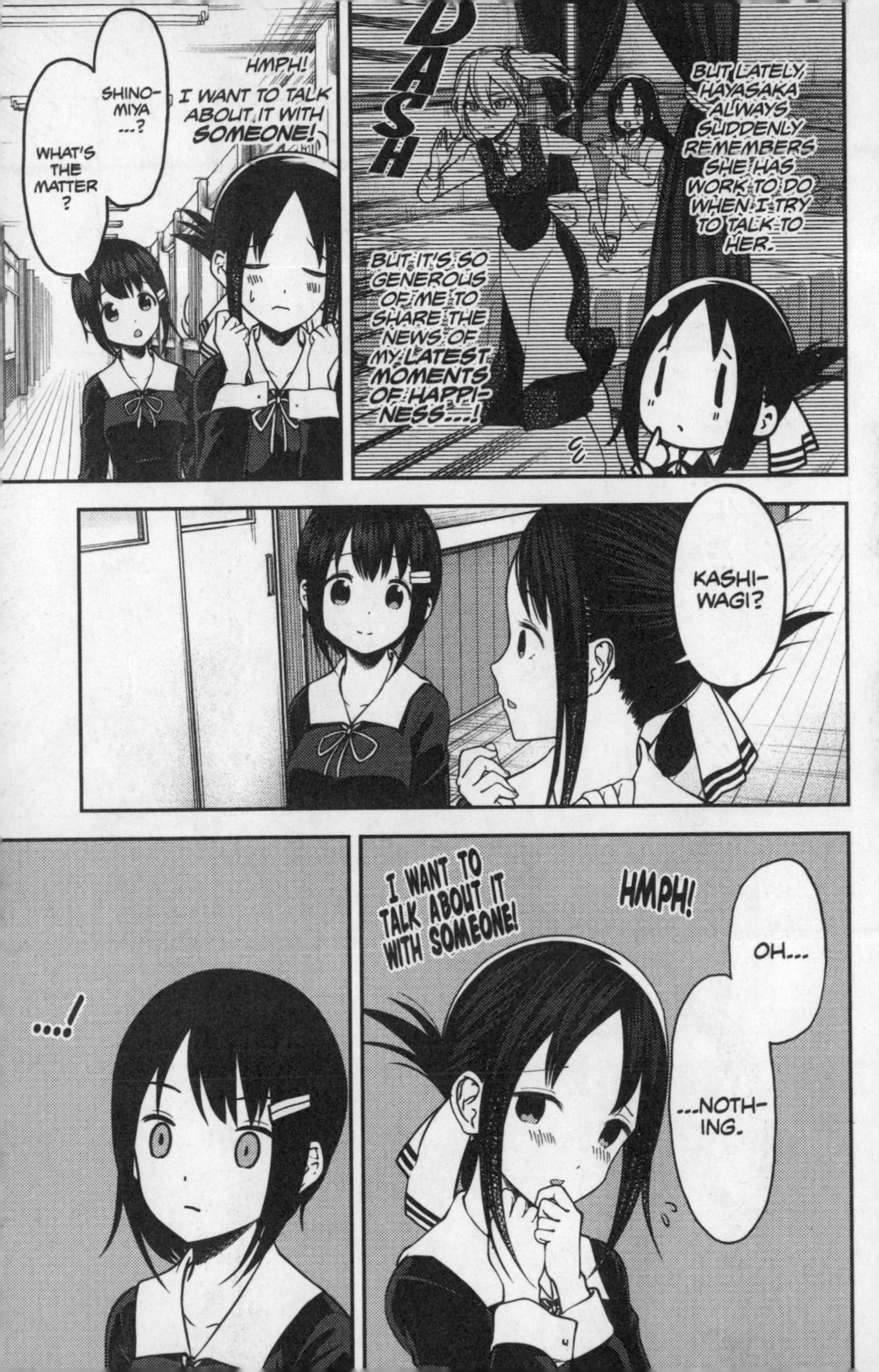
DASH
BUT LATELY, HAYASAKA ALWAYS SUDDENLY REMEMBERS SHE HAS WORK TO DO WHEN I TRY TO TALK TO HER.
BUT IT'S SO GENEROUS OF ME TO SHARE THE NEWS OF MY LATEST MOMENTS OF HAPPINESS...!
HMPH! I WANT TO TALK ABOUT IT WITH SOMEONE!
SHINOMIYA...? WHAT'S THE MATTER?
KASHIWAGI?
HMPH!
I WANT TO TALK ABOUT IT WITH SOMEONE!
OH... ...NOTHING.
...!

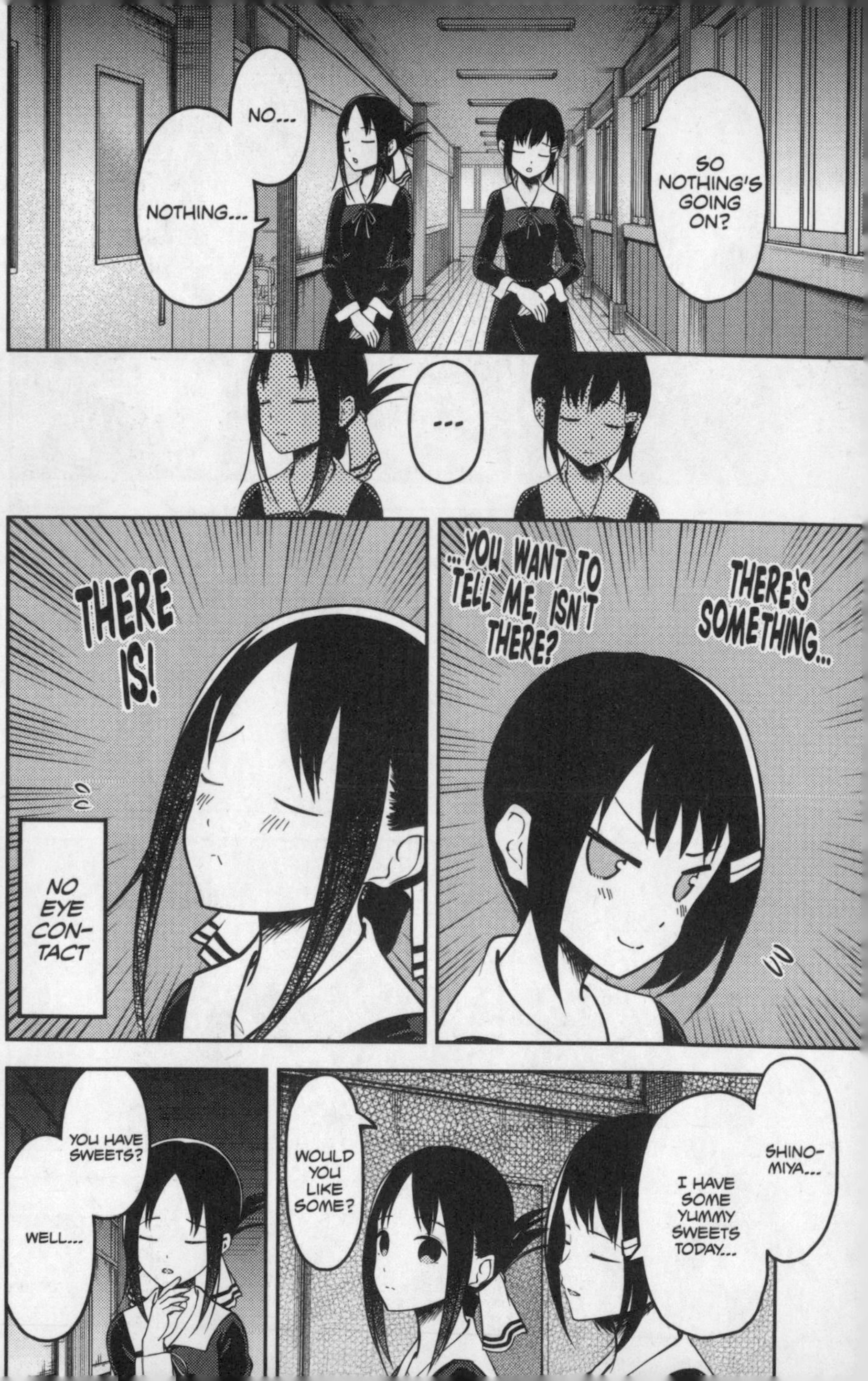
SO NOTHING'S GOING ON?
NO...
NOTHING...
...
THERE'S SOMETHING...
...YOU WANT TO TELL ME, ISN'T THERE?
THERE IS!
NO EYE CON-TACT
SHINO-MIYA...
I HAVE SOME YUMMY SWEETS TODAY...
WOULD YOU LIKE SOME?
YOU HAVE SWEETS?
WELL...

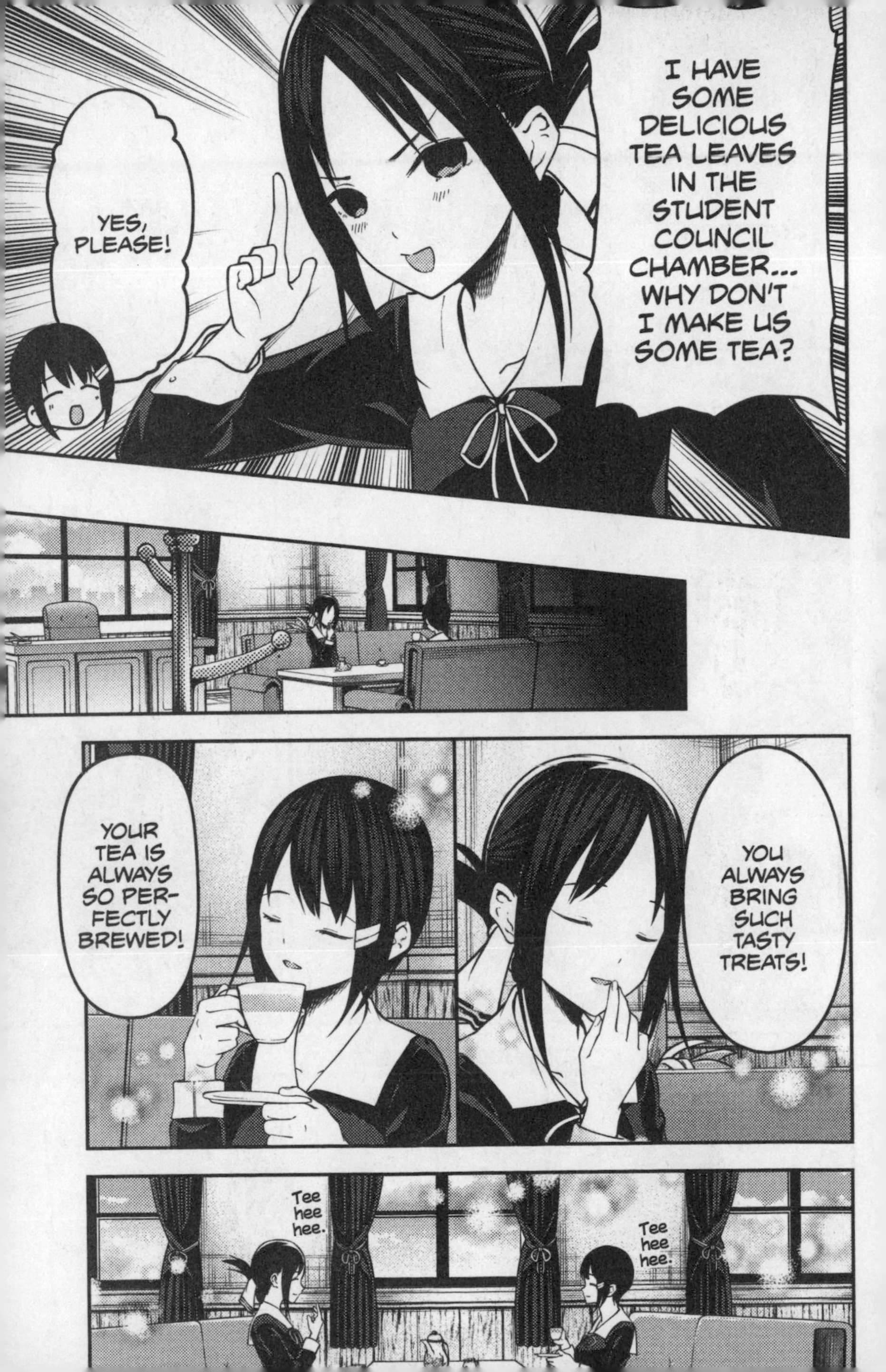
I HAVE SOME DELICIOUS TEA LEAVES IN THE STUDENT COUNCIL CHAMBER... WHY DON'T I MAKE US SOME TEA?
YES, PLEASE!
YOU ALWAYS BRING SUCH TASTY TREATS!
YOUR TEA IS ALWAYS SO PER-FECTLY BREWED!
Tee hee hee.
Tee hee hee.

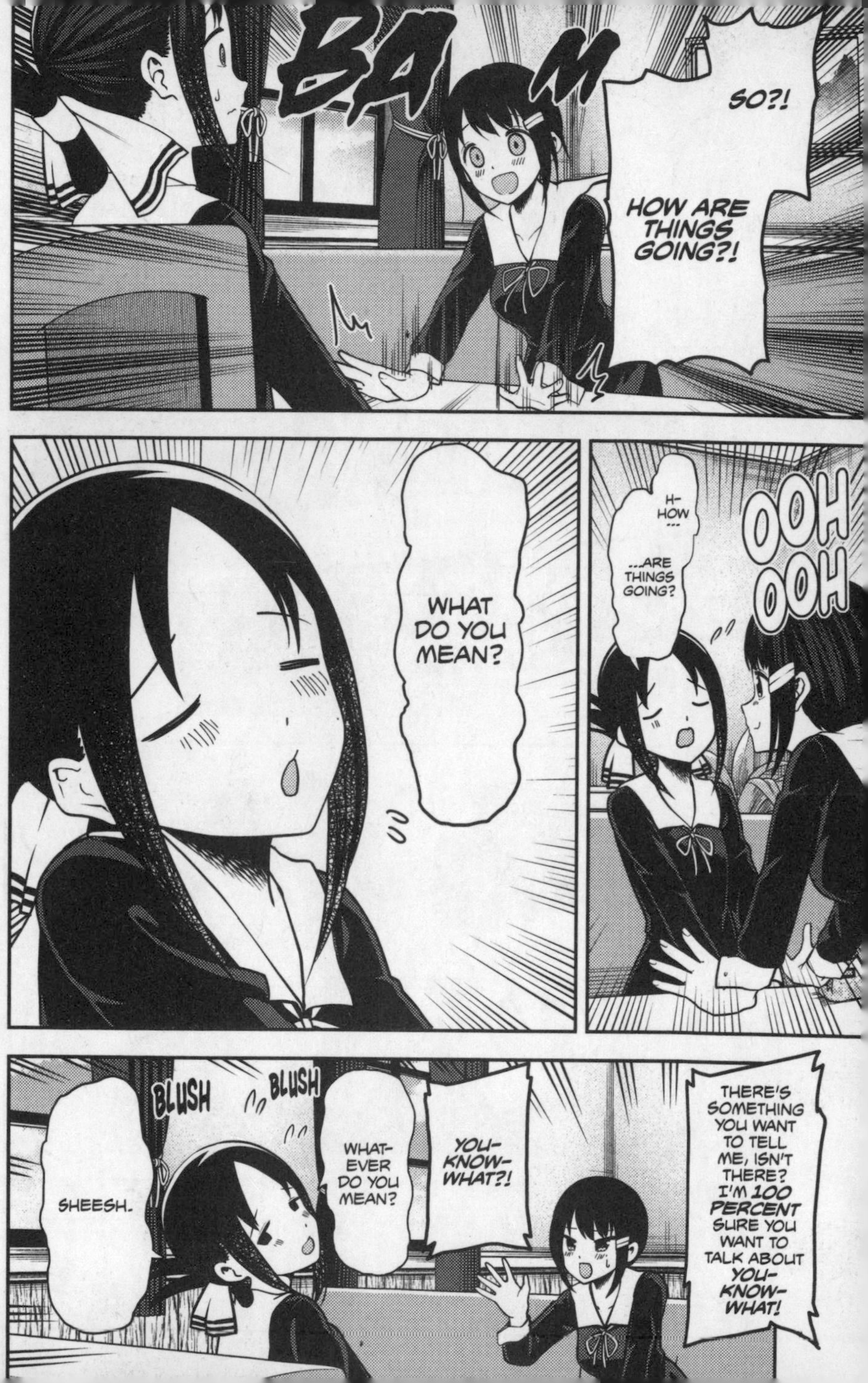
SO?!
HOW ARE THINGS GOING?!
BAM
OOH OOH
H-HOW...
...ARE THINGS GOING?
WHAT DO YOU MEAN?
THERE'S SOMETHING YOU WANT TO TELL ME, ISN'T THERE? I'M 100 PERCENT SURE YOU WANT TO TALK ABOUT YOU-KNOW-WHAT!
YOU-KNOW-WHAT?!
WHAT-EVER DO YOU MEAN?
BLUSH
BLUSH
SHEESH.

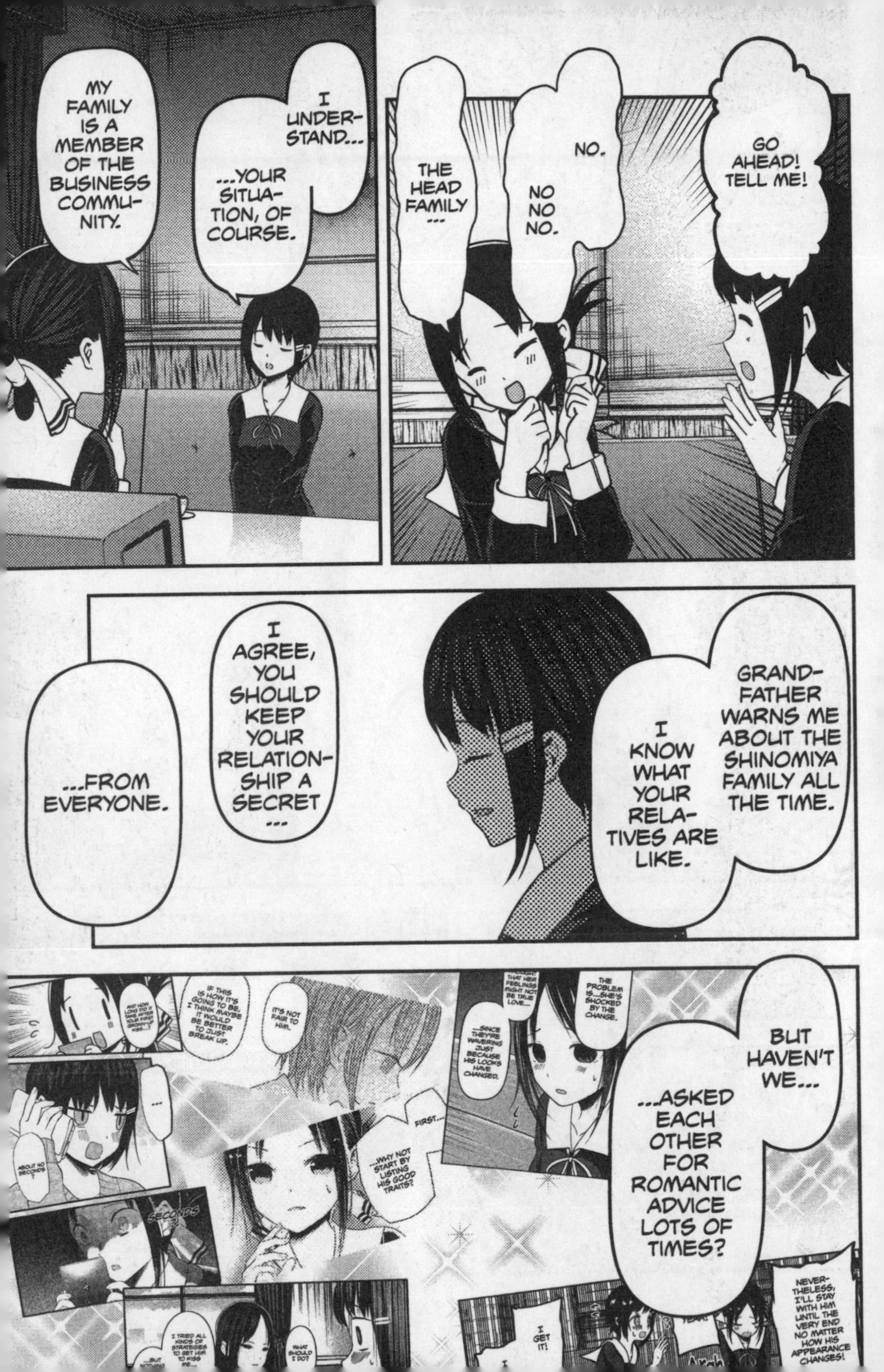
GO AHEAD! TELL ME!
NO.
NO NO NO.
THE HEAD FAMILY...
I UNDERSTAND...
...YOUR SITUATION, OF COURSE.
MY FAMILY IS A MEMBER OF THE BUSINESS COMMUNITY.
GRANDFATHER WARNS ME ABOUT THE SHINOMIYA FAMILY ALL THE TIME.
I KNOW WHAT YOUR RELATIVES ARE LIKE.
I AGREE, YOU SHOULD KEEP YOUR RELATIONSHIP A SECRET...
...FROM EVERYONE.
BUT HAVEN'T WE...
...ASKED EACH OTHER FOR ROMANTIC ADVICE LOTS OF TIMES?
THE PROBLEM IS...SHE'S SHOCKED BY THE CHANGE.
THAT HER FEELINGS MIGHT NOT BE TRUE LOVE...
...SINCE THEY'RE WAVERING JUST BECAUSE HIS LOOKS HAVE CHANGED.
IT'S NOT FAIR TO HIM.
IF THIS IS HOW IT'S GOING TO BE, I THINK MAYBE IT WOULD BE BETTER TO JUST BREAK UP.
AND HOW LONG DID IT TAKE AFTER YOUR FIRST GROWN-UP KISS...?
FIRST...
...WHY NOT START BY LISTING HIS GOOD TRAITS?
...
ABOUT 10 SECONDS?
SECONDS?!
NEVERTHELESS, I'LL STAY WITH HIM UNTIL THE VERY END NO MATTER HOW HIS APPEARANCE CHANGES!
I GET IT!
WHAT SHOULD I DO?
I TRIED ALL KINDS OF STRATEGIES TO GET HIM TO KISS ME...

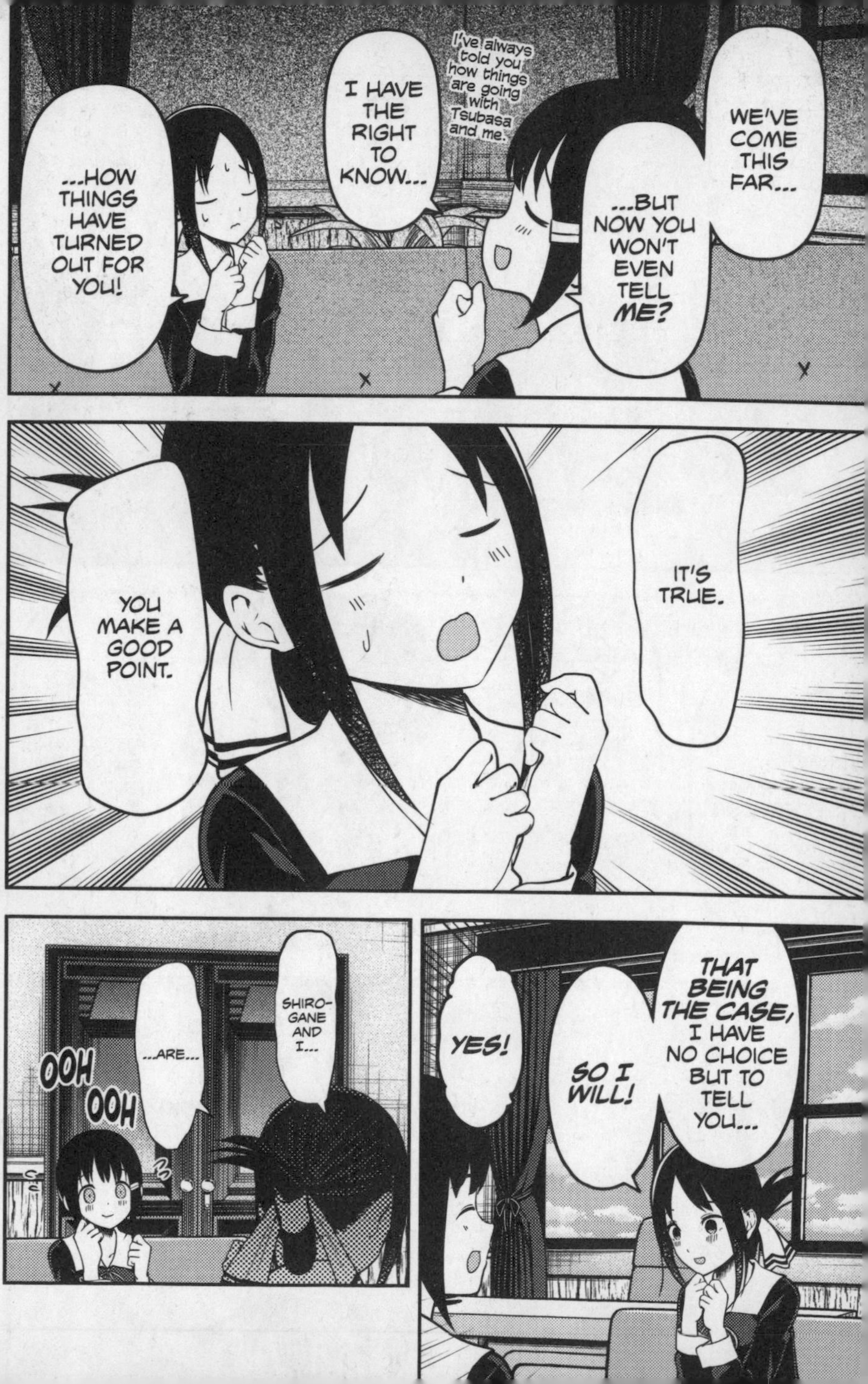
WE'VE COME THIS FAR...
...BUT NOW YOU WON'T EVEN TELL *ME?*
I've always told you how things are going with Tsubasa and me.
I HAVE THE RIGHT TO KNOW...
...HOW THINGS HAVE TURNED OUT FOR YOU!
IT'S TRUE.
YOU MAKE A GOOD POINT.
THAT BEING THE CASE, I HAVE NO CHOICE BUT TO TELL YOU...
SO I WILL!
YES!
SHIRO-GANE AND I...
...ARE...
OOH OOH

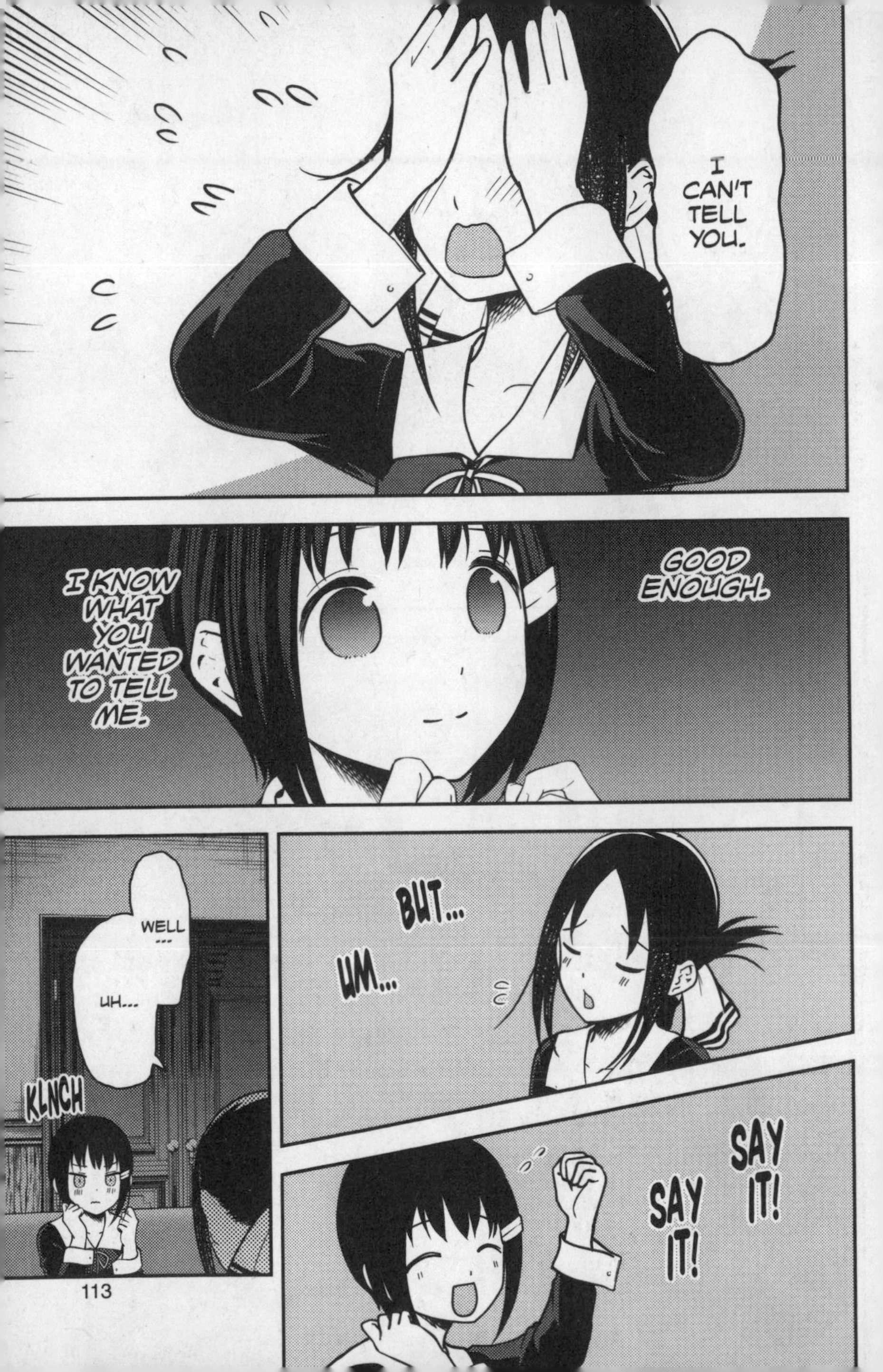
I CAN'T TELL YOU.
GOOD ENOUGH.
I KNOW WHAT YOU WANTED TO TELL ME.
BUT...
UM...
SAY IT!
SAY IT!
WELL...
UH...
KLNCH

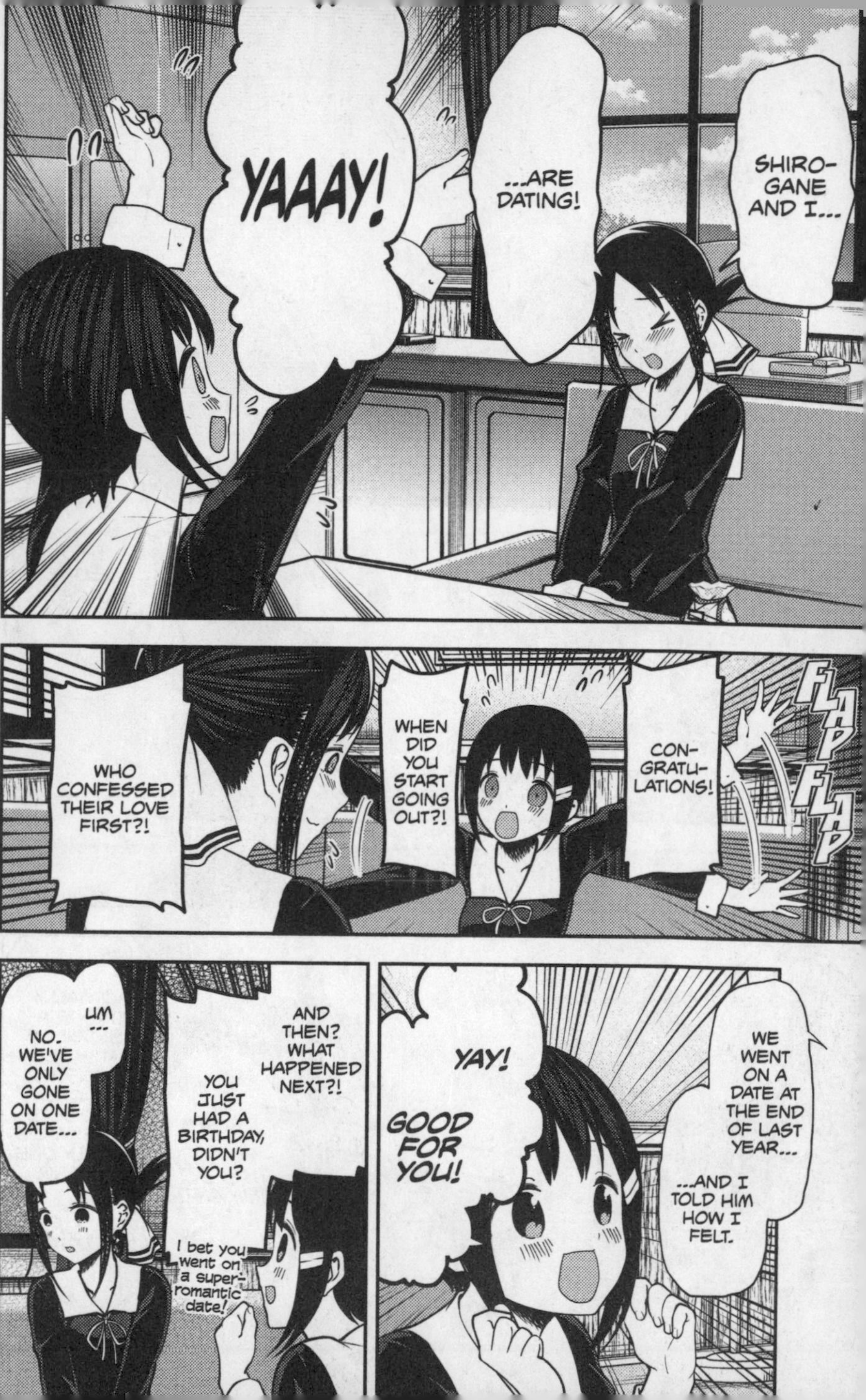
SHIRO-GANE AND I...
...ARE DATING!
YAAAY!
FLAP FLAP
CON-GRATU-LATIONS!
WHEN DID YOU START GOING OUT?!
WHO CONFESSED THEIR LOVE FIRST?!
WE WENT ON A DATE AT THE END OF LAST YEAR...
...AND I TOLD HIM HOW I FELT.
YAY!
GOOD FOR YOU!
AND THEN? WHAT HAPPENED NEXT?!
YOU JUST HAD A BIRTHDAY, DIDN'T YOU?
I bet you went on a super-romantic date!
UM ...
NO. WE'VE ONLY GONE ON ONE DATE...

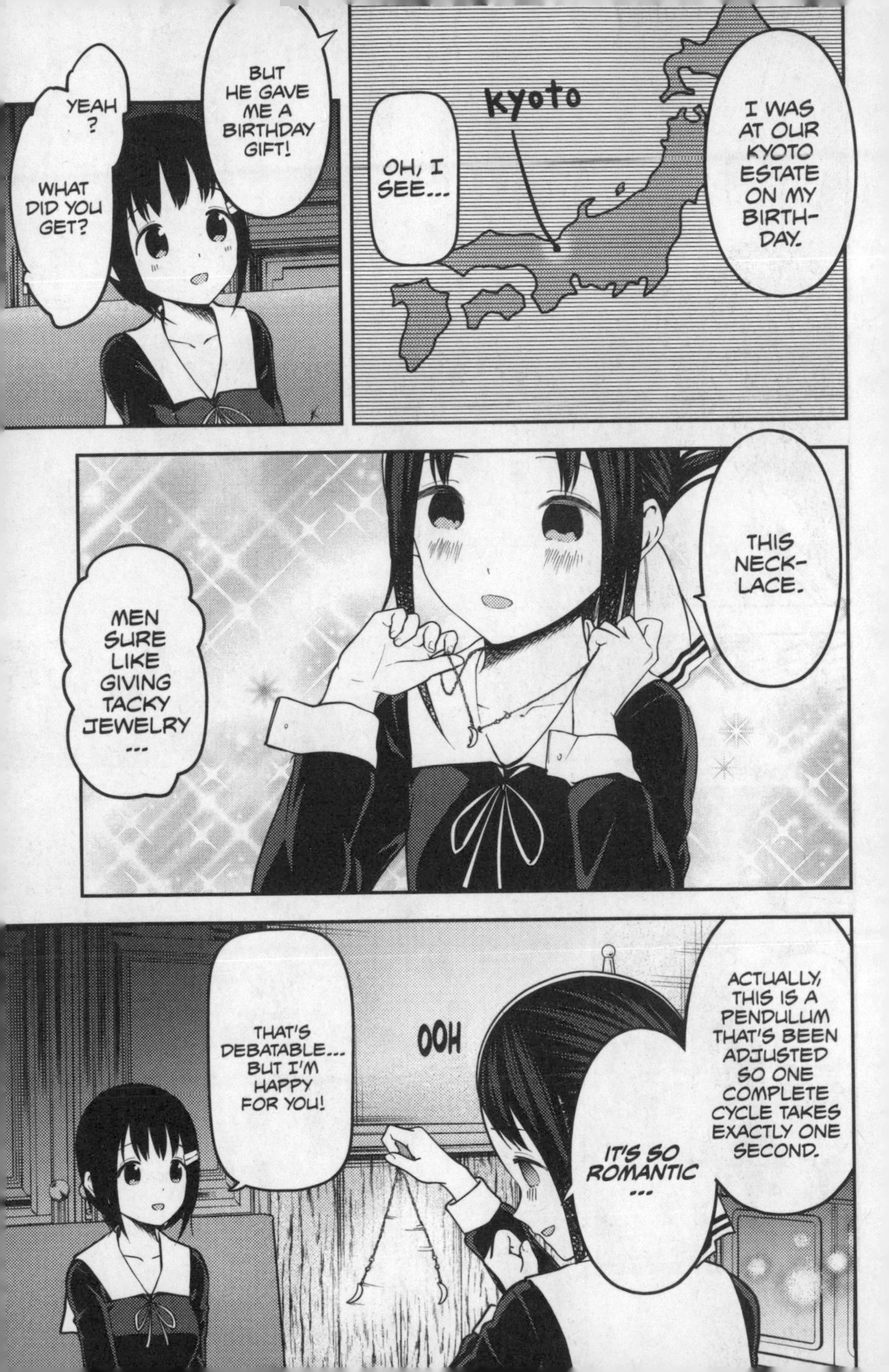
I WAS AT OUR KYOTO ESTATE ON MY BIRTH-DAY.
KYOTO
OH, I SEE...
BUT HE GAVE ME A BIRTHDAY GIFT!
YEAH? WHAT DID YOU GET?
THIS NECK-LACE.
MEN SURE LIKE GIVING TACKY JEWELRY...
ACTUALLY, THIS IS A PENDULUM THAT'S BEEN ADJUSTED SO ONE COMPLETE CYCLE TAKES EXACTLY ONE SECOND.
IT'S SO ROMANTIC...
OOH
THAT'S DEBATABLE... BUT I'M HAPPY FOR YOU!

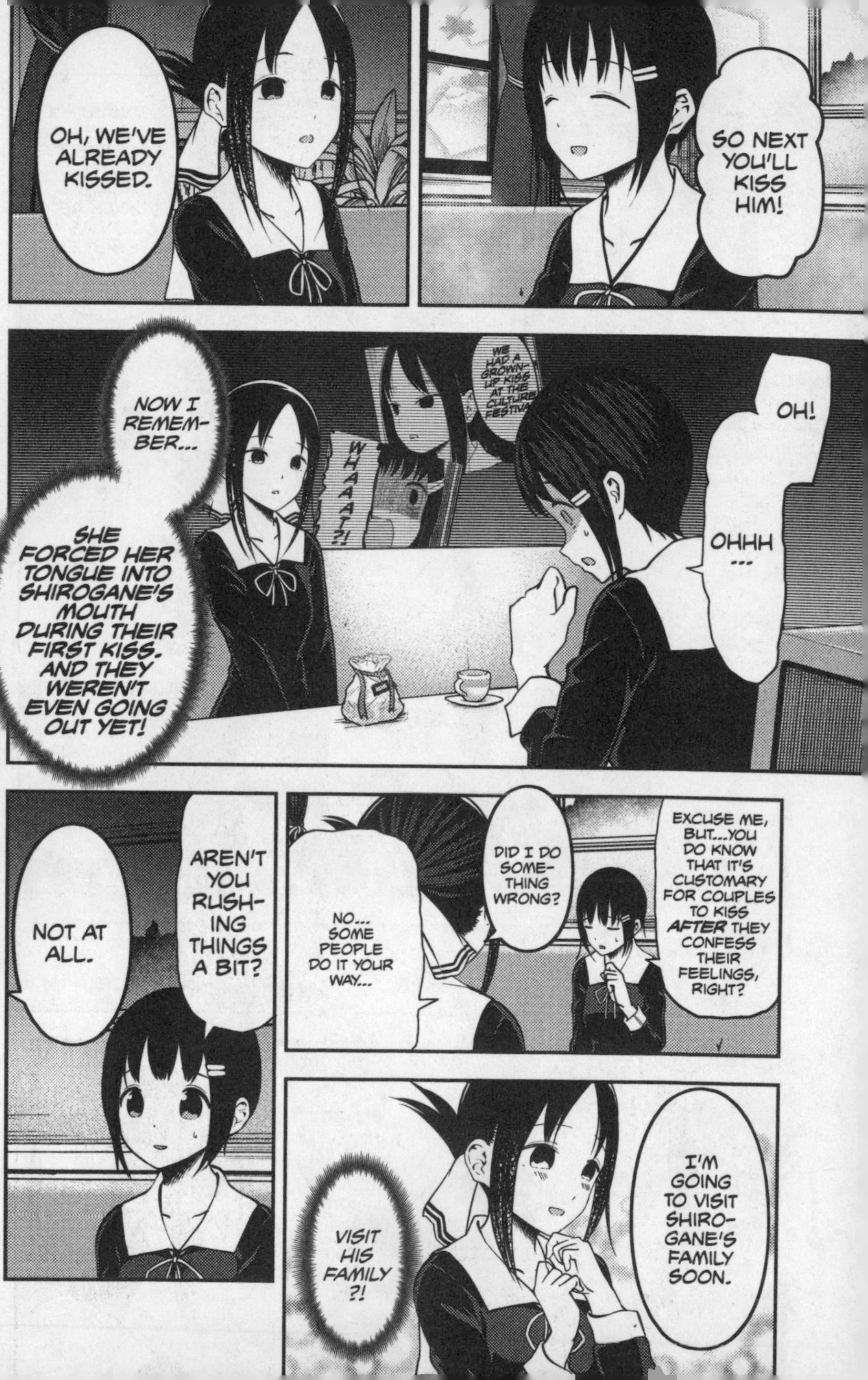
SO NEXT YOU'LL KISS HIM!
OH, WE'VE ALREADY KISSED.
OH!
OHHH...
WE HAD A GROWN-UP KISS AT THE CULTURE FESTIVA
WHAAAAT?!
NOW I REMEMBER...
SHE FORCED HER TONGUE INTO SHIROGANE'S MOUTH DURING THEIR FIRST KISS. AND THEY WEREN'T EVEN GOING OUT YET!
EXCUSE ME, BUT...YOU DO KNOW THAT IT'S CUSTOMARY FOR COUPLES TO KISS *AFTER* THEY CONFESS THEIR FEELINGS, RIGHT?
DID I DO SOMETHING WRONG?
NO... SOME PEOPLE DO IT YOUR WAY...
I'M GOING TO VISIT SHIROGANE'S FAMILY SOON.
VISIT HIS FAMILY?!
AREN'T YOU RUSHING THINGS A BIT?
NOT AT ALL.

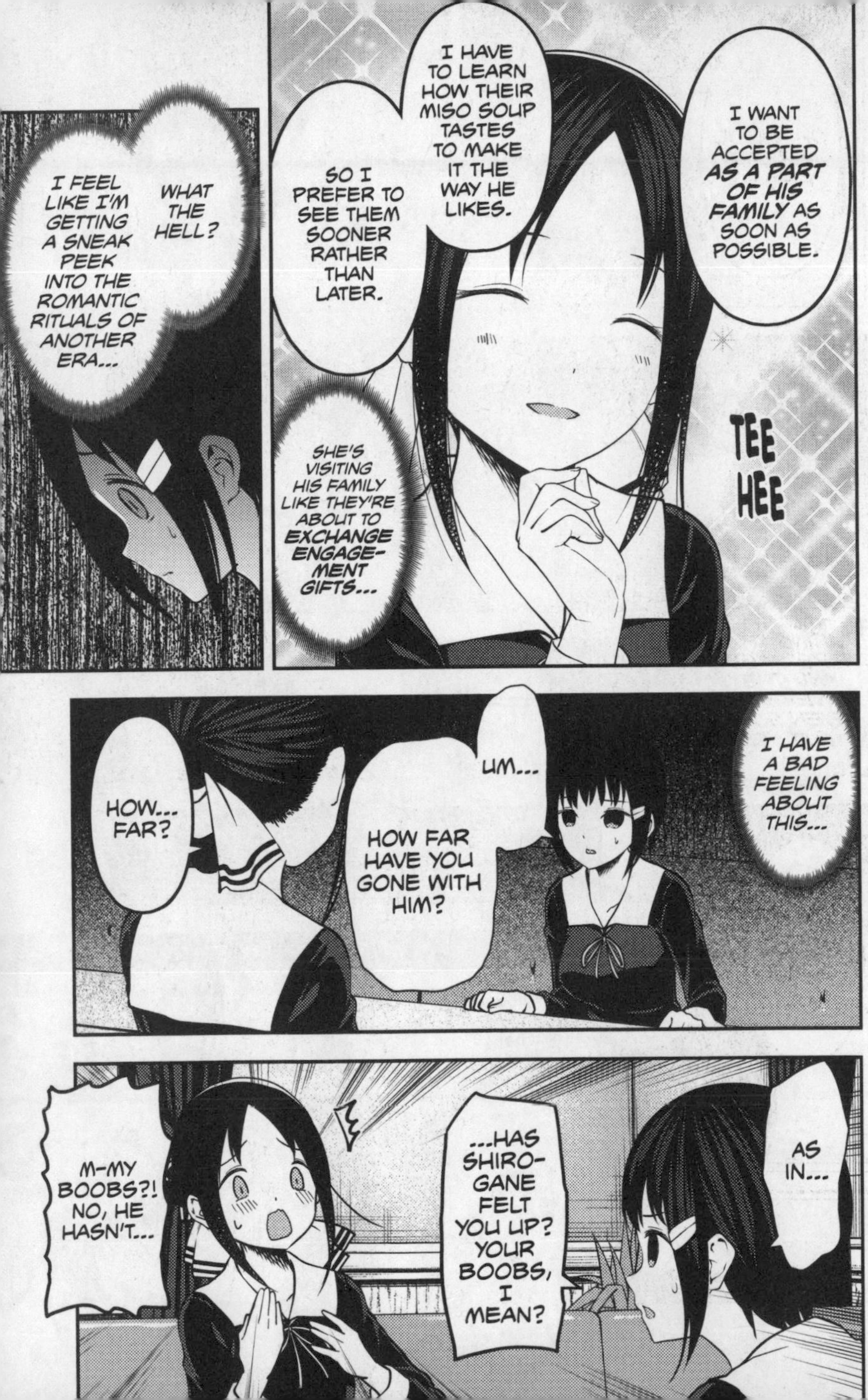
I WANT TO BE ACCEPTED AS A PART OF HIS FAMILY AS SOON AS POSSIBLE.
I HAVE TO LEARN HOW THEIR MISO SOUP TASTES TO MAKE IT THE WAY HE LIKES.
SO I PREFER TO SEE THEM SOONER RATHER THAN LATER.
TEE HEE
SHE'S VISITING HIS FAMILY LIKE THEY'RE ABOUT TO EXCHANGE ENGAGEMENT GIFTS...
WHAT THE HELL?
I FEEL LIKE I'M GETTING A SNEAK PEEK INTO THE ROMANTIC RITUALS OF ANOTHER ERA...
I HAVE A BAD FEELING ABOUT THIS...
UM...
HOW FAR HAVE YOU GONE WITH HIM?
HOW... FAR?
AS IN...
...HAS SHIROGANE FELT YOU UP? YOUR BOOBS, I MEAN?
M-MY BOOBS?! NO, HE HASN'T...

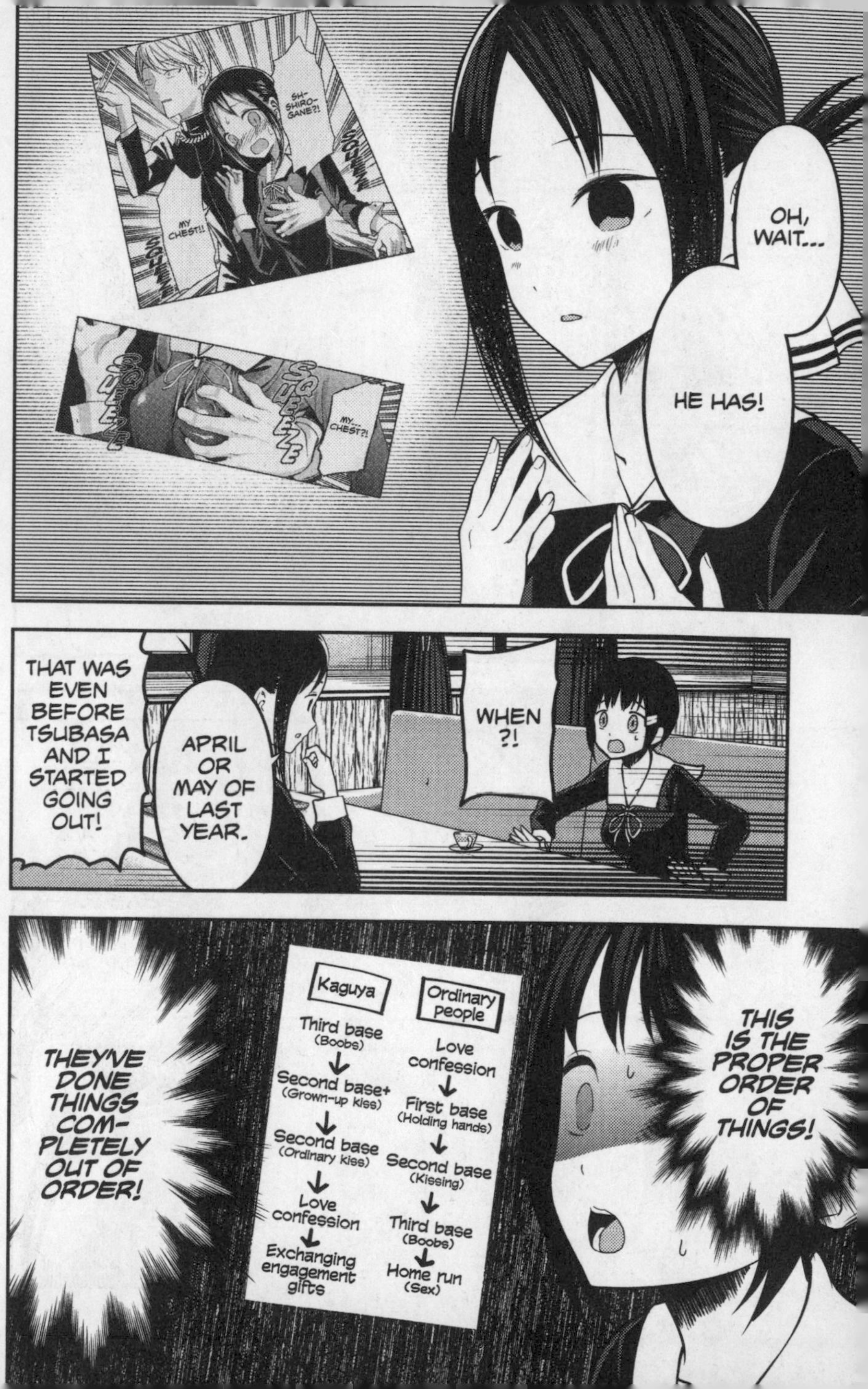
OH, WAIT...
HE HAS!
SH-SHIRO-GANE?!
SQUEEZE
MY CHEST?!
SQUEEZE
SQUEEZE
MY... CHEST?!
SQUEEZE
WHEN?!
APRIL OR MAY OF LAST YEAR.
THAT WAS EVEN BEFORE TSUBASA AND I STARTED GOING OUT!
THIS IS THE PROPER ORDER OF THINGS!
Kaguya
Third base (Boobs)
Second base+ (Grown-up kiss)
Second base (Ordinary kiss)
Love confession
Exchanging engagement gifts
Ordinary people
Love confession
First base (Holding hands)
Second base (Kissing)
Third base (Boobs)
Home run (Sex)
THEY'VE DONE THINGS COM-PLETELY OUT OF ORDER!

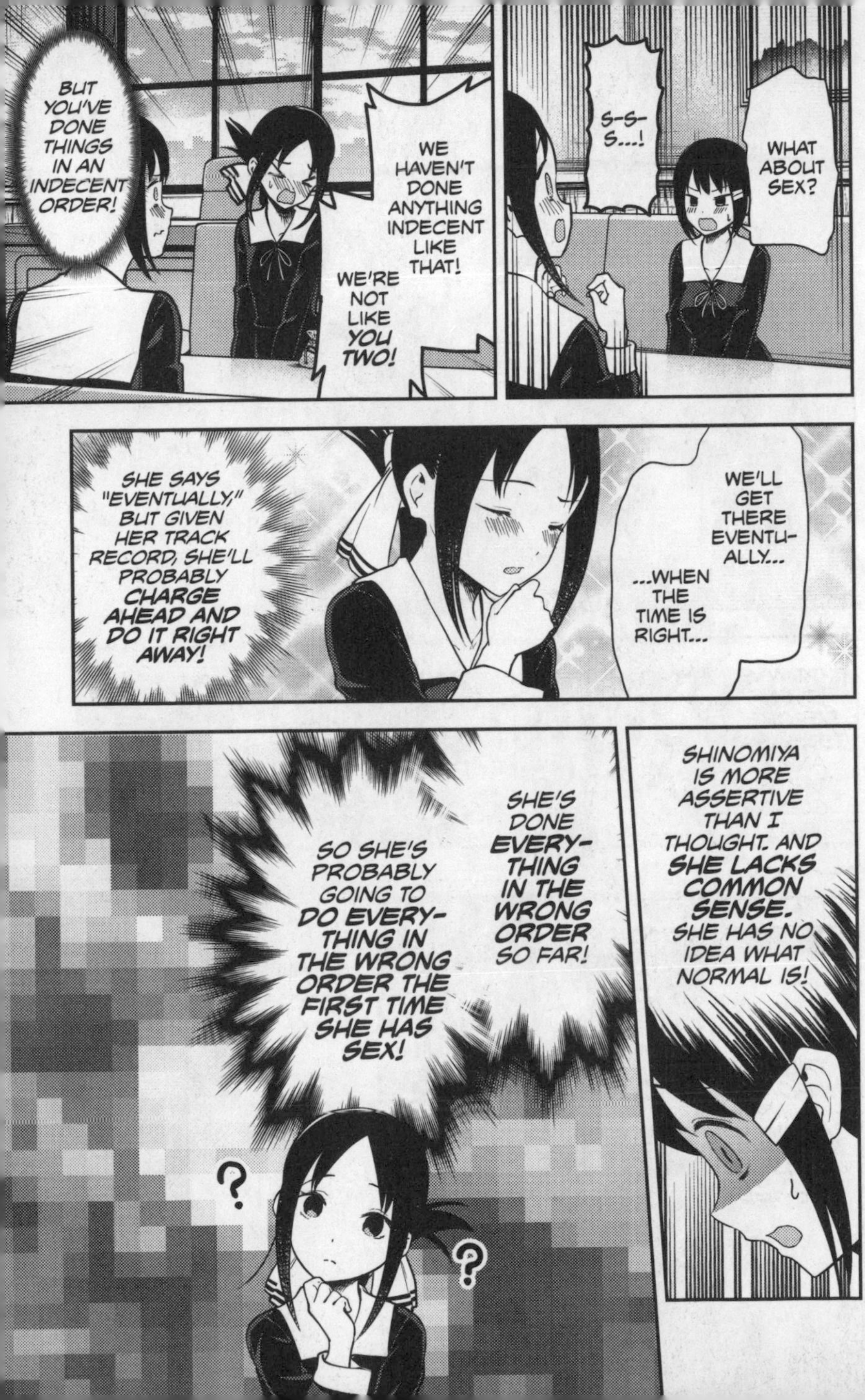
WHAT ABOUT SEX?
S-S-S...!
WE HAVEN'T DONE ANYTHING INDECENT LIKE THAT!
WE'RE NOT LIKE YOU TWO!
BUT YOU'VE DONE THINGS IN AN INDECENT ORDER!
WE'LL GET THERE EVENTUALLY...
...WHEN THE TIME IS RIGHT...
SHE SAYS "EVENTUALLY," BUT GIVEN HER TRACK RECORD, SHE'LL PROBABLY CHARGE AHEAD AND DO IT RIGHT AWAY!
SHINOMIYA IS MORE ASSERTIVE THAN I THOUGHT. AND SHE LACKS COMMON SENSE. SHE HAS NO IDEA WHAT NORMAL IS!
SHE'S DONE EVERYTHING IN THE WRONG ORDER SO FAR!
SO SHE'S PROBABLY GOING TO DO EVERYTHING IN THE WRONG ORDER THE FIRST TIME SHE HAS SEX!
?
?

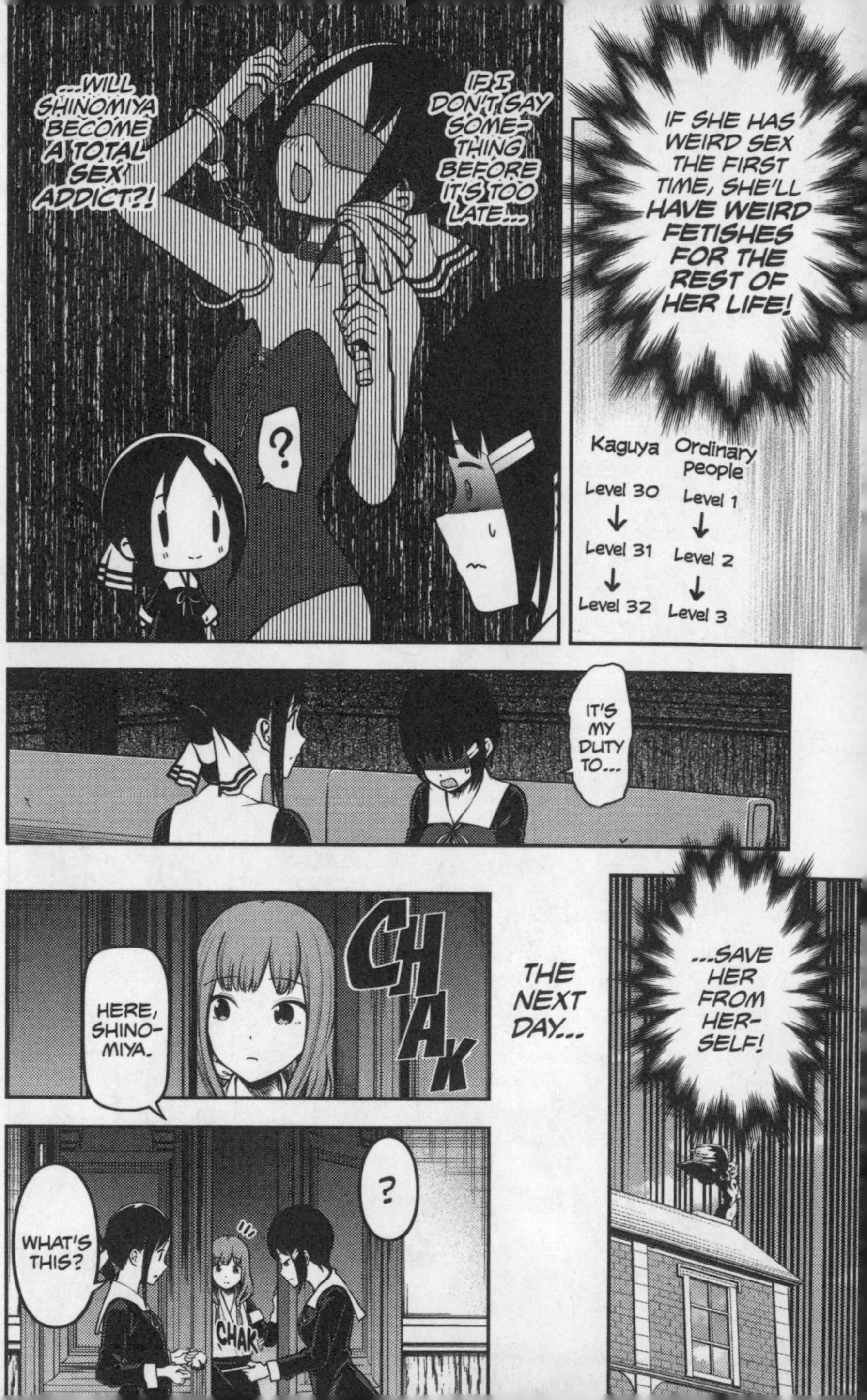
IF SHE HAS WEIRD SEX THE FIRST TIME, SHE'LL HAVE WEIRD FETISHES FOR THE REST OF HER LIFE!
Kaguya
Level 30
Level 31
Level 32
Ordinary People
Level 1
Level 2
Level 3
IF I DON'T SAY SOME-THING BEFORE IT'S TOO LATE...
...WILL SHINOMIYA BECOME A TOTAL SEX ADDICT?!
?
IT'S MY DUTY TO...
...SAVE HER FROM HER-SELF!
THE NEXT DAY...
CHAK
HERE, SHINO-MIYA.
?
WHAT'S THIS?
CHAK

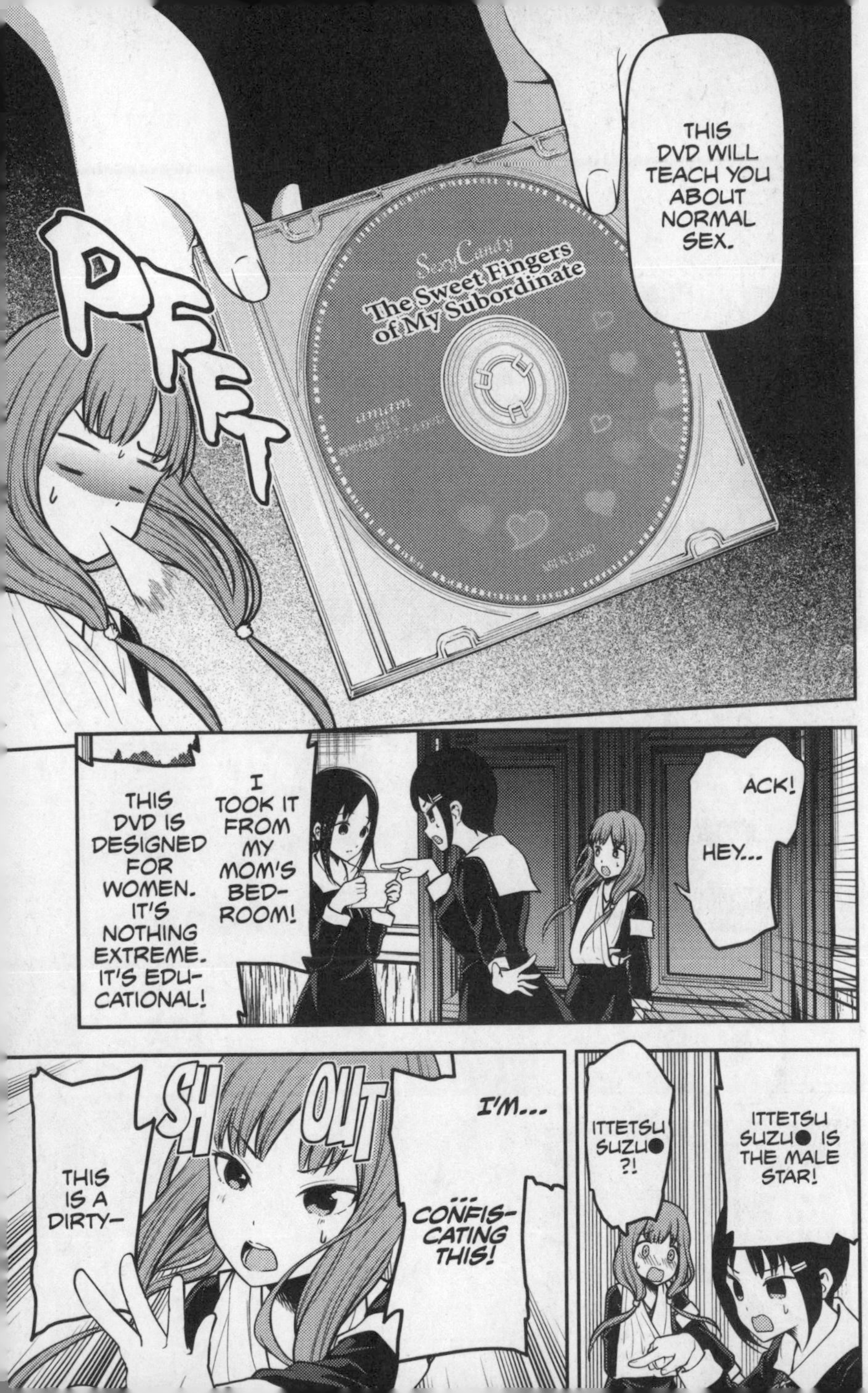
THIS DVD WILL TEACH YOU ABOUT NORMAL SEX.
PFFFT
The Sweet Fingers of My Subordinate
ACK!
HEY...
I TOOK IT FROM MY MOM'S BEDROOM!
THIS DVD IS DESIGNED FOR WOMEN. IT'S NOTHING EXTREME. IT'S EDUCATIONAL!
ITTETSU SUZU● IS THE MALE STAR!
ITTETSU SUZU● ?!
SHOUT
I'M...
...CONFISCATING THIS!
THIS IS A DIRTY—

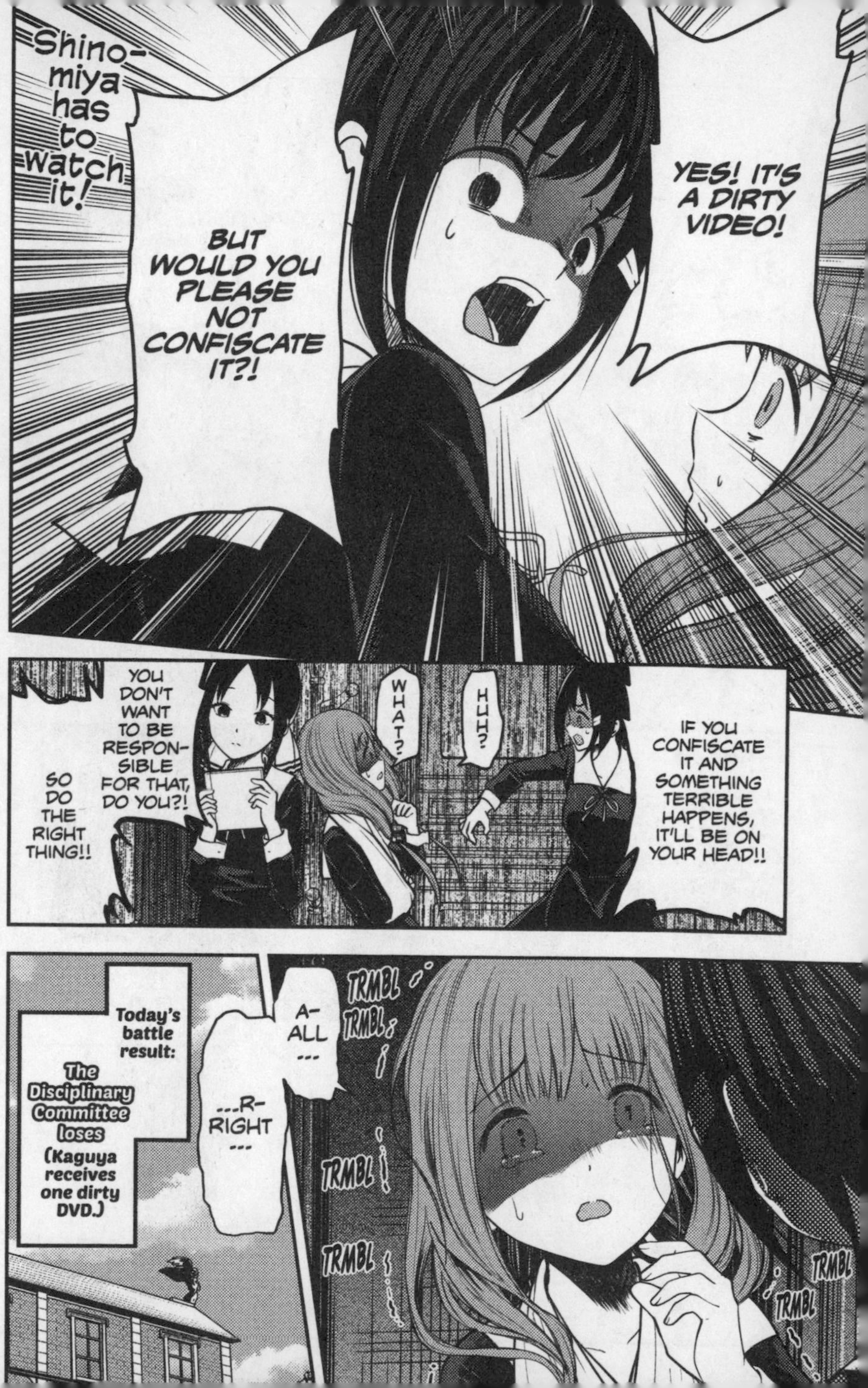
YES! IT'S A DIRTY VIDEO!
BUT WOULD YOU PLEASE NOT CONFISCATE IT?!
Shinomiya has to watch it!
IF YOU CONFISCATE IT AND SOMETHING TERRIBLE HAPPENS, IT'LL BE ON YOUR HEAD!!
HUH?
WHAT?
YOU DON'T WANT TO BE RESPONSIBLE FOR THAT, DO YOU?!
SO DO THE RIGHT THING!!
TRMBL TRMBL
TRMBL TRMBL
TRMBL
TRMBL
TRMBL
A-ALL...
...R-RIGHT...
Today's battle result:
The Disciplinary Committee loses
(Kaguya receives one dirty DVD.)

NAGISA KASHIWAGI

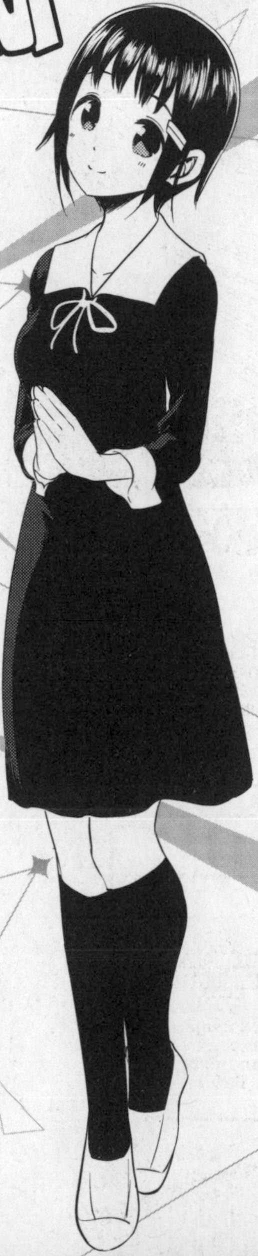

Nagisa Kashiwagi

- Shuchiin Academy High School Second-Year
- Volunteering Club President
- Notable characteristics: fully developed
- Tsubasa Tanuma's girlfriend

As the daughter of the chairman of a large shipbuilding company and the granddaughter of a Japanese Business Federation director, she's tough and calculating. Nagisa is often amazed at Kaguya's idealistic notions about love, but she's good friends with her because they are both cold and calculating and share similar values.

You can tell Nagisa has high ideals, has a lot of pride and easily becomes jealous by the way she deals with Tsubasa. But she is basically gentle, caring, very affectionate and peace loving.

Like most teenagers, Nagisa often neglects to think for herself. She's sensitive to the opinions of the people around her and is easily swayed by others. Nagisa adores Maki Shijo because Maki is a genius and has great strength of will. She's possessive of Maki and has an unachievable desire to be just like her.

Nagisa's relationship with Tsubasa is going well, but they've hit a plateau. They often fight over what their future together will be after they graduate. But they still enjoy kissing and making up after quarrels.

KAGUYA-SAMA

LOVE IS WAR

Battle 168
Their First Encounter

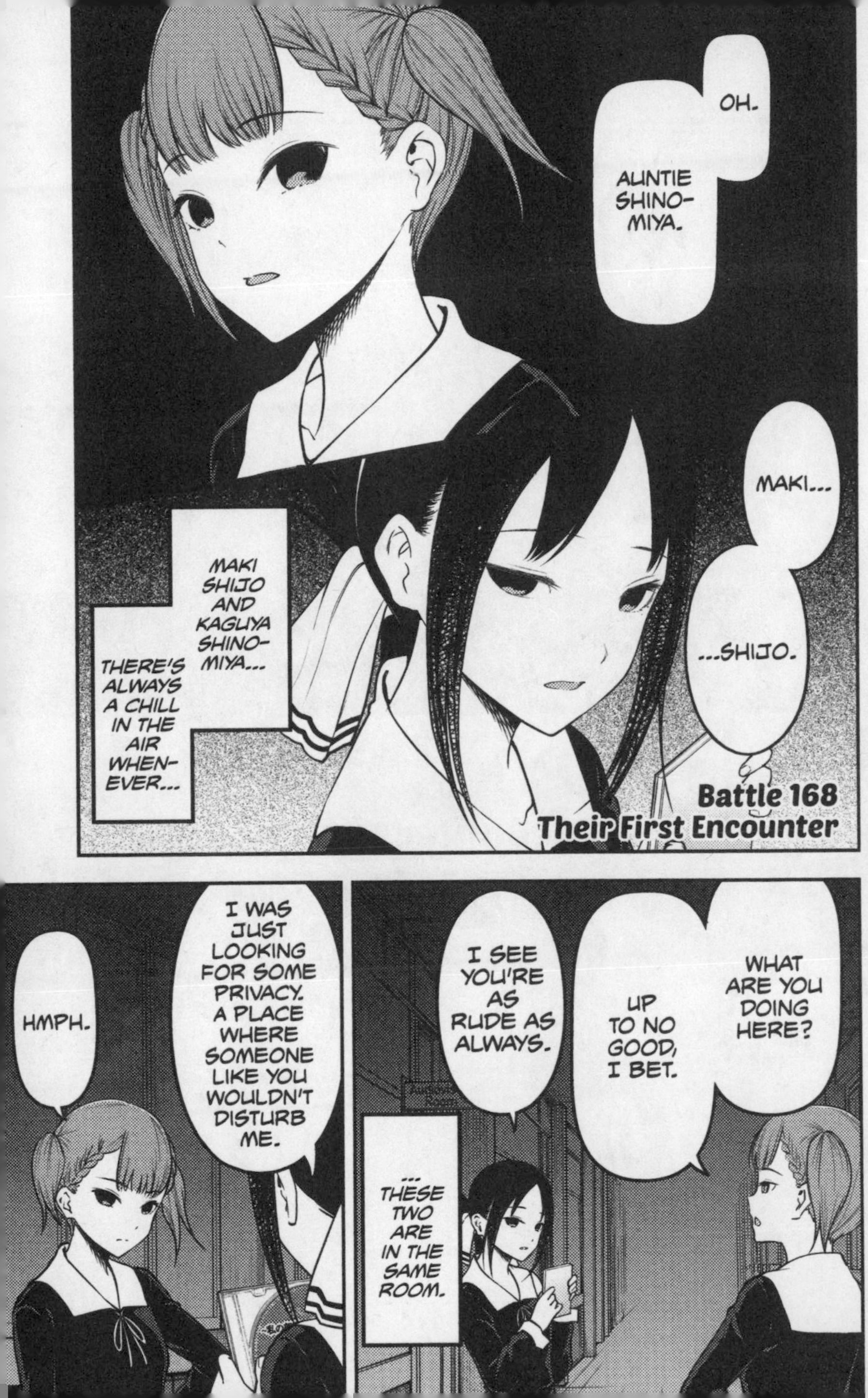
OH.
AUNTIE SHINOMIYA.
MAKI...
...SHIJO.
MAKI SHIJO AND KAGUYA SHINOMIYA... THERE'S ALWAYS A CHILL IN THE AIR WHENEVER...
WHAT ARE YOU DOING HERE?
UP TO NO GOOD, I BET.
I SEE YOU'RE AS RUDE AS ALWAYS.
...THESE TWO ARE IN THE SAME ROOM.
I WAS JUST LOOKING FOR SOME PRIVACY. A PLACE WHERE SOMEONE LIKE YOU WOULDN'T DISTURB ME.
HMPH.

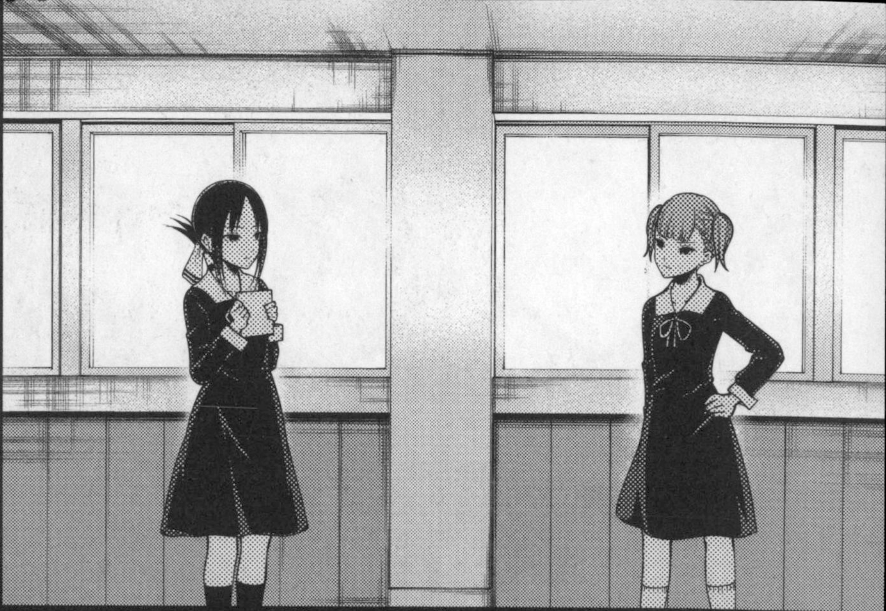

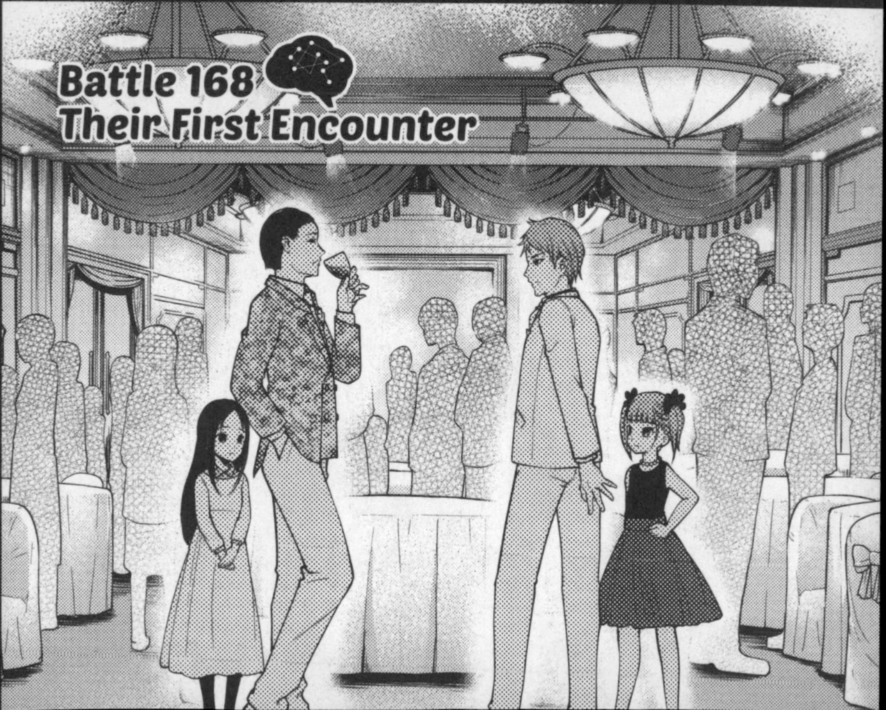
Battle 168
Their First Encounter

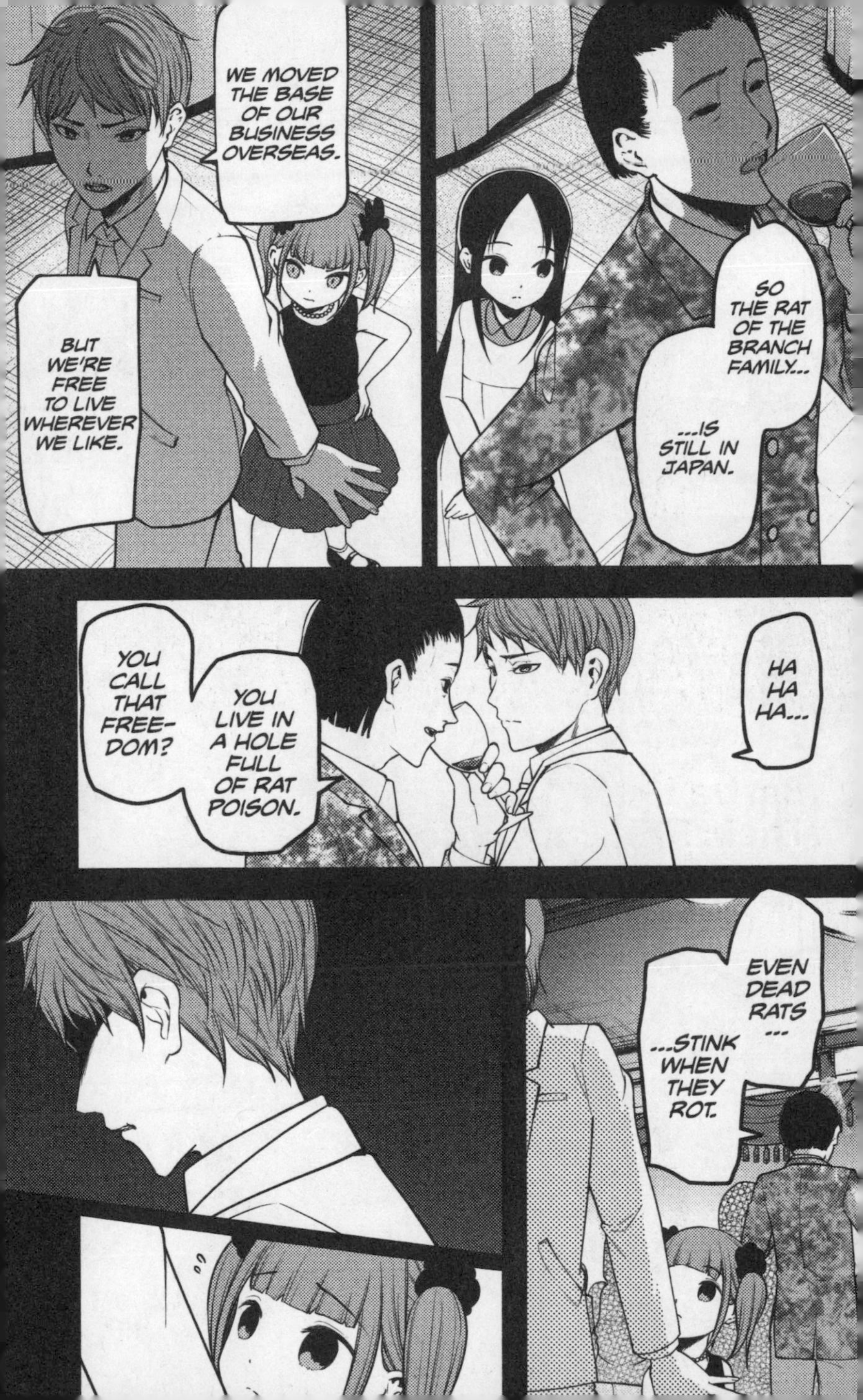

SO THE RAT OF THE BRANCH FAMILY...
...IS STILL IN JAPAN.
WE MOVED THE BASE OF OUR BUSINESS OVERSEAS.
BUT WE'RE FREE TO LIVE WHEREVER WE LIKE.
HA HA HA...
YOU LIVE IN A HOLE FULL OF RAT POISON.
YOU CALL THAT FREE-DOM?
EVEN DEAD RATS...
...STINK WHEN THEY ROT.

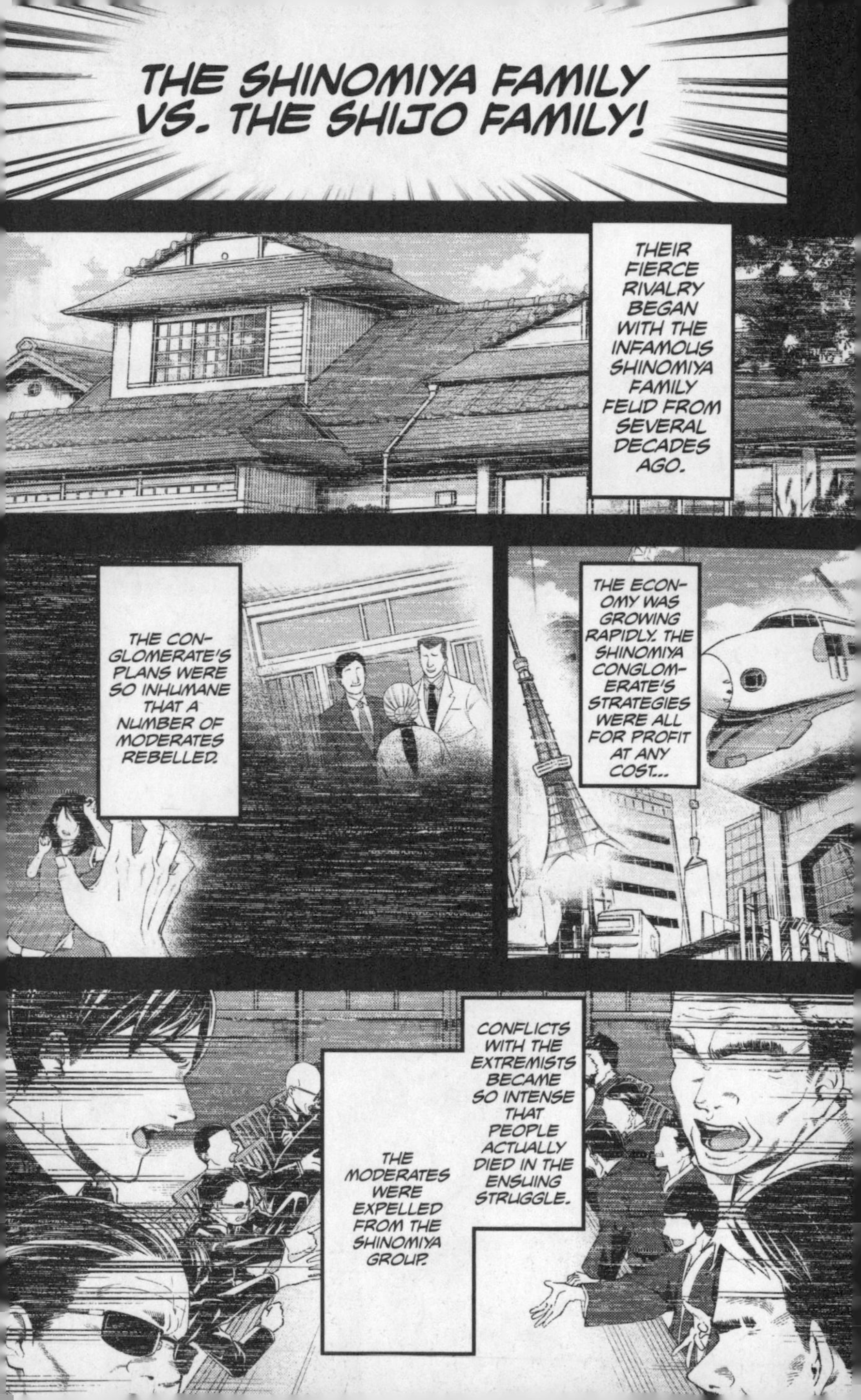
THE SHINOMIYA FAMILY VS. THE SHIJO FAMILY!
THEIR FIERCE RIVALRY BEGAN WITH THE INFAMOUS SHINOMIYA FAMILY FEUD FROM SEVERAL DECADES AGO.
THE ECONOMY WAS GROWING RAPIDLY. THE SHINOMIYA CONGLOMERATE'S STRATEGIES WERE ALL FOR PROFIT AT ANY COST...
THE CONGLOMERATE'S PLANS WERE SO INHUMANE THAT A NUMBER OF MODERATES REBELLED.
CONFLICTS WITH THE EXTREMISTS BECAME SO INTENSE THAT PEOPLE ACTUALLY DIED IN THE ENSUING STRUGGLE.
THE MODERATES WERE EXPELLED FROM THE SHINOMIYA GROUP.

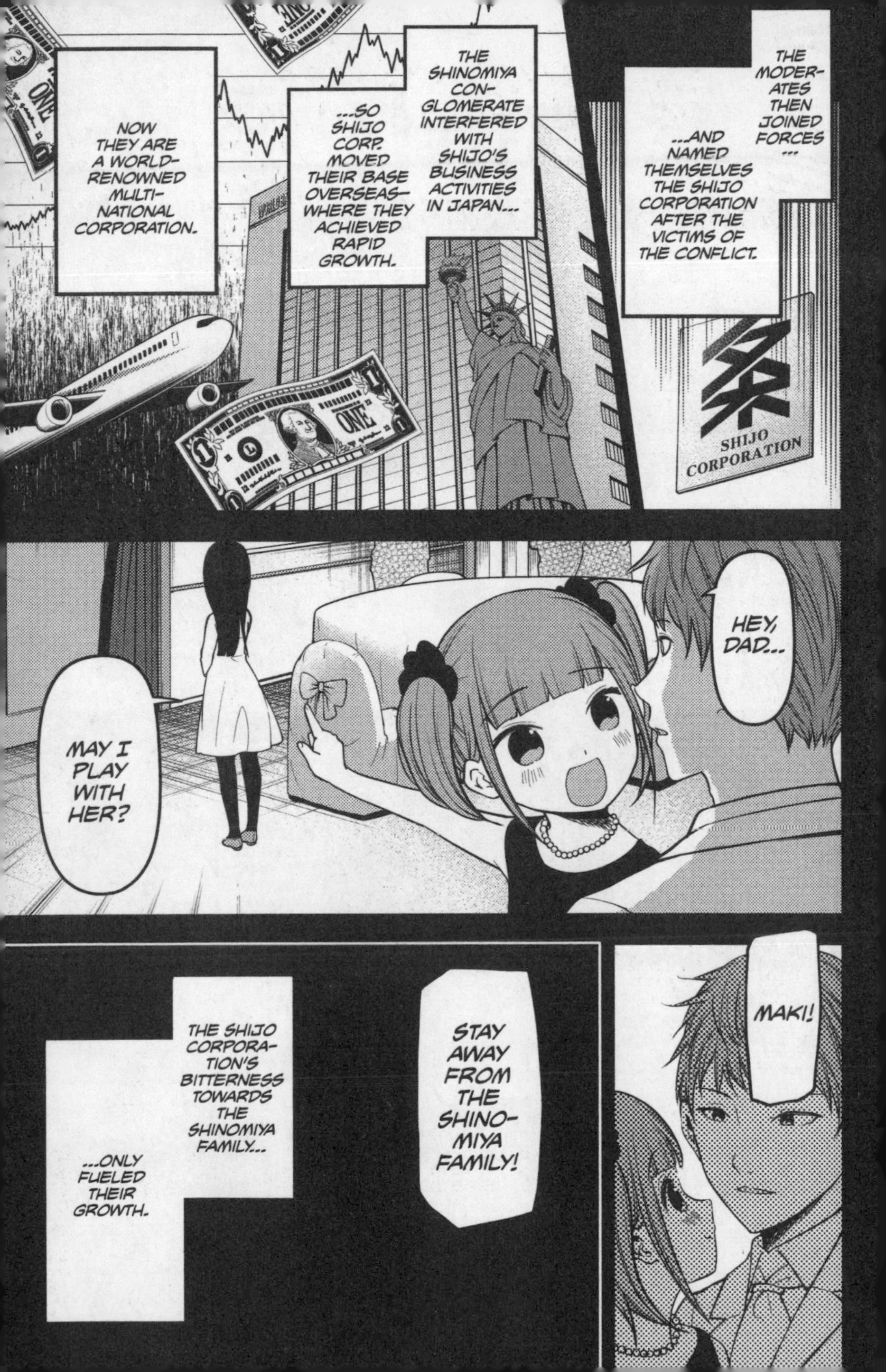
THE MODERATES THEN JOINED FORCES...
...AND NAMED THEMSELVES THE SHIJO CORPORATION AFTER THE VICTIMS OF THE CONFLICT.
SHIJO CORPORATION
THE SHINOMIYA CONGLOMERATE INTERFERED WITH SHIJO'S BUSINESS ACTIVITIES IN JAPAN...
...SO SHIJO CORP. MOVED THEIR BASE OVERSEAS—WHERE THEY ACHIEVED RAPID GROWTH.
NOW THEY ARE A WORLD-RENOWNED MULTINATIONAL CORPORATION.
HEY, DAD...
MAY I PLAY WITH HER?
MAKI!
STAY AWAY FROM THE SHINOMIYA FAMILY!
THE SHIJO CORPORATION'S BITTERNESS TOWARDS THE SHINOMIYA FAMILY...
...ONLY FUELED THEIR GROWTH.

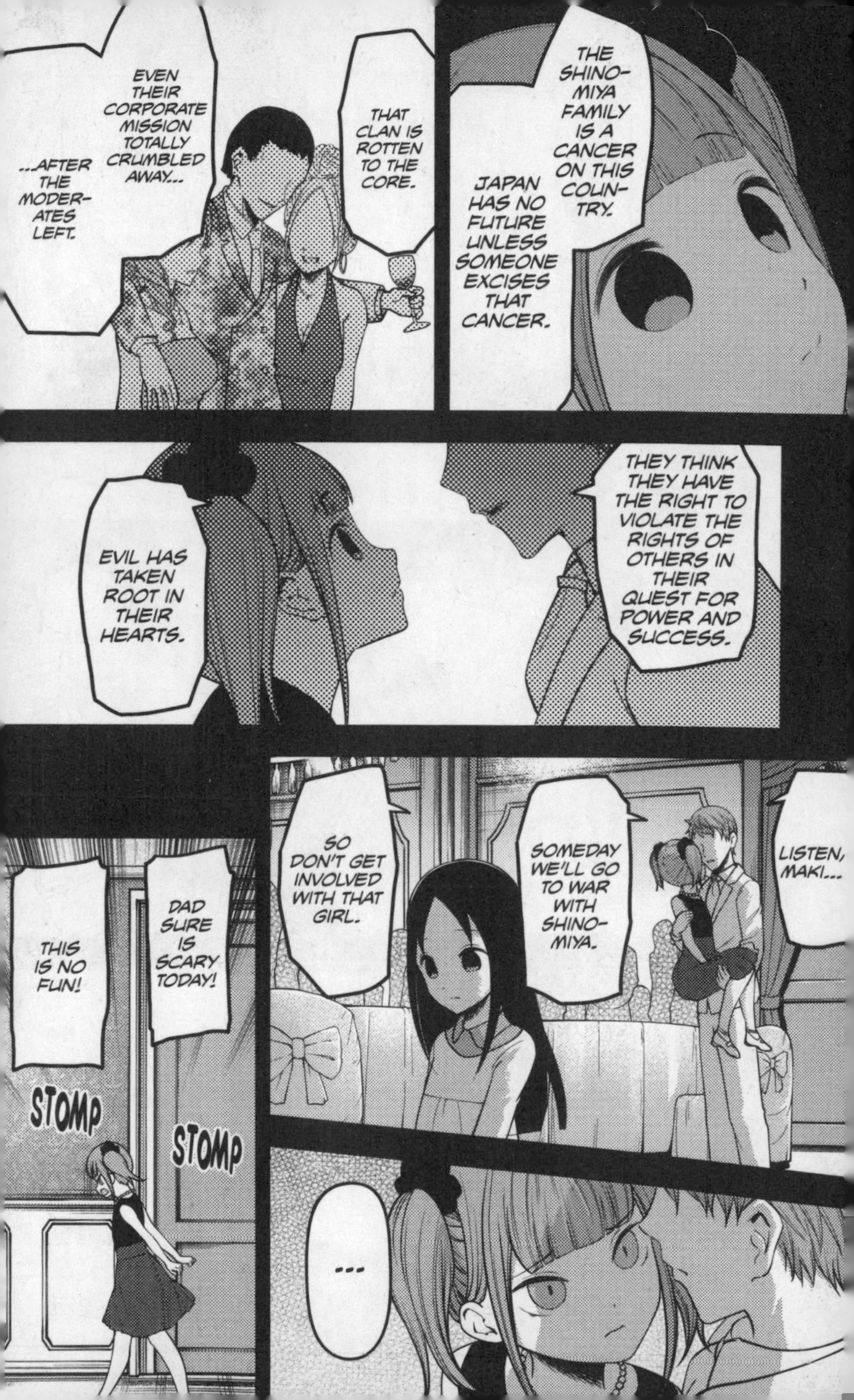
THE SHINOMIYA FAMILY IS A CANCER ON THIS COUNTRY.
JAPAN HAS NO FUTURE UNLESS SOMEONE EXCISES THAT CANCER.
THAT CLAN IS ROTTEN TO THE CORE.
EVEN THEIR CORPORATE MISSION TOTALLY CRUMBLED AWAY...
...AFTER THE MODERATES LEFT.
THEY THINK THEY HAVE THE RIGHT TO VIOLATE THE RIGHTS OF OTHERS IN THEIR QUEST FOR POWER AND SUCCESS.
EVIL HAS TAKEN ROOT IN THEIR HEARTS.
LISTEN, MAKI...
SOMEDAY WE'LL GO TO WAR WITH SHINOMIYA.
SO DON'T GET INVOLVED WITH THAT GIRL.
...
DAD SURE IS SCARY TODAY!
THIS IS NO FUN!
STOMP
STOMP

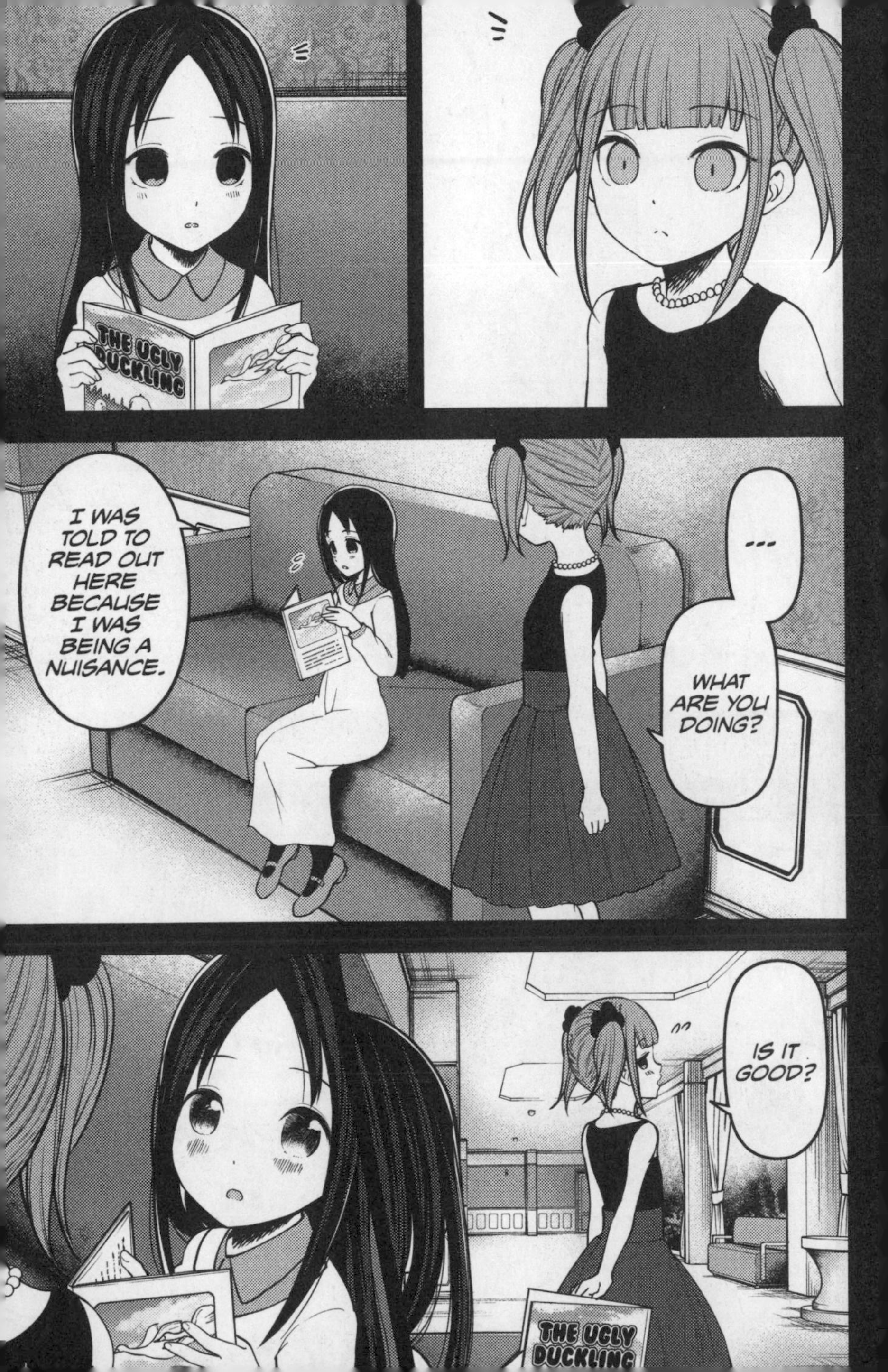

THE UGLY DUCKLING
...
WHAT ARE YOU DOING?
I WAS TOLD TO READ OUT HERE BECAUSE I WAS BEING A NUISANCE.
IS IT GOOD?
THE UGLY DUCKLING

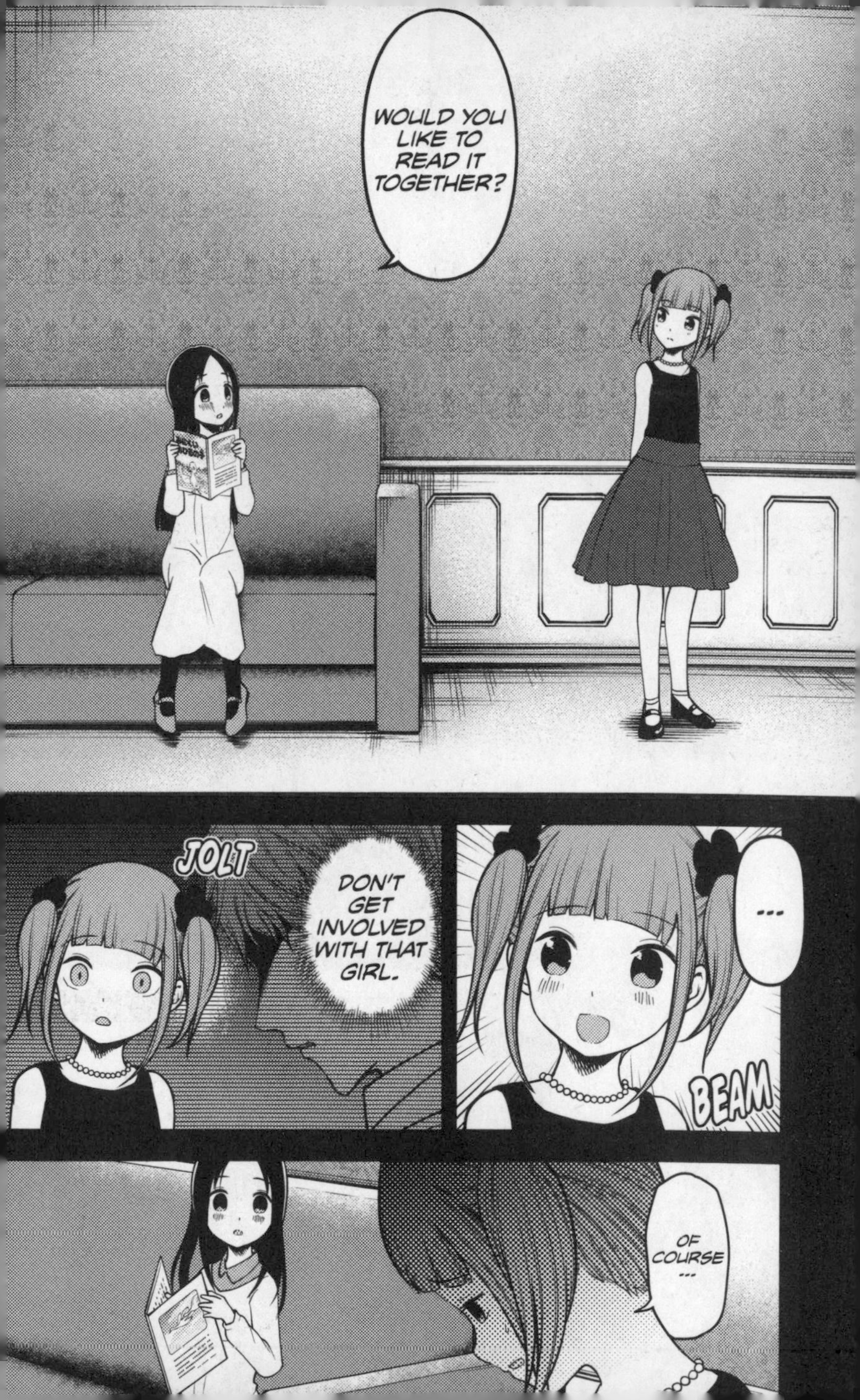
WOULD YOU LIKE TO READ IT TOGETHER?
...
BEAM
JOLT
DON'T GET INVOLVED WITH THAT GIRL.
OF COURSE ...

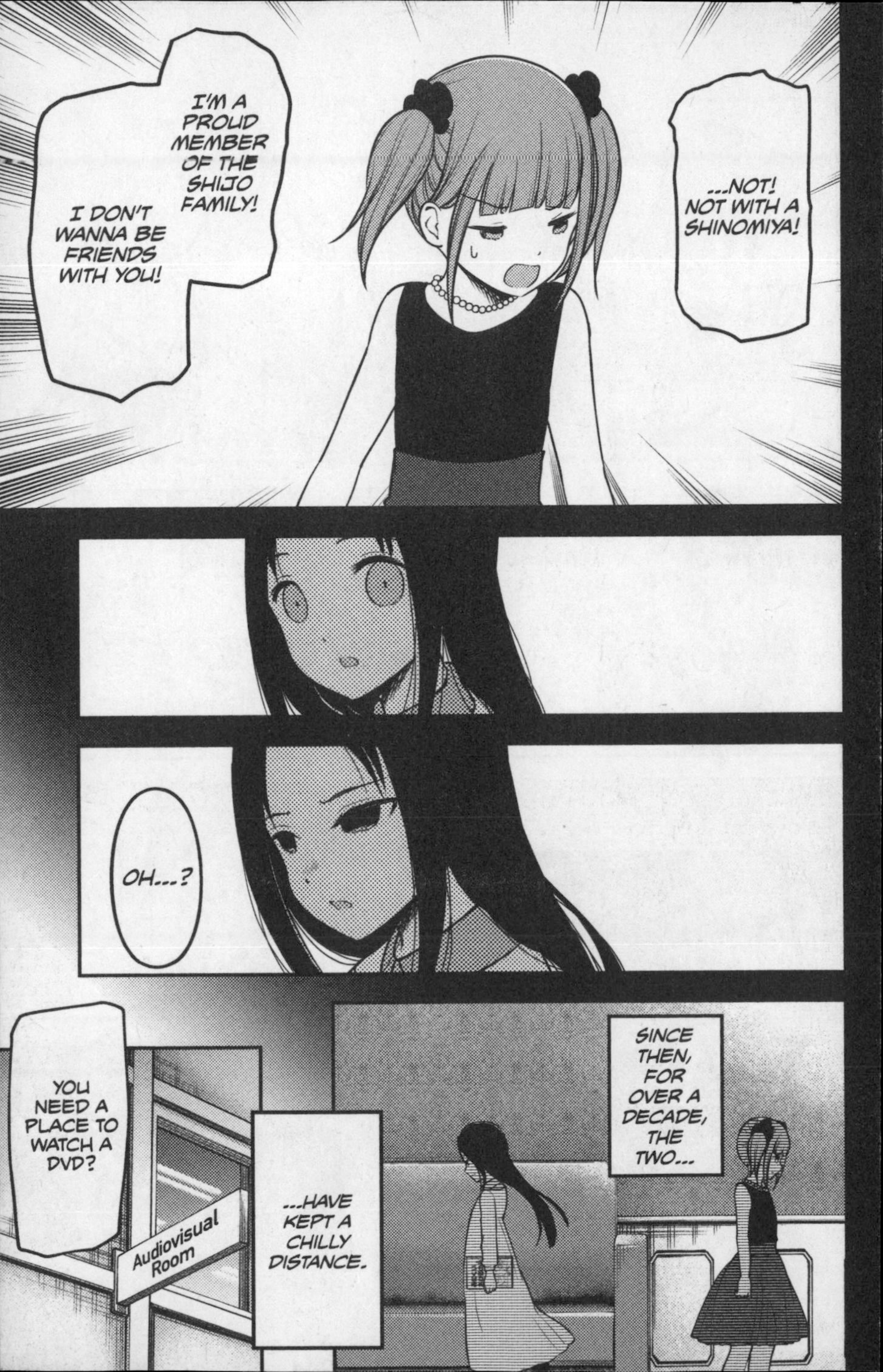
I'M A PROUD MEMBER OF THE SHIJO FAMILY!
I DON'T WANNA BE FRIENDS WITH YOU!
...NOT! NOT WITH A SHINOMIYA!
OH...?
SINCE THEN, FOR OVER A DECADE, THE TWO...
...HAVE KEPT A CHILLY DISTANCE.
YOU NEED A PLACE TO WATCH A DVD?
Audiovisual Room

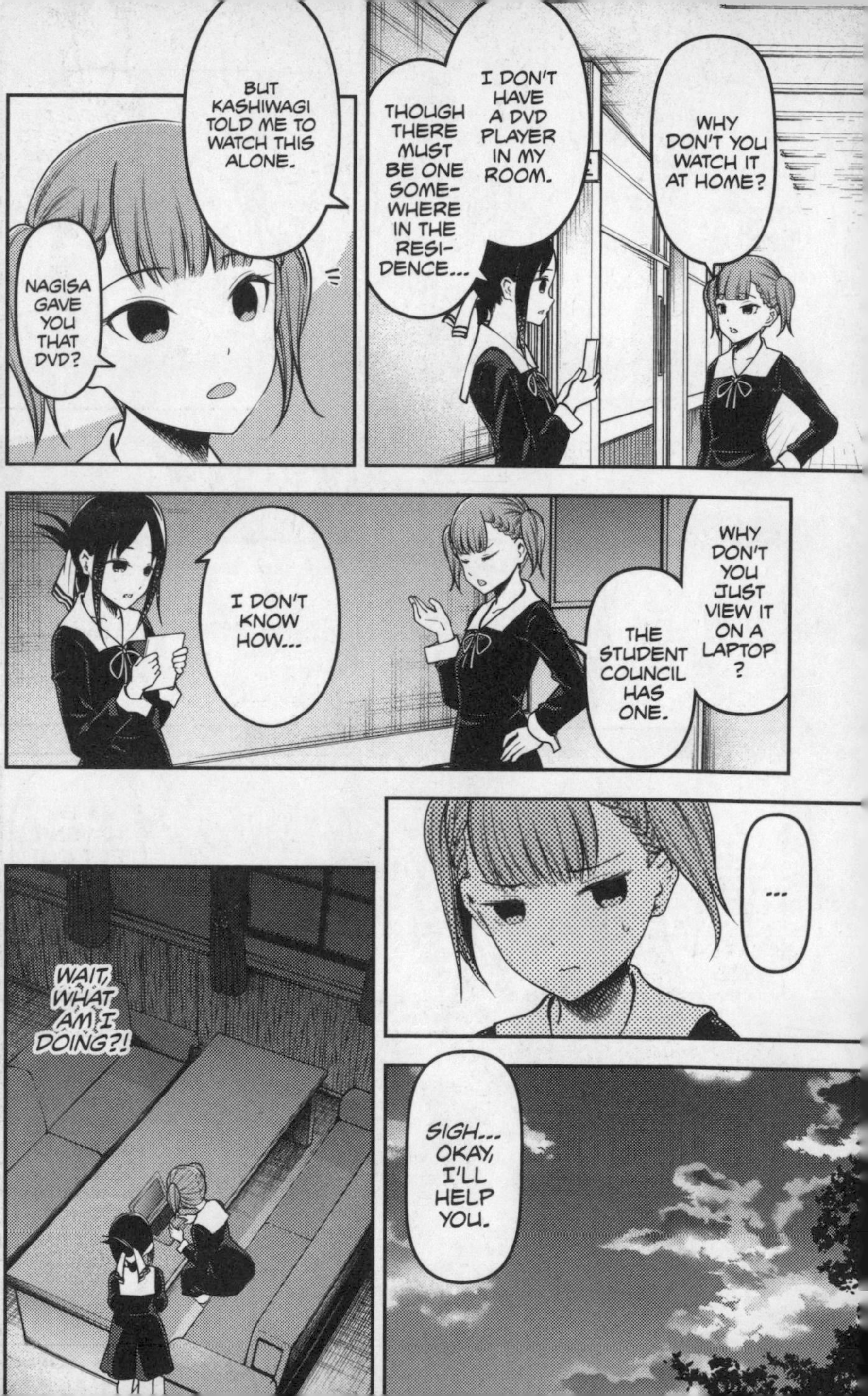
WHY DON'T YOU WATCH IT AT HOME?
I DON'T HAVE A DVD PLAYER IN MY ROOM.
THOUGH THERE MUST BE ONE SOME-WHERE IN THE RESI-DENCE...
BUT KASHIWAGI TOLD ME TO WATCH THIS ALONE.
NAGISA GAVE YOU THAT DVD?
WHY DON'T YOU JUST VIEW IT ON A LAPTOP?
THE STUDENT COUNCIL HAS ONE.
I DON'T KNOW HOW...
...
SIGH... OKAY, I'LL HELP YOU.
WAIT, WHAT AM I DOING?!

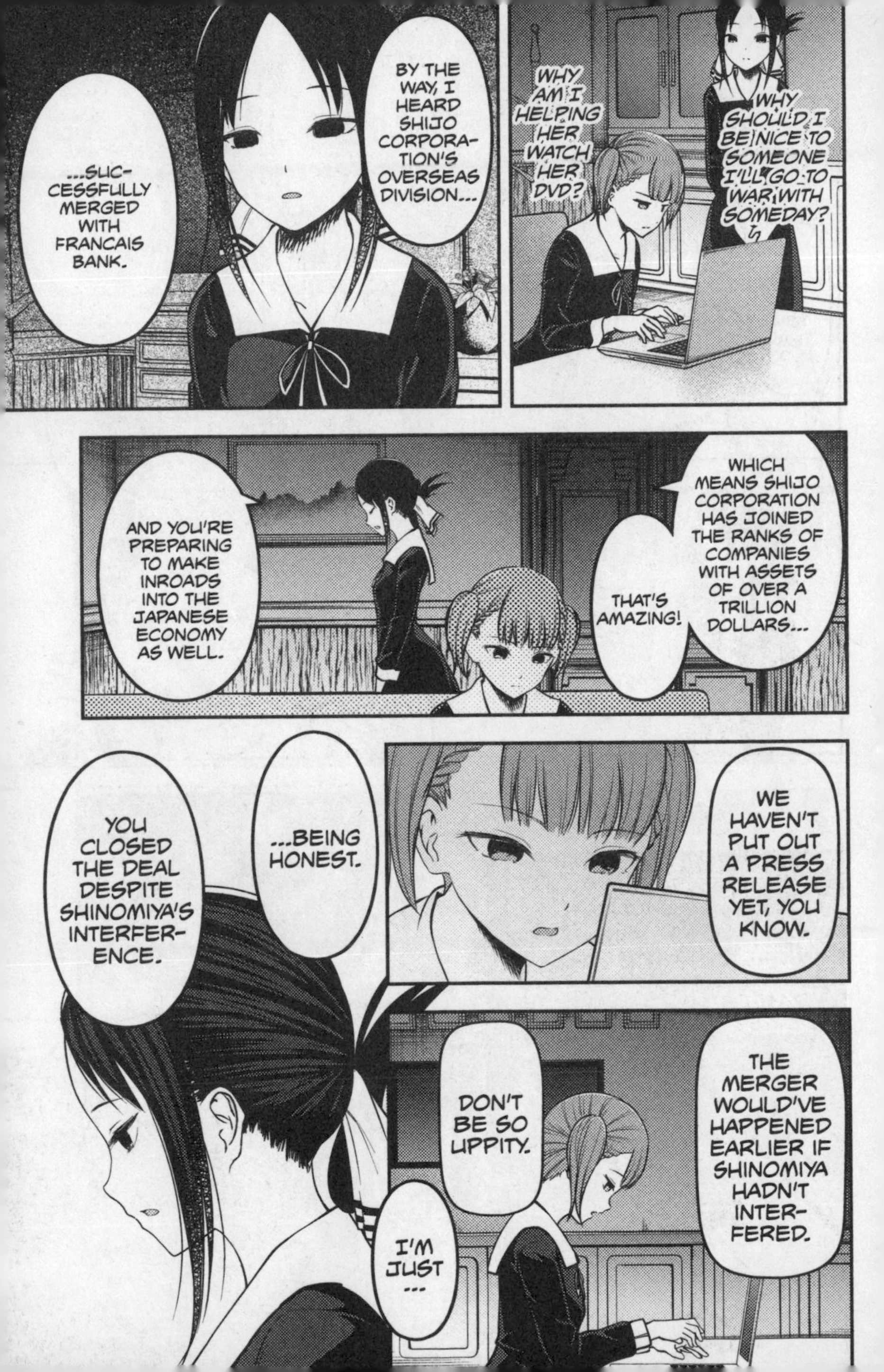
WHY SHOULD I BE NICE TO SOMEONE I'LL GO TO WAR WITH SOMEDAY?
WHY AM I HELPING HER WATCH HER DVD?
BY THE WAY, I HEARD SHIJO CORPORATION'S OVERSEAS DIVISION...
...SUC-CESSFULLY MERGED WITH FRANCAIS BANK.
WHICH MEANS SHIJO CORPORATION HAS JOINED THE RANKS OF COMPANIES WITH ASSETS OF OVER A TRILLION DOLLARS...
THAT'S AMAZING!
AND YOU'RE PREPARING TO MAKE INROADS INTO THE JAPANESE ECONOMY AS WELL.
WE HAVEN'T PUT OUT A PRESS RELEASE YET, YOU KNOW.
YOU CLOSED THE DEAL DESPITE SHINOMIYA'S INTERFER-ENCE.
THE MERGER WOULD'VE HAPPENED EARLIER IF SHINOMIYA HADN'T INTER-FERED.
DON'T BE SO UPPITY.
I'M JUST...
...BEING HONEST.

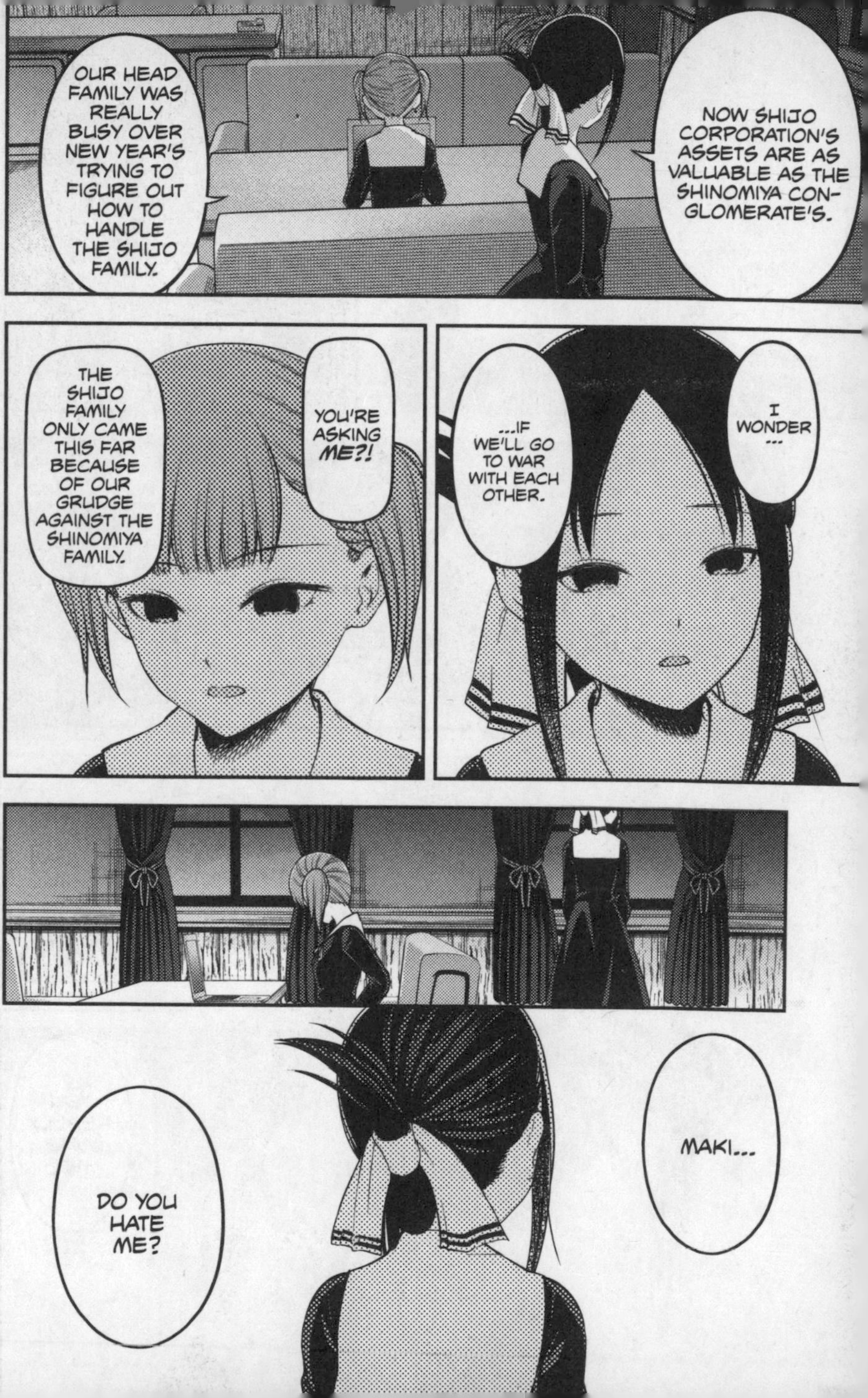
NOW SHIJO CORPORATION'S ASSETS ARE AS VALUABLE AS THE SHINOMIYA CONGLOMERATE'S.
OUR HEAD FAMILY WAS REALLY BUSY OVER NEW YEAR'S TRYING TO FIGURE OUT HOW TO HANDLE THE SHIJO FAMILY.
I WONDER...
...IF WE'LL GO TO WAR WITH EACH OTHER.
YOU'RE ASKING *ME?!*
THE SHIJO FAMILY ONLY CAME THIS FAR BECAUSE OF OUR GRUDGE AGAINST THE SHINOMIYA FAMILY.
MAKI...
DO YOU HATE ME?

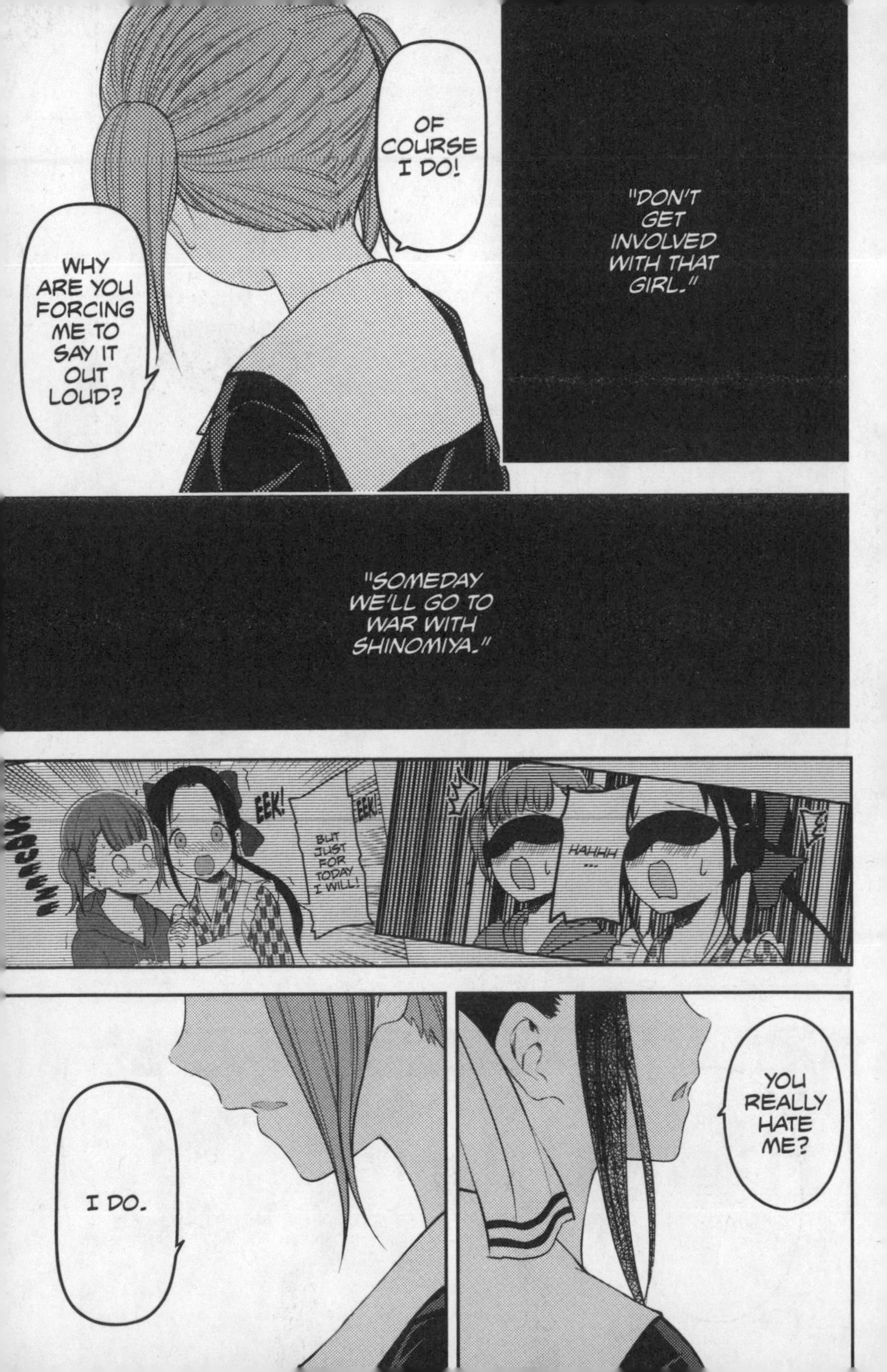
"DON'T GET INVOLVED WITH THAT GIRL."
OF COURSE I DO!
WHY ARE YOU FORCING ME TO SAY IT OUT LOUD?
"SOMEDAY WE'LL GO TO WAR WITH SHINOMIYA."
HAHHH...
EEK!
EEK!
BUT JUST FOR TODAY I WILL!
YOU REALLY HATE ME?
I DO.

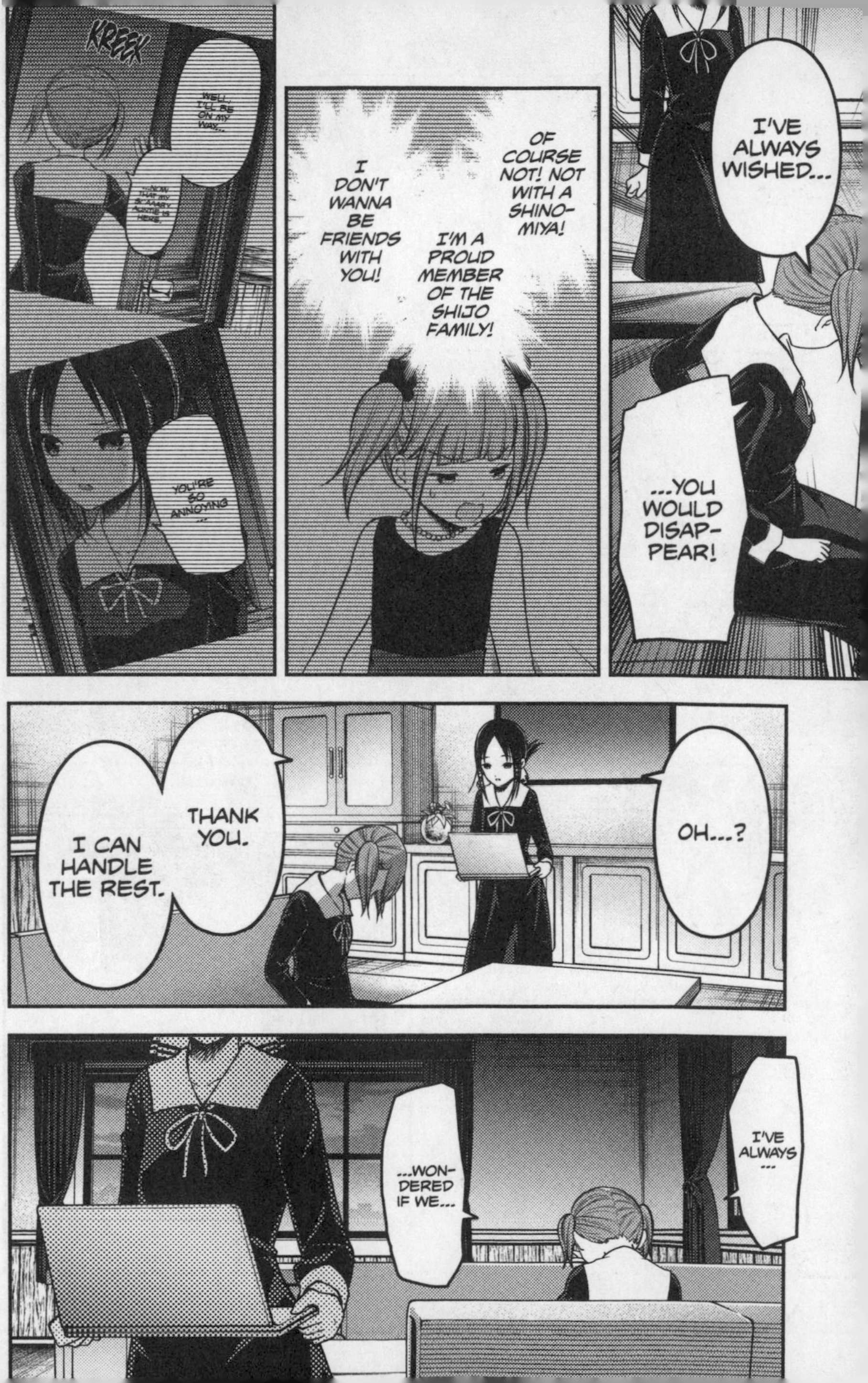

I'VE ALWAYS WISHED...
...YOU WOULD DISAPPEAR!
OF COURSE NOT! NOT WITH A SHINOMIYA!
I'M A PROUD MEMBER OF THE SHIJO FAMILY!
I DON'T WANNA BE FRIENDS WITH YOU!
KREEK
WELL, I'LL BE ON MY WAY...
YOU'RE SO ANNOYING...
OH...?
THANK YOU.
I CAN HANDLE THE REST.
I'VE ALWAYS...
...WONDERED IF WE...

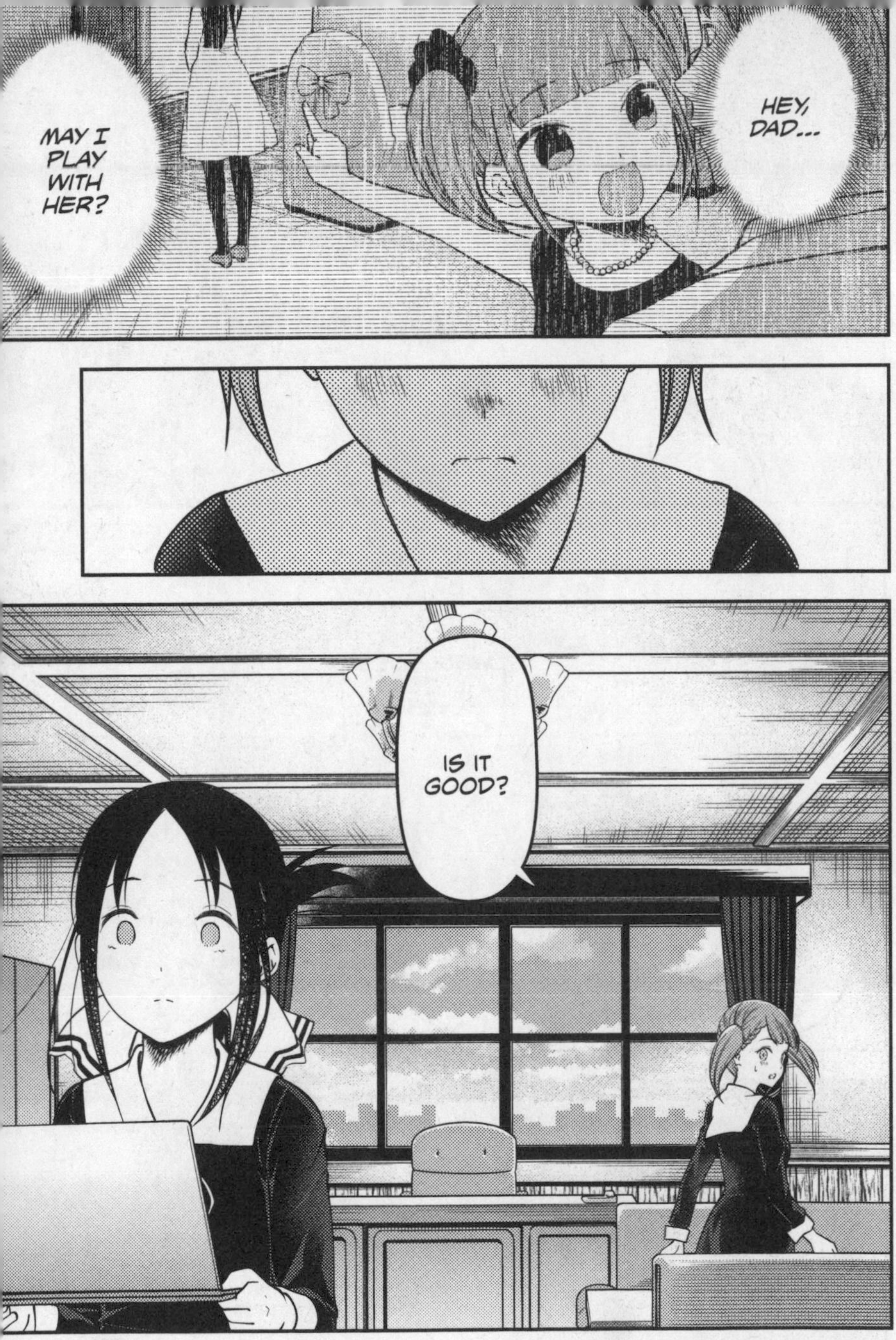
HEY, DAD...
MAY I PLAY WITH HER?
IS IT GOOD?

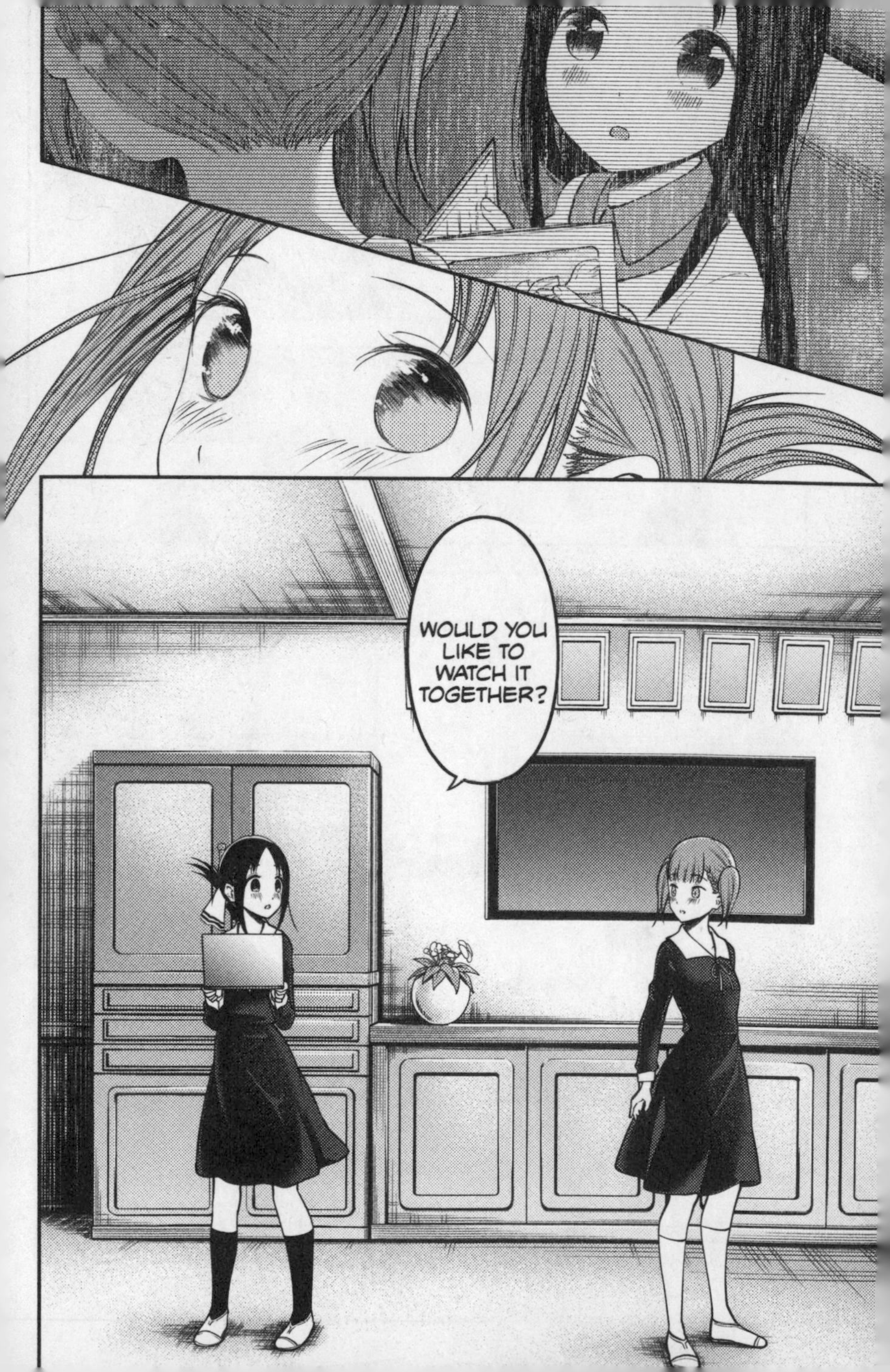
WOULD YOU LIKE TO WATCH IT TOGETHER?

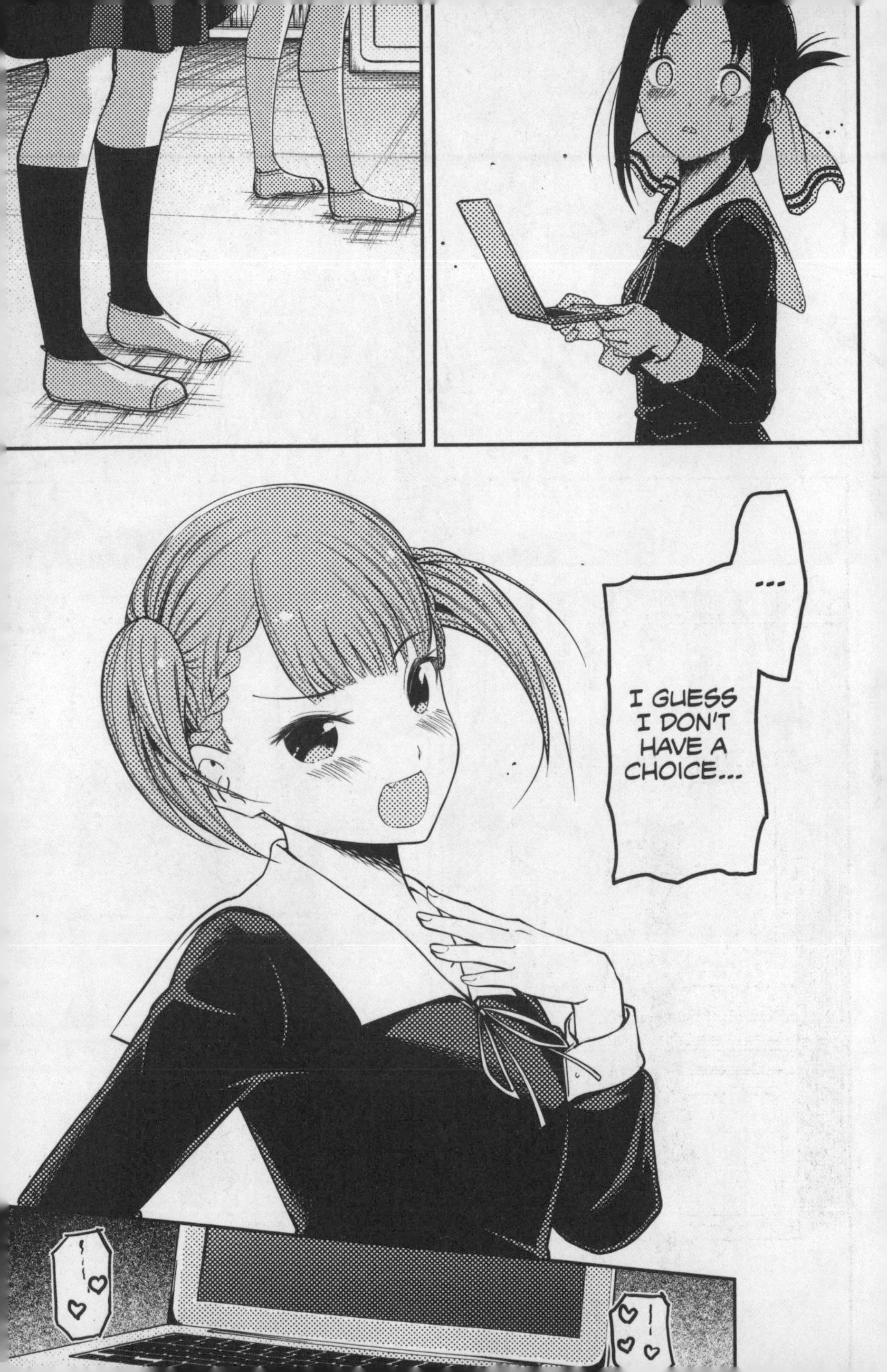
...
I GUESS I DON'T HAVE A CHOICE...

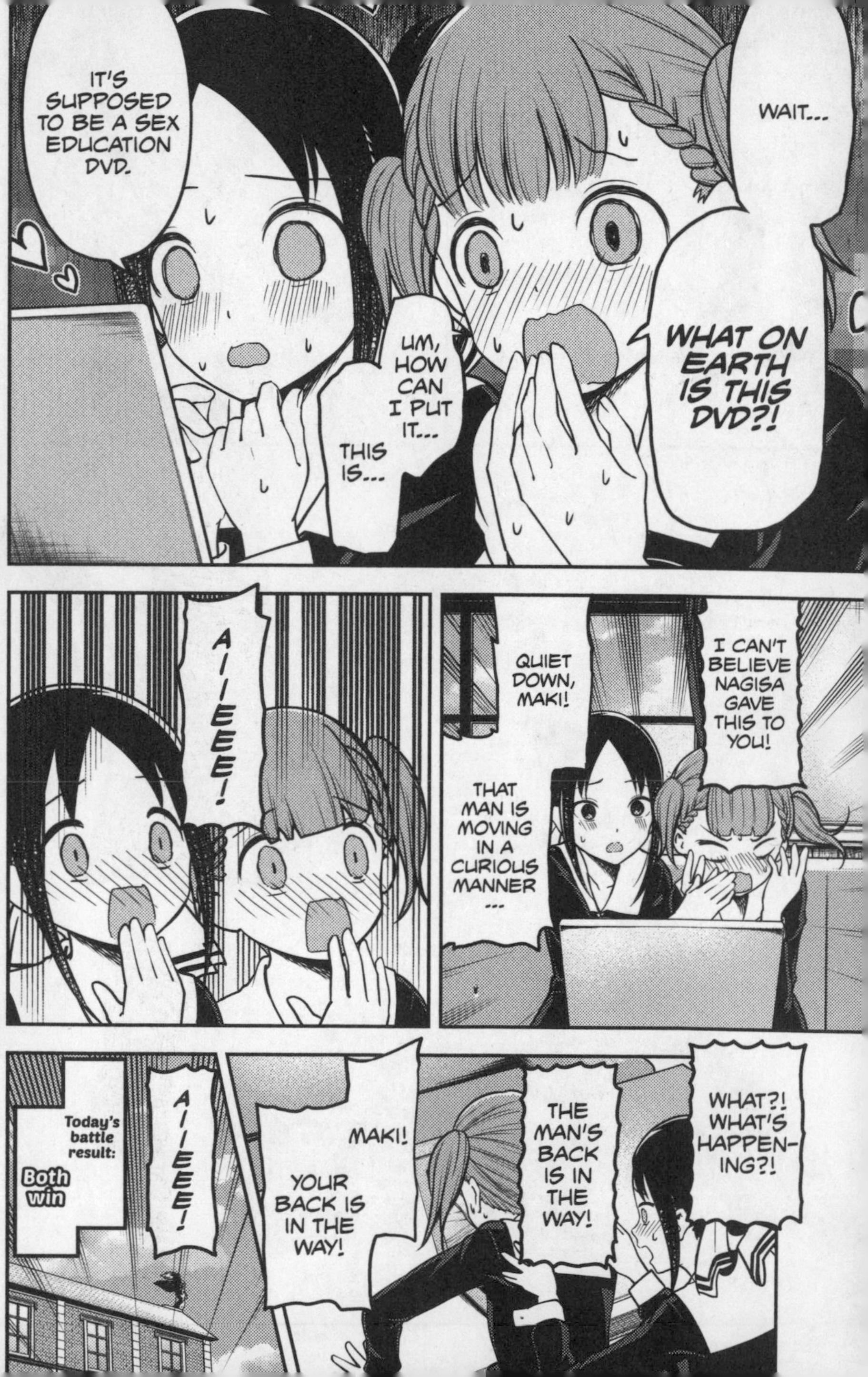
WAIT...
WHAT ON EARTH IS THIS DVD?!
UM, HOW CAN I PUT IT...
THIS IS...
IT'S SUPPOSED TO BE A SEX EDUCATION DVD.
I CAN'T BELIEVE NAGISA GAVE THIS TO YOU!
QUIET DOWN, MAKI!
THAT MAN IS MOVING IN A CURIOUS MANNER...
AIIEEE!
WHAT?! WHAT'S HAPPEN-ING?!
THE MAN'S BACK IS IN THE WAY!
MAKI!
YOUR BACK IS IN THE WAY!
AIIEEE!
Today's battle result:
Both win

MAKI SHIJO

Maki Shijo

- Shuchiin Academy High School Second-Year
- Volunteering Club Member
- Notable characteristics: stunning beauty
- Used to be the star of the bonus pages

A daughter of the Shijo family, a branch family of the Shinomiya family. The two families are currently feuding, which is upsetting for Maki.

Maki is ranked third in her grade. She's not doing her absolute best, and she believes she could be in first place if she applied herself more.

Maki is as talented as Kaguya, but they have different strengths and weaknesses. Kaguya's genius was developed through her Spartan education. She thinks fast and has great mimicry skills as well as a photographic memory. Maki's genius was developed through her advanced, cutting-edge education. She has excellent critical-thinking skills, is adaptable and has a photographic memory for the things she cares to remember. Their thought processes are polar opposites—nevertheless, they somehow tend to reach similar conclusions.

Maki has a full social life, so she's not as pessimistic about humanity as Kaguya. However, she's still quite wary of other people.

Maki is innocent and pure of heart, and she possesses great inner strength. It's clear she's a nice person because even though she still wants to be with Tsubasa, she doesn't hate her friend for dating him.

Maki has a twin brother. He enrolled in a nearby public high school because he wanted to continue to play soccer with his neighborhood friends. His parents are worried about him, so he studies hard in order to rank first in national practice exams to assuage their concern. He also managed to get his weak local soccer club to participate in Japan's interscholastic athletic competition. Thus he's a genius in his own way.

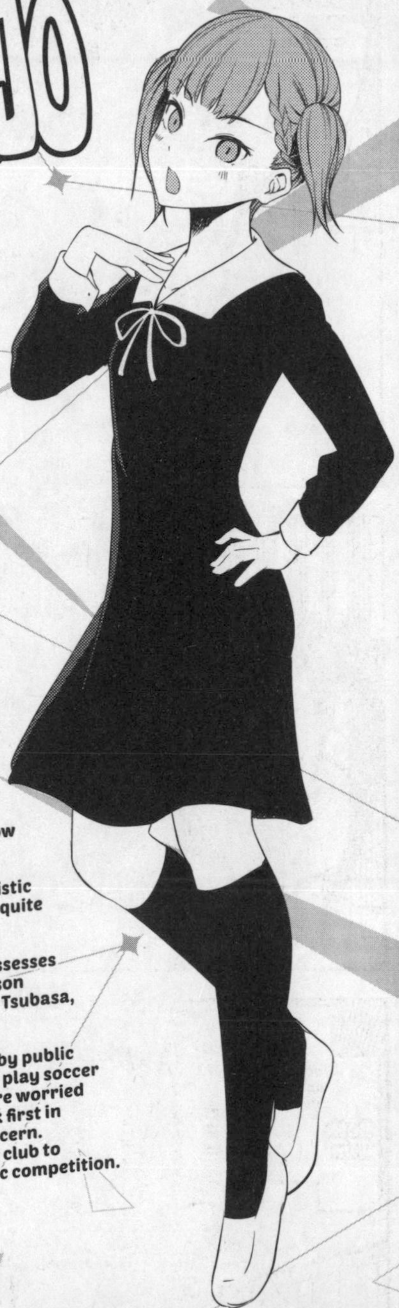

KAGUYA-SAMA
LOVE IS WAR

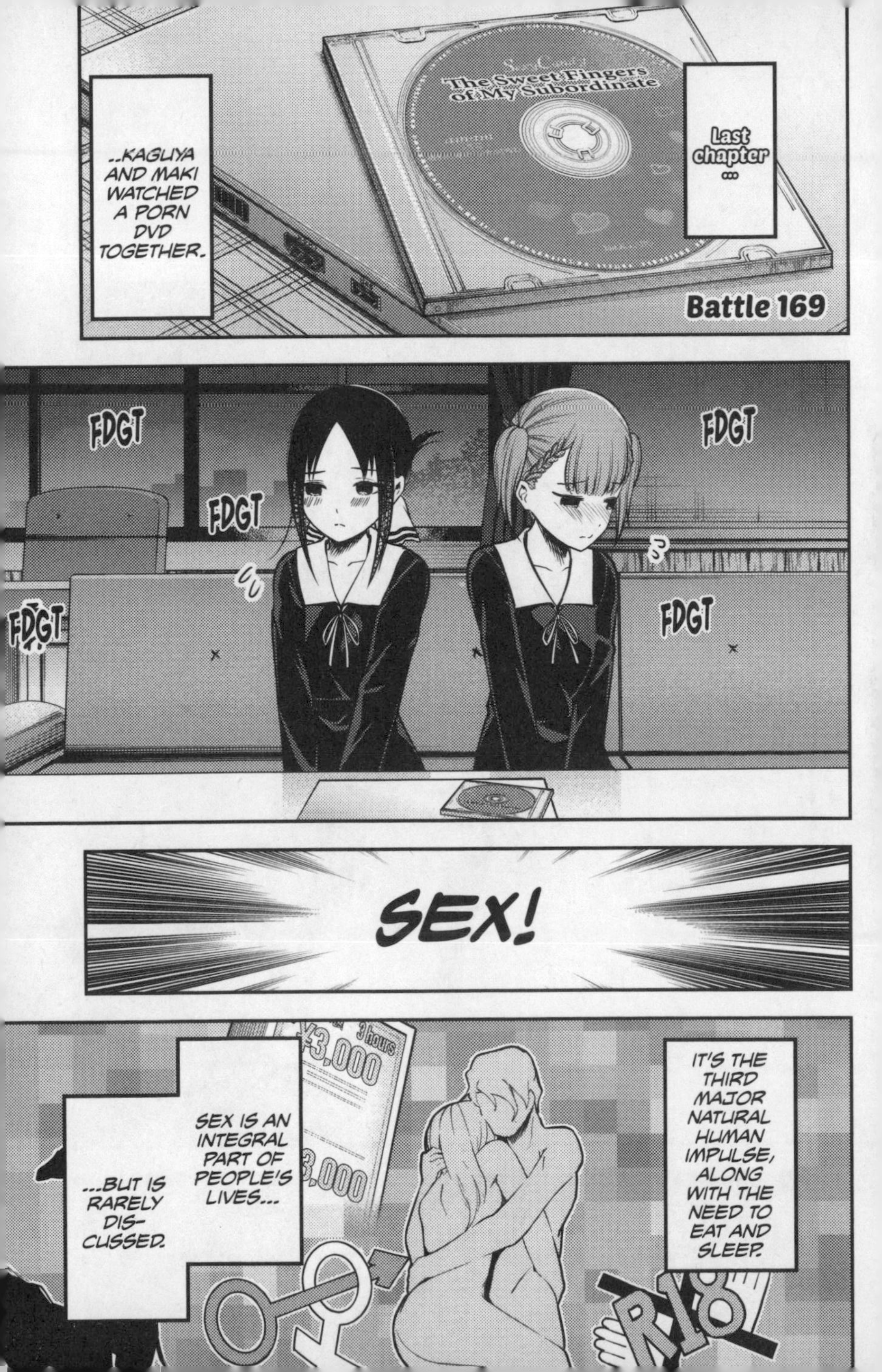
The Sweet Fingers of My Subordinate
Last chapter...
...Kaguya and Maki watched a porn DVD together.
Battle 169
FDGT
FDGT
FDGT
FDGT
FDGT
SEX!
It's the third major natural human impulse, along with the need to eat and sleep.
3 hours
¥3,000
Sex is an integral part of people's lives...
...but is rarely dis-cussed.
R18

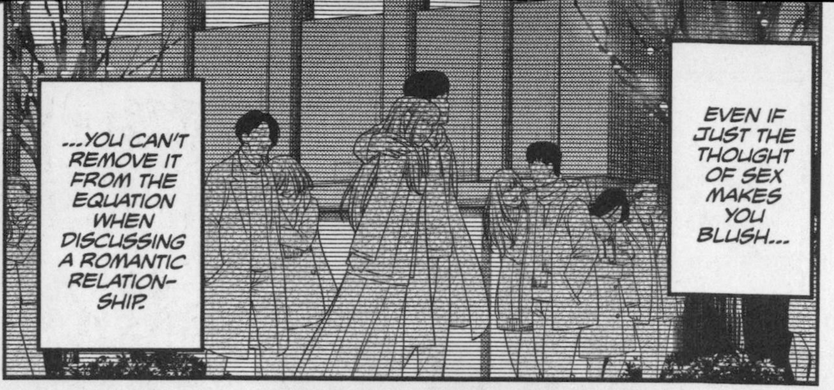
EVEN IF JUST THE THOUGHT OF SEX MAKES YOU BLUSH...
...YOU CAN'T REMOVE IT FROM THE EQUATION WHEN DISCUSSING A ROMANTIC RELATION-SHIP.

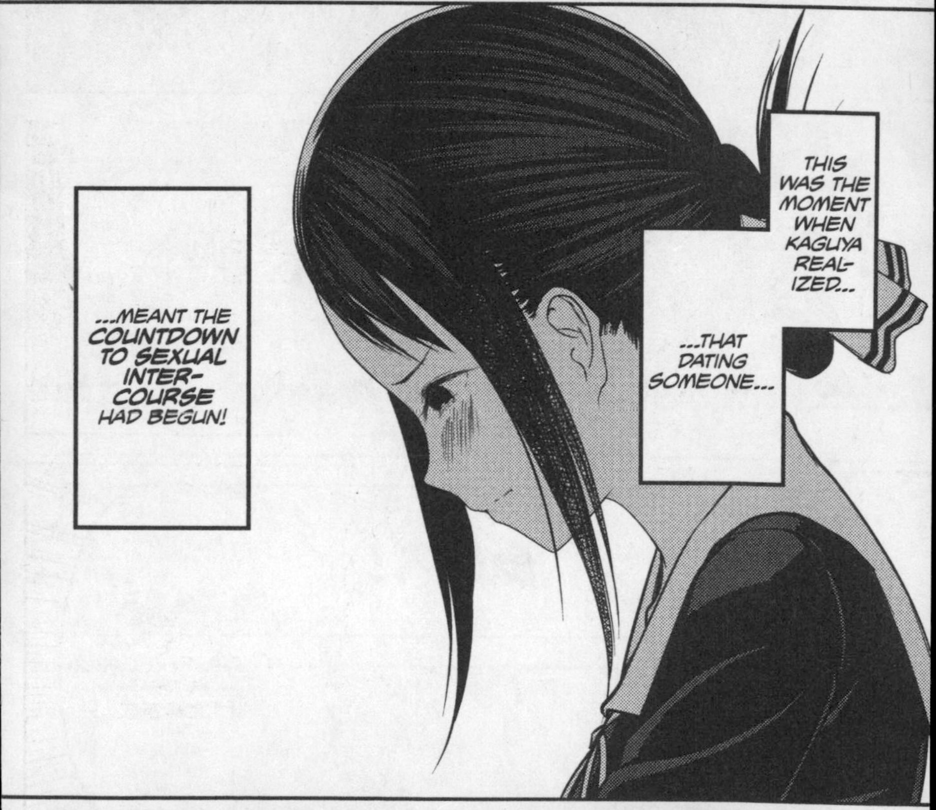
THIS WAS THE MOMENT WHEN KAGUYA REAL-IZED...
...THAT DATING SOMEONE...
...MEANT THE COUNTDOWN TO SEXUAL INTER-COURSE HAD BEGUN!

Battle 169
The ABC's of Lovers, Part 1

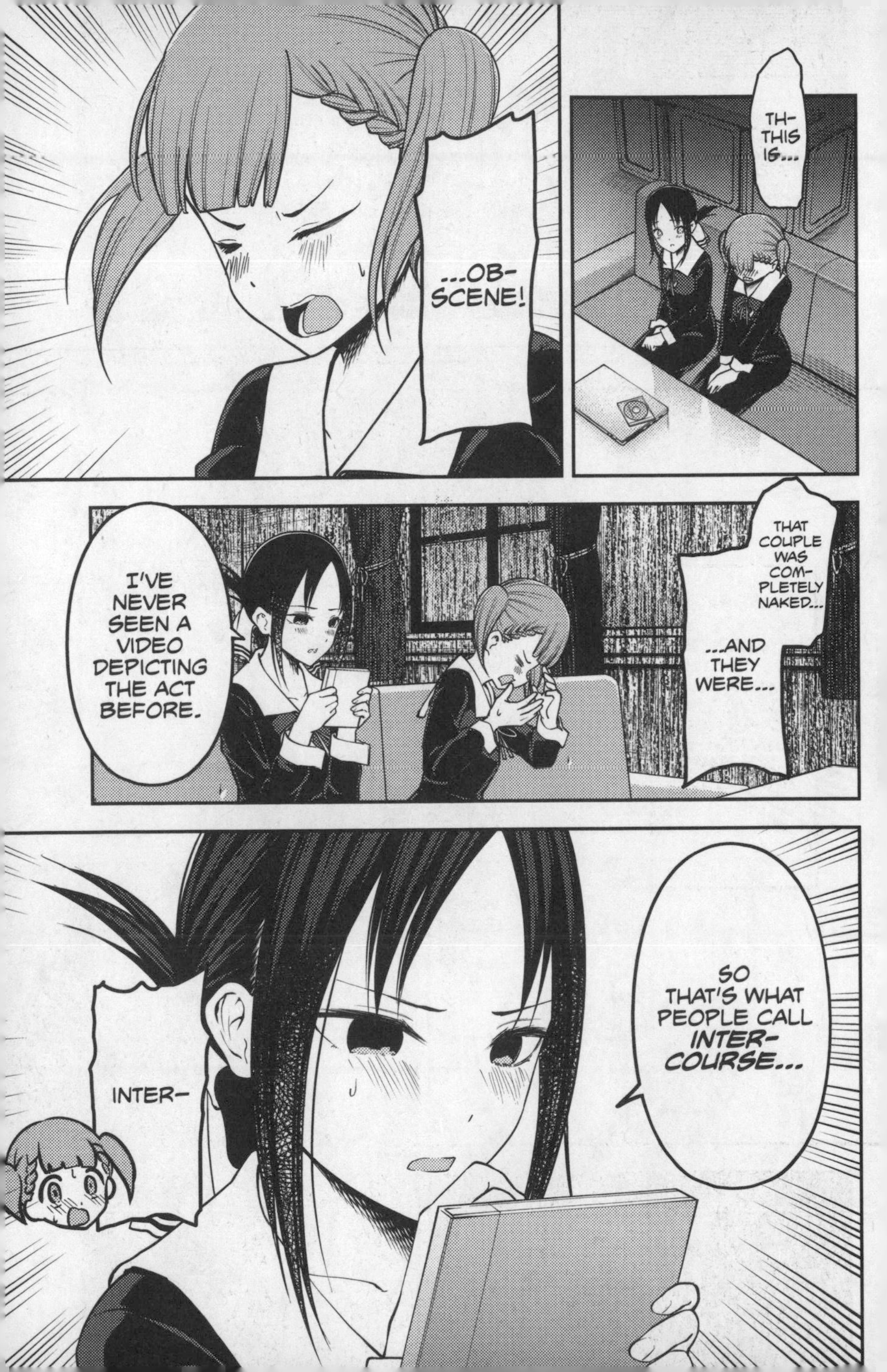
TH- THIS IS...
...OB- SCENE!
THAT COUPLE WAS COM- PLETELY NAKED...
...AND THEY WERE...
I'VE NEVER SEEN A VIDEO DEPICTING THE ACT BEFORE.
SO THAT'S WHAT PEOPLE CALL INTER- COURSE...
INTER-

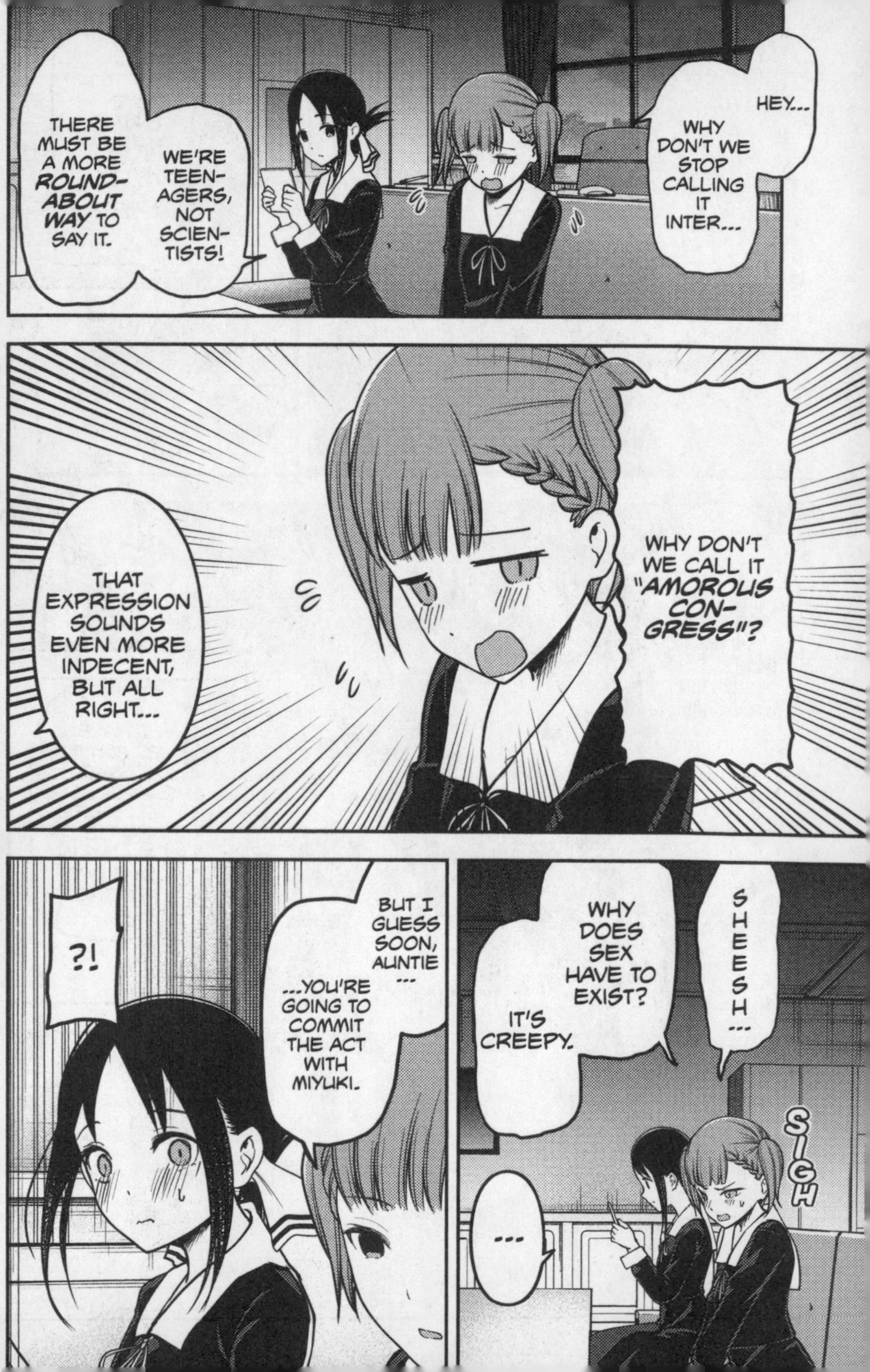
HEY...
WHY DON'T WE STOP CALLING IT INTER...
WE'RE TEEN-AGERS, NOT SCIEN-TISTS!
THERE MUST BE A MORE ROUND-ABOUT WAY TO SAY IT.
WHY DON'T WE CALL IT "AMOROUS CON-GRESS"?
THAT EXPRESSION SOUNDS EVEN MORE INDECENT, BUT ALL RIGHT...
SHEESH...
WHY DOES SEX HAVE TO EXIST?
IT'S CREEPY.
SIGH
...
BUT I GUESS SOON, AUNTIE...
...YOU'RE GOING TO COMMIT THE ACT WITH MIYUKI.
?!

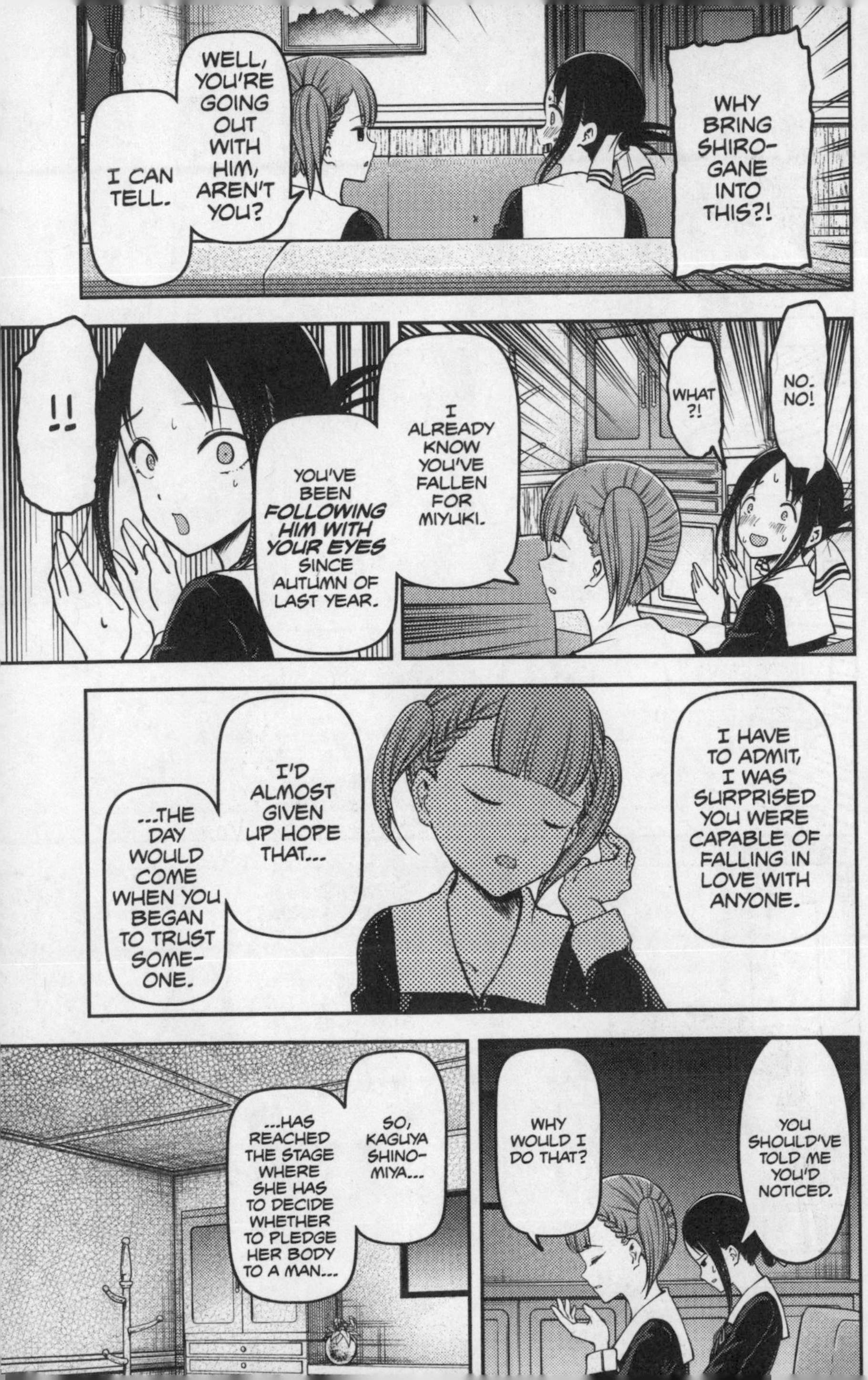
WHY BRING SHIRO-GANE INTO THIS?!
WELL, YOU'RE GOING OUT WITH HIM, AREN'T YOU?
I CAN TELL.
NO. NO!
WHAT?!
I ALREADY KNOW YOU'VE FALLEN FOR MIYUKI.
YOU'VE BEEN *FOLLOWING HIM WITH YOUR EYES* SINCE AUTUMN OF LAST YEAR.
!!
I HAVE TO ADMIT, I WAS SURPRISED YOU WERE CAPABLE OF FALLING IN LOVE WITH ANYONE.
I'D ALMOST GIVEN UP HOPE THAT...
...THE DAY WOULD COME WHEN YOU BEGAN TO TRUST SOME-ONE.
YOU SHOULD'VE TOLD ME YOU'D NOTICED.
WHY WOULD I DO THAT?
SO, KAGUYA SHINO-MIYA...
...HAS REACHED THE STAGE WHERE SHE HAS TO DECIDE WHETHER TO PLEDGE HER BODY TO A MAN...

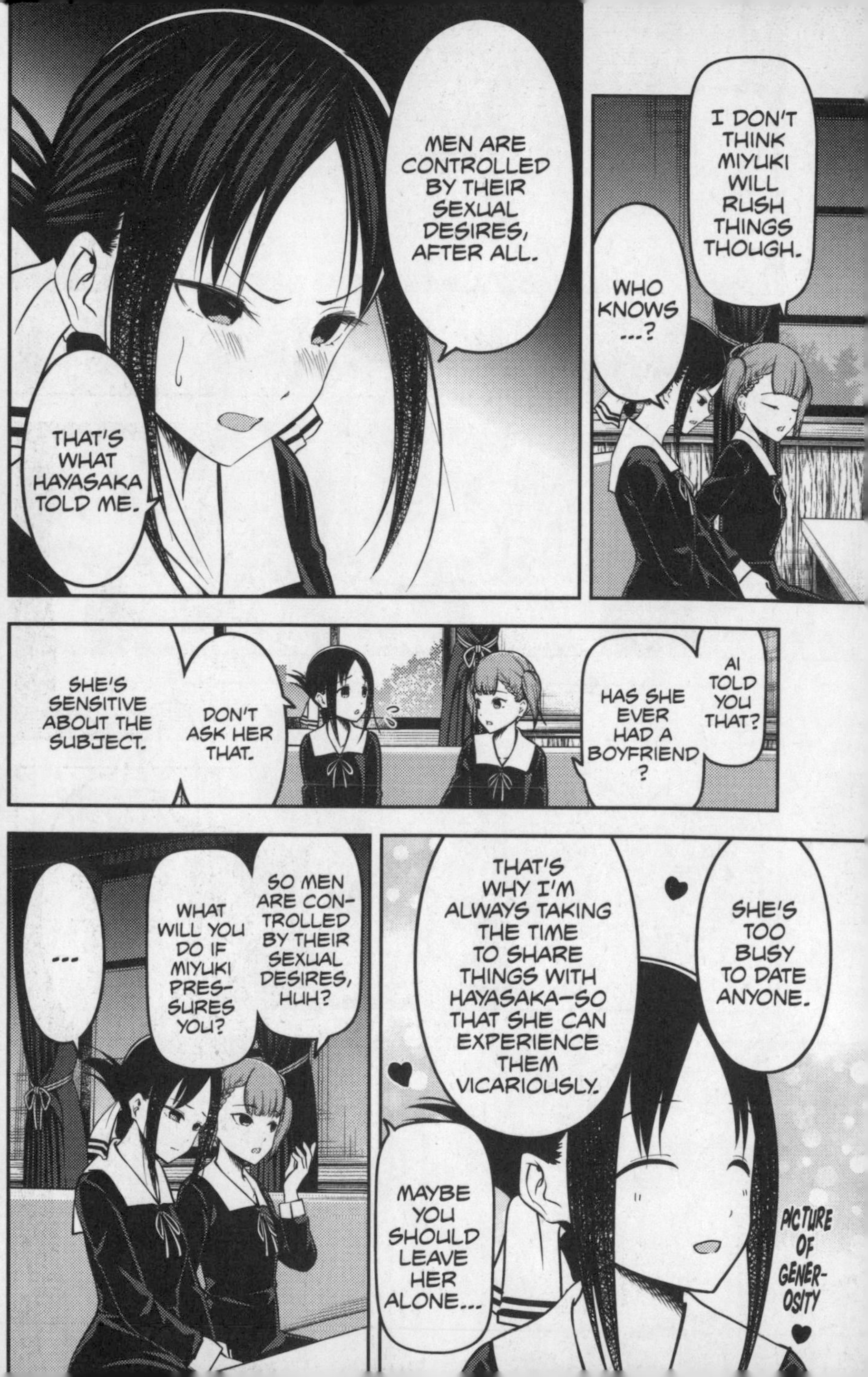
I DON'T THINK MIYUKI WILL RUSH THINGS THOUGH.
WHO KNOWS ...?
MEN ARE CONTROLLED BY THEIR SEXUAL DESIRES, AFTER ALL.
THAT'S WHAT HAYASAKA TOLD ME.
AI TOLD YOU THAT?
HAS SHE EVER HAD A BOYFRIEND?
DON'T ASK HER THAT.
SHE'S SENSITIVE ABOUT THE SUBJECT.
SHE'S TOO BUSY TO DATE ANYONE.
THAT'S WHY I'M ALWAYS TAKING THE TIME TO SHARE THINGS WITH HAYASAKA—SO THAT SHE CAN EXPERIENCE THEM VICARIOUSLY.
PICTURE OF GENEROSITY
MAYBE YOU SHOULD LEAVE HER ALONE...
SO MEN ARE CONTROLLED BY THEIR SEXUAL DESIRES, HUH?
WHAT WILL YOU DO IF MIYUKI PRESSURES YOU?
...

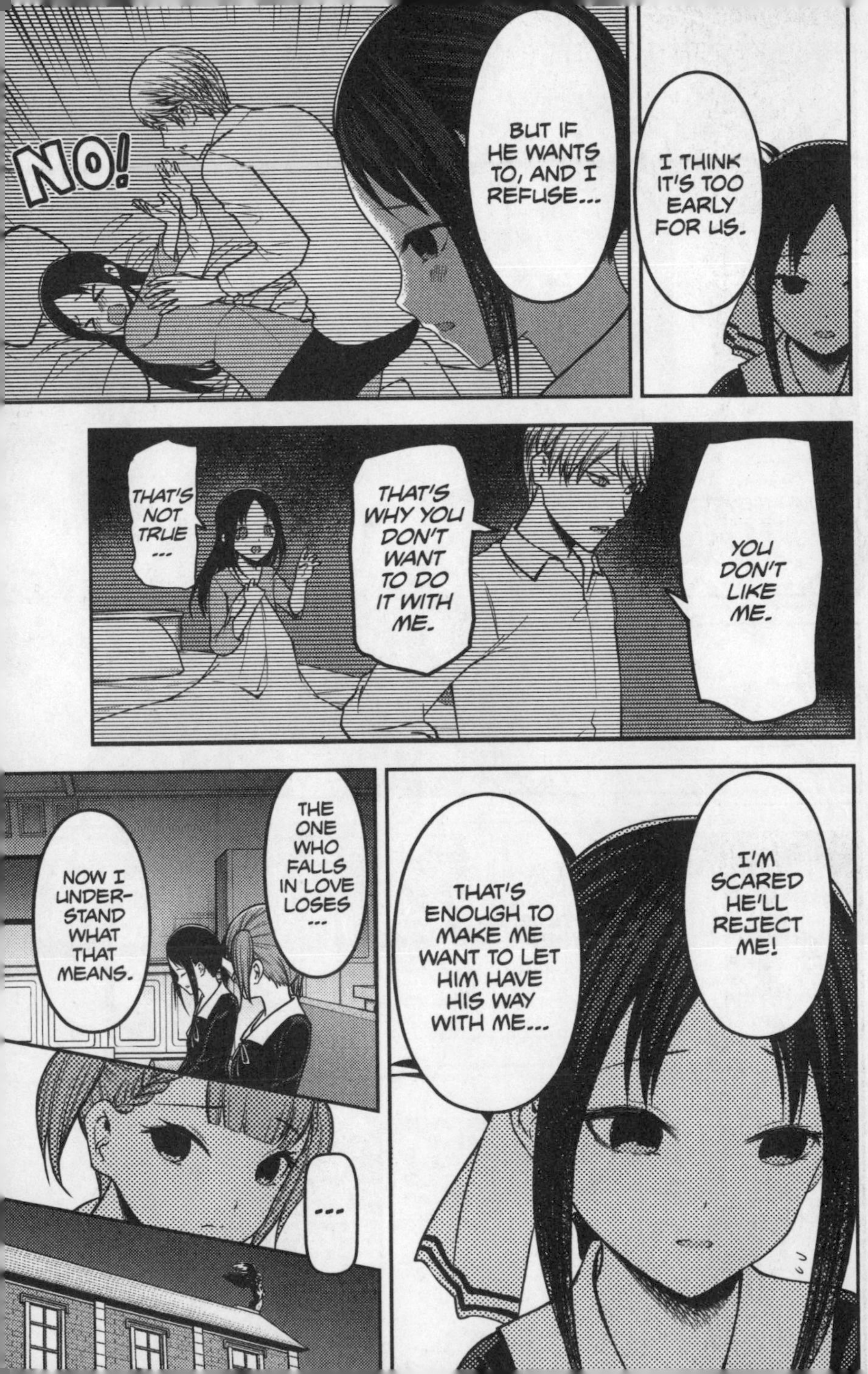
I THINK IT'S TOO EARLY FOR US.
BUT IF HE WANTS TO, AND I REFUSE...
NO!
YOU DON'T LIKE ME.
THAT'S WHY YOU DON'T WANT TO DO IT WITH ME.
THAT'S NOT TRUE ...
I'M SCARED HE'LL REJECT ME!
THAT'S ENOUGH TO MAKE ME WANT TO LET HIM HAVE HIS WAY WITH ME...
THE ONE WHO FALLS IN LOVE LOSES ...
NOW I UNDER-STAND WHAT THAT MEANS.
...

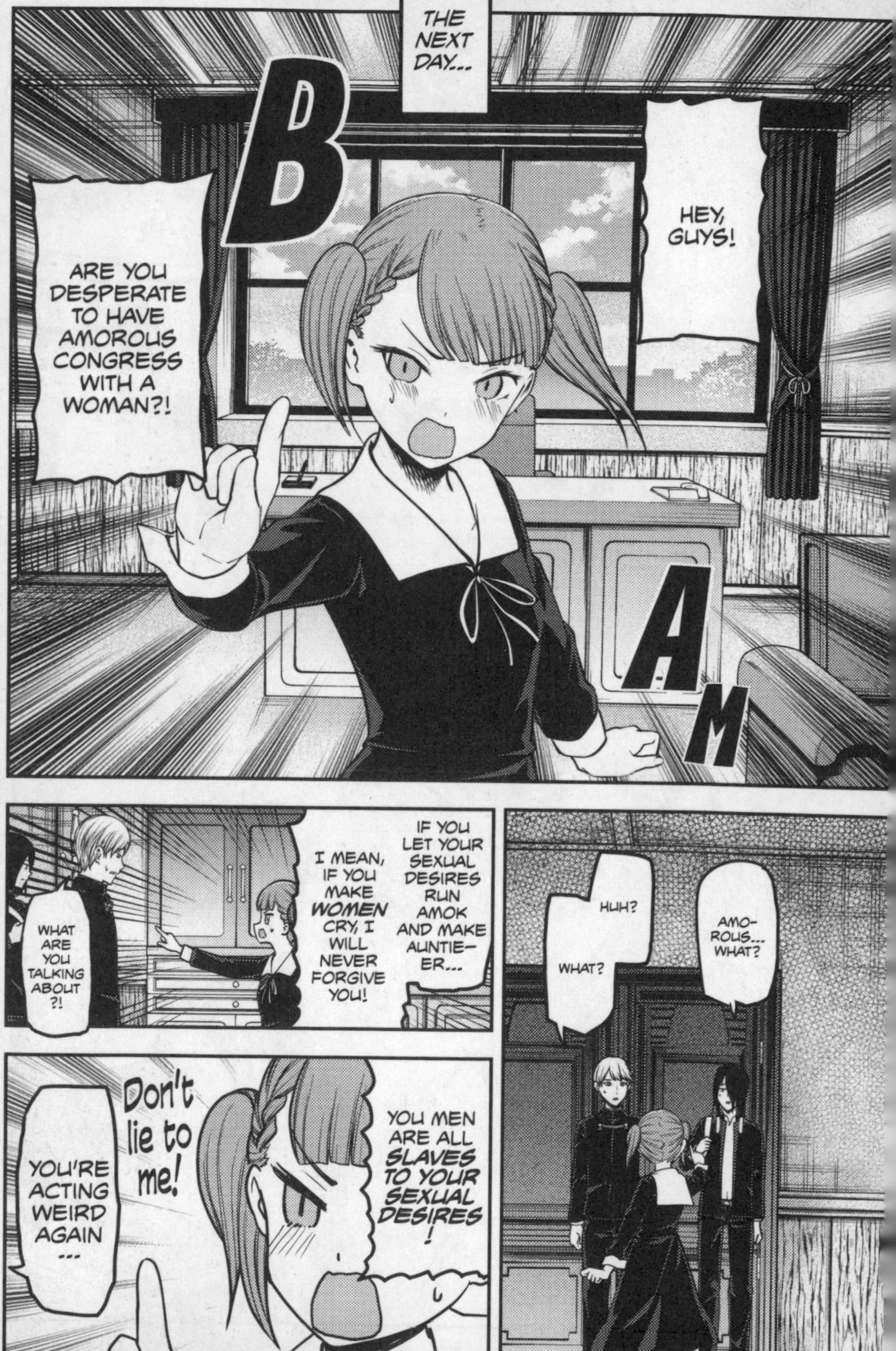
THE NEXT DAY...
HEY, GUYS!
BAM
ARE YOU DESPERATE TO HAVE AMOROUS CONGRESS WITH A WOMAN?!
AMOROUS... WHAT?
HUH?
WHAT?
IF YOU LET YOUR SEXUAL DESIRES RUN AMOK AND MAKE AUNTIE— ER...
I MEAN, IF YOU MAKE WOMEN CRY, I WILL NEVER FORGIVE YOU!
WHAT ARE YOU TALKING ABOUT?!
YOU MEN ARE ALL SLAVES TO YOUR SEXUAL DESIRES!
Don't lie to me!
YOU'RE ACTING WEIRD AGAIN...

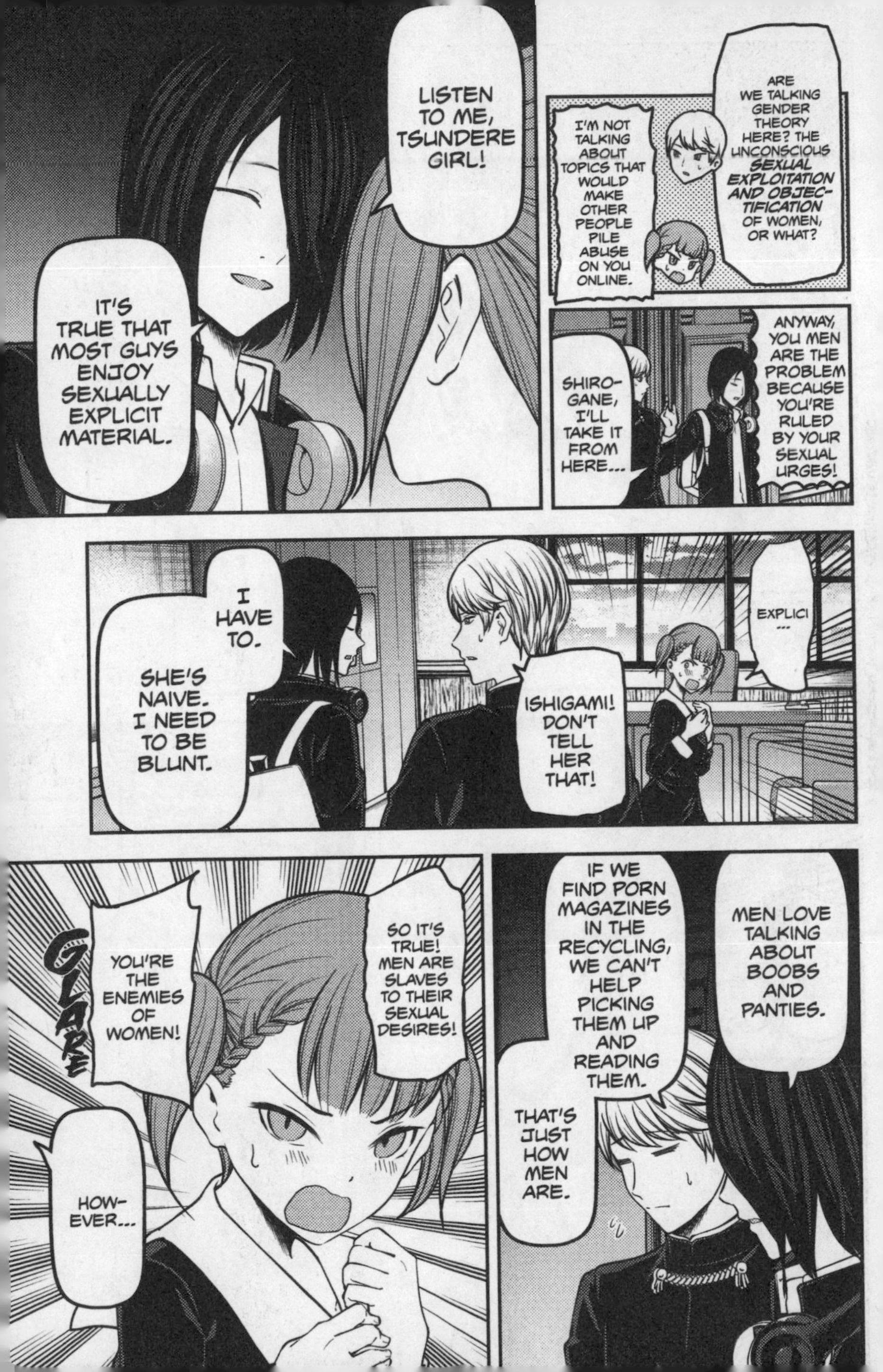

ARE WE TALKING GENDER THEORY HERE? THE UNCONSCIOUS ***SEXUAL EXPLOITATION AND OBJECTIFICATION*** OF WOMEN, OR WHAT?
I'M NOT TALKING ABOUT TOPICS THAT WOULD MAKE OTHER PEOPLE PILE ABUSE ON YOU ONLINE.
ANYWAY, YOU MEN ARE THE PROBLEM BECAUSE YOU'RE RULED BY YOUR SEXUAL URGES!
SHIROGANE, I'LL TAKE IT FROM HERE...
LISTEN TO ME, TSUNDERE GIRL!
IT'S TRUE THAT MOST GUYS ENJOY SEXUALLY EXPLICIT MATERIAL.
EXPLICI...
ISHIGAMI! DON'T TELL HER THAT!
I HAVE TO.
SHE'S NAIVE. I NEED TO BE BLUNT.
MEN LOVE TALKING ABOUT BOOBS AND PANTIES.
IF WE FIND PORN MAGAZINES IN THE RECYCLING, WE CAN'T HELP PICKING THEM UP AND READING THEM.
THAT'S JUST HOW MEN ARE.
SO IT'S TRUE! MEN ARE SLAVES TO THEIR SEXUAL DESIRES!
GLARE
YOU'RE THE ENEMIES OF WOMEN!
HOW-EVER...

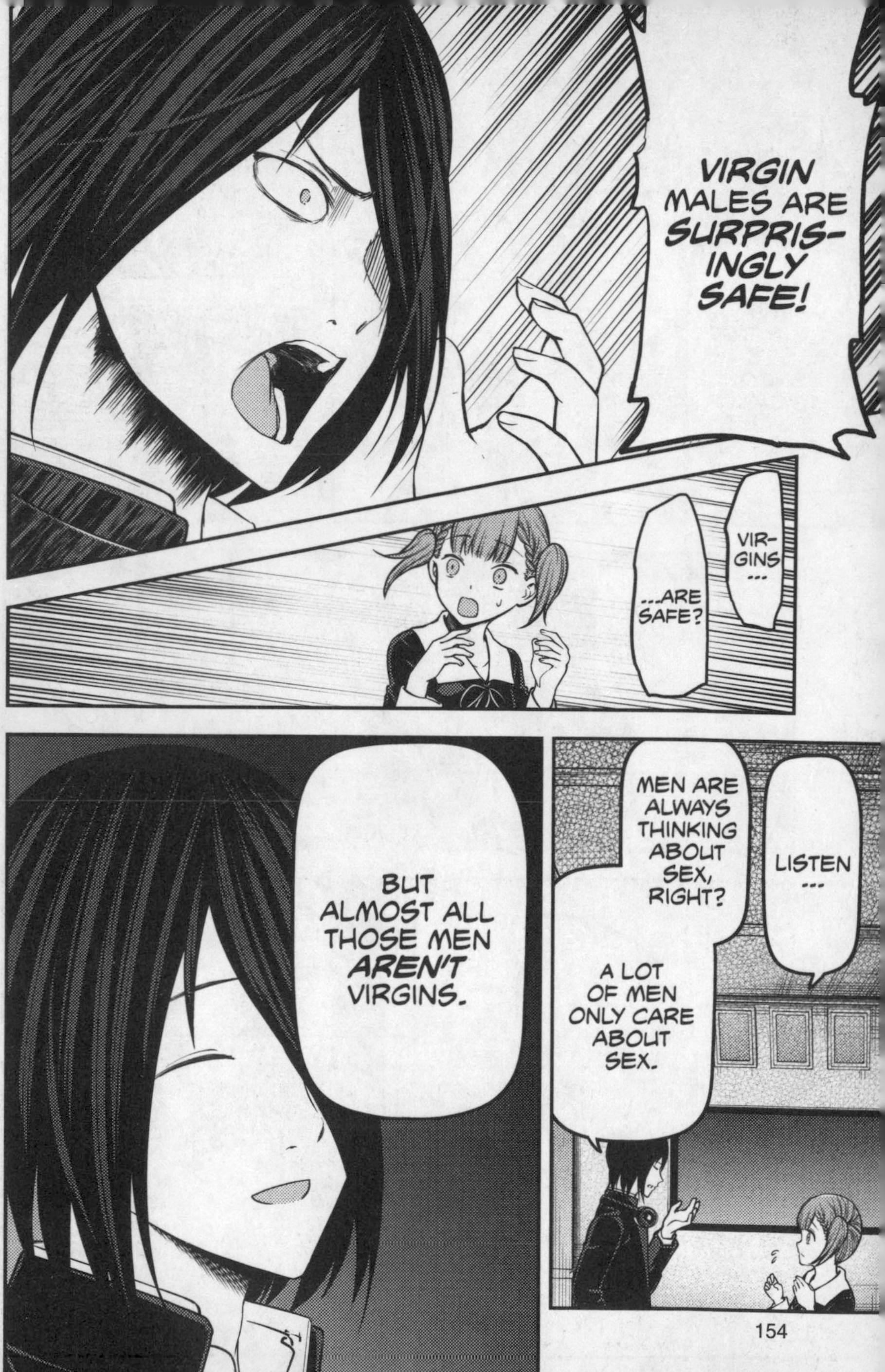
VIRGIN MALES ARE SURPRIS-INGLY SAFE!
VIR-GINS...
...ARE SAFE?
LISTEN...
MEN ARE ALWAYS THINKING ABOUT SEX, RIGHT?
A LOT OF MEN ONLY CARE ABOUT SEX.
BUT ALMOST ALL THOSE MEN AREN'T VIRGINS.

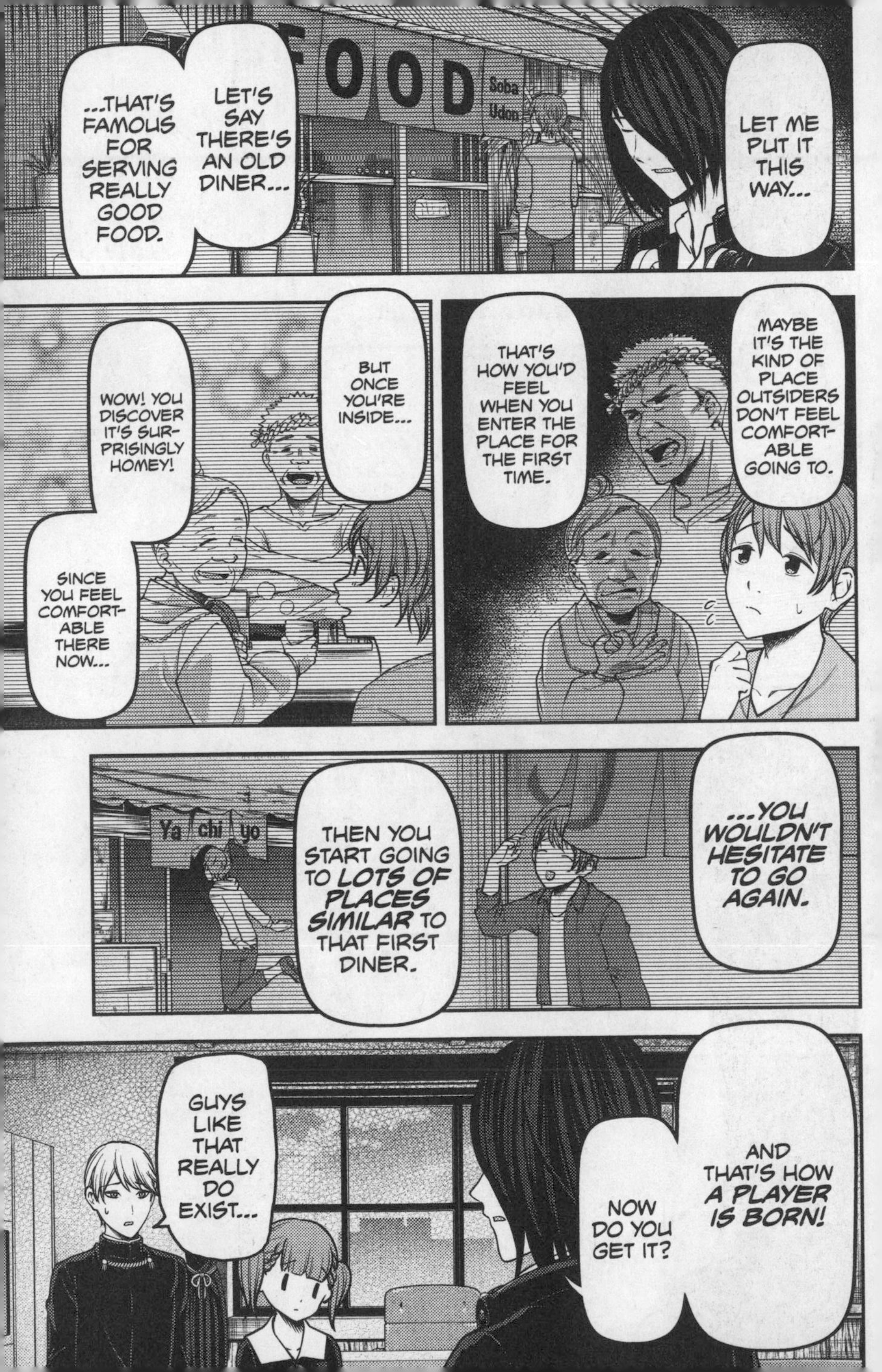
LET ME PUT IT THIS WAY...
FOOD
Soba Udon
LET'S SAY THERE'S AN OLD DINER...
...THAT'S FAMOUS FOR SERVING REALLY GOOD FOOD.
MAYBE IT'S THE KIND OF PLACE OUTSIDERS DON'T FEEL COMFORTABLE GOING TO.
THAT'S HOW YOU'D FEEL WHEN YOU ENTER THE PLACE FOR THE FIRST TIME.
BUT ONCE YOU'RE INSIDE...
WOW! YOU DISCOVER IT'S SURPRISINGLY HOMEY!
SINCE YOU FEEL COMFORTABLE THERE NOW...
...YOU WOULDN'T HESITATE TO GO AGAIN.
THEN YOU START GOING TO LOTS OF PLACES SIMILAR TO THAT FIRST DINER.
Ya chi yo
AND THAT'S HOW A PLAYER IS BORN!
NOW DO YOU GET IT?
GUYS LIKE THAT REALLY DO EXIST...

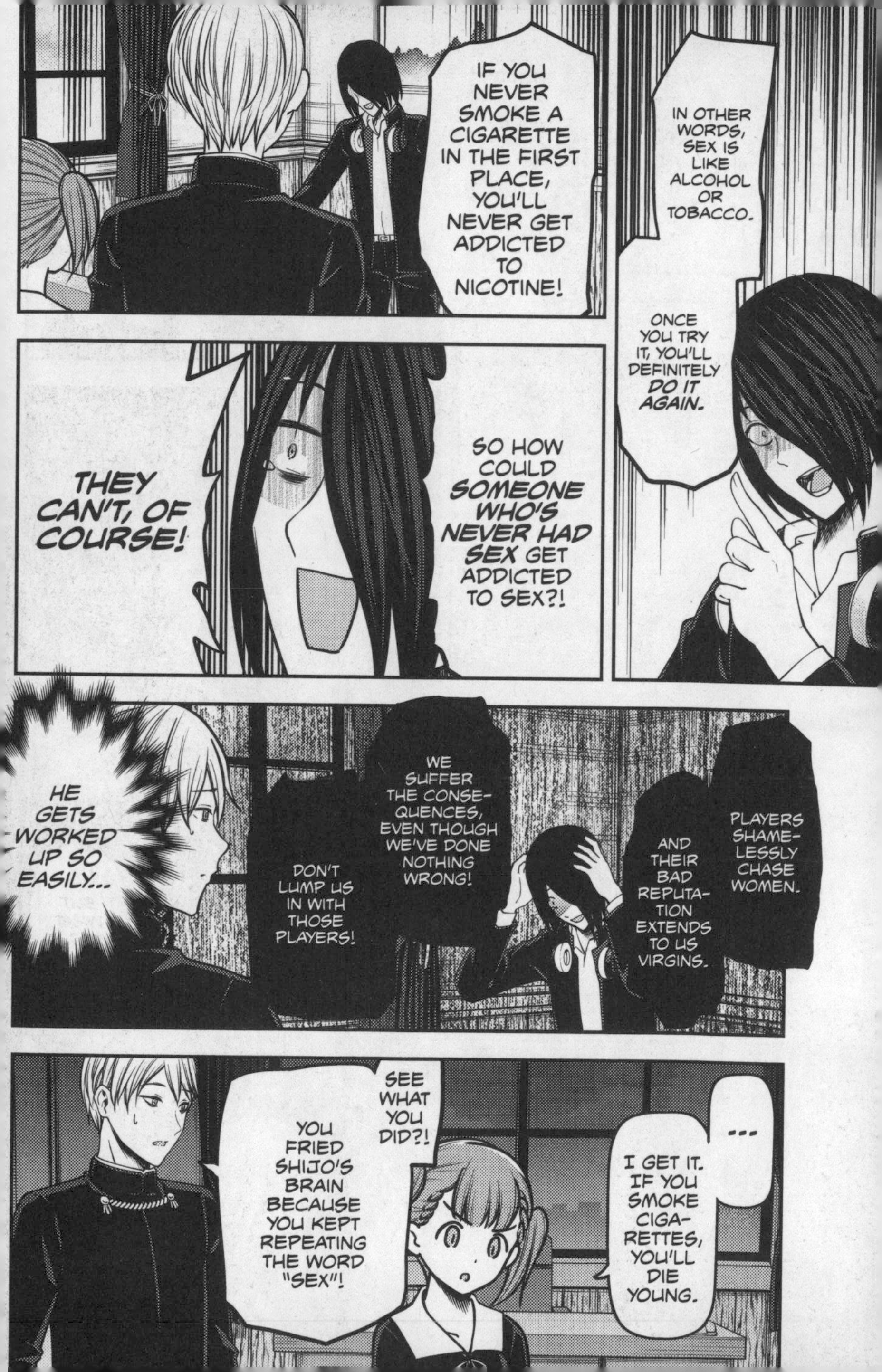
IN OTHER WORDS, SEX IS LIKE ALCOHOL OR TOBACCO.
ONCE YOU TRY IT, YOU'LL DEFINITELY DO IT AGAIN.
IF YOU NEVER SMOKE A CIGARETTE IN THE FIRST PLACE, YOU'LL NEVER GET ADDICTED TO NICOTINE!
SO HOW COULD SOMEONE WHO'S NEVER HAD SEX GET ADDICTED TO SEX?!
THEY CAN'T, OF COURSE!
PLAYERS SHAMELESSLY CHASE WOMEN.
AND THEIR BAD REPUTATION EXTENDS TO US VIRGINS.
WE SUFFER THE CONSEQUENCES, EVEN THOUGH WE'VE DONE NOTHING WRONG!
DON'T LUMP US IN WITH THOSE PLAYERS!
HE GETS WORKED UP SO EASILY...
...
I GET IT. IF YOU SMOKE CIGARETTES, YOU'LL DIE YOUNG.
SEE WHAT YOU DID?!
YOU FRIED SHIJO'S BRAIN BECAUSE YOU KEPT REPEATING THE WORD "SEX"!

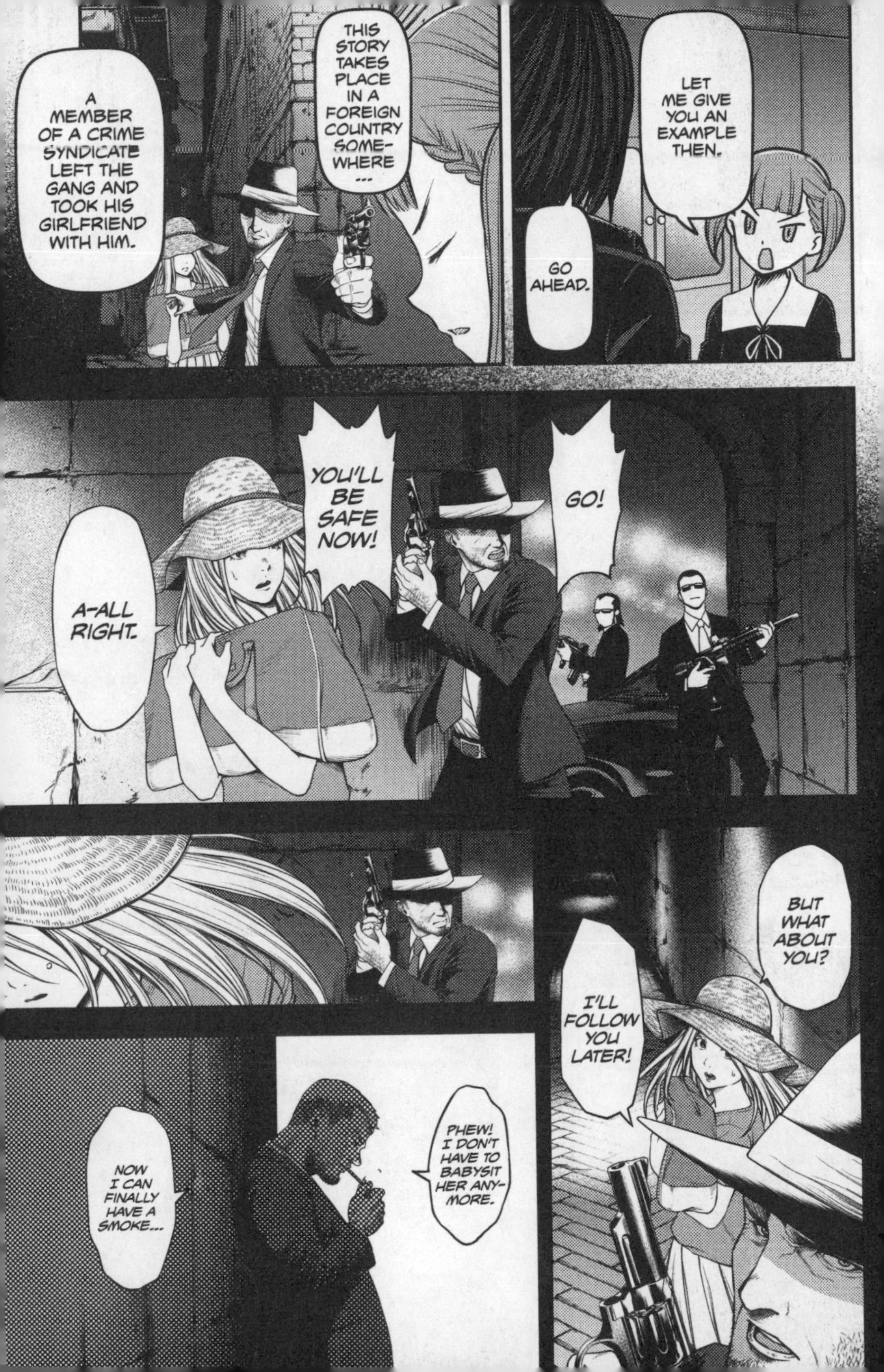
LET ME GIVE YOU AN EXAMPLE THEN.
GO AHEAD.
THIS STORY TAKES PLACE IN A FOREIGN COUNTRY SOMEWHERE...
A MEMBER OF A CRIME SYNDICATE LEFT THE GANG AND TOOK HIS GIRLFRIEND WITH HIM.
GO!
YOU'LL BE SAFE NOW!
A-ALL RIGHT.
BUT WHAT ABOUT YOU?
I'LL FOLLOW YOU LATER!
PHEW! I DON'T HAVE TO BABYSIT HER ANYMORE.
NOW I CAN FINALLY HAVE A SMOKE...

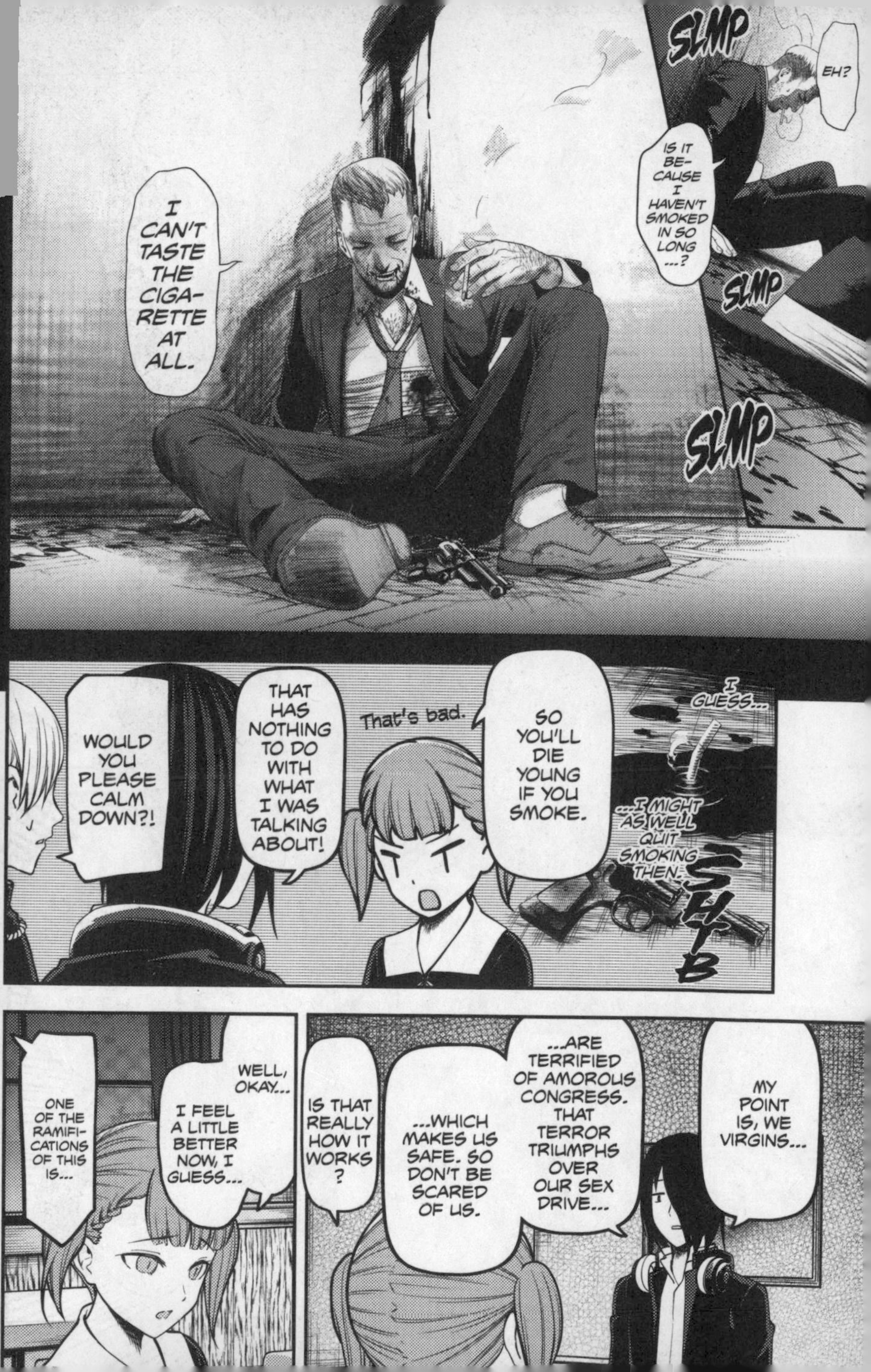
SLMP
EH?
IS IT BECAUSE I HAVEN'T SMOKED IN SO LONG...?
SLMP
SLMP
I CAN'T TASTE THE CIGARETTE AT ALL.
I GUESS...
...I MIGHT AS WELL QUIT SMOKING THEN.
SHB
SO YOU'LL DIE YOUNG IF YOU SMOKE.
That's bad.
THAT HAS NOTHING TO DO WITH WHAT I WAS TALKING ABOUT!
WOULD YOU PLEASE CALM DOWN?!
MY POINT IS, WE VIRGINS...
...ARE TERRIFIED OF AMOROUS CONGRESS. THAT TERROR TRIUMPHS OVER OUR SEX DRIVE...
...WHICH MAKES US SAFE. SO DON'T BE SCARED OF US.
IS THAT REALLY HOW IT WORKS?
WELL, OKAY...
I FEEL A LITTLE BETTER NOW, I GUESS...
ONE OF THE RAMIFICATIONS OF THIS IS...

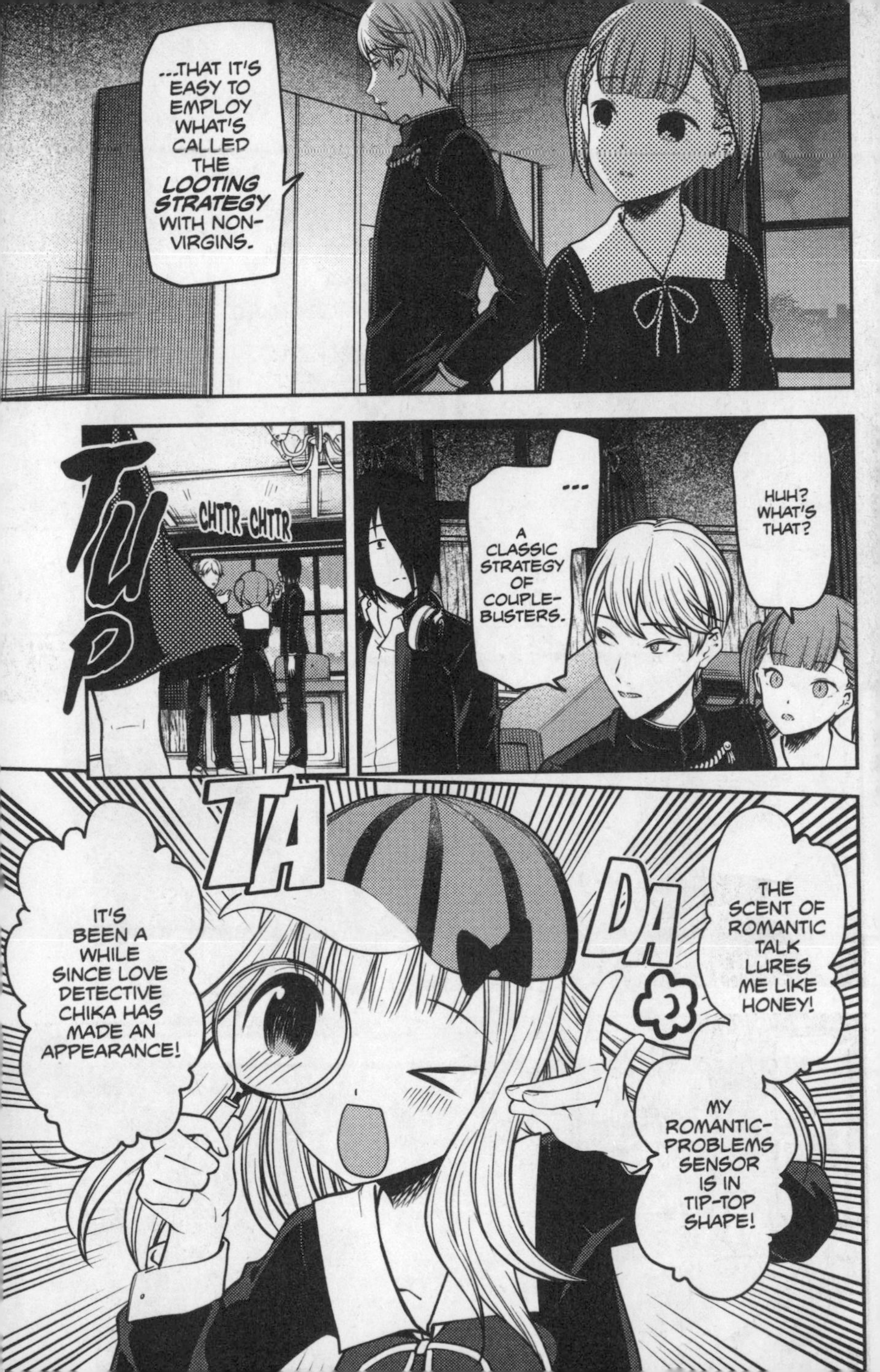
...THAT IT'S EASY TO EMPLOY WHAT'S CALLED THE *LOOTING STRATEGY* WITH NON-VIRGINS.
HUH? WHAT'S THAT?
...
A CLASSIC STRATEGY OF COUPLE-BUSTERS.
TUP
CHTTR-CHTTR
TA
THE SCENT OF ROMANTIC TALK LURES ME LIKE HONEY!
DA
IT'S BEEN A WHILE SINCE LOVE DETECTIVE CHIKA HAS MADE AN APPEARANCE!
MY ROMANTIC-PROBLEMS SENSOR IS IN TIP-TOP SHAPE!

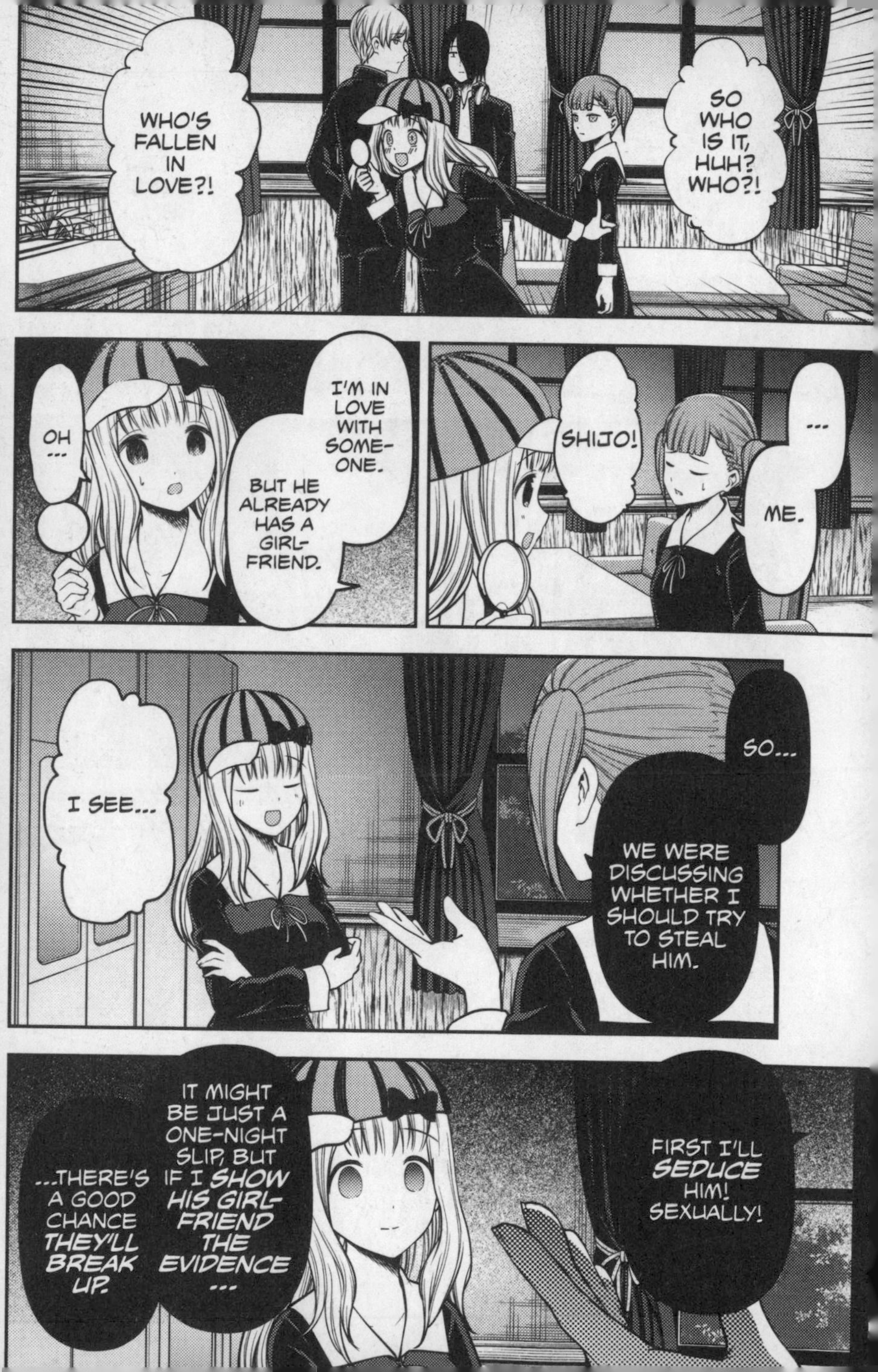
SO WHO IS IT, HUH? WHO?!
WHO'S FALLEN IN LOVE?!
... ME.
SHIJO!
I'M IN LOVE WITH SOMEONE.
BUT HE ALREADY HAS A GIRLFRIEND.
OH...
SO...
WE WERE DISCUSSING WHETHER I SHOULD TRY TO STEAL HIM.
I SEE...
FIRST I'LL *SEDUCE* HIM! SEXUALLY!
IT MIGHT BE JUST A ONE-NIGHT SLIP, BUT IF I *SHOW HIS GIRLFRIEND THE EVIDENCE*...
...THERE'S A GOOD CHANCE *THEY'LL BREAK UP.*

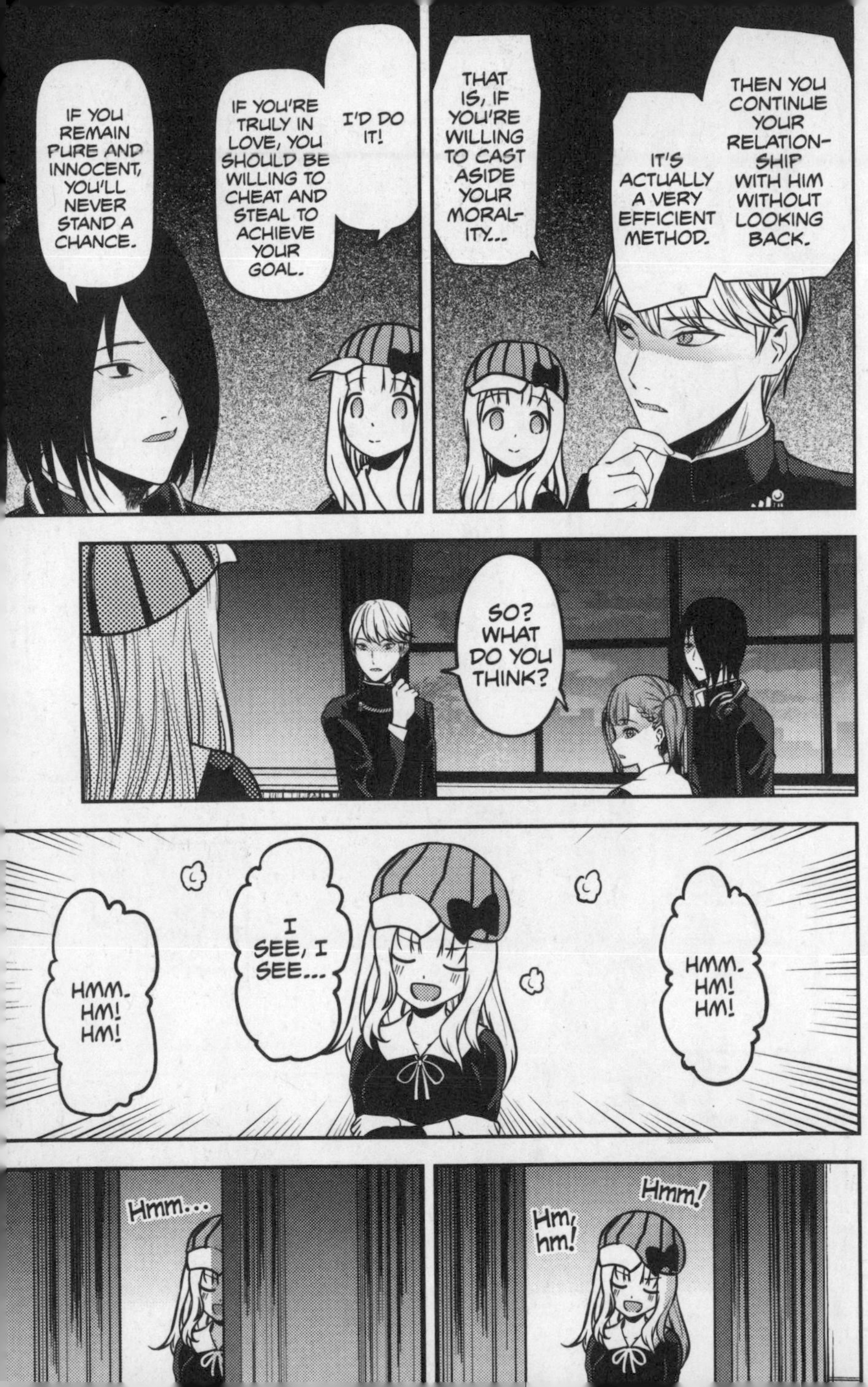
THEN YOU CONTINUE YOUR RELATIONSHIP WITH HIM WITHOUT LOOKING BACK.
IT'S ACTUALLY A VERY EFFICIENT METHOD.
THAT IS, IF YOU'RE WILLING TO CAST ASIDE YOUR MORALITY...
I'D DO IT!
IF YOU'RE TRULY IN LOVE, YOU SHOULD BE WILLING TO CHEAT AND STEAL TO ACHIEVE YOUR GOAL.
IF YOU REMAIN PURE AND INNOCENT, YOU'LL NEVER STAND A CHANCE.
SO? WHAT DO YOU THINK?
HMM. HM! HM!
I SEE, I SEE...
HMM. HM! HM!
Hmm!
Hm, hm!
Hmm...

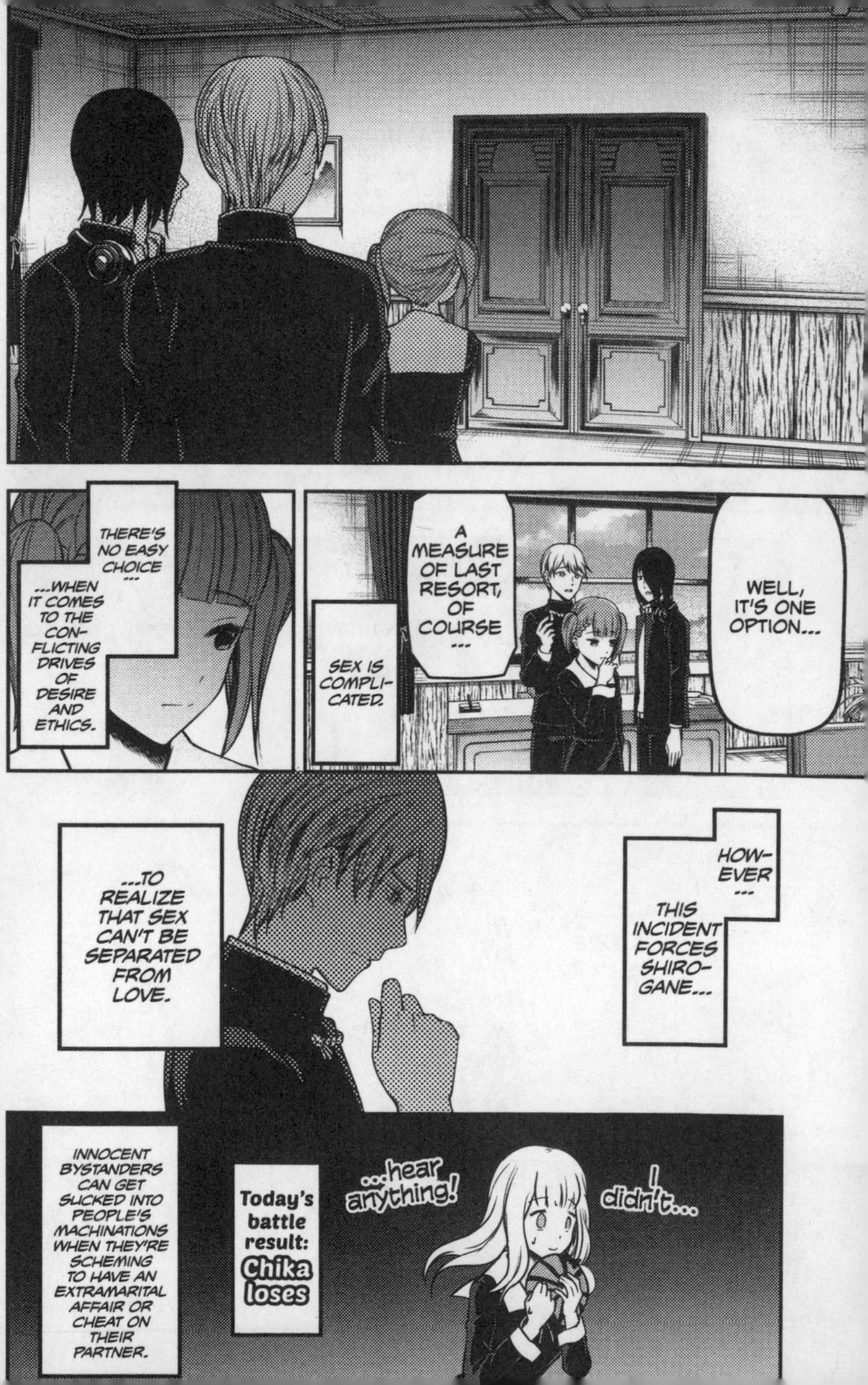
WELL, IT'S ONE OPTION...
A MEASURE OF LAST RESORT, OF COURSE...
SEX IS COMPLICATED.
THERE'S NO EASY CHOICE...
...WHEN IT COMES TO THE CONFLICTING DRIVES OF DESIRE AND ETHICS.
HOWEVER...
THIS INCIDENT FORCES SHIROGANE...
...TO REALIZE THAT SEX CAN'T BE SEPARATED FROM LOVE.
I didn't...
...hear anything!
Today's battle result: Chika loses
INNOCENT BYSTANDERS CAN GET SUCKED INTO PEOPLE'S MACHINATIONS WHEN THEY'RE SCHEMING TO HAVE AN EXTRAMARITAL AFFAIR OR CHEAT ON THEIR PARTNER.

A. I
THINK
IT IS.

Q. ISN'T
THE
STORY
GETTING
A LITTLE
TOO
PRURIENT
?

Sexy Candy
The Sweet Fingers
of My Subordinate

amami

KAGUYA-SAMA

LOVE IS WAR

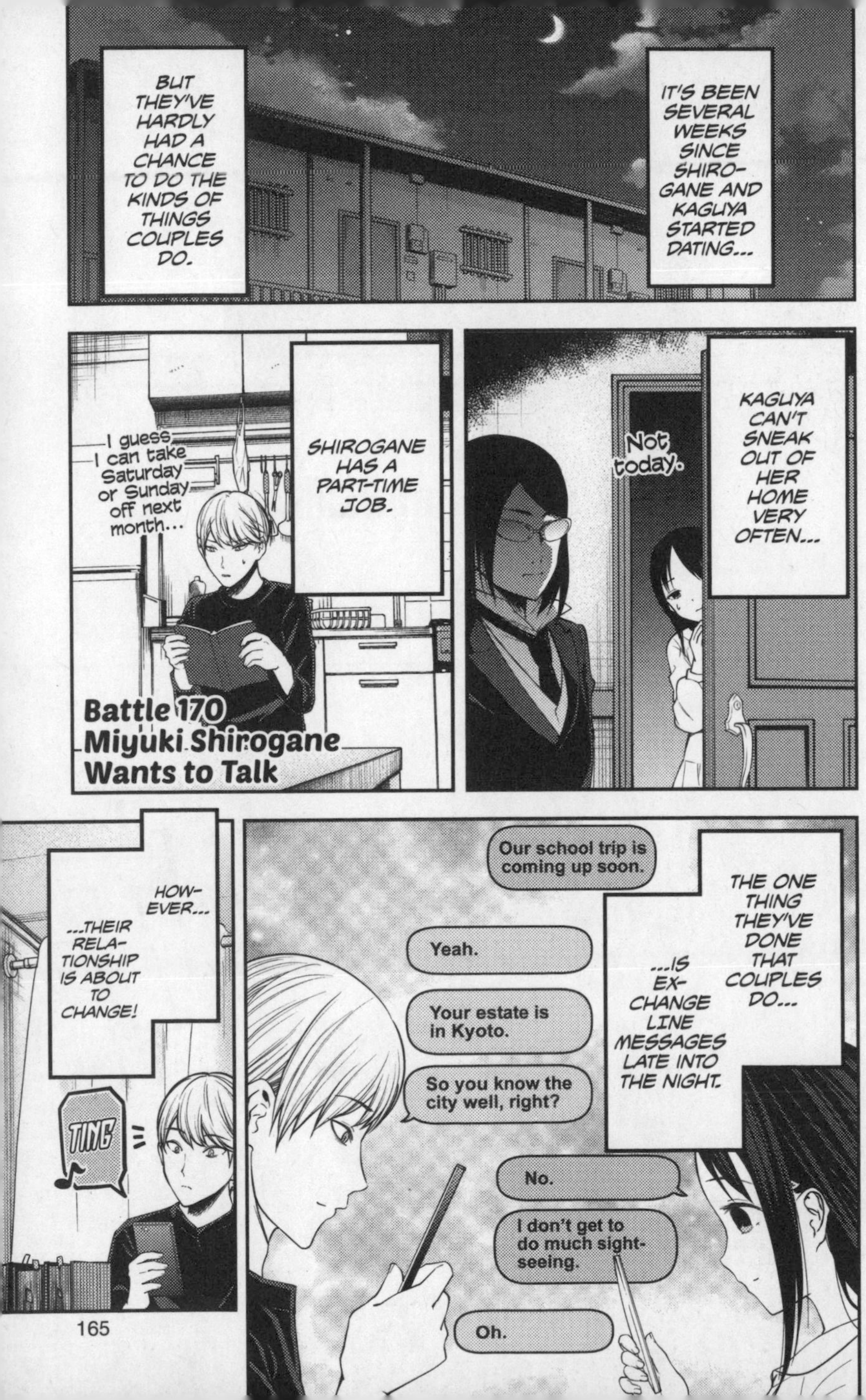
IT'S BEEN SEVERAL WEEKS SINCE SHIROGANE AND KAGUYA STARTED DATING...
BUT THEY'VE HARDLY HAD A CHANCE TO DO THE KINDS OF THINGS COUPLES DO.
KAGUYA CAN'T SNEAK OUT OF HER HOME VERY OFTEN...
Not today.
SHIROGANE HAS A PART-TIME JOB.
I guess I can take Saturday or Sunday off next month...
Battle 170 Miyuki Shirogane Wants to Talk
THE ONE THING THEY'VE DONE THAT COUPLES DO...
...IS EXCHANGE LINE MESSAGES LATE INTO THE NIGHT.
Our school trip is coming up soon.
Yeah.
Your estate is in Kyoto.
So you know the city well, right?
No.
I don't get to do much sightseeing.
Oh.
HOWEVER...
...THEIR RELATIONSHIP IS ABOUT TO CHANGE!
TING

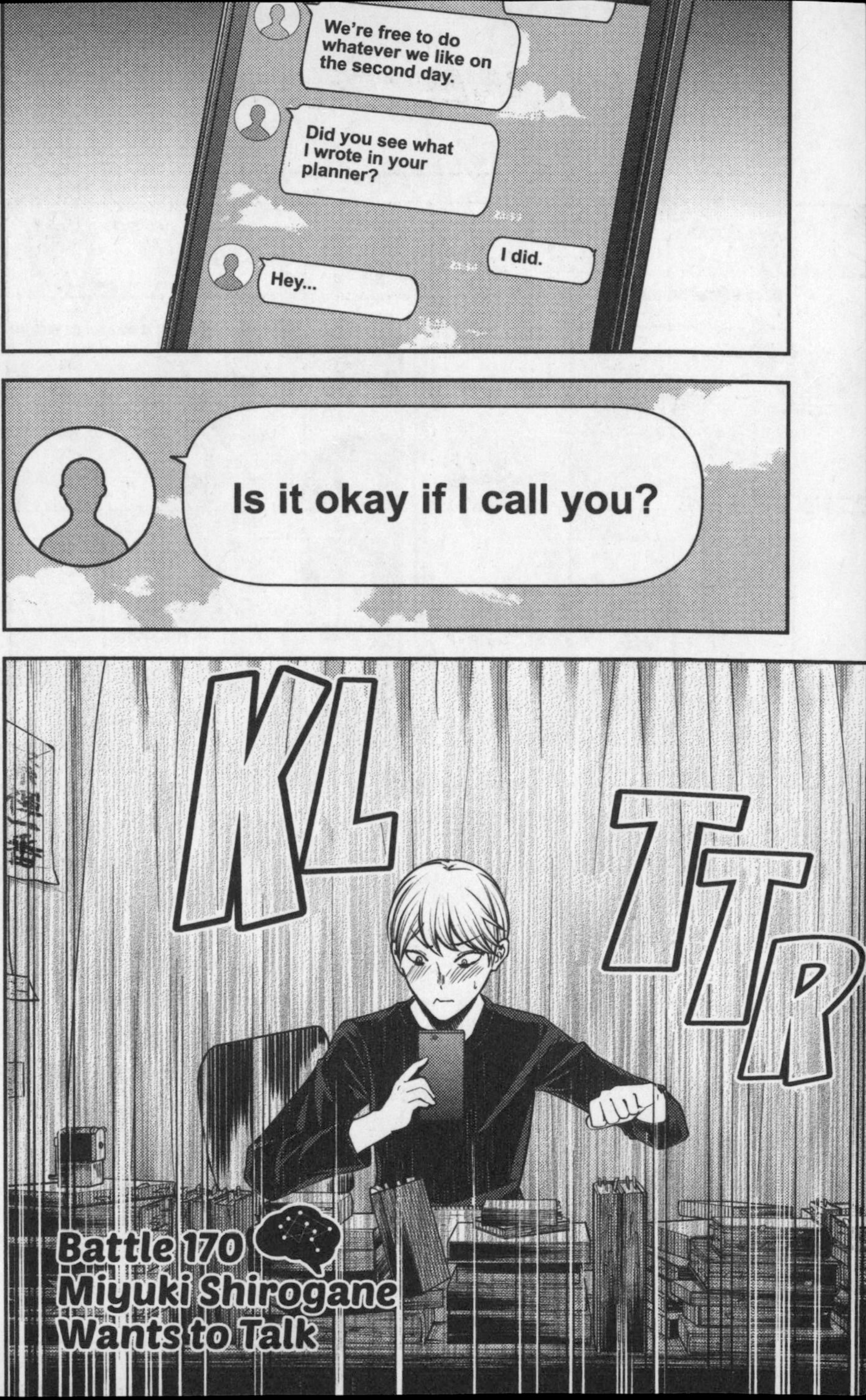
We're free to do whatever we like on the second day.
Did you see what I wrote in your planner?
I did.
Hey...
Is it okay if I call you?
KLTTR
Battle 170
Miyuki Shirogane Wants to Talk

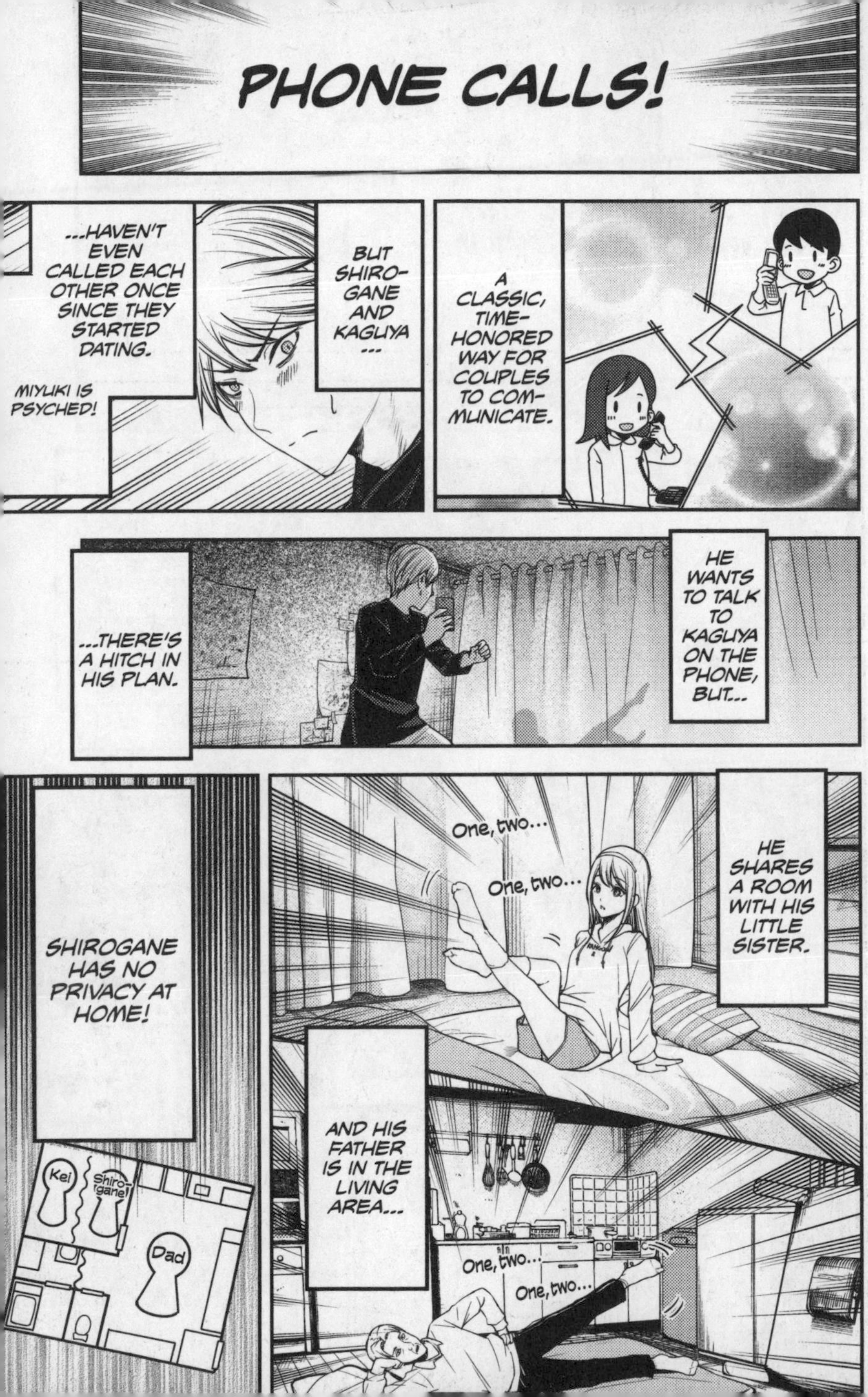
PHONE CALLS!
A CLASSIC, TIME-HONORED WAY FOR COUPLES TO COMMUNICATE.
BUT SHIROGANE AND KAGUYA ...
...HAVEN'T EVEN CALLED EACH OTHER ONCE SINCE THEY STARTED DATING.
MIYUKI IS PSYCHED!
HE WANTS TO TALK TO KAGUYA ON THE PHONE, BUT...
...THERE'S A HITCH IN HIS PLAN.
HE SHARES A ROOM WITH HIS LITTLE SISTER.
One, two...
One, two...
AND HIS FATHER IS IN THE LIVING AREA...
One, two...
One, two...
SHIROGANE HAS NO PRIVACY AT HOME!
Kei
Shirogane
Dad

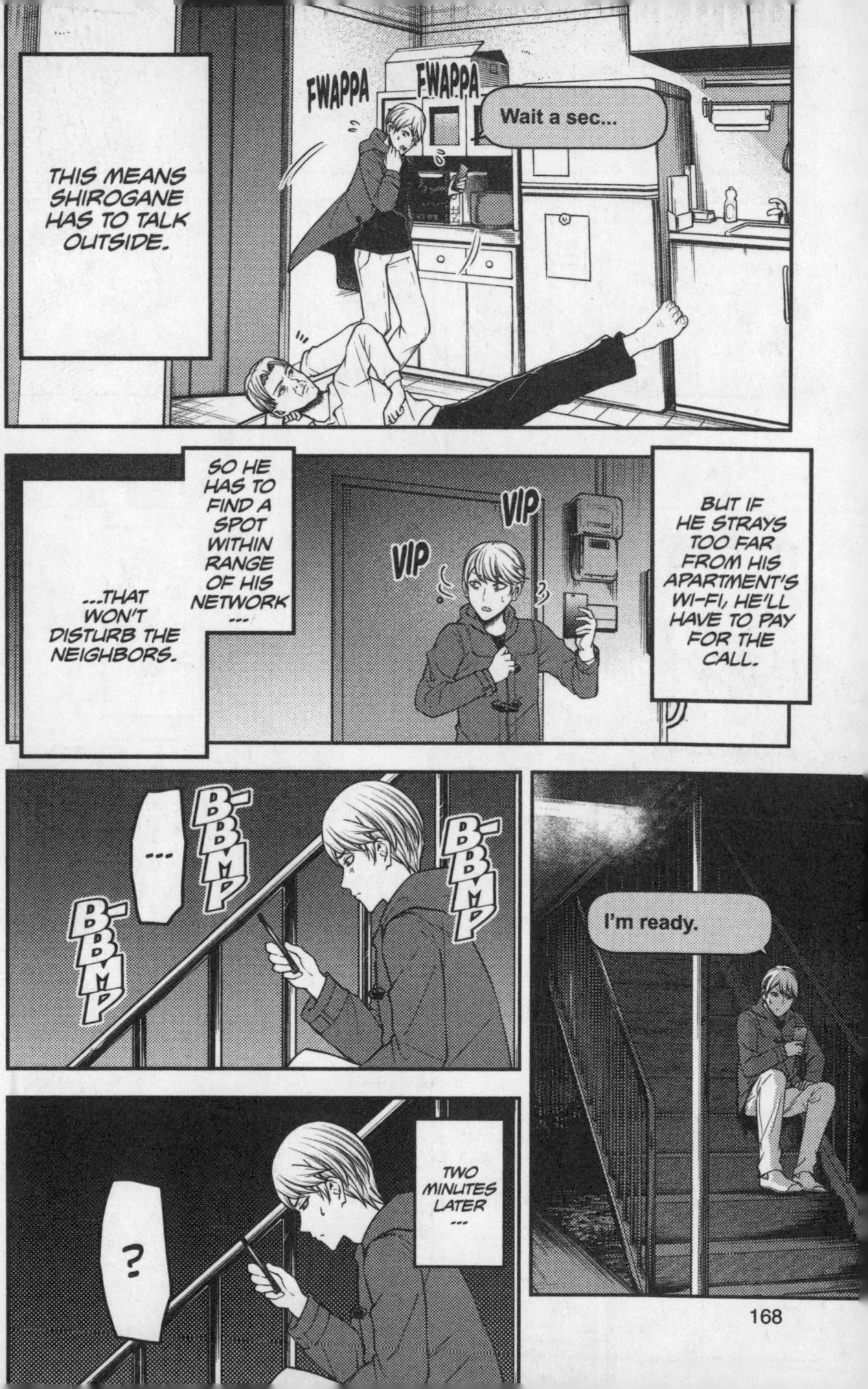
Wait a sec...
FWAPPA
FWAPPA
THIS MEANS SHIROGANE HAS TO TALK OUTSIDE.
BUT IF HE STRAYS TOO FAR FROM HIS APARTMENT'S WI-FI, HE'LL HAVE TO PAY FOR THE CALL.
VIP
VIP
SO HE HAS TO FIND A SPOT WITHIN RANGE OF HIS NETWORK...
...THAT WON'T DISTURB THE NEIGHBORS.
I'm ready.
B-BBMP
...
B-BBMP
TWO MINUTES LATER...
?

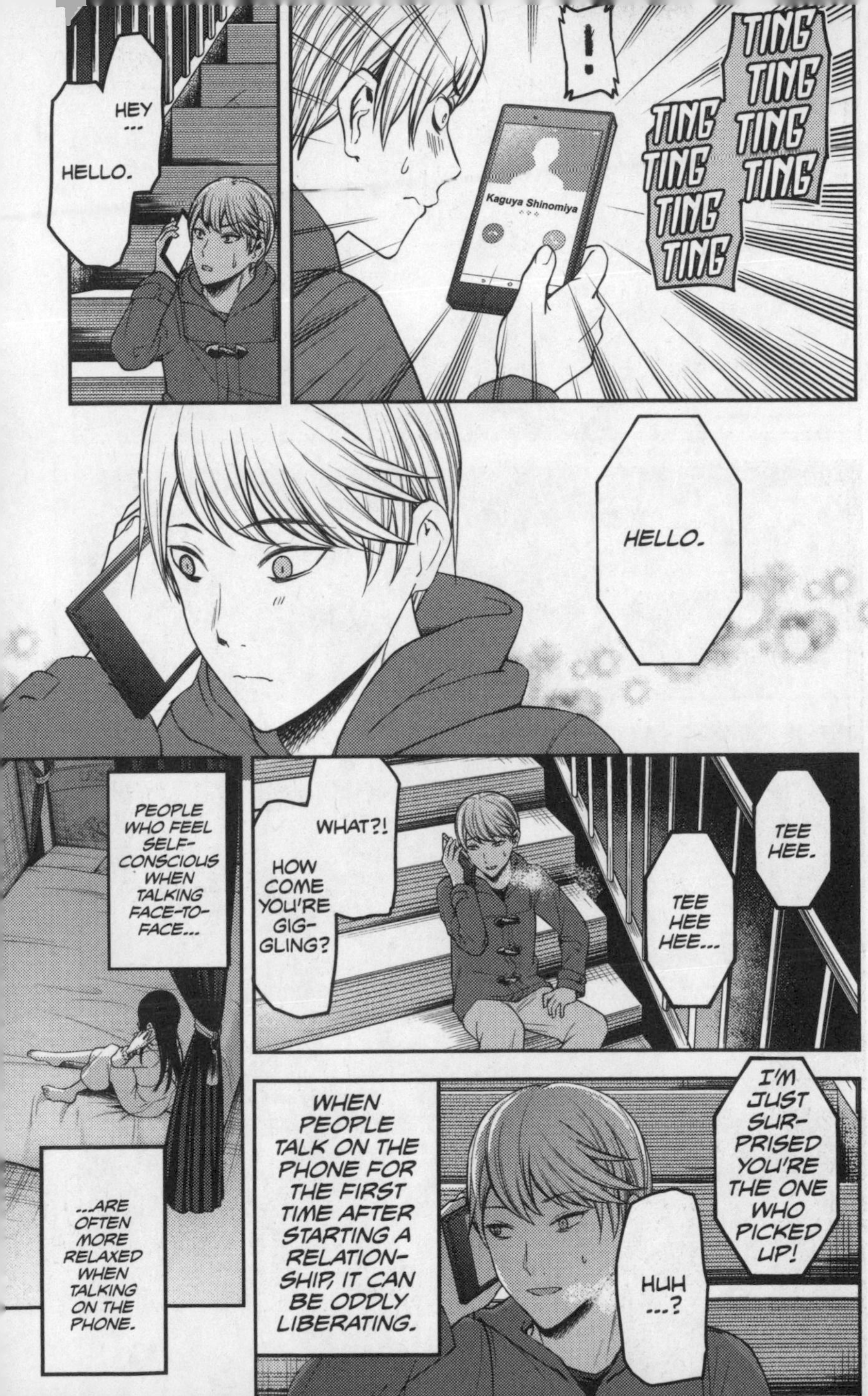
TING TING TING TING
TING TING TING TING
!
Kaguya Shinomiya
HEY... HELLO.
HELLO.
TEE HEE.
TEE HEE HEE...
WHAT?! HOW COME YOU'RE GIG-GLING?
I'M JUST SUR-PRISED YOU'RE THE ONE WHO PICKED UP!
HUH...?
WHEN PEOPLE TALK ON THE PHONE FOR THE FIRST TIME AFTER STARTING A RELATION-SHIP, IT CAN BE ODDLY LIBERATING.
PEOPLE WHO FEEL SELF-CONSCIOUS WHEN TALKING FACE-TO-FACE...
...ARE OFTEN MORE RELAXED WHEN TALKING ON THE PHONE.

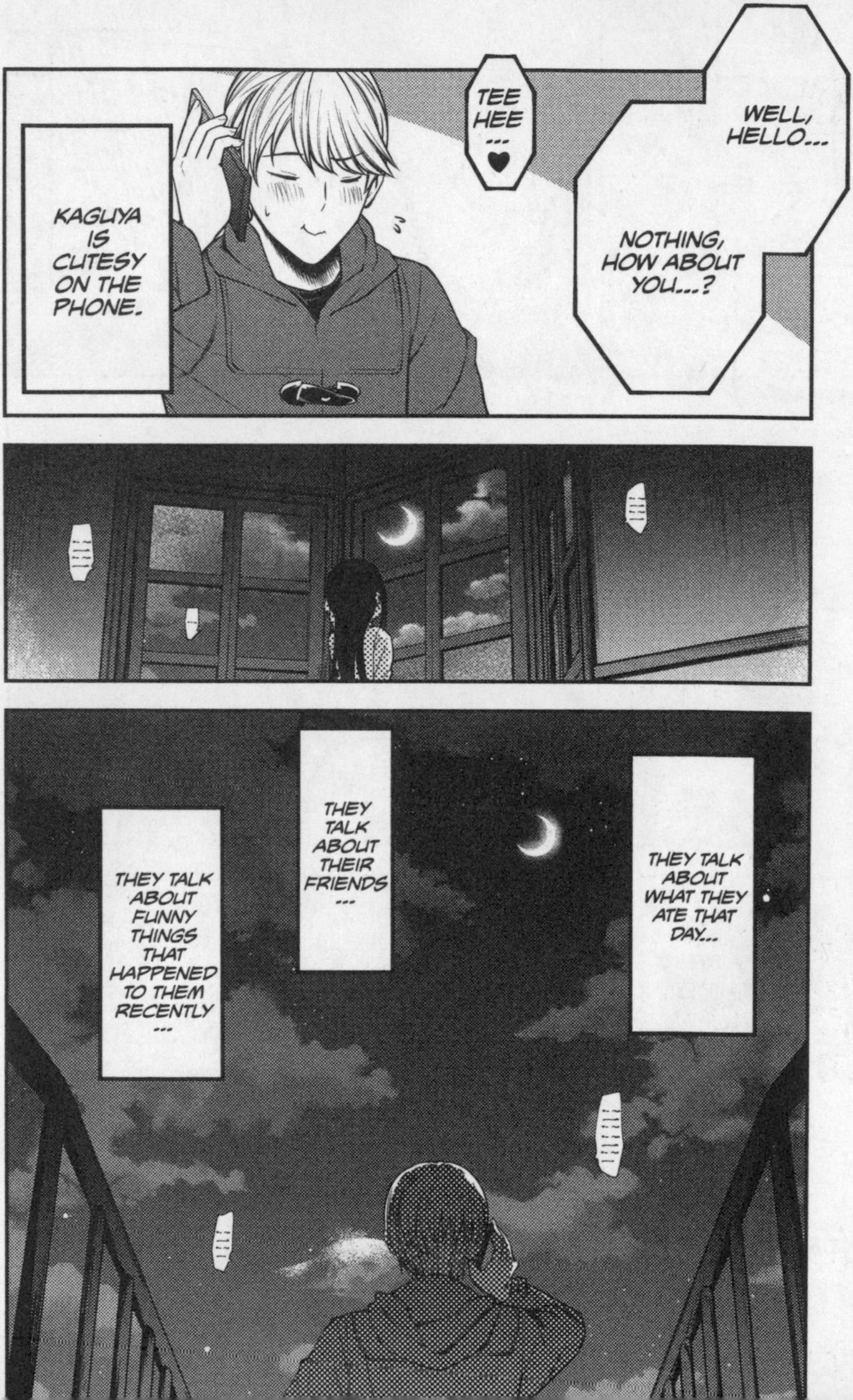
WELL, HELLO...
NOTHING, HOW ABOUT YOU...?
TEE HEE ... ♥
KAGUYA IS CUTESY ON THE PHONE.
THEY TALK ABOUT WHAT THEY ATE THAT DAY...
THEY TALK ABOUT THEIR FRIENDS ...
THEY TALK ABOUT FUNNY THINGS THAT HAPPENED TO THEM RECENTLY ...

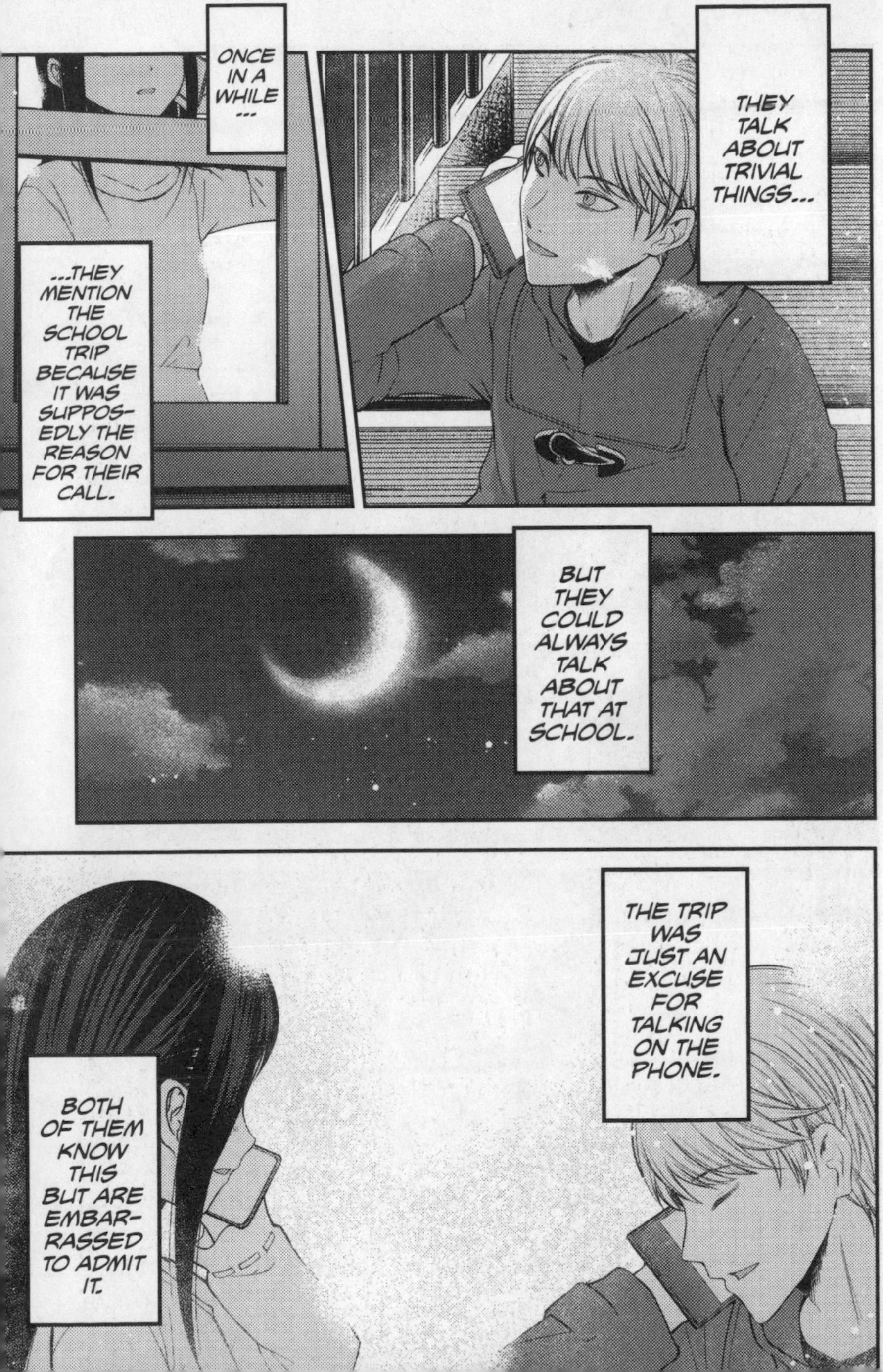
THEY TALK ABOUT TRIVIAL THINGS...
ONCE IN A WHILE...
...THEY MENTION THE SCHOOL TRIP BECAUSE IT WAS SUPPOSEDLY THE REASON FOR THEIR CALL.
BUT THEY COULD ALWAYS TALK ABOUT THAT AT SCHOOL.
THE TRIP WAS JUST AN EXCUSE FOR TALKING ON THE PHONE.
BOTH OF THEM KNOW THIS BUT ARE EMBARRASSED TO ADMIT IT.

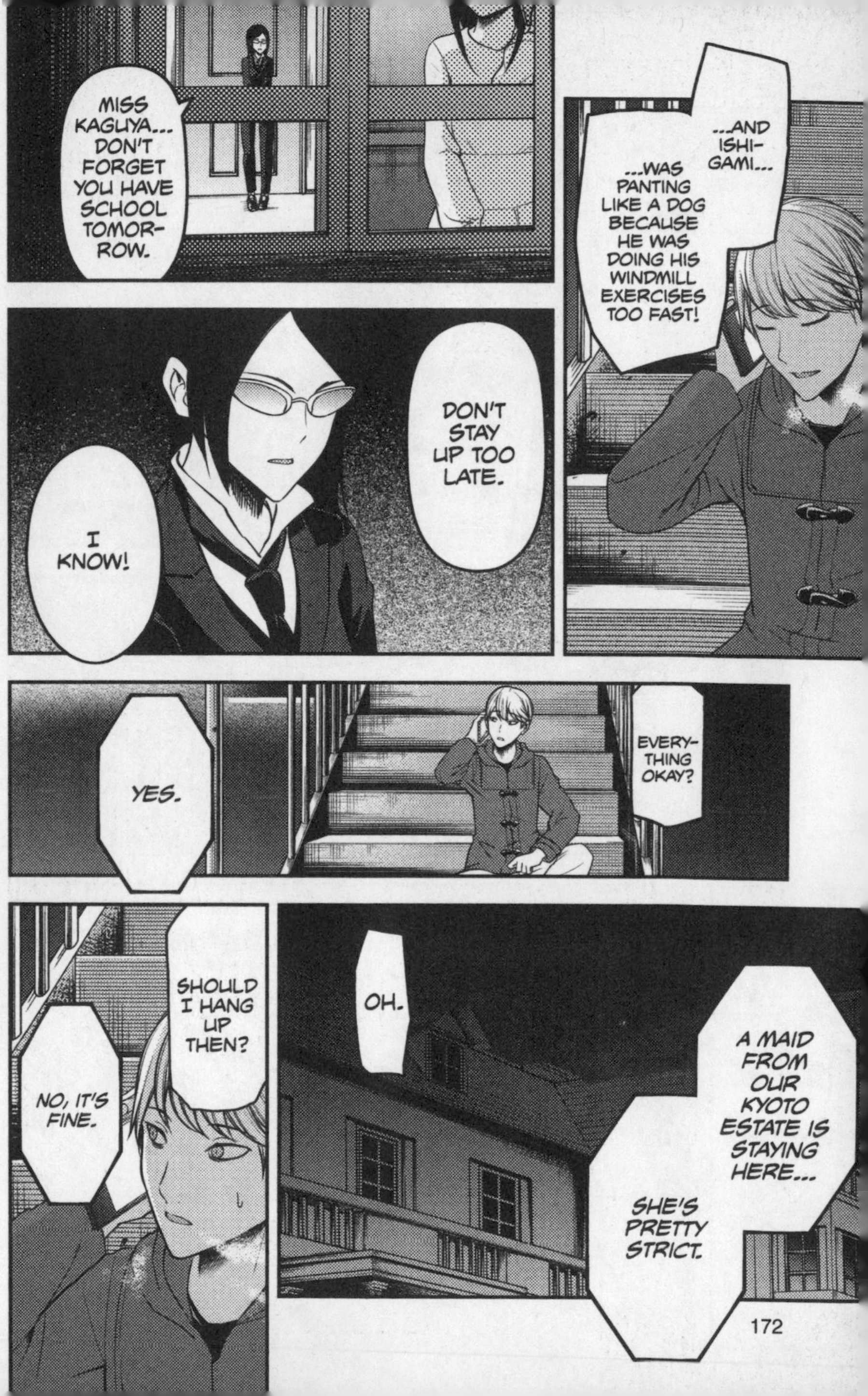
...AND ISHI-GAMI...
...WAS PANTING LIKE A DOG BECAUSE HE WAS DOING HIS WINDMILL EXERCISES TOO FAST!
MISS KAGUYA... DON'T FORGET YOU HAVE SCHOOL TOMOR-ROW.
DON'T STAY UP TOO LATE.
I KNOW!
EVERY-THING OKAY?
YES.
A MAID FROM OUR KYOTO ESTATE IS STAYING HERE...
SHE'S PRETTY STRICT.
OH.
SHOULD I HANG UP THEN?
NO, IT'S FINE.

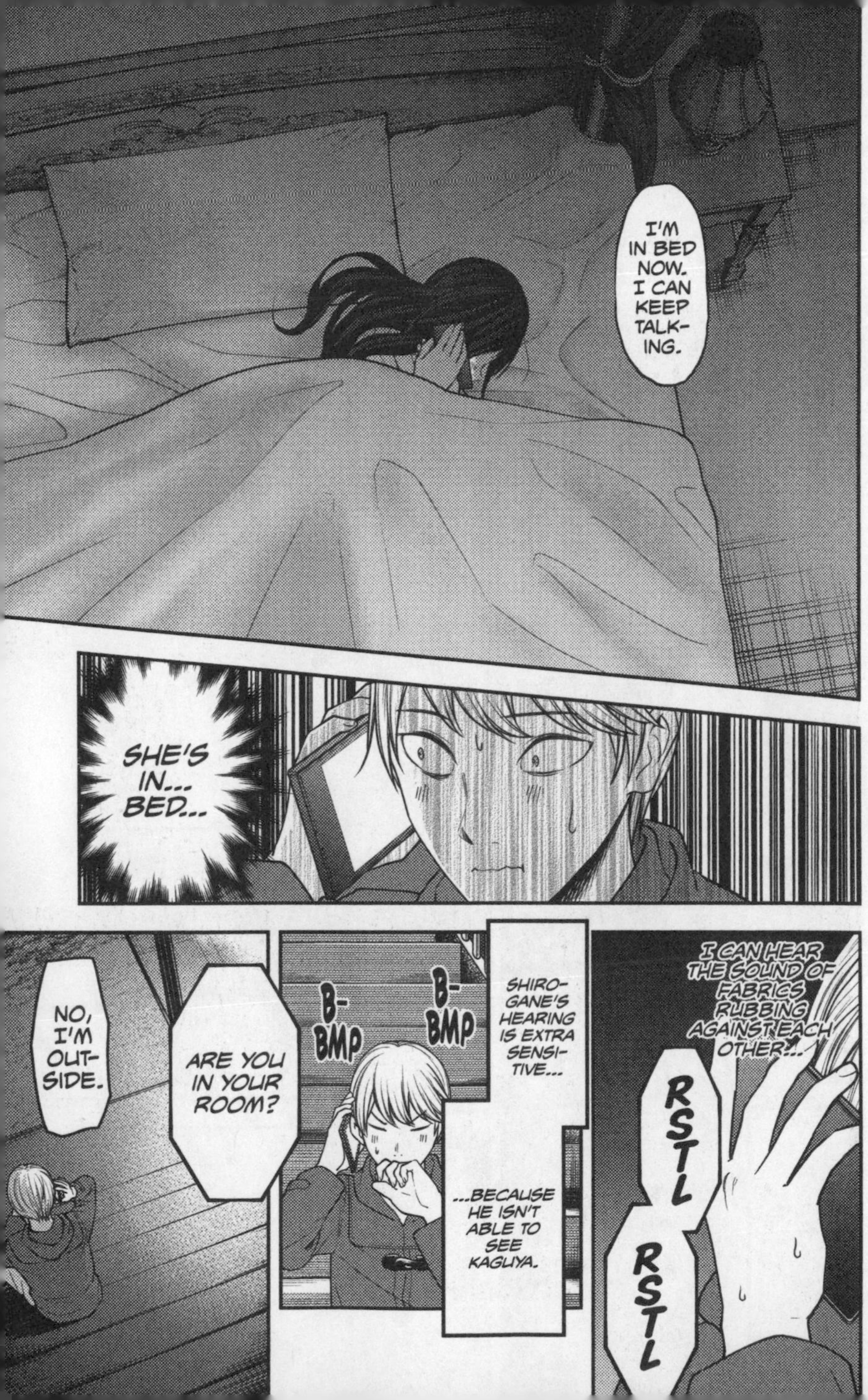
I'M IN BED NOW. I CAN KEEP TALK-ING.
SHE'S IN... BED...
I CAN HEAR THE SOUND OF FABRICS RUBBING AGAINST EACH OTHER...
RSTL
RSTL
SHIRO-GANE'S HEARING IS EXTRA SENSI-TIVE...
...BECAUSE HE ISN'T ABLE TO SEE KAGUYA.
B-BMP
B-BMP
ARE YOU IN YOUR ROOM?
NO, I'M OUT-SIDE.

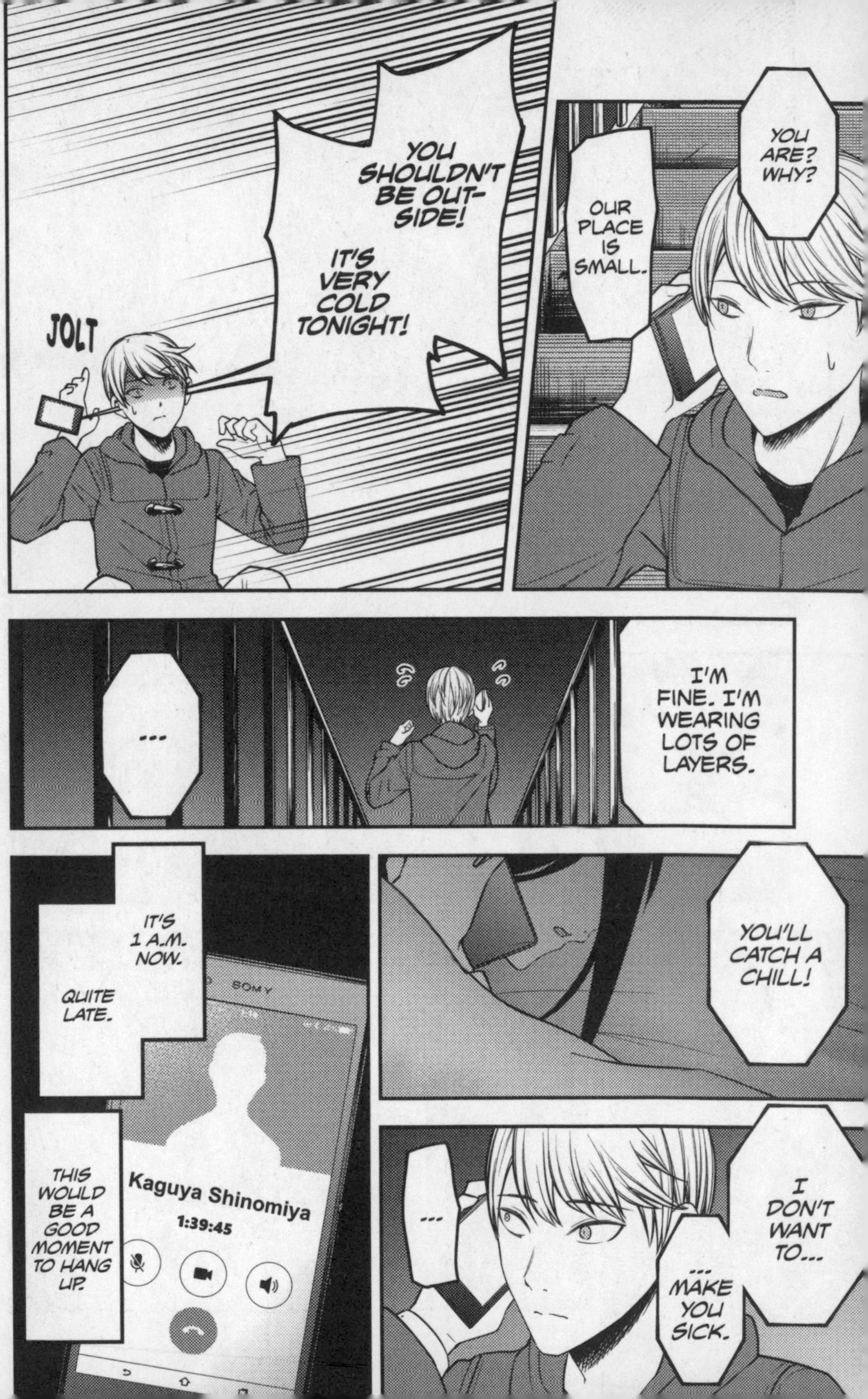
YOU ARE? WHY?
OUR PLACE IS SMALL.
YOU SHOULDN'T BE OUT-SIDE!
IT'S VERY COLD TONIGHT!
JOLT
I'M FINE. I'M WEARING LOTS OF LAYERS.
...
YOU'LL CATCH A CHILL!
I DON'T WANT TO...
... MAKE YOU SICK.
...
IT'S 1 A.M. NOW.
QUITE LATE.
SONY
Kaguya Shinomiya
1:39:45
THIS WOULD BE A GOOD MOMENT TO HANG UP.

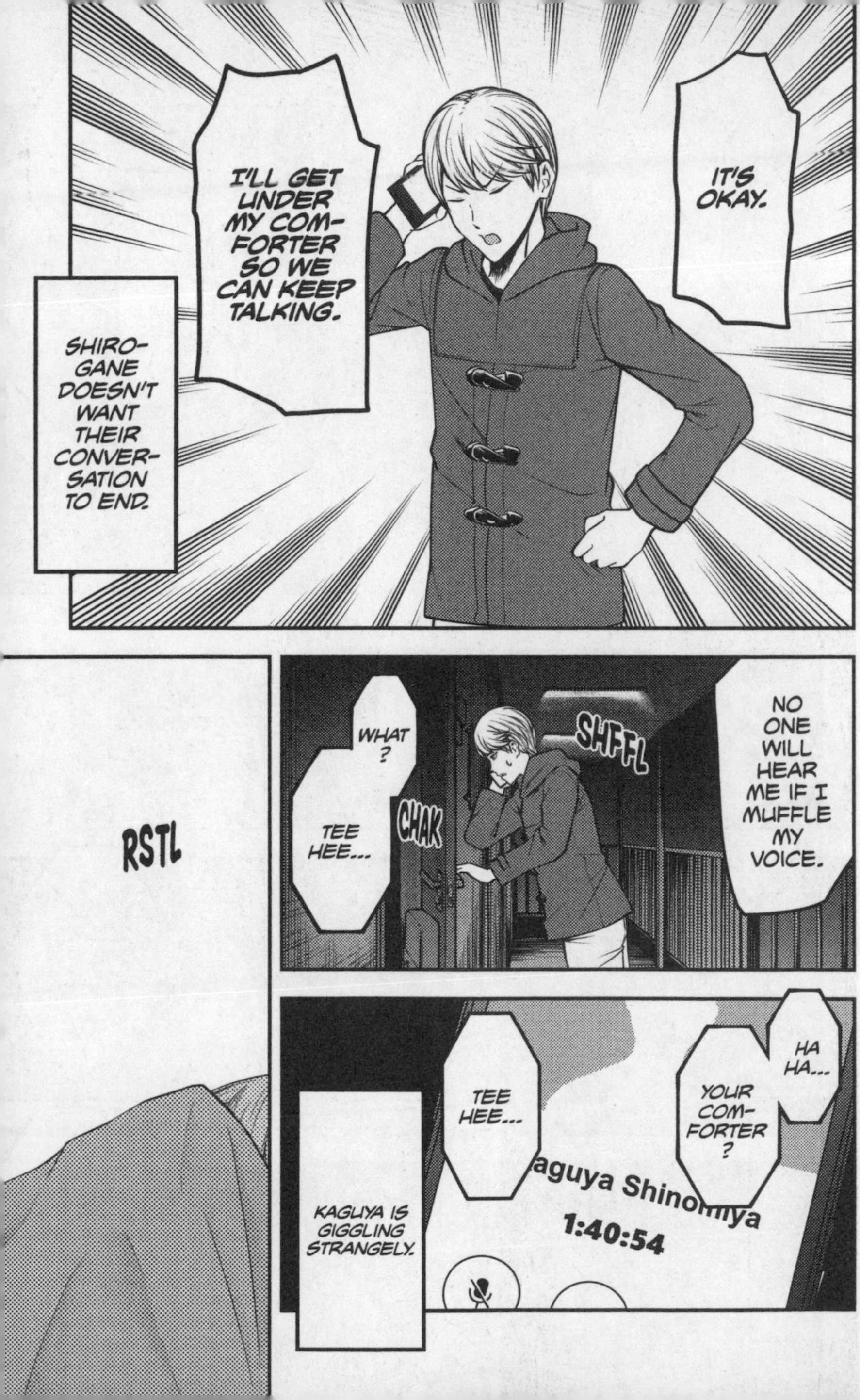
IT'S OKAY.
I'LL GET UNDER MY COM-FORTER SO WE CAN KEEP TALKING.
SHIRO-GANE DOESN'T WANT THEIR CONVER-SATION TO END.
NO ONE WILL HEAR ME IF I MUFFLE MY VOICE.
SHFFL
CHAK
WHAT?
TEE HEE...
HA HA...
YOUR COM-FORTER?
TEE HEE...
aguya Shinomiya
1:40:54
KAGUYA IS GIGGLING STRANGELY.
RSTL

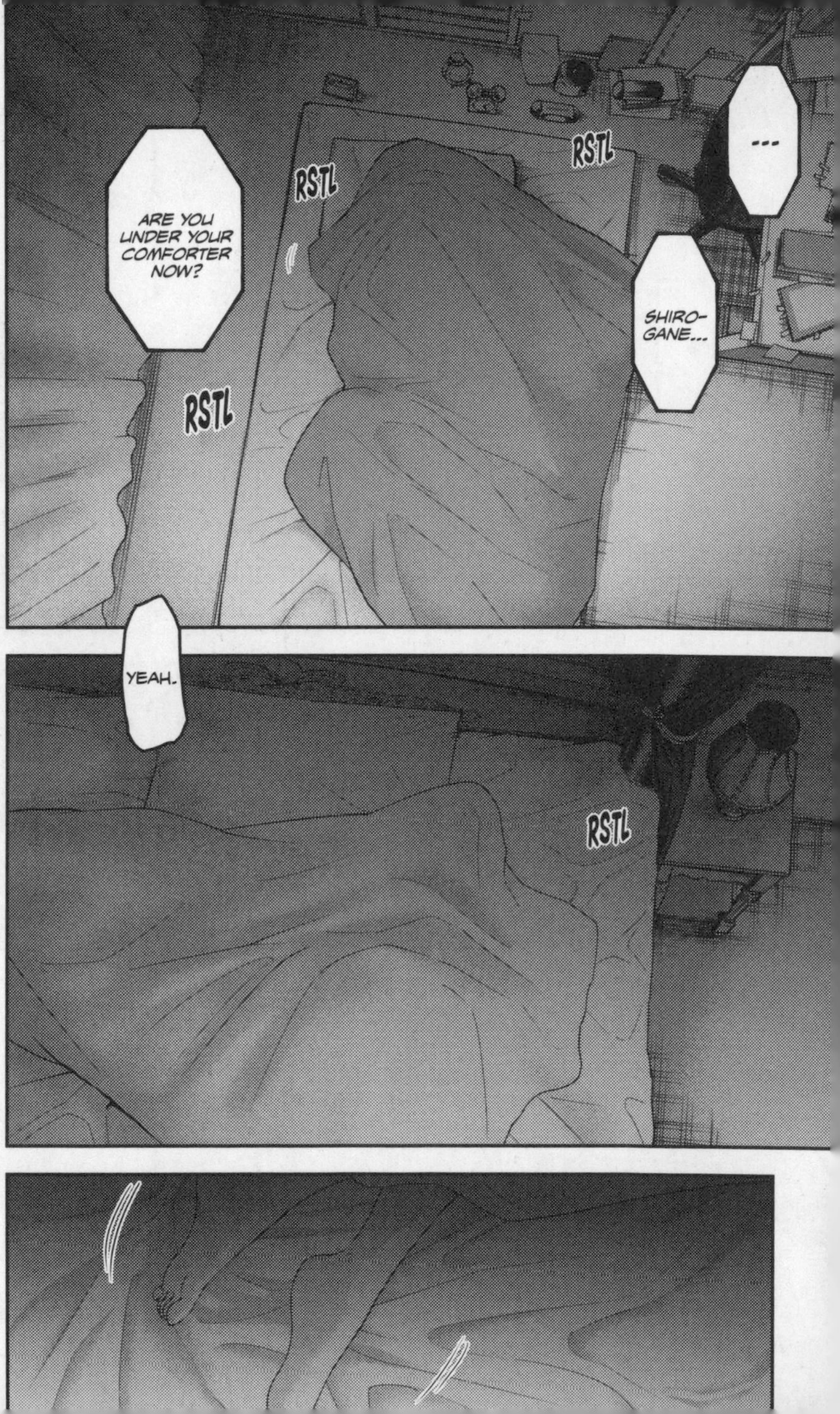
...
SHIRO-GANE...
RSTL
ARE YOU UNDER YOUR COMFORTER NOW?
RSTL
RSTL
YEAH.
RSTL

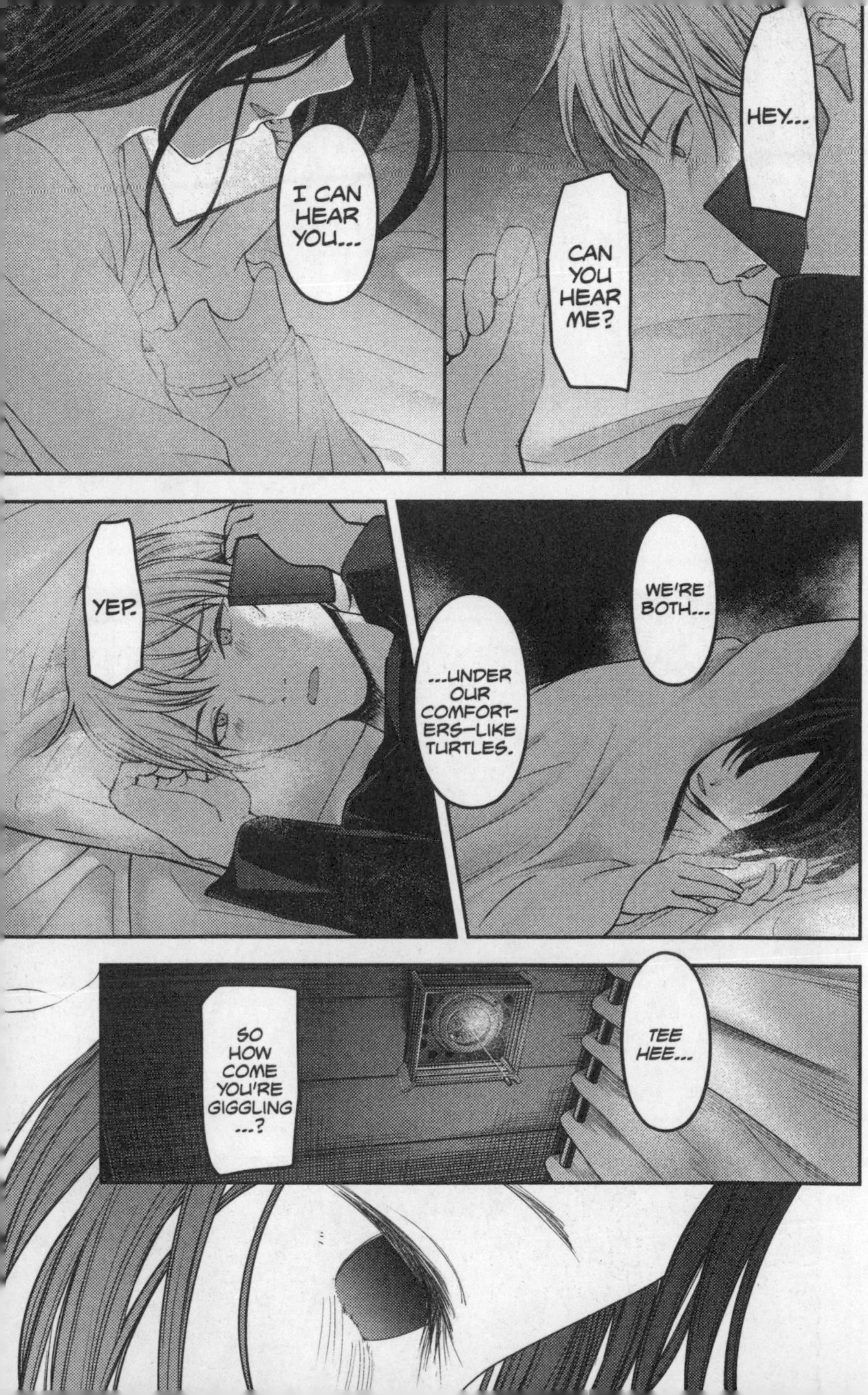
HEY...
CAN YOU HEAR ME?
I CAN HEAR YOU...
WE'RE BOTH...
...UNDER OUR COMFORTERS—LIKE TURTLES.
YEP.
TEE HEE...
SO HOW COME YOU'RE GIGGLING...?

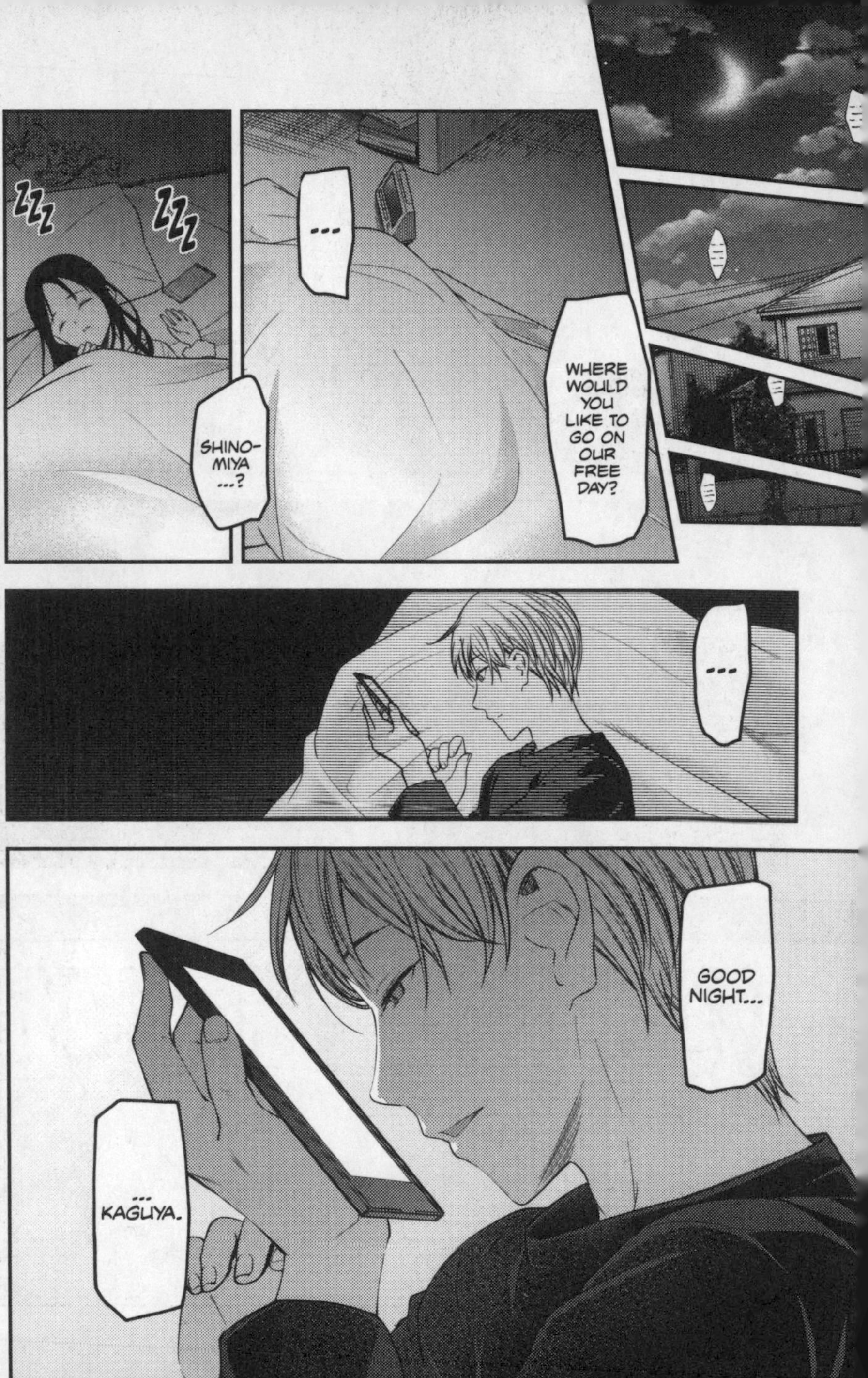
WHERE WOULD YOU LIKE TO GO ON OUR FREE DAY?
...
SHINO-MIYA ...?
ZZZ
ZZZ
...
GOOD NIGHT...
... KAGUYA.

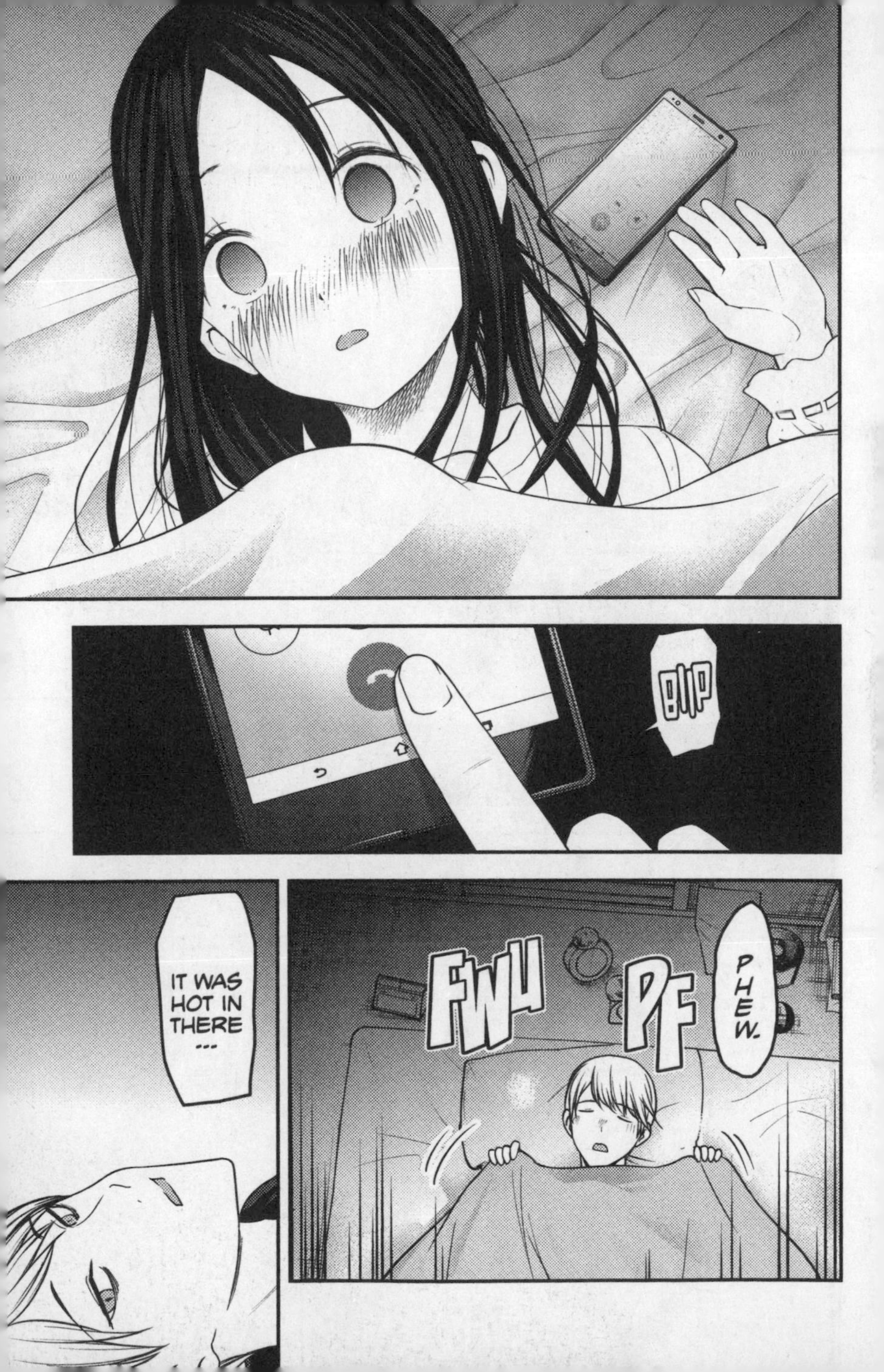
BLIP
FWUPF
PHEW.
IT WAS HOT IN THERE...

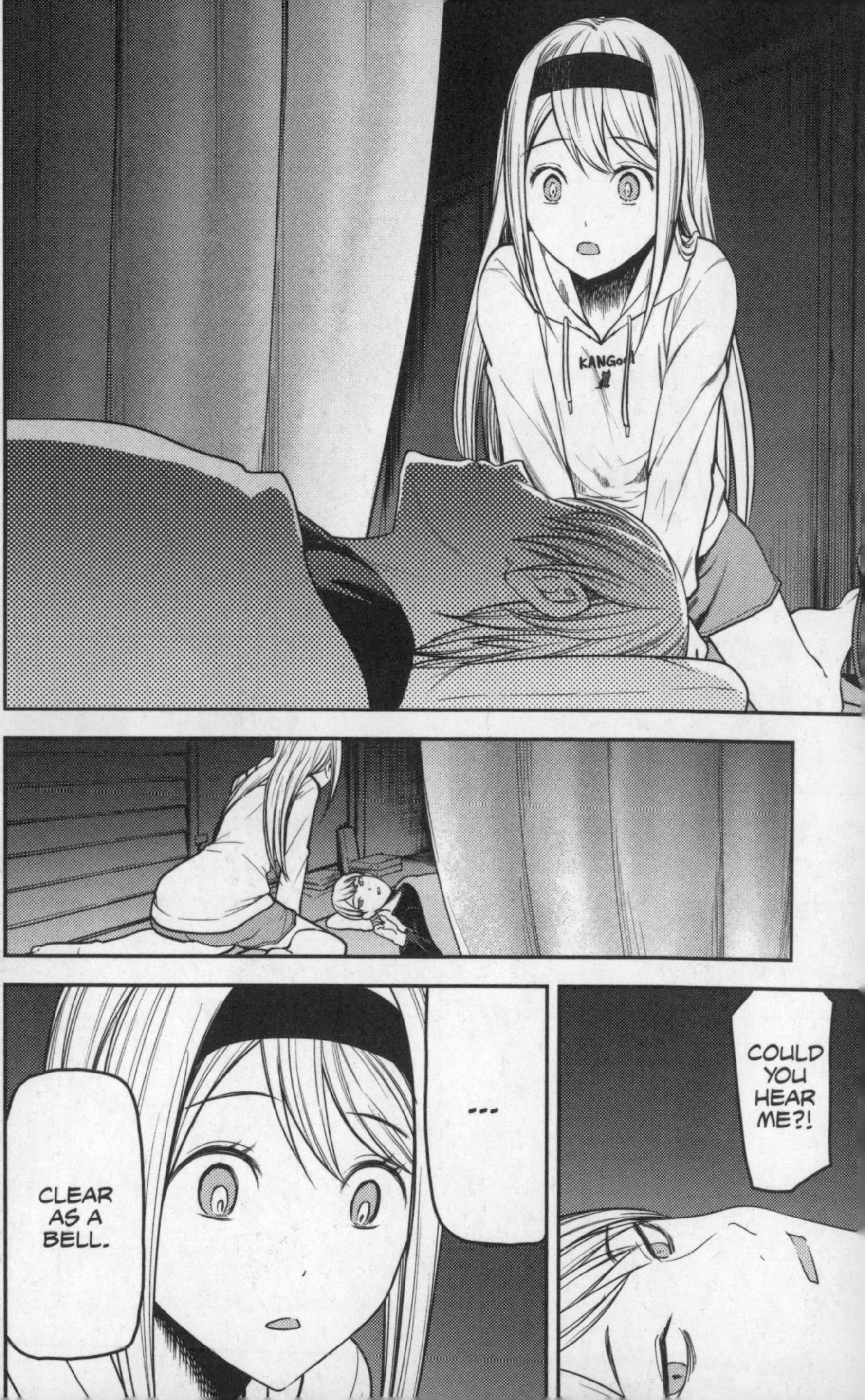
COULD YOU HEAR ME?!
...
CLEAR AS A BELL.

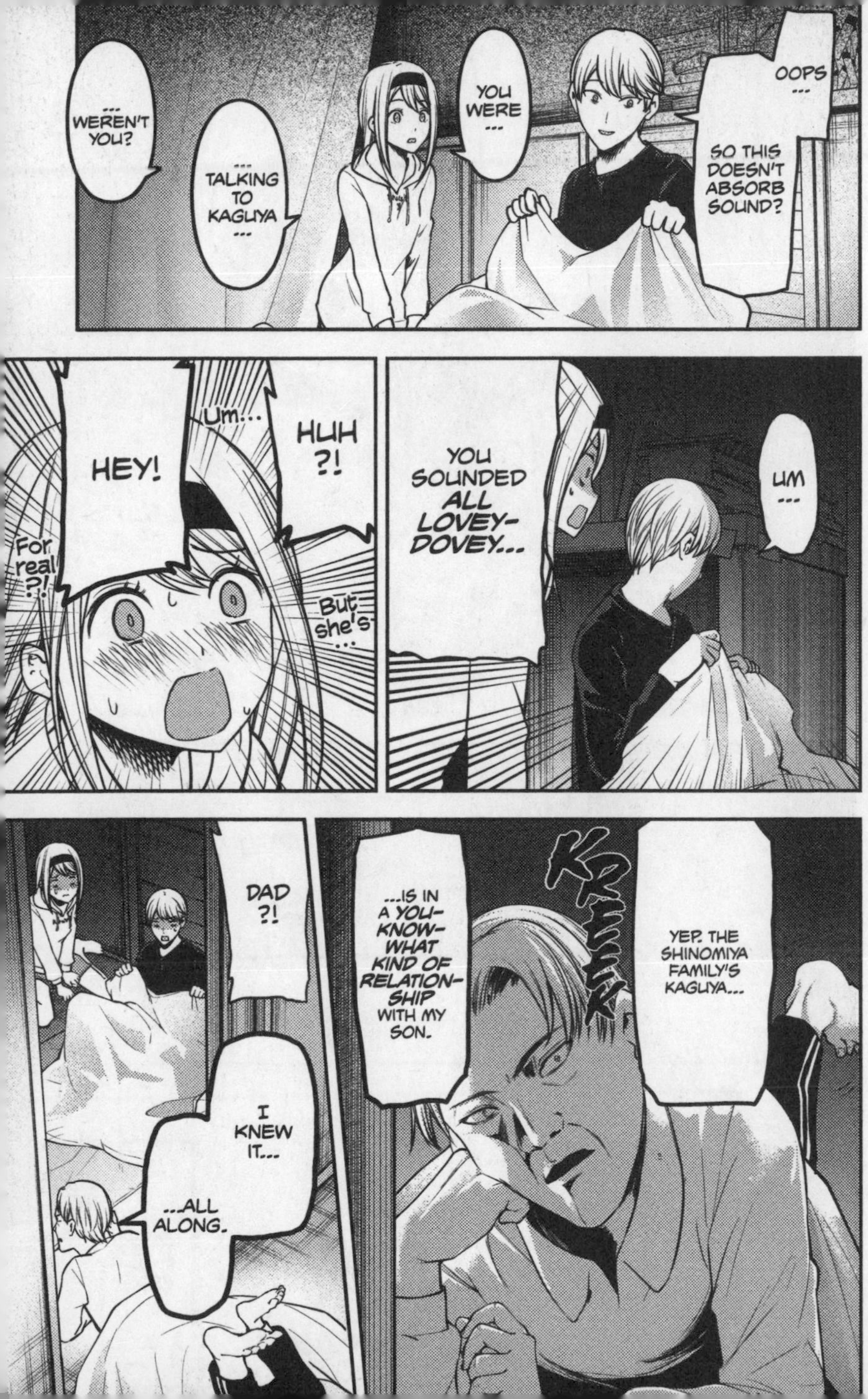
OOPS ...
SO THIS DOESN'T ABSORB SOUND?
YOU WERE ...
... TALKING TO KAGUYA ...
... WEREN'T YOU?
UM ...
YOU SOUNDED ALL LOVEY-DOVEY...
HUH ?!
Um...
HEY!
But she's...
For real ?!
YEP. THE SHINOMIYA FAMILY'S KAGUYA...
...IS IN A YOU-KNOW-WHAT KIND OF RELATIONSHIP WITH MY SON.
DAD ?!
I KNEW IT...
...ALL ALONG.

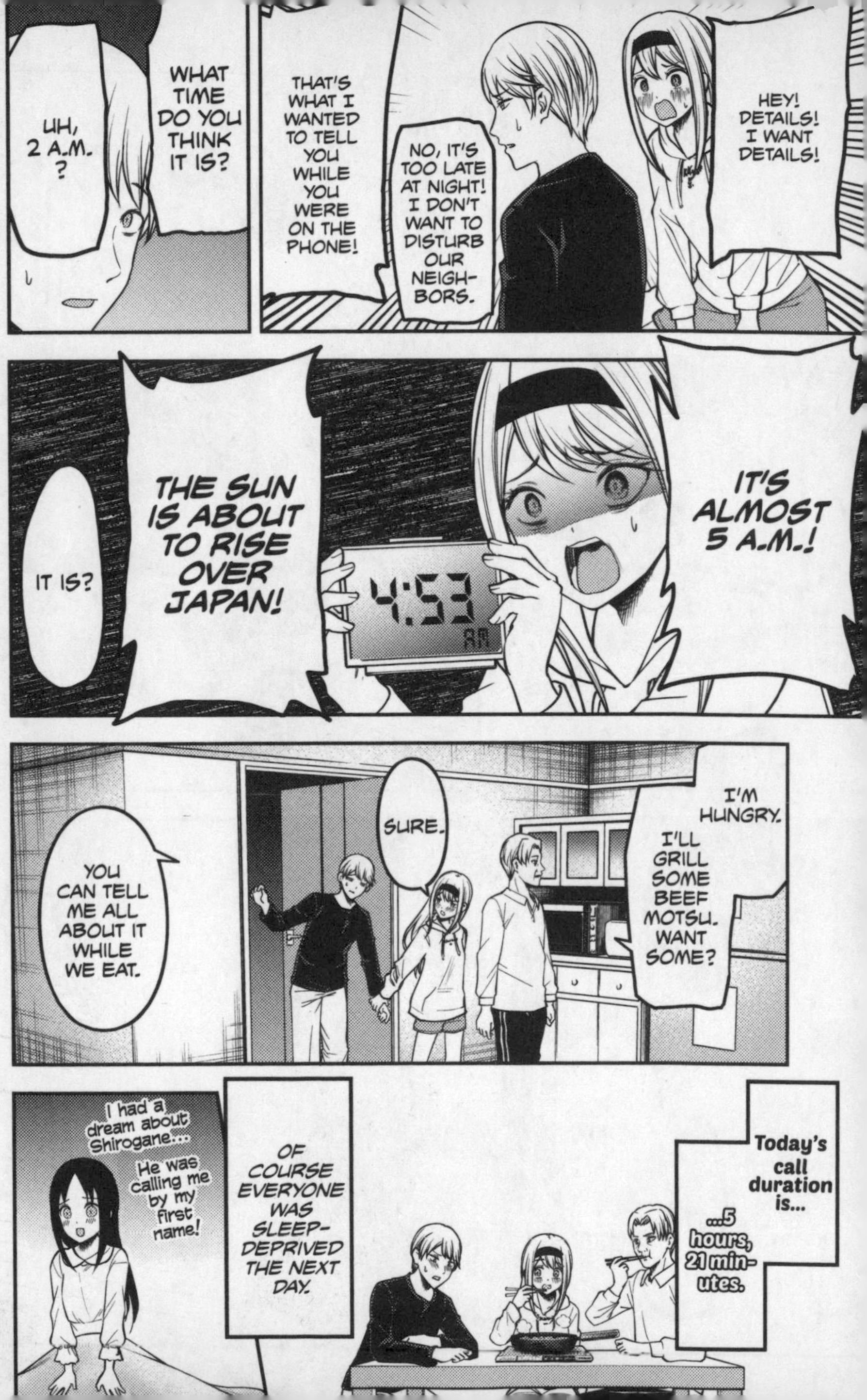
HEY! DETAILS! I WANT DETAILS!
NO, IT'S TOO LATE AT NIGHT! I DON'T WANT TO DISTURB OUR NEIGHBORS.
THAT'S WHAT I WANTED TO TELL YOU WHILE YOU WERE ON THE PHONE!
WHAT TIME DO YOU THINK IT IS?
UH, 2 A.M.?
IT'S ALMOST 5 A.M.!
4:53 AM
THE SUN IS ABOUT TO RISE OVER JAPAN!
IT IS?
I'M HUNGRY. I'LL GRILL SOME BEEF MOTSU. WANT SOME?
SURE.
YOU CAN TELL ME ALL ABOUT IT WHILE WE EAT.
Today's call duration is...
...5 hours, 21 minutes.
OF COURSE EVERYONE WAS SLEEP-DEPRIVED THE NEXT DAY.
I had a dream about Shirogane...
He was calling me by my first name!

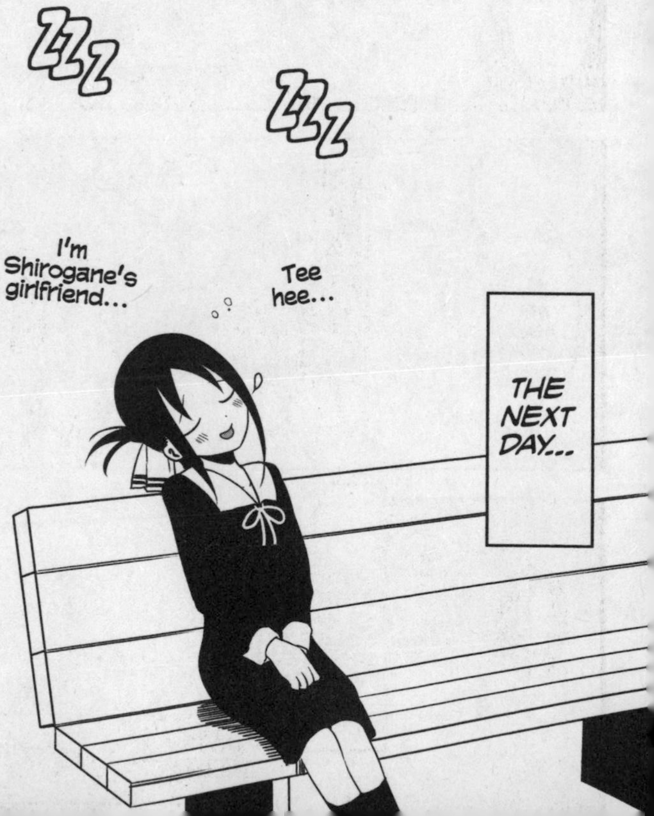
ZZZ
ZZZ
THE NEXT DAY...
Tee hee...
I'm Shirogane's girlfriend...

KAGUYA-SAMA
LOVE IS WAR

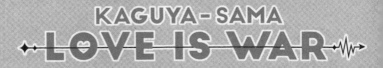

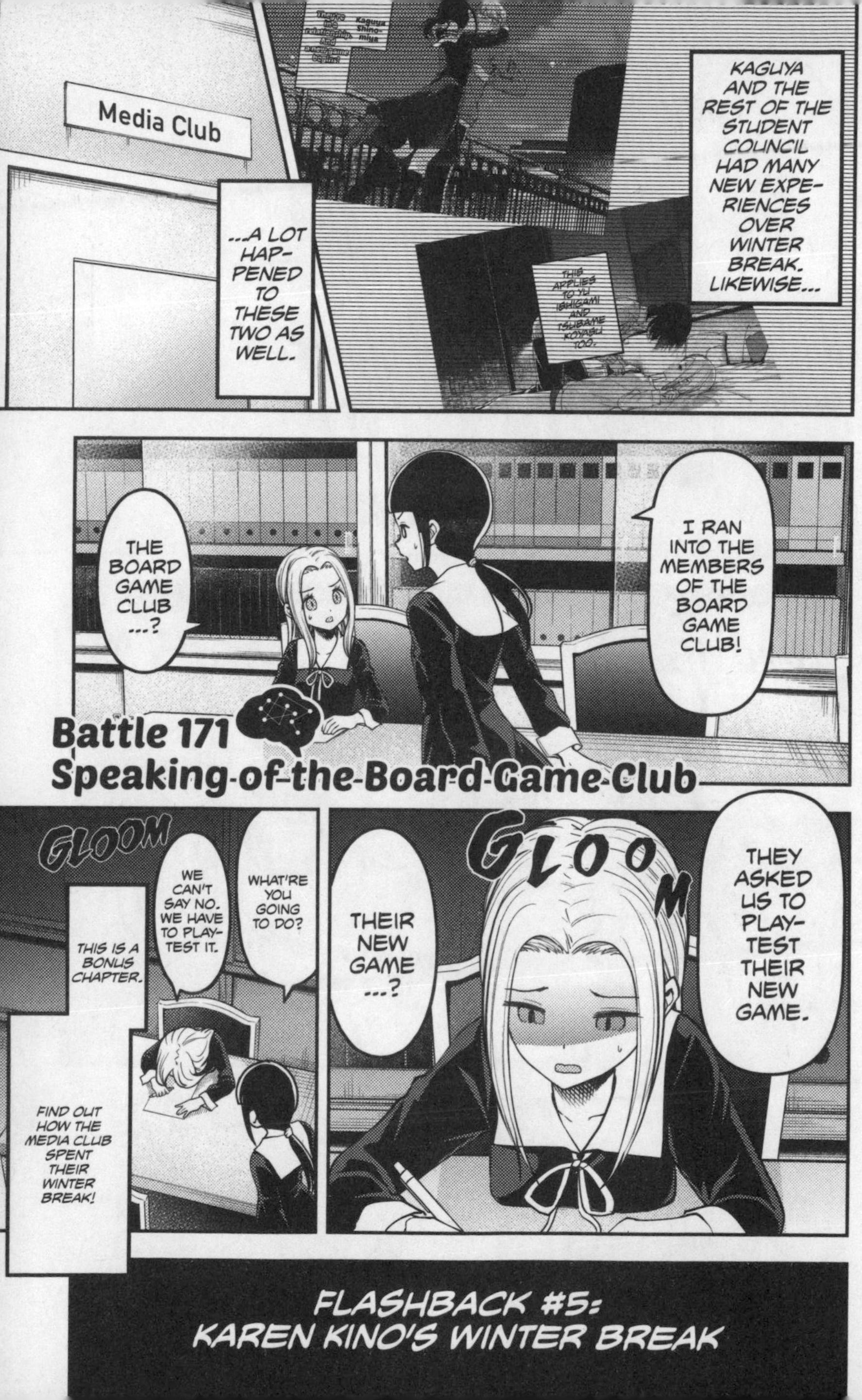
Kaguya Shinomiya
KAGUYA AND THE REST OF THE STUDENT COUNCIL HAD MANY NEW EXPERIENCES OVER WINTER BREAK. LIKEWISE...
THIS APPLIES TO YU ISHIGAMI AND TSUBAME KOYASU TOO.
...A LOT HAPPENED TO THESE TWO AS WELL.
Media Club
I RAN INTO THE MEMBERS OF THE BOARD GAME CLUB!
THE BOARD GAME CLUB ...?
Battle 171
Speaking of the Board Game Club
THEY ASKED US TO PLAYTEST THEIR NEW GAME.
GLOOM
THEIR NEW GAME ...?
WHAT'RE YOU GOING TO DO?
WE CAN'T SAY NO. WE HAVE TO PLAYTEST IT.
GLOOM
THIS IS A BONUS CHAPTER.
FIND OUT HOW THE MEDIA CLUB SPENT THEIR WINTER BREAK!
FLASHBACK #5: KAREN KINO'S WINTER BREAK

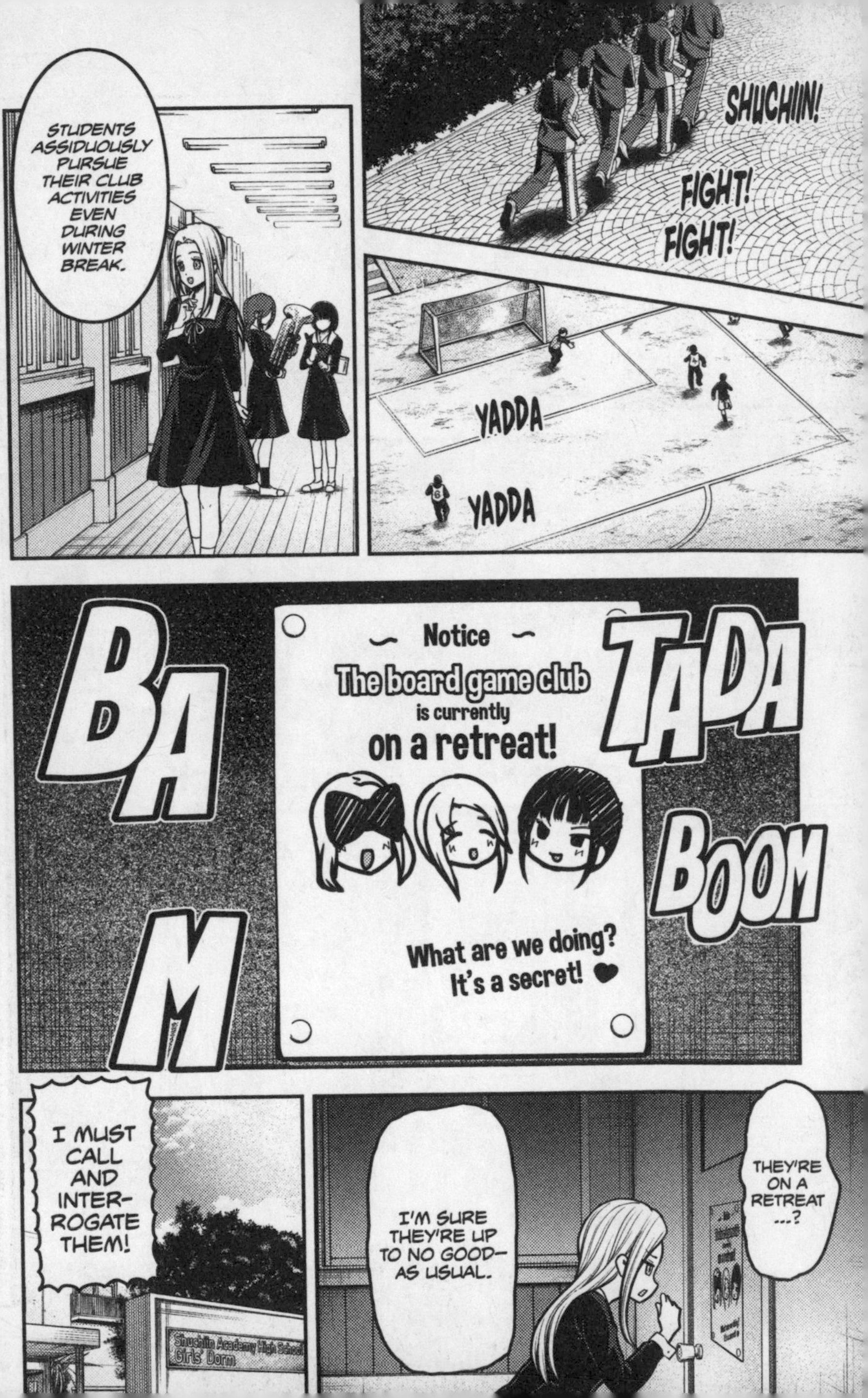
SHUCHIIN!
FIGHT! FIGHT!
YADDA
YADDA
STUDENTS ASSIDUOUSLY PURSUE THEIR CLUB ACTIVITIES EVEN DURING WINTER BREAK.
TADA
BOOM
~ Notice ~
The board game club is currently on a retreat!
What are we doing? It's a secret! ♥
BAM
THEY'RE ON A RETREAT...?
I'M SURE THEY'RE UP TO NO GOOD— AS USUAL.
I MUST CALL AND INTER-ROGATE THEM!
Shuchiin Academy High School Girls' Dorm

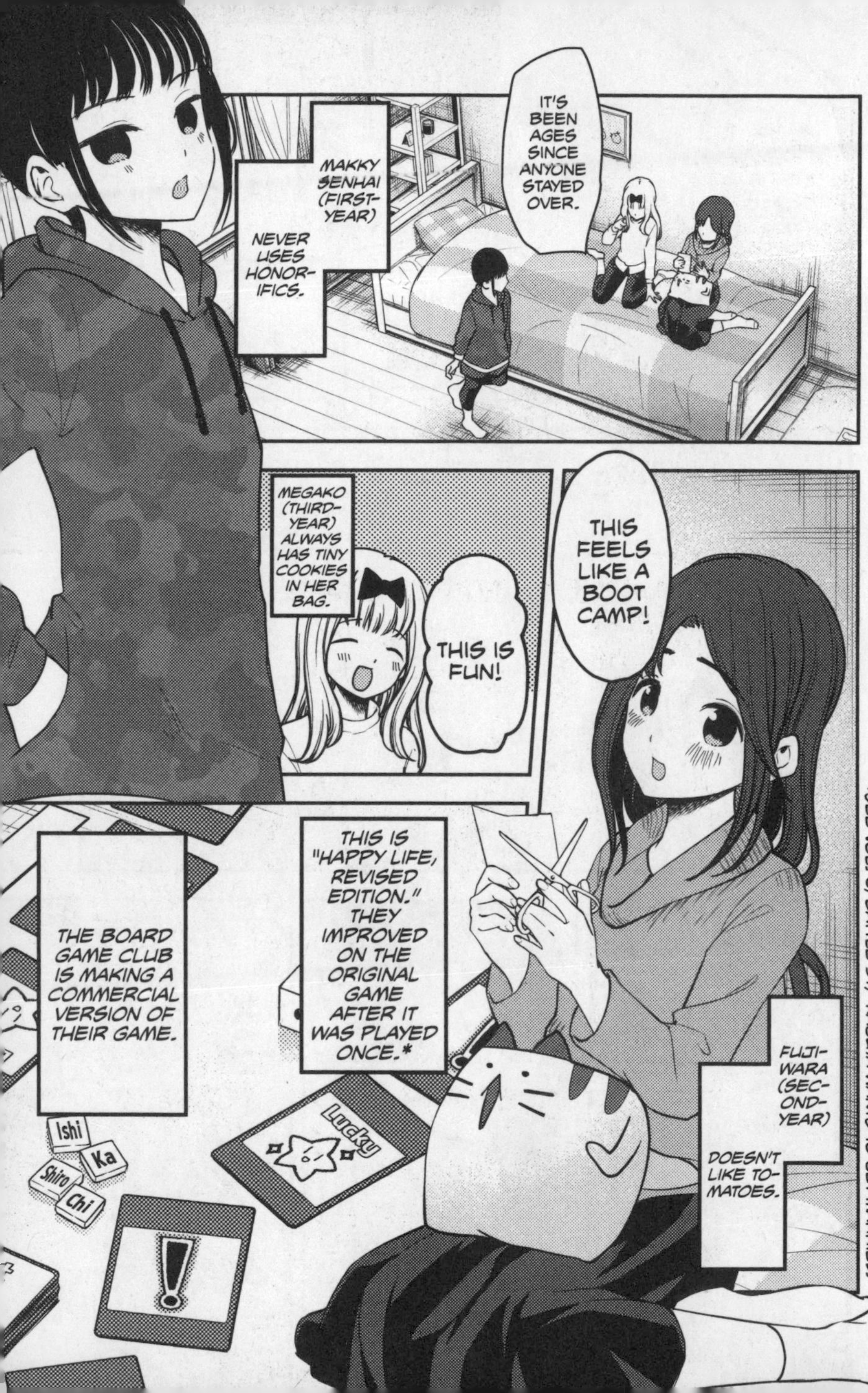
IT'S BEEN AGES SINCE ANYONE STAYED OVER.
THIS FEELS LIKE A BOOT CAMP!
MEGAKO (THIRD-YEAR) ALWAYS HAS TINY COOKIES IN HER BAG.
THIS IS FUN!
MAKKY SENHAI (FIRST-YEAR)
NEVER USES HONORIFICS.
FUJIWARA (SECOND-YEAR)
DOESN'T LIKE TOMATOES.
THIS IS "HAPPY LIFE, REVISED EDITION." THEY IMPROVED ON THE ORIGINAL GAME AFTER IT WAS PLAYED ONCE.*
THE BOARD GAME CLUB IS MAKING A COMMERCIAL VERSION OF THEIR GAME.
Lucky
Ishi
Ka
Shiro
Chi

*SEE VOL. 6, BATTLE 57, "KAGUYA WANTS TO GET MARRIED."

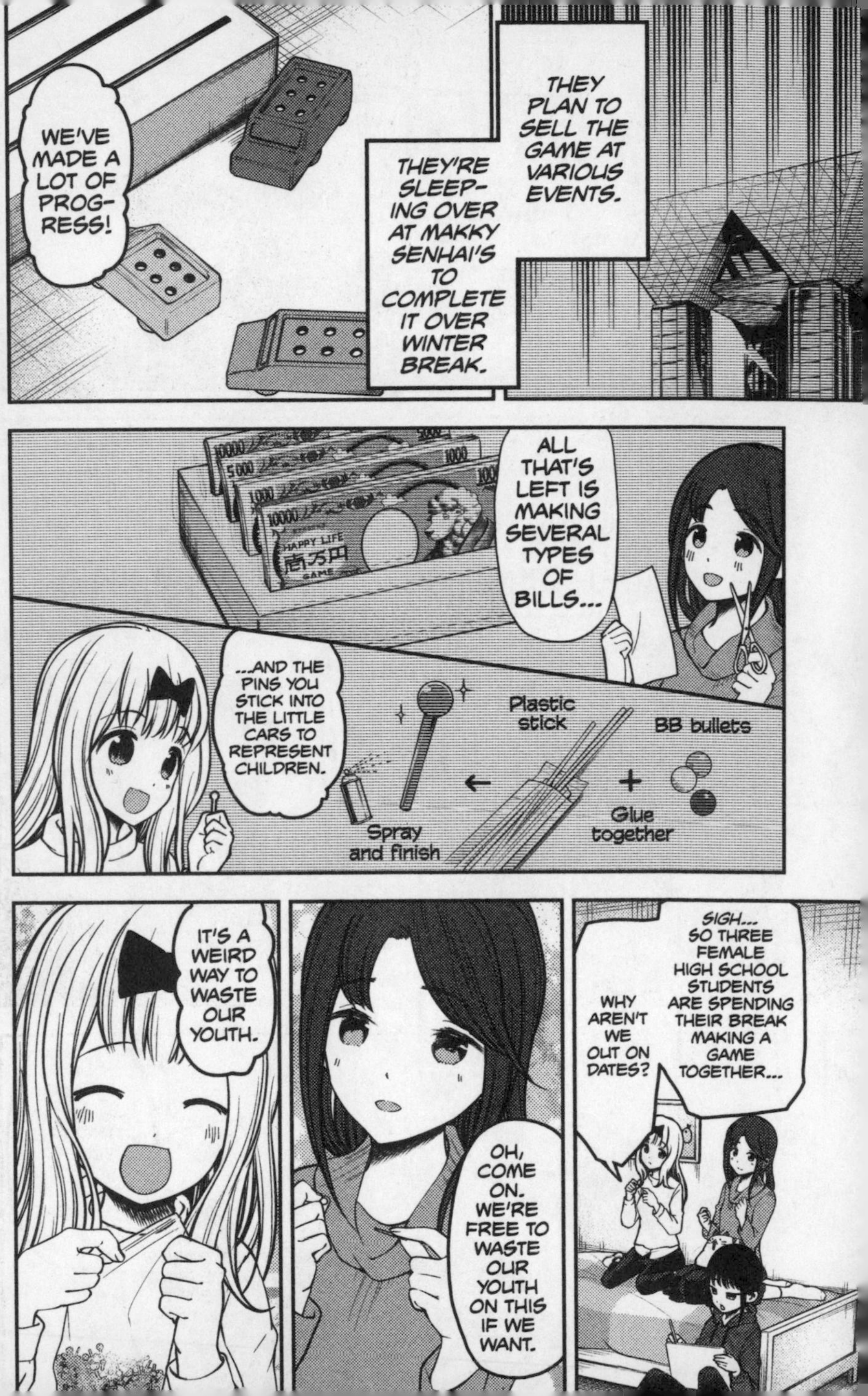
THEY PLAN TO SELL THE GAME AT VARIOUS EVENTS.
THEY'RE SLEEPING OVER AT MAKKY SENHAI'S TO COMPLETE IT OVER WINTER BREAK.
WE'VE MADE A LOT OF PROGRESS!
ALL THAT'S LEFT IS MAKING SEVERAL TYPES OF BILLS...
...AND THE PINS YOU STICK INTO THE LITTLE CARS TO REPRESENT CHILDREN.
Plastic stick
BB bullets
Glue together
Spray and finish
SIGH... SO THREE FEMALE HIGH SCHOOL STUDENTS ARE SPENDING THEIR BREAK MAKING A GAME TOGETHER...
WHY AREN'T WE OUT ON DATES?
OH, COME ON. WE'RE FREE TO WASTE OUR YOUTH ON THIS IF WE WANT.
IT'S A WEIRD WAY TO WASTE OUR YOUTH.

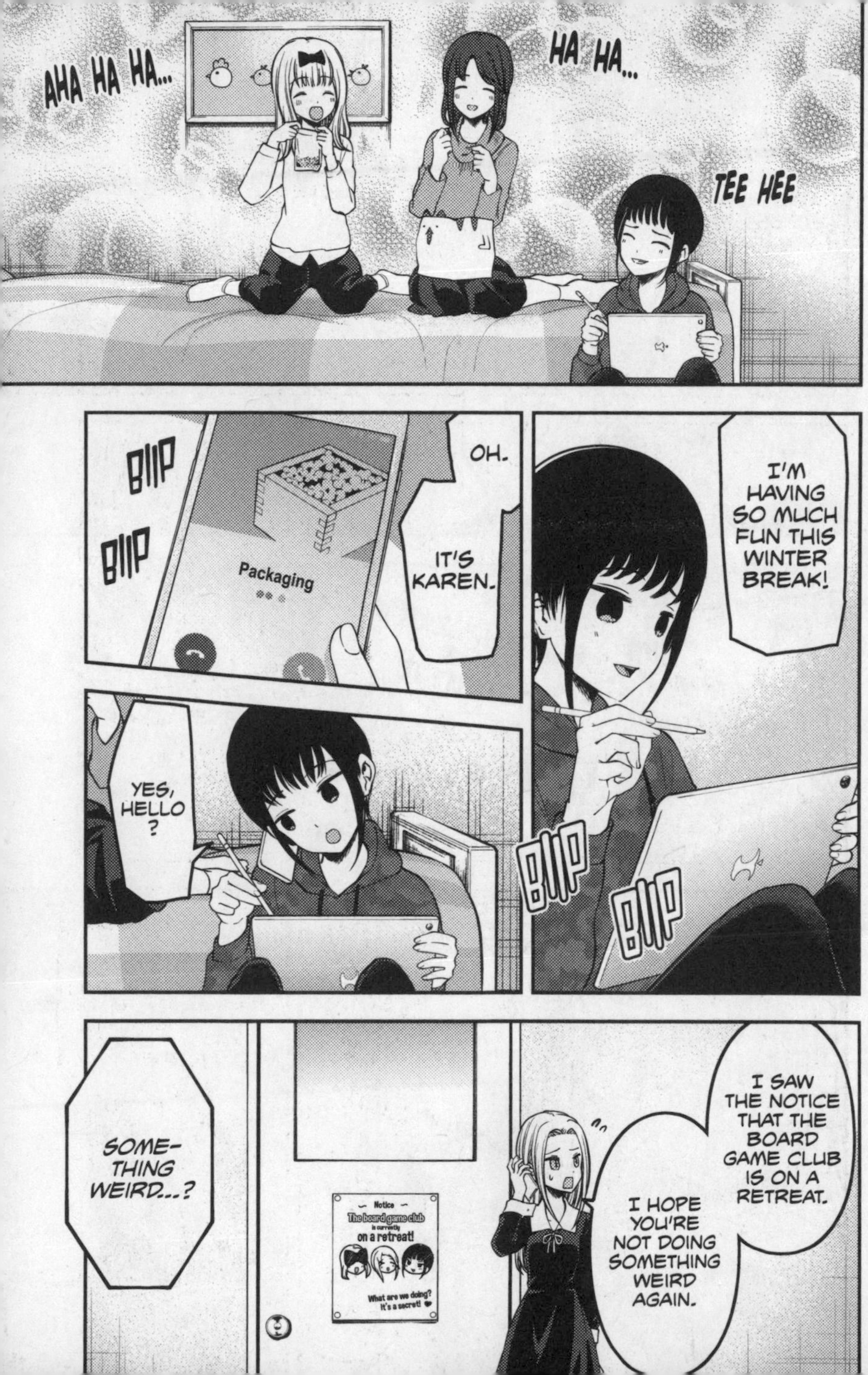
TEE HEE
HA HA...
AHA HA HA...
I'M HAVING SO MUCH FUN THIS WINTER BREAK!
BIIP
BIIP
OH.
IT'S KAREN.
BIIP
BIIP
Packaging
YES, HELLO?
I SAW THE NOTICE THAT THE BOARD GAME CLUB IS ON A RETREAT.
I HOPE YOU'RE NOT DOING SOMETHING WEIRD AGAIN.
Notice
The board game club is currently on a retreat!
What are we doing? It's a secret!
SOME-THING WEIRD...?

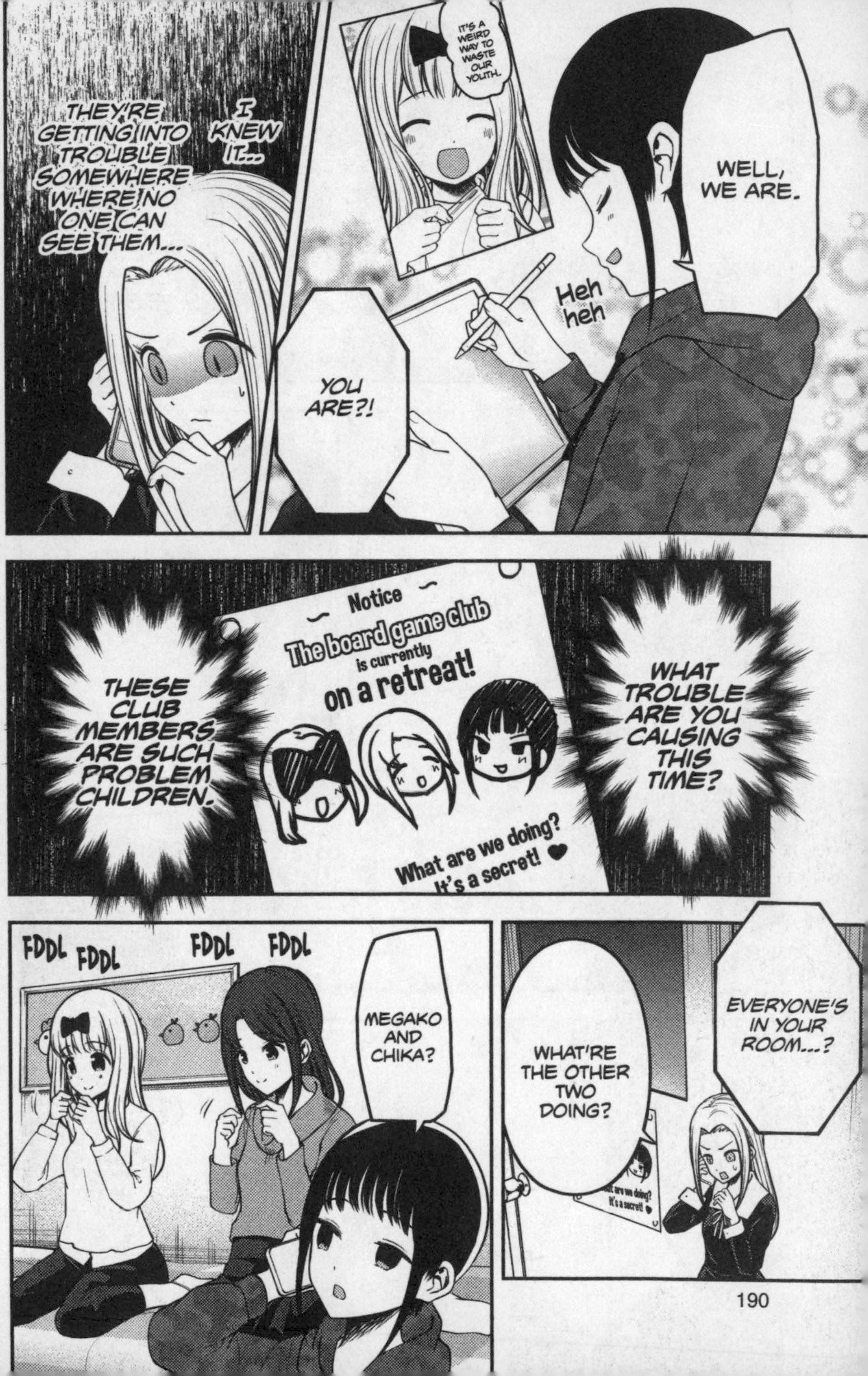
WELL, WE ARE.
Heh heh
IT'S A WEIRD WAY TO WASTE OUR YOUTH.
YOU ARE?!
I KNEW IT...
THEY'RE GETTING INTO TROUBLE SOMEWHERE WHERE NO ONE CAN SEE THEM...
WHAT TROUBLE ARE YOU CAUSING THIS TIME?
Notice
The board game club is currently on a retreat!
What are we doing? It's a secret! ❤
THESE CLUB MEMBERS ARE SUCH PROBLEM CHILDREN.
EVERYONE'S IN YOUR ROOM...?
WHAT'RE THE OTHER TWO DOING?
MEGAKO AND CHIKA?
FDDL
FDDL
FDDL
FDDL

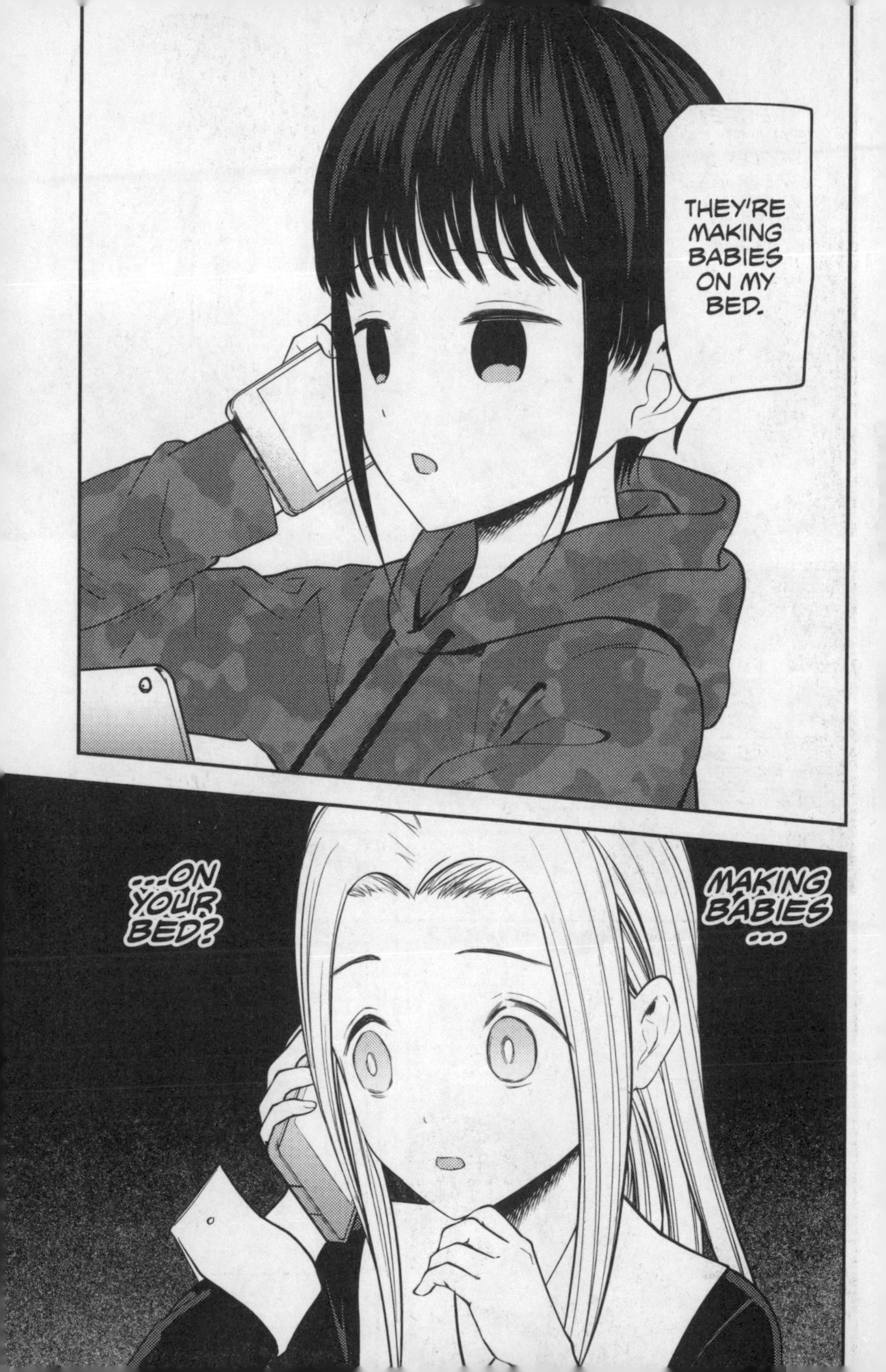
THEY'RE MAKING BABIES ON MY BED.
MAKING BABIES...
...ON YOUR BED?

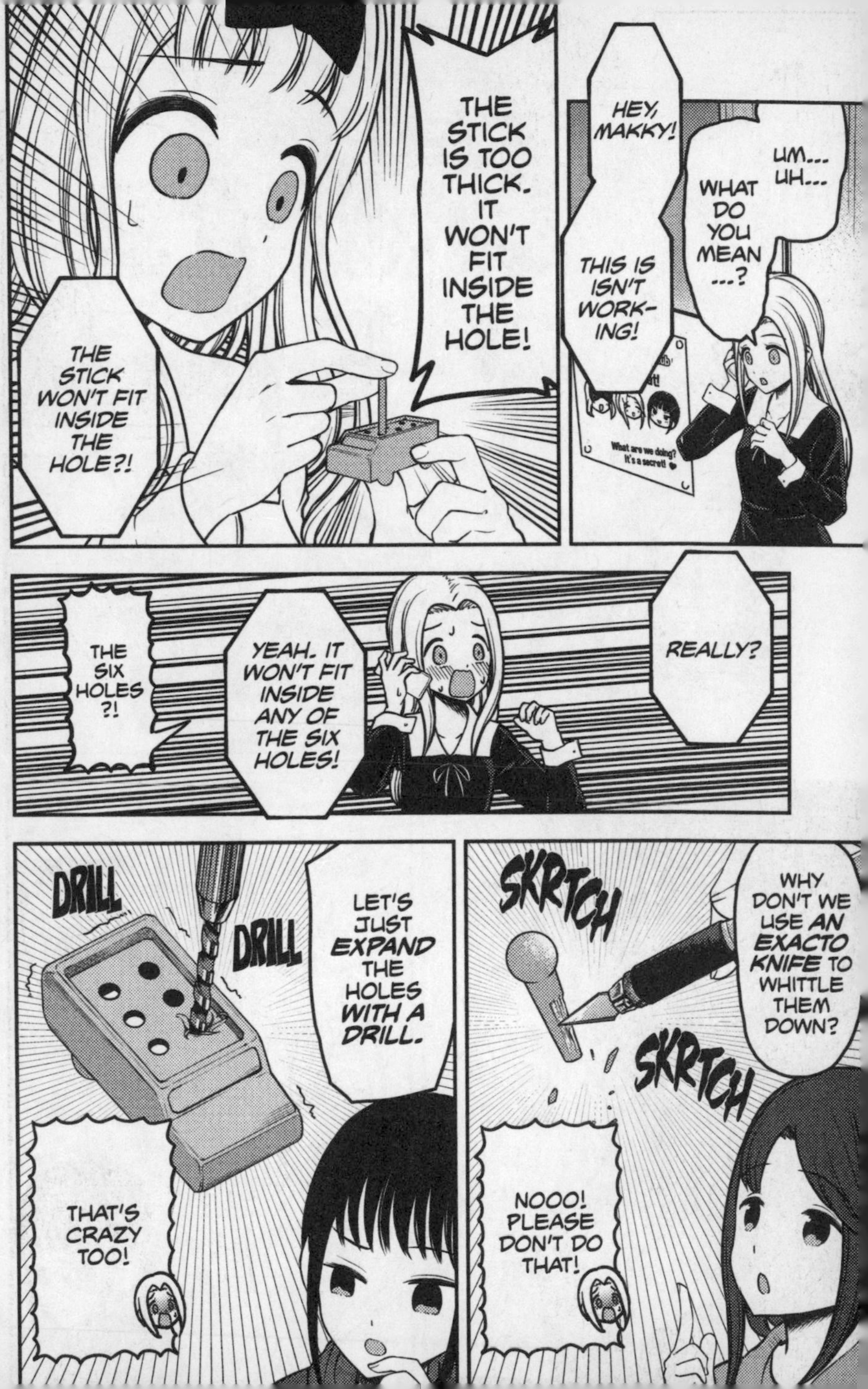
HEY, MAKKY!
THIS IS ISN'T WORKING!
UM... UH...
WHAT DO YOU MEAN ...?
What are we doing? It's a secret!
THE STICK IS TOO THICK. IT WON'T FIT INSIDE THE HOLE!
THE STICK WON'T FIT INSIDE THE HOLE?!
REALLY?
YEAH. IT WON'T FIT INSIDE ANY OF THE SIX HOLES!
THE SIX HOLES ?!
SKRTCH
WHY DON'T WE USE AN EXACTO KNIFE TO WHITTLE THEM DOWN?
SKRTCH
NOOO! PLEASE DON'T DO THAT!
DRILL
DRILL
LET'S JUST EXPAND THE HOLES WITH A DRILL.
THAT'S CRAZY TOO!

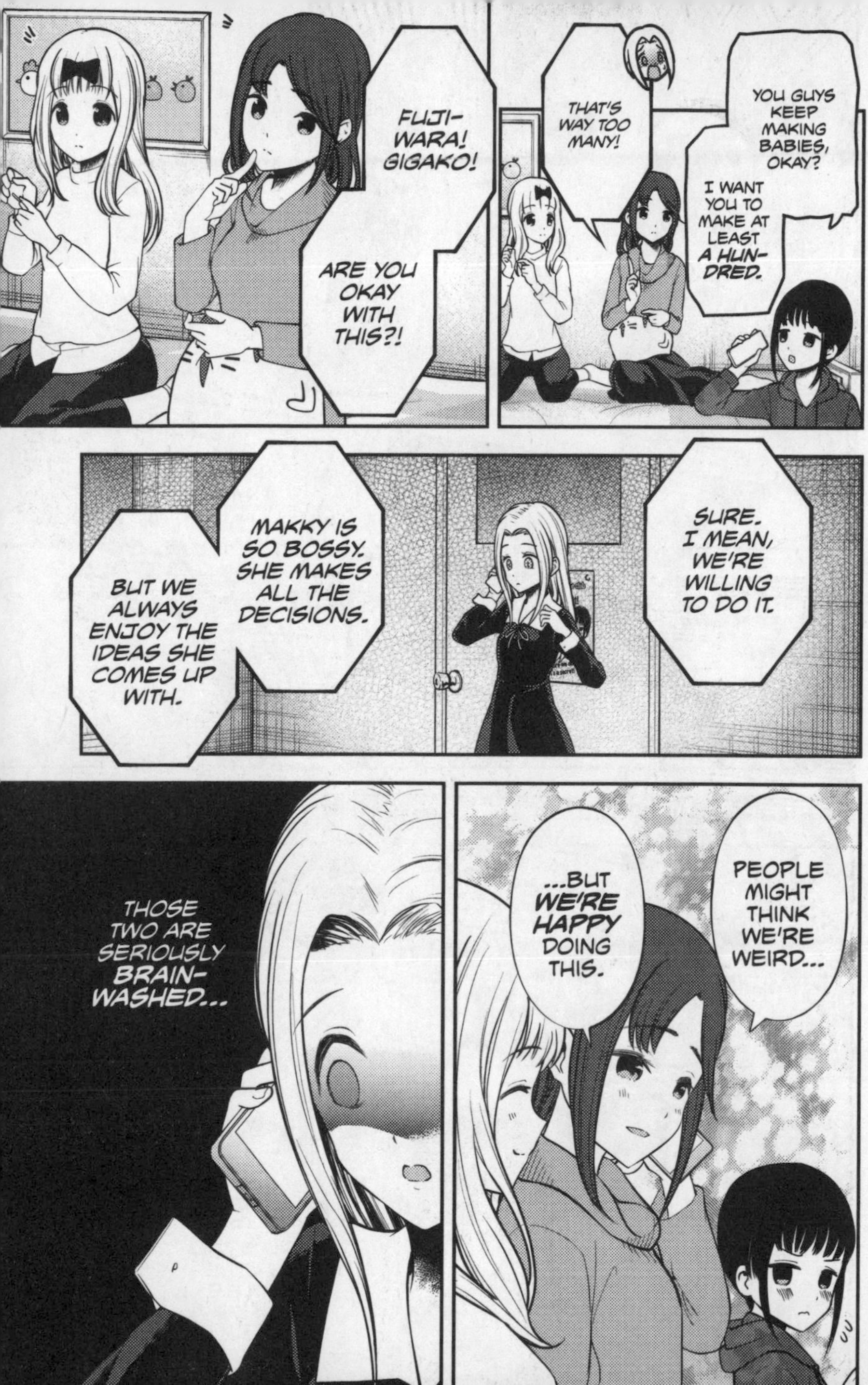
YOU GUYS KEEP MAKING BABIES, OKAY?
I WANT YOU TO MAKE AT LEAST A HUNDRED.
THAT'S WAY TOO MANY!
FUJIWARA! GIGAKO!
ARE YOU OKAY WITH THIS?!
SURE. I MEAN, WE'RE WILLING TO DO IT.
MAKKY IS SO BOSSY. SHE MAKES ALL THE DECISIONS.
BUT WE ALWAYS ENJOY THE IDEAS SHE COMES UP WITH.
PEOPLE MIGHT THINK WE'RE WEIRD...
...BUT WE'RE HAPPY DOING THIS.
THOSE TWO ARE SERIOUSLY BRAIN-WASHED...

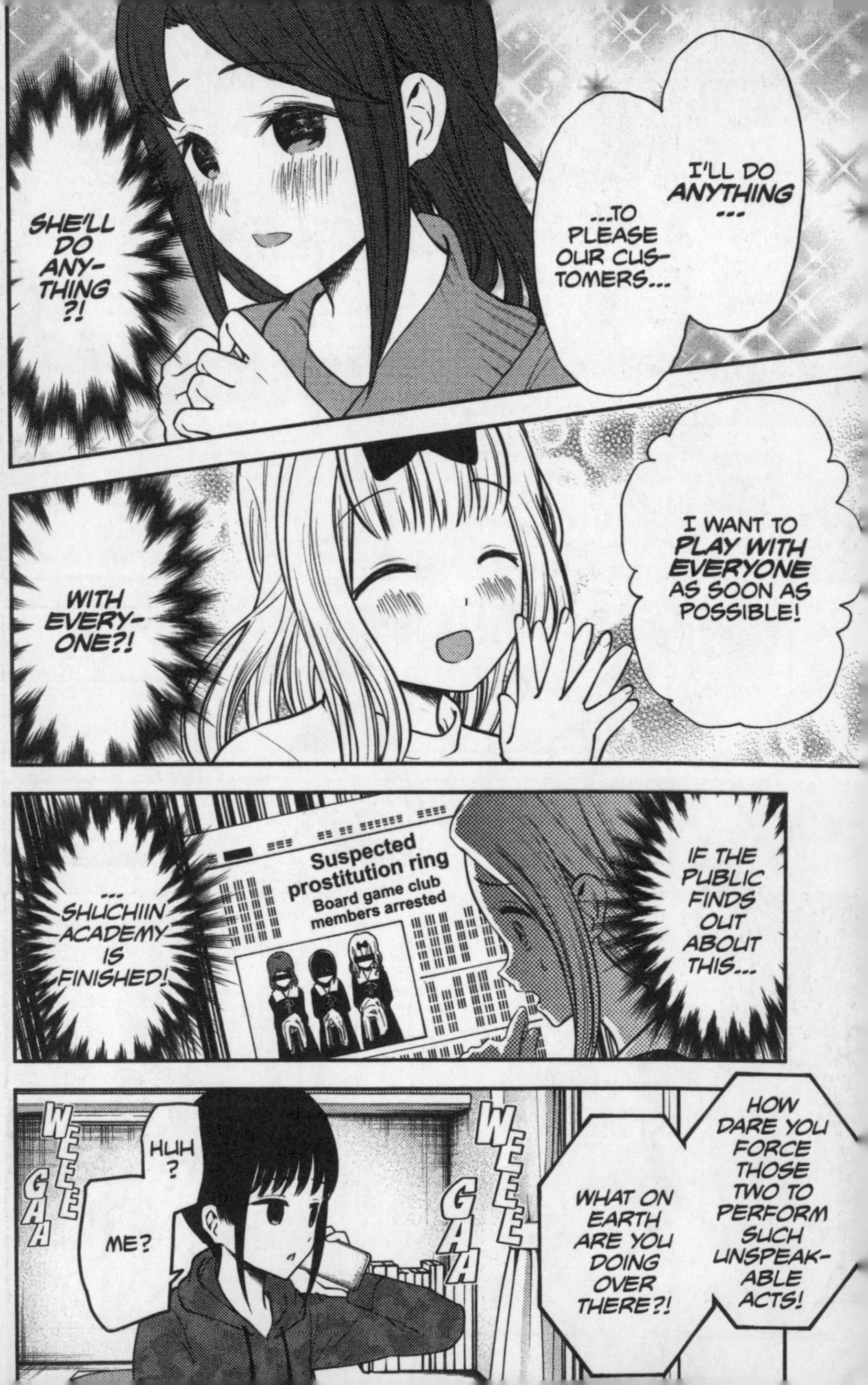
I'LL DO ANYTHING...
...TO PLEASE OUR CUSTOMERS...
SHE'LL DO ANYTHING?!
I WANT TO PLAY WITH EVERYONE AS SOON AS POSSIBLE!
WITH EVERYONE?!
IF THE PUBLIC FINDS OUT ABOUT THIS...
Suspected prostitution ring
Board game club members arrested
...SHUCHIIN ACADEMY IS FINISHED!
HOW DARE YOU FORCE THOSE TWO TO PERFORM SUCH UNSPEAKABLE ACTS!
WHAT ON EARTH ARE YOU DOING OVER THERE?!
WEEEGAA
HUH?
ME?
WEEEGAA

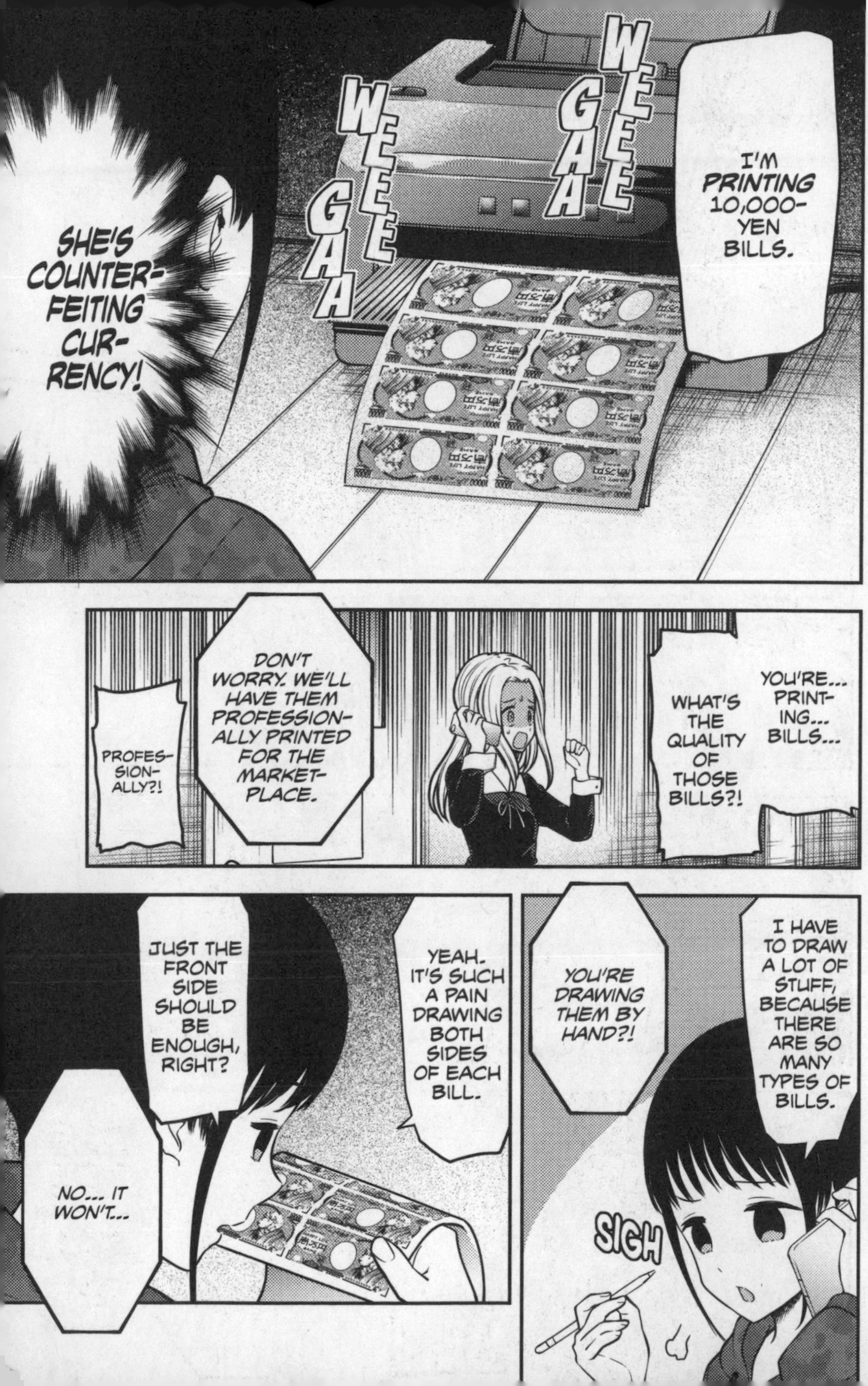
I'M PRINTING 10,000-YEN BILLS.
WEEEGAAA
WEEEGAAA
SHE'S COUNTERFEITING CURRENCY!
YOU'RE... PRINTING... BILLS...
WHAT'S THE QUALITY OF THOSE BILLS?!
DON'T WORRY. WE'LL HAVE THEM PROFESSIONALLY PRINTED FOR THE MARKETPLACE.
PROFESSIONALLY?!
I HAVE TO DRAW A LOT OF STUFF, BECAUSE THERE ARE SO MANY TYPES OF BILLS.
YOU'RE DRAWING THEM BY HAND?!
SIGH
YEAH. IT'S SUCH A PAIN DRAWING BOTH SIDES OF EACH BILL.
JUST THE FRONT SIDE SHOULD BE ENOUGH, RIGHT?
NO... IT WON'T...

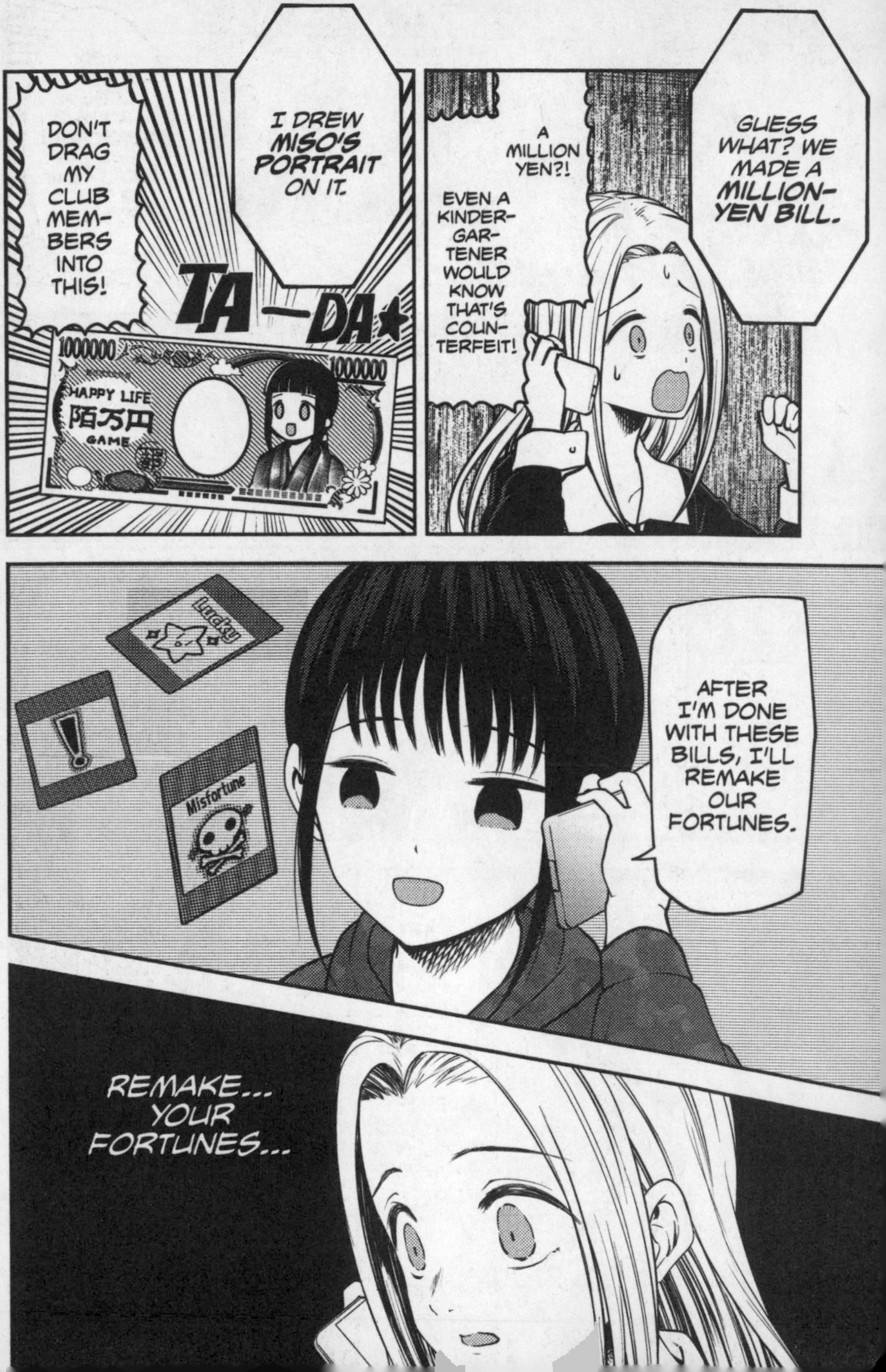
GUESS WHAT? WE MADE A MILLION-YEN BILL.
A MILLION YEN?!
EVEN A KINDERGARTENER WOULD KNOW THAT'S COUNTERFEIT!
I DREW MISO'S PORTRAIT ON IT.
DON'T DRAG MY CLUB MEMBERS INTO THIS!
TA—DA★
1000000
1000000
HAPPY LIFE
陌万円
GAME
AFTER I'M DONE WITH THESE BILLS, I'LL REMAKE OUR FORTUNES.
Lucky
Misfortune
REMAKE... YOUR FORTUNES...

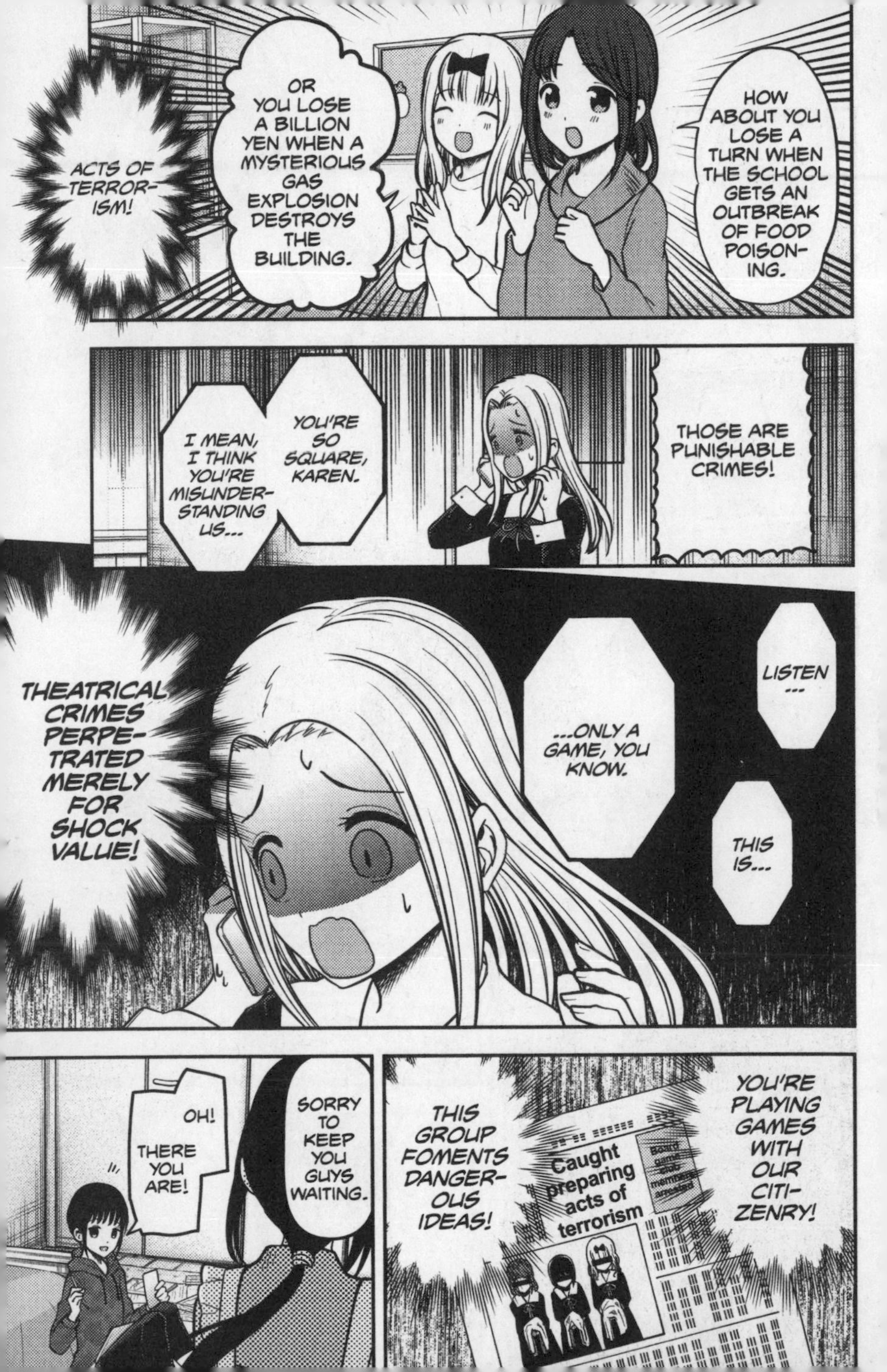
HOW ABOUT YOU LOSE A TURN WHEN THE SCHOOL GETS AN OUTBREAK OF FOOD POISONING.
OR YOU LOSE A BILLION YEN WHEN A MYSTERIOUS GAS EXPLOSION DESTROYS THE BUILDING.
ACTS OF TERRORISM!
THOSE ARE PUNISHABLE CRIMES!
YOU'RE SO SQUARE, KAREN.
I MEAN, I THINK YOU'RE MISUNDERSTANDING US...
LISTEN...
THIS IS...
...ONLY A GAME, YOU KNOW.
THEATRICAL CRIMES PERPETRATED MERELY FOR SHOCK VALUE!
YOU'RE PLAYING GAMES WITH OUR CITIZENRY!
THIS GROUP FOMENTS DANGEROUS IDEAS!
Caught preparing acts of terrorism
SORRY TO KEEP YOU GUYS WAITING.
OH!
THERE YOU ARE!

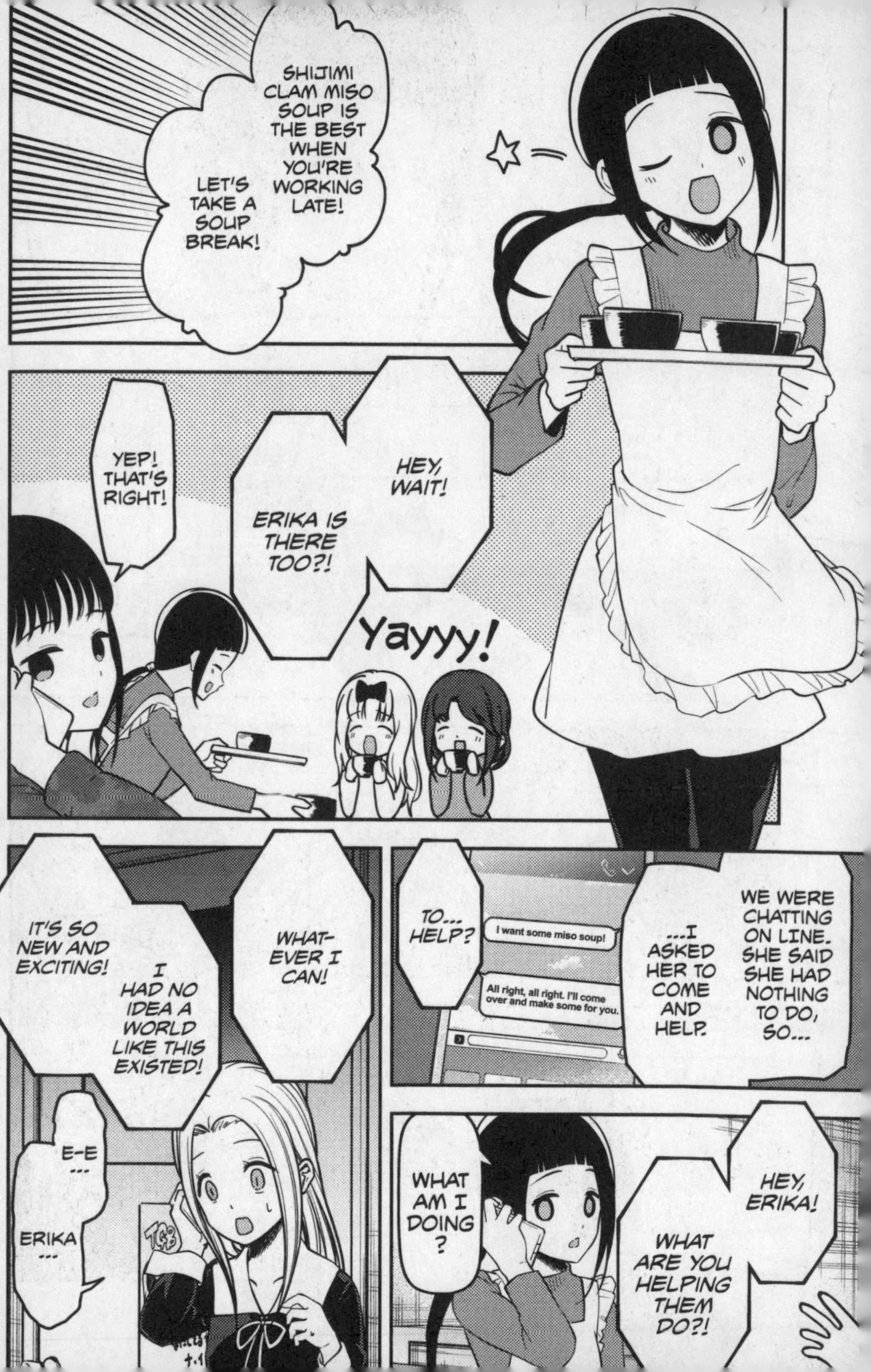
SHIJIMI CLAM MISO SOUP IS THE BEST WHEN YOU'RE WORKING LATE!
LET'S TAKE A SOUP BREAK!
HEY, WAIT! ERIKA IS THERE TOO?!
YEP! THAT'S RIGHT!
Yayyy!
WE WERE CHATTING ON LINE. SHE SAID SHE HAD NOTHING TO DO, SO...
...I ASKED HER TO COME AND HELP.
I want some miso soup!
All right, all right. I'll come over and make some for you.
TO... HELP?
HEY, ERIKA! WHAT ARE YOU HELPING THEM DO?!
WHAT AM I DOING?
WHAT-EVER I CAN!
IT'S SO NEW AND EXCITING!
I HAD NO IDEA A WORLD LIKE THIS EXISTED!
E-E... ERIKA...

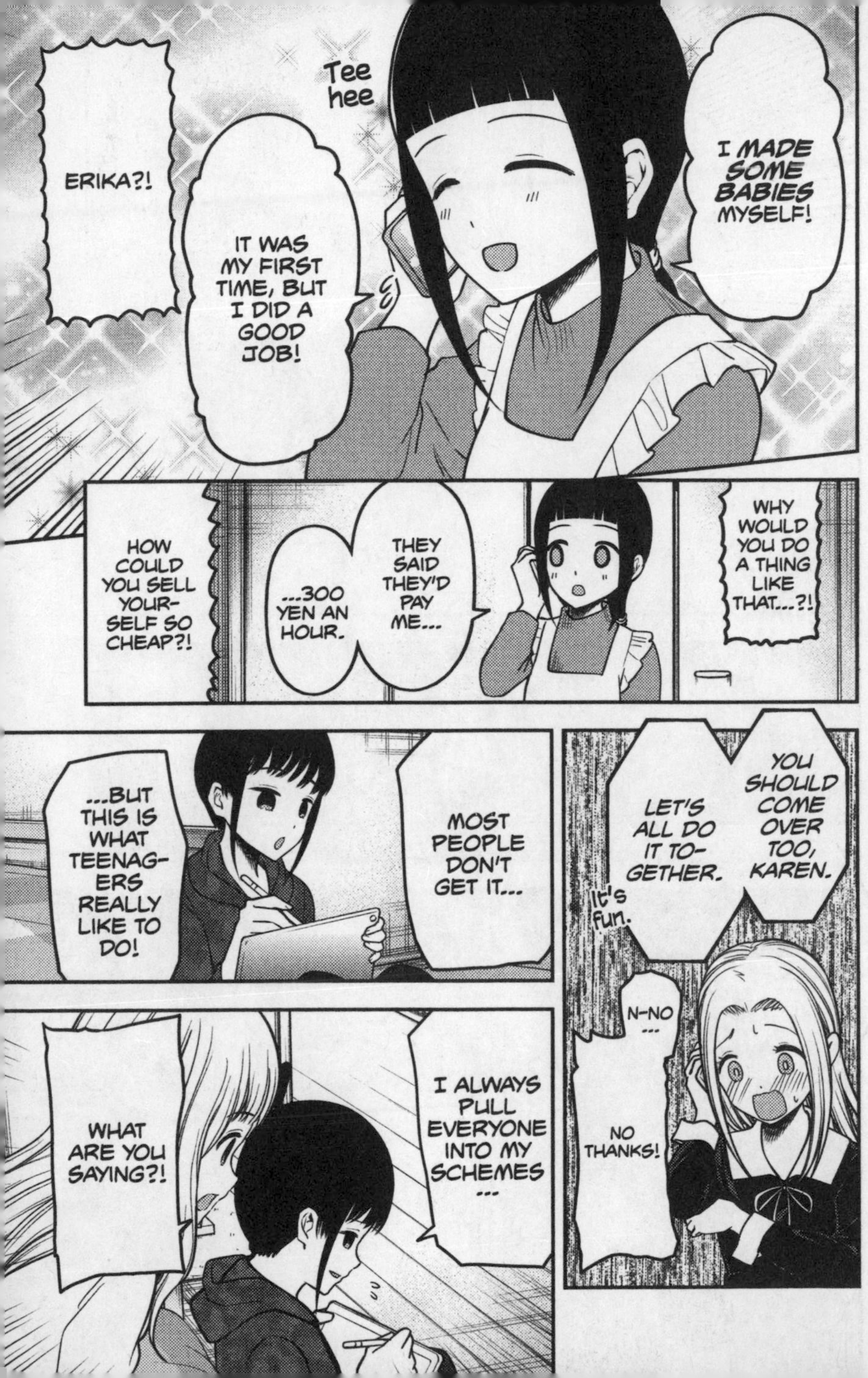
I MADE SOME BABIES MYSELF!
Tee hee
IT WAS MY FIRST TIME, BUT I DID A GOOD JOB!
ERIKA?!
WHY WOULD YOU DO A THING LIKE THAT...?!
THEY SAID THEY'D PAY ME...
...300 YEN AN HOUR.
HOW COULD YOU SELL YOUR-SELF SO CHEAP?!
YOU SHOULD COME OVER TOO, KAREN.
LET'S ALL DO IT TO-GETHER.
It's fun.
N-NO ...
NO THANKS!
MOST PEOPLE DON'T GET IT...
...BUT THIS IS WHAT TEENAG-ERS REALLY LIKE TO DO!
I ALWAYS PULL EVERYONE INTO MY SCHEMES ...
WHAT ARE YOU SAYING?!

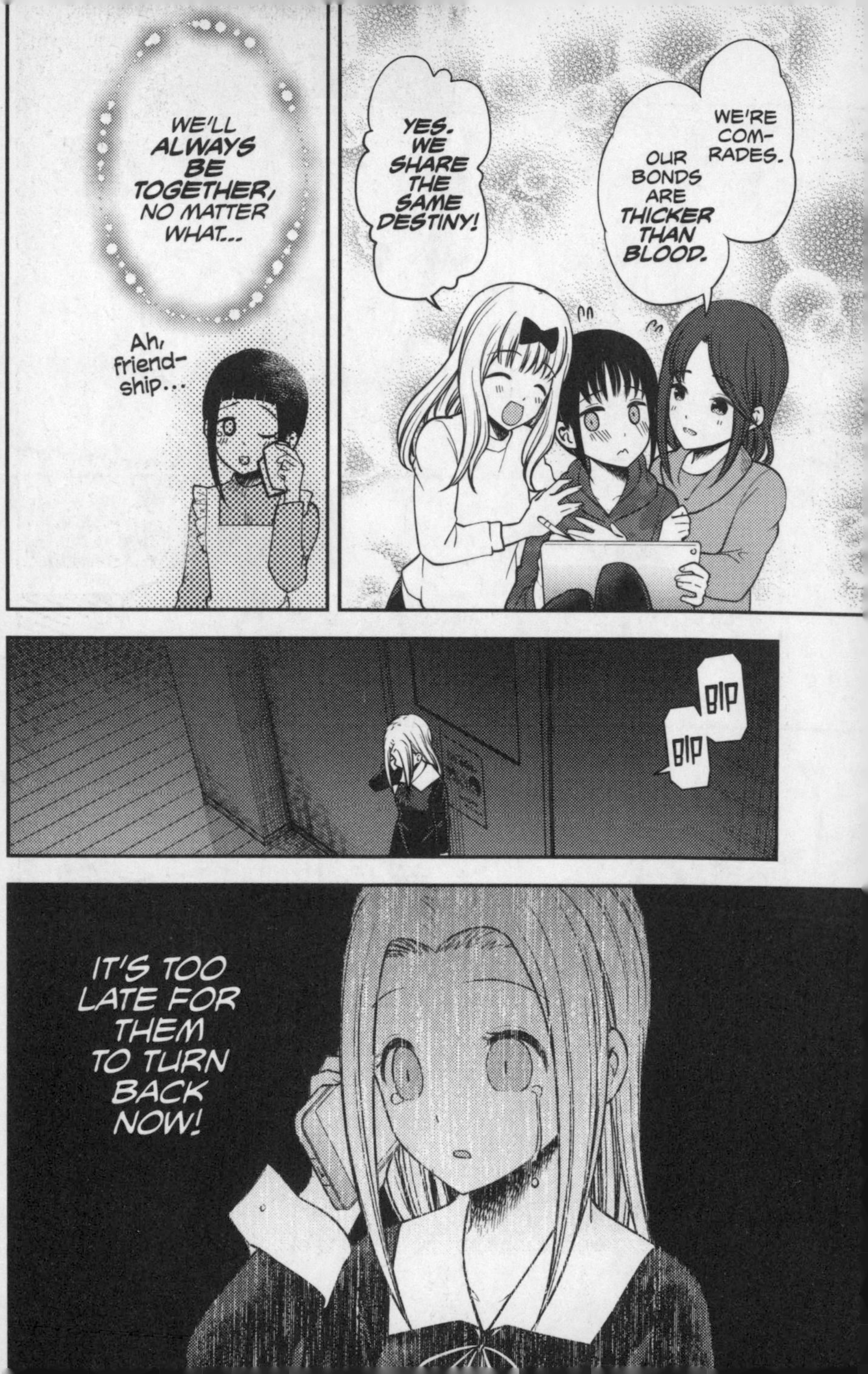
WE'RE COM-RADES. OUR BONDS ARE THICKER THAN BLOOD.
YES. WE SHARE THE SAME DESTINY!
WE'LL ALWAYS BE TOGETHER, NO MATTER WHAT...
Ah, friend-ship...
BIP
BIP
IT'S TOO LATE FOR THEM TO TURN BACK NOW!

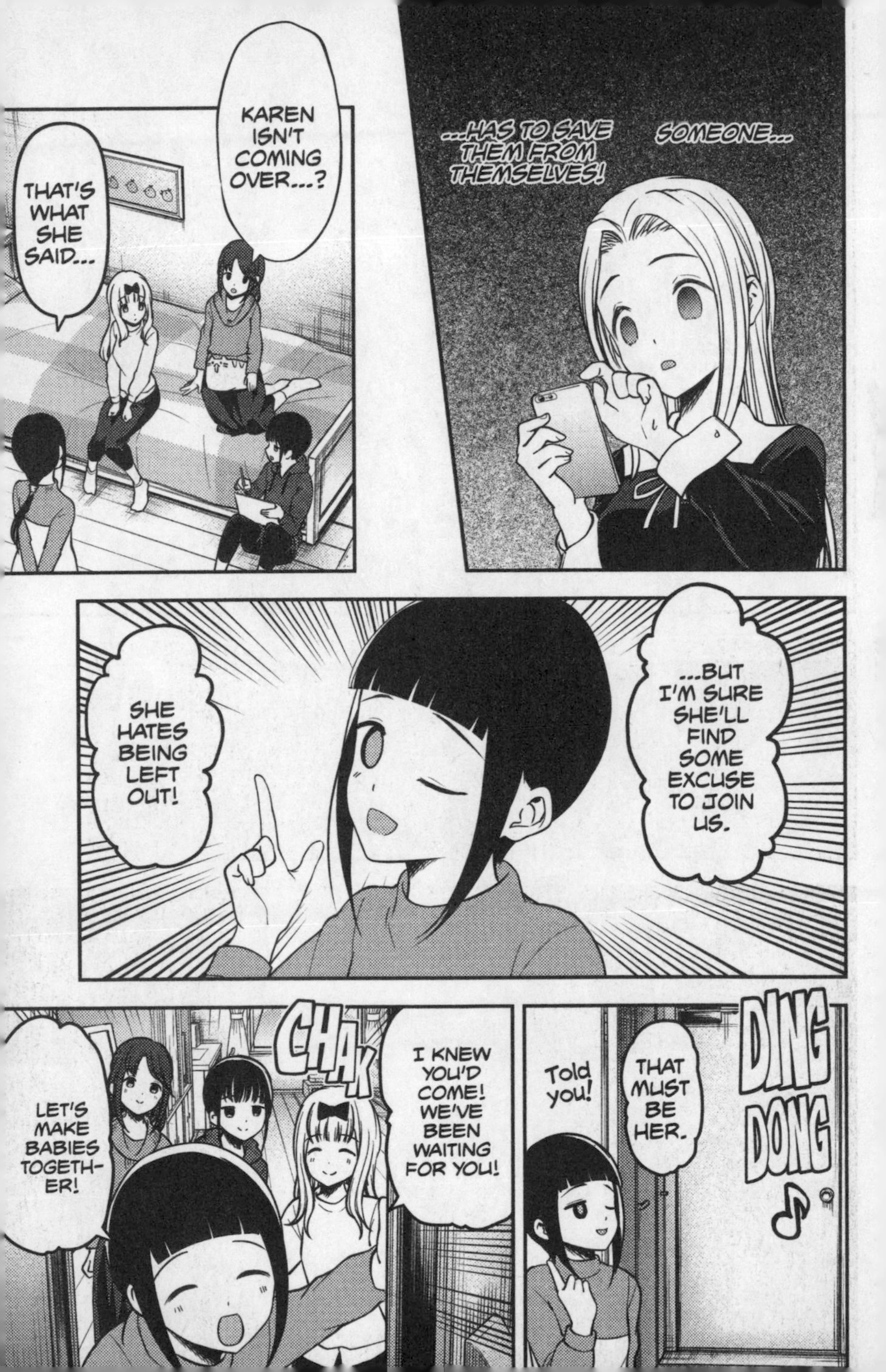
SOMEONE...
...HAS TO SAVE THEM FROM THEMSELVES!
KAREN ISN'T COMING OVER...?
THAT'S WHAT SHE SAID...
...BUT I'M SURE SHE'LL FIND SOME EXCUSE TO JOIN US.
SHE HATES BEING LEFT OUT!
DING DONG
THAT MUST BE HER.
Told you!
CHAK
I KNEW YOU'D COME! WE'VE BEEN WAITING FOR YOU!
LET'S MAKE BABIES TOGETH-ER!

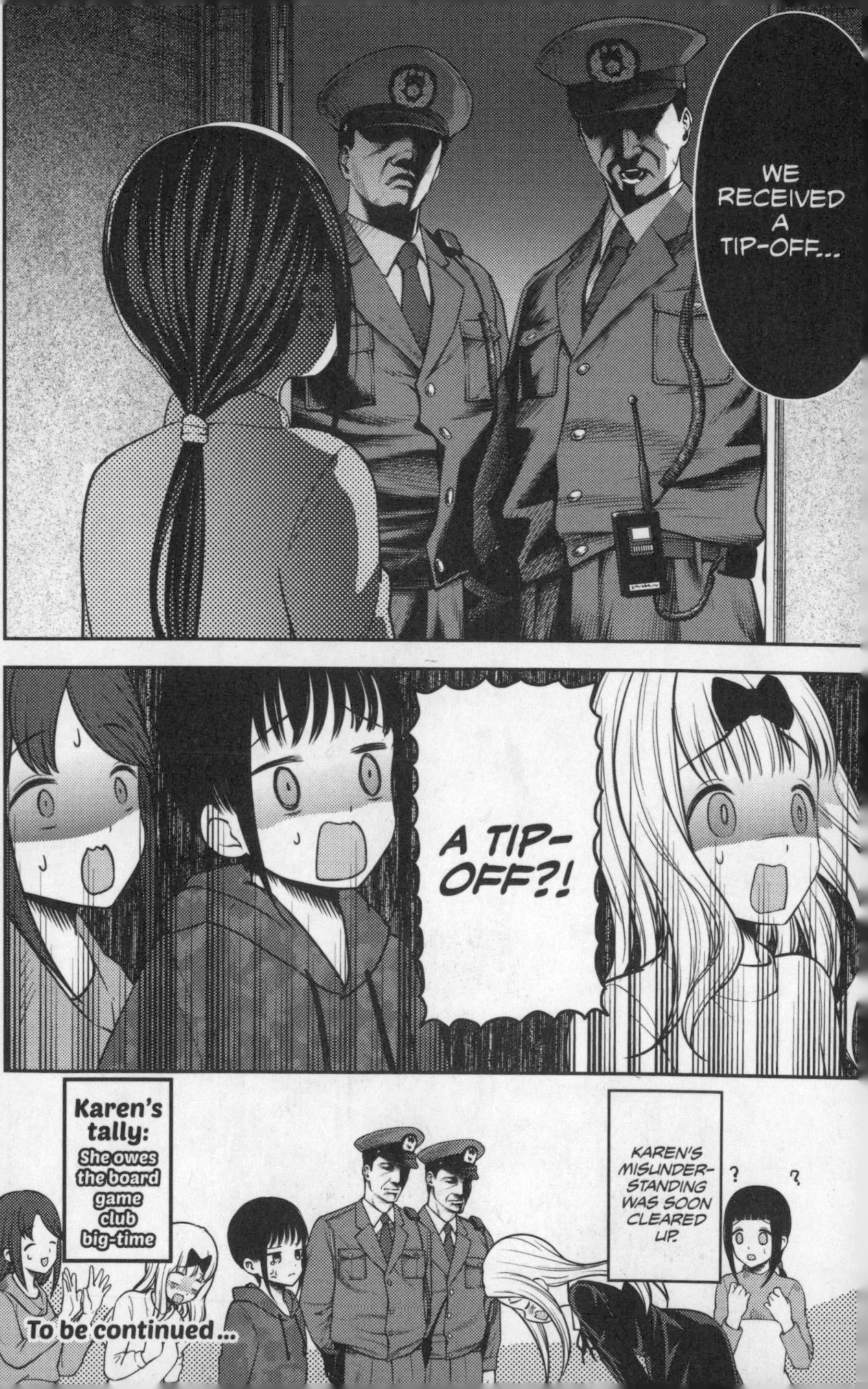
WE RECEIVED A TIP-OFF...
A TIP-OFF?!
KAREN'S MISUNDERSTANDING WAS SOON CLEARED UP.
? ?
Karen's tally:
She owes the board game club big-time
To be continued...

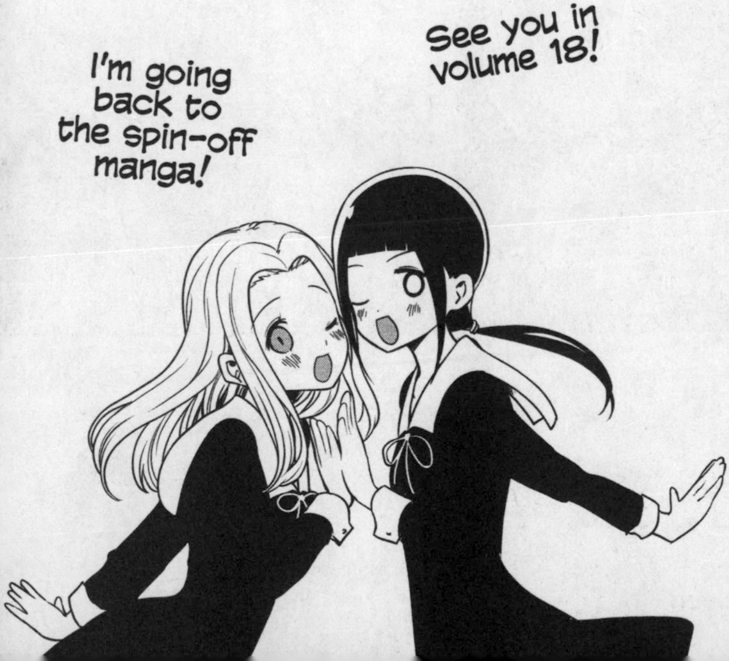
See you in volume 18!
I'm going back to the spin-off manga!

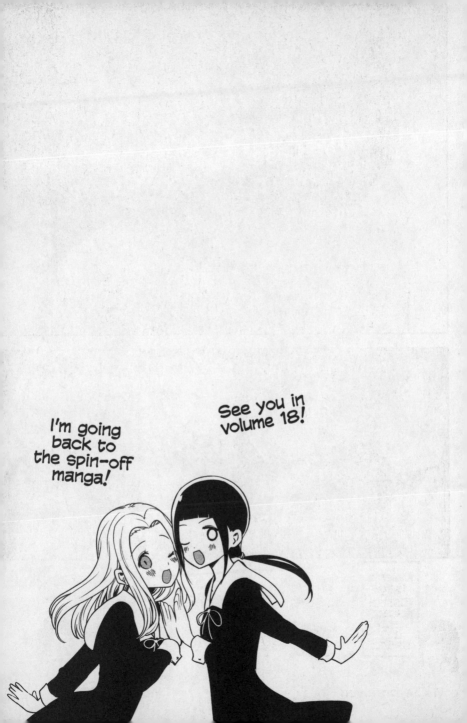

THE WORD "LOVE" IS MEANINGLESS UNTIL YOU'VE FALLEN IN IT.

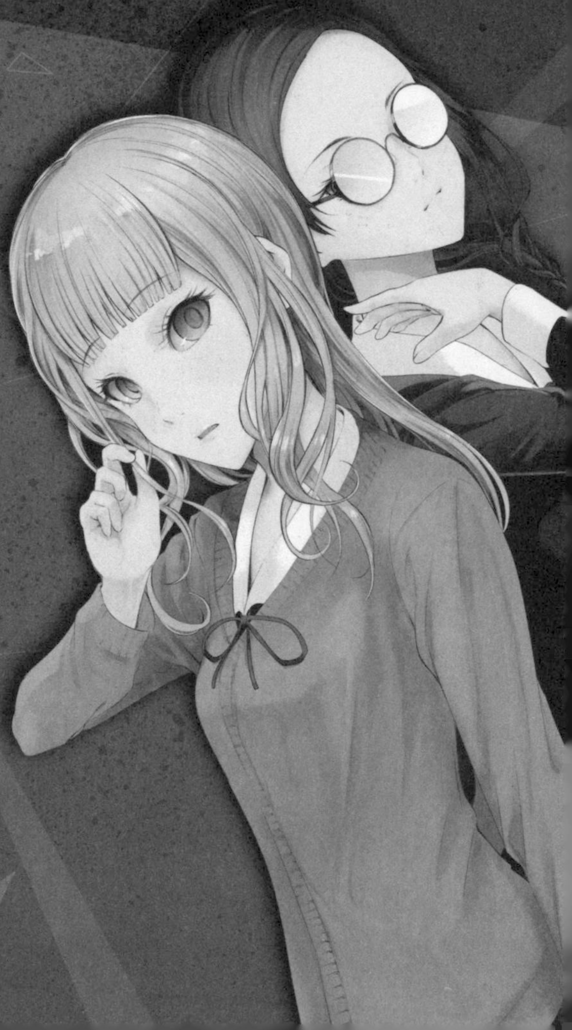

Aka Akasaka

Aka Akasaka got his start as an assistant to Jinsei Kataoka and Kazuma Kondou, the creators of *Deadman Wonderland*. His first serialized manga was an adaptation of the light novel series *Sayonara Piano Sonata*, published by Kadokawa in 2011. *Kaguya-sama: Love Is War* began serialization in *Miracle Jump* in 2015 but was later moved to *Weekly Young Jump* in 2016 due to its popularity.

If you answer truthfully, you'll learn what you're subconsciously thinking!

KAGUYA-SAMA
LOVE IS WAR

Which student council member do you like...?!

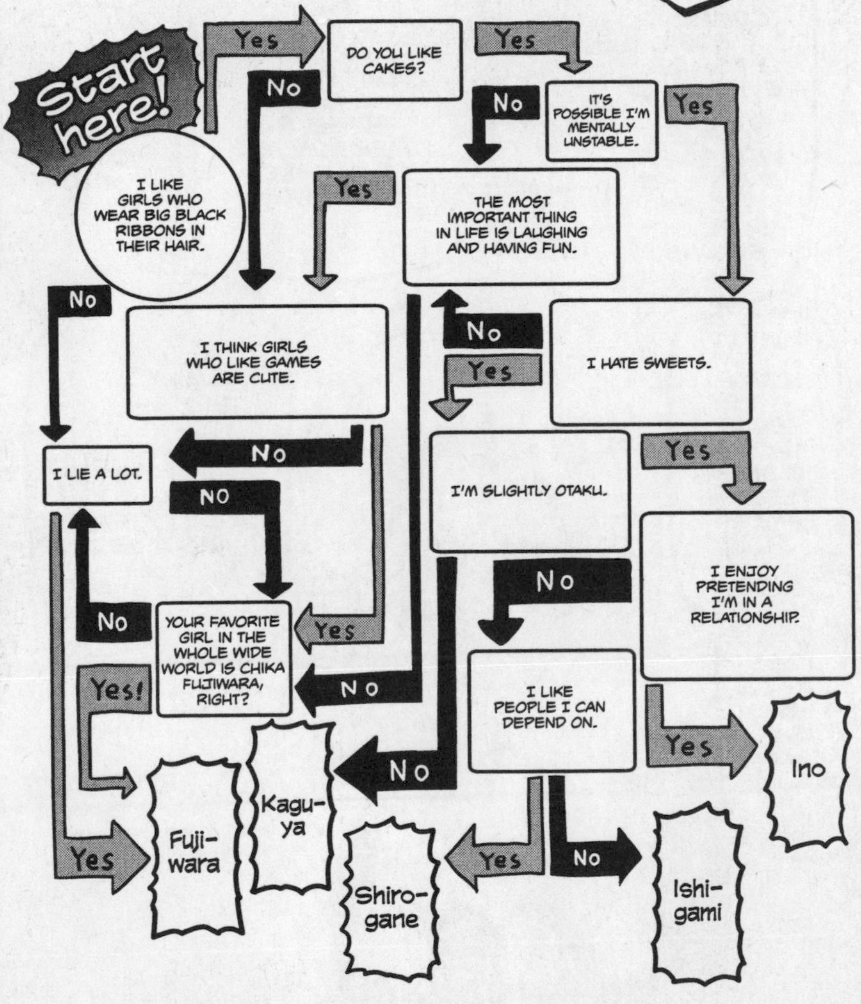
Start here!
Yes
DO YOU LIKE CAKES?
Yes
No
No
IT'S POSSIBLE I'M MENTALLY UNSTABLE.
Yes
I LIKE GIRLS WHO WEAR BIG BLACK RIBBONS IN THEIR HAIR.
Yes
THE MOST IMPORTANT THING IN LIFE IS LAUGHING AND HAVING FUN.
No
I THINK GIRLS WHO LIKE GAMES ARE CUTE.
No
Yes
I HATE SWEETS.
I LIE A LOT.
No
NO
I'M SLIGHTLY OTAKU.
Yes
No
I ENJOY PRETENDING I'M IN A RELATIONSHIP.
No
YOUR FAVORITE GIRL IN THE WHOLE WIDE WORLD IS CHIKA FUJIWARA, RIGHT?
Yes
NO
I LIKE PEOPLE I CAN DEPEND ON.
Yes!
Yes
Ino
No
Kagu-ya
Fuji-wara
Yes
Yes
No
Shiro-gane
Ishi-gami

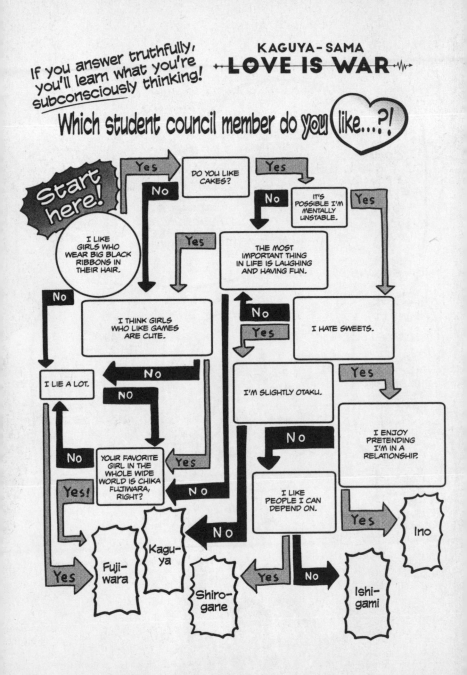

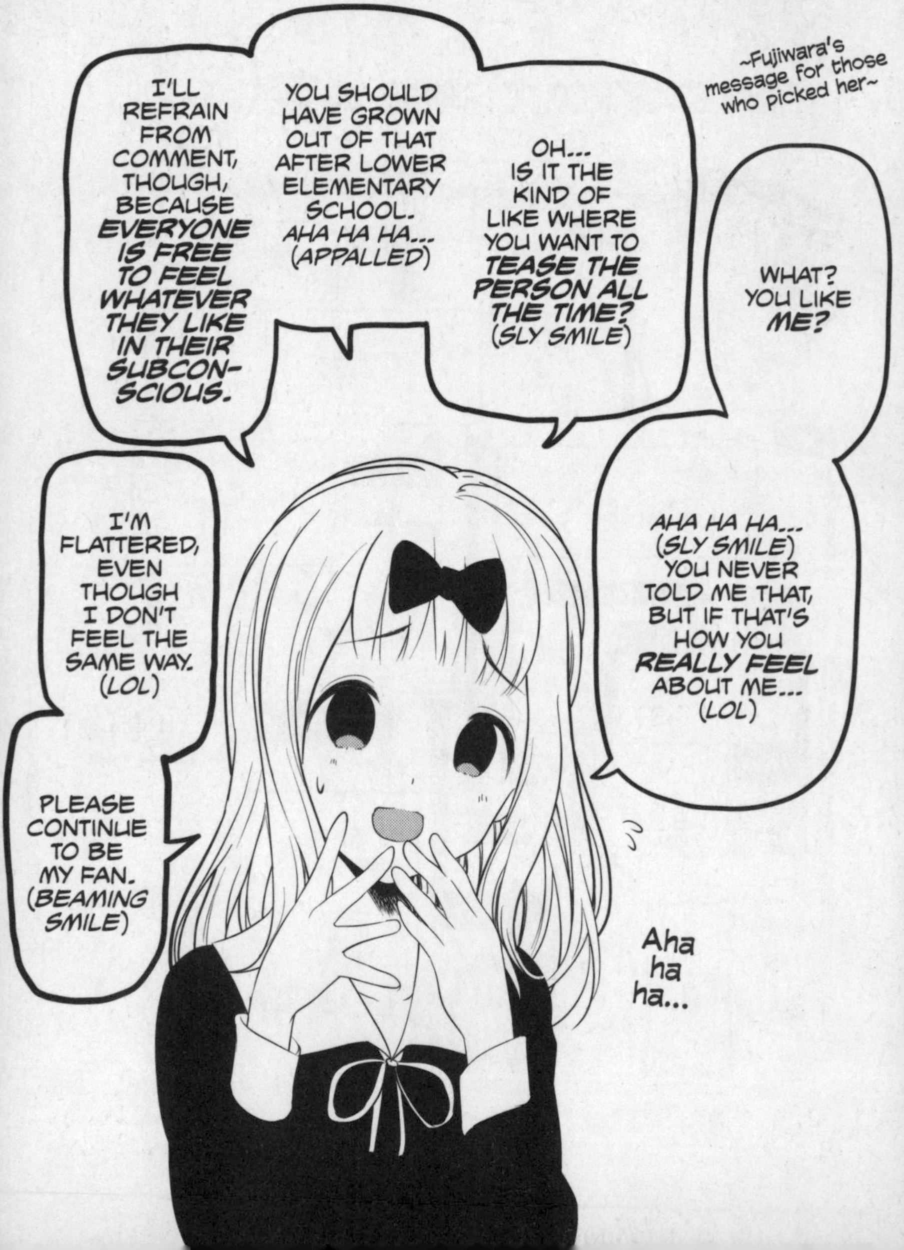
~Fujiwara's message for those who picked her~
WHAT? YOU LIKE *ME?*
AHA HA HA... (*SLY SMILE*) YOU NEVER TOLD ME THAT, BUT IF THAT'S HOW YOU *REALLY FEEL* ABOUT ME... (*LOL*)
OH... IS IT THE KIND OF LIKE WHERE YOU WANT TO *TEASE THE PERSON ALL THE TIME?* (*SLY SMILE*)
YOU SHOULD HAVE GROWN OUT OF THAT AFTER LOWER ELEMENTARY SCHOOL. *AHA HA HA...* (*APPALLED*)
I'LL REFRAIN FROM COMMENT, THOUGH, BECAUSE *EVERYONE IS FREE TO FEEL WHATEVER THEY LIKE IN THEIR SUBCONSCIOUS.*
I'M FLATTERED, EVEN THOUGH I DON'T FEEL THE SAME WAY. (*LOL*)
PLEASE CONTINUE TO BE MY FAN. (*BEAMING SMILE*)
Aha ha ha...